THE SEARCH FOR BEAUTY IN ISLAM

And say: O my Lord, increase me in knowledge (XX:114)

By: Mohammad Agha Miri

THE SEARCH FOR BEAUTY IN ISLAM

A CONFERENCE OF THE BOOKS

Khaled Abou El Fadl

Rowman & Littlefield Publishers, Inc.

LANHAM • BOULDER • NEW YORK • TORONTO • OXFORD

ROWMAN & LITTLEFIELD PUBLISHERS, INC.

Published in the United States of America
by Rowman & Littlefield Publishers, Inc.
A wholly owned subsidiary of The Rowman & Littlefield Publishing Group, Inc.
4501 Forbes Boulevard, Suite 200, Lanham, Maryland 20706
www.rowmanlittlefield.com

PO Box 317
Oxford
OX2 9RU, UK

British Library Cataloguing in Publication Information Available

Library of Congress Cataloging-in-Publication Data

Abou El Fadl, Khaled, 1963–
  The search for beauty in Islam : a conference of the books / Khaled M. Abou El Fadl.
    p. cm.
  Originally published: Conference of the books. Lanham : University Press of America,
  2001.
  Includes index.
  ISBN 0-7425-5093-1 (cloth : alk. paper) — ISBN 0-7425-5094-X (pbk. : alk. paper)
  1. Islam—Appreciation. 2. Islam—Essence, genius, nature. 3. Sufism. I. Abou El
  Fadl, Khaled, 1963- Conference of the books. II. Title.

  BP163.A258 2005
  297.2—dc22   2005018902

Printed in the United States of America

♾™ The paper used in this publication meets the minimum requirements of American
National Standard for Information Sciences—Permanence of Paper for Printed Library
Materials, ANSI/NISO Z39.48-1992.

This book is dedicated to my sons, Cherif and Medhat;
may the Conference find them and may they find beauty.

Acknowledgments

These essays were written over a time period spanning a decade or more. All of the essays were inspired by a single compulsion: the search for beauty in Islam—what is beautiful in Islam, about Islam, and in the lives of those who adhere to the Islamic faith. Often this search has forced me to wrestle with the challenge of understanding the beauty of the Divine as well as the divinity of beauty. This, however, is not a book of philosophical speculation. The essays take full account of the ugliness that often plagues Muslim realities, and it is through the process of engaging those unseemly realities that the search for beauty takes place. The overwhelming majority of the chapters that comprise this book resulted from actual encounters with Muslims and non-Muslims, but I have avoided using names, and have changed some of the facts to dilute the identity of those involved. I apologize if I have been unjust or unfair to anyone who unwittingly inspired the writing of one of these essays. I owe an enormous debt of gratitude to all those who knowingly or unknowingly and directly or indirectly played a role in this search for beauty.

The publication of this book in its current form owes its existence entirely to the dedicated readers from different parts of the world who, believing in the mission of these essays, accompanied me in the search for beauty in Islam. It is their consistent and overwhelming enthusiasm and encouragement that led to the publication of *The Search for Beauty in Islam*. A large number of readers wrote me describing the profound impact that the essays now printed in this book have had on their lives—on their understanding of Islam and relationship with God. To each one of these readers I can only say that I am deeply humbled and honored to have been able to contribute to and possibly enrich their own personal journeys while seeking to understand what is beautiful about the Islamic faith and the reasons for the ugliness that exists in Muslim life.

I am extremely grateful to so many people who contributed time, effort, and encouragement to this project. I am most grateful to my parents Medhat Abou El Fadl and Afaf El Nimr, and to the teachers and *Shaykhs* who molded me, gave me the love of knowledge and beauty, and taught me that the height of beauty is God. I cannot find the words to thank my wife Grace and son Cherif for helping and encouraging me, and for being my most trusted and critical readers. They became the pulse that kept this project alive through many hurdles, and I am grateful to them both. I have had the very distinct privilege of working with Jeremy Langford, a truly honorable and dedicated editor at Rowman and Littlefield who I am proud to call a friend. He continued to believe in the importance of this work and expended every effort to ensure it was promptly published. I express my sincere gratitude to Naheed Fakoor, Omar Fadel, and Hisham Mahmoud for their unfailing support, valuable insights, and for reading and editing this work. I also thank Mazen Asbahi, Lena Shahbandar, and Assim Mohammad. I would like to express my very special gratitude to Mr. Mohammad Fareed for his faith in my work, and for his unwavering moral support. Lastly, I would be quite remiss not to thank those without whom these essays could never have been written: my books who kept *The Search* going night after night, and who are the joy of my life; and also the jurists of Islam, my everlasting companions in the search for beauty.

Contents

Preface for the New Edition

The precursor to this book was a collection of essays published in 2001 under the title *The Conference of the Books: The Search for Beauty in Islam*. Since the original publication, what began as a humble collection of essays, written with the hope of igniting a spark of interest in the Islamic intellectual heritage, has exceeded all expectations in striking a meaningful chord in enough hearts and minds so as to set off a flurry of interest around the world. In its pre-9/11 publication, *The Conference of the Books* was a difficult book to publish. Few publishers were interested in a book that tackled the nuanced and complex notions of a concept as elusive and amorphous as beauty in Islam. When the book was finally published it was very expensive, limited in its initial printing, and distributed largely through word of mouth. Nevertheless, somehow, this book has managed not only to survive, but rather thrive despite its inauspicious beginnings.

The events of 9/11 tragically demonstrated the further importance and prescience of *The Conference*. Written long before the 9/11 tragedies, *The Conference* had already detailed the potential dangers, threats, and long-term effects of the ugliness of the puritanical Wahhabi movement upon Muslims and the world. Today it is even more urgent and necessary that Muslims reconnect with what is beautiful in their tradition and reclaim what has been lost to the puritanical forces within their religion. It is nothing short of devastating to witness the persistence, severity, and uniformity of the ugliness that has been committed across the Muslim world. Rather than finding peace and tranquility in a shared understanding of beauty, today's Muslims find more shared commonality in bitter understandings of violence, hatred, ignorance, pain, and tragedy.

Since 2001, I have received numerous powerful, impassioned, heart-wrenching, and beautiful letters from people around the world about how *The Conference* has somehow touched them, moved them, given them hope, and even changed their lives. To non-Muslims, *The Conference* offered an opportunity to gain an insider's view to the struggles, problems, and pains of contemporary Muslims as well as to understand what the Islamic tradition had to offer humanity. To Muslims, *The Conference* has allowed many to discover an Islam they never knew existed outside of their hearts, and for some, it provided an open door back to the faith that they had abandoned because of the ugly modern realities of Muslims. This is not a testament as to the power of my writing, rather it is a testament to the power and draw of the longing for beauty and the divinity of the search. It is evidence of a collective longing to reconnect with the Creator in beauty. It is also clear evidence that many Muslims are longing to reclaim the lost beauty many of their co-religionists had seemingly abandoned, when there seemed to be no road back.

The demand for *The Conference* has been nothing short of astonishing, and this new printing demonstrates that the book has grown and developed as a result of the incredible demand for the search to continue.

The *Conference* transcends all cultural, geographic, political, and sociological boundaries, and has managed to touch people in all corners of the world. *The Conference* has been translated into several languages, and I have received correspondence from people as far away as Indonesia, Singapore, Nigeria, the Netherlands, South Africa, Australia, Europe, and the Middle East. One of the most amazing stories I have heard was relayed by a former student of mine who, while visiting her Persian relatives ended up in a remote village in the mountains so isolated that she was astonished to know people lived there. In polite regard for their guest, the villagers were eager to offer my student some form of entertainment during her stay, and collectively mustered a search for a book for her to read. In this far away village, hundreds of miles from civilization, the villagers were able to produce only two non-Persian books, a German book on engineering and *The Conference of the Books*. My student was shocked and astonished that the *Conference* had somehow made the trek to this remote village in Iran.

This universal appeal of the search for beauty is evidence of the innateness of the idea and also of the power of our shared humanity. Beauty is a universal concept, a unifying force, and a source of hope for a better future. It is with this in mind that I humbly submit this complete collection of essays documenting the trials, the tribulations, and occasionally, the jubilation of one Muslim's struggles to find beauty amidst the challenges that confront contemporary Islam, and to discover beauty in the past that once was Islam. In all cases, the search for beauty should continue and never end. While the efforts of one searcher might bring us a little closer to comprehending the divinity of beauty and the beauty of the Divine, neither Divinity nor beauty can be fully realized. Therefore, I present this modest work with the enduring hope that this is only the beginning of the search, not the end.

Introduction

The *Search for Beauty in Islam* is a collection of studies in the ethos of the Islamic intellectual heritage and the contemporary Muslim reality. The studies presented in this book arose from my encounters, as a jurist and teacher, with Muslims in the United States and other parts of the world. The essays were written in response to actual recurring problems in the Muslim community that are directly relevant to the moral and ethical definition of Islam in the contemporary world. The range of topics addressed in this book are quite broad; among others, the topics include censorship, political oppression, terrorism, the veil and the treatment of women, marriage, parental rights, the role of Islamic law, the dynamics between law and morality, and the character of the Prophet Muhammad. The range of topics was dictated by the types of issues raised by the people I encountered, as well as by my own spiritual and moral development. Therefore, there is a noticeable evolvement in these essays, and I leave it to the reader to decide on the direction and merit of this evolution.

The essays, however, do not represent a systematic argument toward a specific conclusion, nor is this book intended as a scholastic discourse on the contemporary Muslim reality. The essays do not assume an air of detachment or academic objectivity, but rather reflect a variety of moods; they are passionate, jubilant, angry, and sometimes, sarcastic, but they are invariably committed. Each essay was written in the context of an imagined conference of books that occurs every night. The books represented here are the books of my personal library, which contains books on a variety of subjects including Judaism, Christianity, law, philosophy, and literature. However, the books represented in this conference are mostly classical Islamic texts, and these texts engage their readers in reflections about the contemporary Muslim reality. Books, in general, preserve snapshots of the intellectual activity of their authors. Classical Islamic texts are the repository of the intellects of the past—the intellects that eventually transformed into books. And, it is my belief that of all God's wondrous creations, the intellect is the most wondrous of all, and it is also my belief that a book is the gift of God that preserves the intellect for generations to come. With this in mind, I engaged the intellects of the past in addressing the intellects of the present. A Muslim may read these essays as the testament of a Muslim jurist on the problems that confront us today. A non-Muslim may read these essays for their sociological significance and for their relevance to comparative insights on law and theology. Yet, as the Islamic message was addressed to human beings at large, I wrote these essays for Muslims and non-Muslims alike.

Each essay in this collection is designed to stand on its own merit, so the book may be read selectively or out of order. Nevertheless, there are unifying themes in this book, and these unifying themes are this work's basic message. My primary focus is on the ethos of knowledge and beauty in modern Islam. Furthermore, this book seeks to create a nexus and bond between the Islamic intellectual heritage of the past and contemporary Muslim thought. Muslims today are uprooted from their intellectual tradition, and the result has been that Muslims have lost the ethos of knowledge, as well as their moral and intellectual grounding. The Islamic message started with a single book—the Qur'an—a book of remarkable moral vision and beauty. And, this single book has inspired an intellectual heritage of beauty and magnificence. It is my hope that the *Conference of the Books* will help rekindle the interest of Muslims in the book, and in their rich intellectual heritage.

The Muslim jurist and theologian *Imam al-Haramayn* al-Juwayni (d. 478/1085) once wrote that the requisites for the pursuit of knowledge are intelligence, diligence, poverty, the instruction of teachers, travel in foreign land, and a long commitment of time. This statement reflected a particular ethos toward knowledge that prevailed in the Islamic classical age. The same ethos is also reflected in the oft-repeated statement: the pursuit of knowledge mandates an exertion of the intellect and a long and arduous struggle (*jahd al-nafs wa badhl al-qariha*). Classical Muslim scholars often expressed the conviction that the pursuit of knowledge (*talab al-'ilm*) is an essential component of the Divine Will or plan, and that God values the search for knowledge more than the results of the search.

The ethos of which I speak, consisted of the belief in the difficulty and elusiveness of knowledge, the belief that the more important the field of knowledge, the greater the demand for exertion, and that the elusiveness and inaccessibility of knowledge served a Divine purpose or plan. Integral to this ethos was the conviction that the pursuit of knowledge was a religious and ethical act, and that the pursuit of elusive and difficult knowledge was particularly pleasing to God. The attainment of knowledge was considered to be a cumulative and gradual process by which students built upon the insights of their masters, and scholars engaged each other in constant debate. All knowledge was thought to belong to God, and while God is all-knowing, human beings had to diligently seek this knowledge. Human beings, however, will never be able to attain but a fraction of God's truth. This did not necessarily mean that truth is relative, but it did mean that truth is partial. Diligence and persistence in searching, as well as debate and engagement, would yield greater insights into God's infinite knowledge, but at all times the knowledge attained would be partial and incomplete.

Symptomatic of this ethos were the numerous traditions or reports emphasizing that the pursuit of knowledge is an act of permanent worship (*talab al-'ilm 'ibada da'ima*). Some reports elevated the pursuit of religious knowledge to a status higher than prayer or ritualistic practice, even stating that the scholars are the inheritors of Prophets. Several traditions, or reports, asserted that a pious scholar is far superior to a pious but ignorant worshipper. In fact, the merit of a scholar over the ignorant is akin to the merit of the Prophet over the lowliest of people. Other reports emphasized that the best kind of travel is that which is done in pursuit of knowledge, and that this kind of travel is the mandatory *hijra* (religious duty of migration) that never ends. Still other reports demanded that Muslims travel even to the farthest reaches of the earth in pursuit of knowledge.

Classical Muslim scholars proffered several justifications for this ethos. They often argued that the complexity of knowledge is a function of the richness of God and of the complexity of God's creation. Muslim scholars also argued that the mind's worship is in the pursuit of the subtleties of the Divine Will, while the body's worship is in physical compliance with the law. If knowledge was not complex and elusive, God could not be served through the mechanisms of the intellect, but would only be served through the obedience of the body. This would defeat the whole purpose behind the creation of the intellect, and would reward individuals with lazy and dull minds. Furthermore, Muslim scholars asserted that the existence of diversity in scholarly opinion is a mercy or blessing upon Muslims so that the religious law may be able to accommodate the varied and changing affairs of human beings. Part of God's charge and test to human beings is that they would know how to disagree and debate (*adab al-ikhtilaf*) without falling into strife and animosity (*fitna*).

There are many historical and social, as well as theological reasons for the emergence of this ethos in Islamic classical culture. Among these reasons were the geographic vastness of the Islamic empire and the *de facto* emergence of geographically centered schools of legal and religious practice. Doctrines legitimating and justifying intellectual diversity arose alongside these geographic schools. Furthermore, within the first three hundred years of Islam, a juristic class with its own institutionalized structure, and specialized and technical language, emerged within Islam. This juristic class mediated between the political elites and other social and commercial elites. It also played an important function in mediating between the elites and the masses. The ethos of knowledge helped sustain this class, validated its mediating role in society, and endowed it with theological and moral legitimacy. Importantly, however, the fact that there were historical and social factors that contributed to the emergence of the ethos of knowledge does not in any way minimize or lessen the value or the Islamic authenticity of the ethos itself. The ethos became an essential part of the fabric of Islamic theology and morality. Regardless of the historical reasons, the ethos produced a remarkable richness in the quantity and quality of the intellectual product of the Islamic civilization, and this intellectual richness left its undeniable mark on the world at large.

Significantly, this richness and diversity is, for the most part, lost in contemporary Islam. There has been a sharp and clear deterioration in the ethos of knowledge in the Muslim world today. There are many reasons for this deterioration, among them the legacy of colonialism, the emergence of the puritanical and anti-historical Wahhabi and Salafi movements, economic problems, the breakdown of private endowments supporting educational institutions, and the monopolization by the state of the mechanisms for the production and propagation of information. Unfortunately, the deterioration in the ethos of knowledge has infected Muslims inside and outside the Muslim world, and has contributed to a state of intellectual paralysis, even among Muslims in the West.

Muslim connections to the epistemology, processes, and products of their intellectual heritage have been severed in the modern age, and in my opinion, they are the worse off for it. It is not that this intellectual heritage was ideal or free of problems, but that its ethical and moral potential is far superior to anything that replaced it. Furthermore, this intellectual heritage is more consistent with the moral and ethical spirit of the Islamic message as reflected in the Qur'an and the life of the Prophet Muhammad. As such, this intellectual heritage does not only have the virtue of authenticity, but it is also qualitatively superior to anything followed by contemporary Muslims today. It is important to note, however, that I do not idealize, but rather, I do admire the Islamic intellectual legacy. The reader will find many occasions where I am critical of positions and stands taken by classical Muslim jurists. The mistakes of the past have as much to teach us, as do the successes.

These essays do not only attempt to reinvigorate, but also re-orient the pre-modern methodologies of Islamic knowledge. I argue that there is much beauty in the traditional Islamic methodologies of knowledge, but I also argue that even the traditional methodologies should be re-oriented toward an unrelenting and persistent exploration of a core Islamic value—beauty.

The German orientalist Joseph Schacht once argued that Islamic law is the epitome of Islamic thought and the core and kernel of Islam itself.* The veracity of this

---

*Joseph Schacht, *An Introduction to Islamic Law* (Oxford: Oxford University Press, 1964), 1.

statement depends largely on how we define Islamic law. If by Islamic law we mean the sum total of positive commandments or rules (*ahkam*), this statement is clearly false. If Islamic law means the process, methodology, and normative values of the Islamic religion (*Shari'a*), then this statement is true. One suspects that Schacht meant the former, and in that, he is clearly wrong.

God's law (*Shari'a*) is about a process, methodology, and morality. At the core of this morality is the value of beauty. Human understanding of the law (*fiqh*) engages the process and searches the various normative values of *Shari'a*, but human understanding can never be the embodiment of God's beauty. Furthermore, the rules (*ahkam*) are the product of the human attempt at understanding, but they do not represent God's beauty. As I argue in this book, the positive commandments or rules delineate the outer boundaries of proper behavior, but they do not articulate the substance and soul of Islamic morality. The rules are at the fringe of Islamic morality; they are the external shell that do not express or create substance. The rules are about boundaries. The boundaries could be the product of an attempt to give effect to a certain morality, or they could be the product of circumstance or convenience. Although the rules may have been inspired by a moral vision or normative ideas, they do not express a moral vision or ethos. Put differently, piety creates and pursues the rules, but the rules do not create piety. However, the rules may promote piety if they are carried out with the appropriate intent and moral vision. If the intent and moral vision do not exist, then the rules become meaningless pedantry.

In this collection of essays, I try to promote a cultural ethos of beauty in contemporary Islam. I believe that the core and kernel of Islam is the search for beauty— the search for God's inexhaustible beauty and the beauty of God's creation. The search for God's law must attempt to pursue, express, promote, and re-create God's beauty. The search for beauty will necessarily mean transcending rule-making to the discovery of normative values. The normative values should inspire and direct the process of rule-making, but, as stated above, the rules themselves cannot be equated with morality or the core value of beauty.

Admittedly, speaking in terms of the pursuit of beauty instead of rules is alien to contemporary Islamic culture. I do not hide the fact that I see much ugliness in the reality of Muslims today, and that I think most Muslim discourses are either apologetic and dogmatic, or legalistic and formalistic. In contemporary Muslim discourses, legalism and the pursuit of pedantic rules have replaced the search for moral or normative values. Result-oriented and unprincipled methodologies of inquiry are quite widespread. Even the so-called reformers or liberals rely on the opportunistic concept of public interest (*maslaha*) to justify what they deem to be socially desirable results. Like the traditionalists or conservatives, Muslim liberals are dishonestly selective and noncritical in dealing with the Islamic tradition, and like the traditionalists or conservatives, they do not bother with systematic methodologies of inquiry or with the search for moral or normative values. Authoritarian methodologies of knowledge are commonplace among all types of Muslim intellectual orientations, and this has led to intellectual dishonesty, censorship, and intolerance. Even centuries-old classical texts have been banned, while other classical texts have been censored or cleansed of "offending" passages. The treatment of women in many Muslim communities is simply appalling. The dominance of puritan creeds such as Wahhabism has led to an attitude of disregard and disrespect toward the Islamic intellectual heritage, and to an ahistorical, if not anti-historical, approach to Islam. In the words of a friend, "Wahhabism and Salafism have made Islam in the modern age boring and dull."

I pray that this is a passing phase in the history of Islam, and that Muslims will regain their intellectual vigor and their enlightened spark. I wrote these articles not as an outsider or armchair critic. Rather, I deal with the issues that plague the Islamic world, day-in and day-out, as a professor and teacher. As a Muslim, I live these problems, and as a Muslim, I firmly believe in the beauty and resilience of the Islamic message.

Therefore, in search of the majestic beauty of Islam, I humbly present these essays. And, as classical Muslim jurists would typically say, this is my effort, if I am correct, it is a blessing from God, and if I am wrong, I seek God's forgiveness, for God knows best.

Dr. Khaled Abou El Fadl
Los Angeles, CA

CHAPTER 1

The Conference of Books:
The First Admission

In a small town outside Princeton, New Jersey, in a small crowded apartment, blessed by its immeasurable powers and burdened by its keeper, you will find the Islamic Civilization. The glories, the infamies, the victories, the ecstasies, the soft supplications, the tearful entreats, the dreams, the endless lessons of human follies, and the exacting record of the divine covenant are all here, present every night.

The impregnable, resilient volumes stand side by side in a solemn procession testifying to our deeds. Hasn't the Lord commanded us to recite and to bear witness? Here, in this small crowded space, is the endless recitation and the eternal murmurings of the Conference of Books. Who was ever foolish enough to believe that there is a past and present? There is only the read and unread; otherwise, all times are ever present in this library.

If you listen carefully enough, in the dead of night, you will hear the whispers, the arguments, the debates. You will hear the constant search for the Divine and the aching sublimation. When was this conference first held? "At first, God created the intellect," the Prophet said. With creation, the library was born and, with the library, the numerous books testifying to the glory of the Divine.

Has any civilization honored the book more than we have? And, has any civilization betrayed the book more than we have? In the beginning, we memorized from our Prophet, "An hour's reflection is better than a year's worship." Puzzled, we asked, "Even better than reading the Qur'an?" And he, may he be blessed, said, "And, can the Qur'an be useful without knowledge?" 'Ali (d. 40/661), his student and Companion, then declared, "God did not distribute to His servants anything more to be esteemed than intelligence." Ever since, the Conference of Books re-convened in Islam and for Islam, and what a miraculous Conference it was! In a frenzied celebration, the books of the world gathered around the lands of the Ka'ba. The discussions, the debates, produced a stream of books glittering with the luminous substance that is Divinity.

When was the Conference adjourned and when did it re-convene in the crowded apartment outside of Princeton, New Jersey? When the meretricious exaltations heaped on books mingled with the weapons of dust and neglect. When the reading stopped and the eloquent eulogization began. Then the Conference convened here, and has been here ever since.

I sit here, irrelevant to its majesty, inebriated by its presence. I can only listen in on its conversations and I humbly await my transformation—my transformation into a book. All of you, present in this Conference, were intellects once but without the form. Eventually, the intellect transformed into a book and buried its writer.

I look at you and I can glimpse the spirit of the writer who once wrote you. The thoughts and the arguments are overwhelming except for the fact that once a fallible human being stood behind them. Why is it that in a book the personal legacies, the moments of triumph, the moments of despair, the pain and the sorrows are all lost? Or, are they? My own idiosyncrasies, my own legacy, finds in you companionship and repose. One day only those who love you, as I love you, will glean my remains in the pages and hear my laughter between the words.

I search for myself in you. I open the books of al-Jahiz (d. 255/869)—his arguments vindicating and defending the women of his age mesmerize me. What happened to his school, al-Jahiziyya, and where are its books? In a state of ecstasy, I feel the enormous impact of the books that crushed him to death. At that moment was he as ecstatic as me? My eyes roll to the books of Ibn Taymiyya (d. 728/1328), no less controversial in his age and probably more contentious but, otherwise, so different. Today everyone cites him and very few understand him. Even in his day he bewildered friend and foe. His detractors accused him of insanity, and he was left to die in prison. I shiver at the thought of the numerous times he was beaten for his beliefs and how he rejoiced in his suffering! But isn't torture always a certificate of sincerity issued to the brightest and bravest?

I feel a sharp pain in the chest and my eyes burn. I look around the Conference of Books and despite myself notice all the books whose authors were tortured. Al-Nisa'i (d. 303/915), the collector of *hadith*, was beaten for refusing to praise Mu'awiya (d. 60/680) and died shortly thereafter. Abu Bakr al-Sarakhsi (d. 483/1090), one of the main Hanafi jurists, wrote his *al-Mabsut* in prison. Al-Shaykh 'Ulaysh (d. 1299/1882) was beaten while ill and thrown in prison where he died sick and deserted. Ibn al-Qayyim (d. 751/1350), Ibn Taymiyya's (d. 728/1328) student, was beaten and imprisoned. Drenched in his blood, he was placed on a donkey and taken around the city. But what did it matter? Ibn al-Qayyim loved his books. His endless quest to acquire books became legendary. God, how many book lovers and collectors existed in the Islamic Civilization and how many book conferences were held! Despite any oppression the book always managed to save its writer.

The pain in my chest is too much now. I hear my father's screams of pain exactly forty years ago. I quickly glance toward al-Amidi (d. 631/1233), the jurist, and Taj al-Din al-Subki (d. 771/1370), the Chief Justice of Egypt. Both were brilliant and unrestrained but persecuted by intellectual parasites. But this stream of memories is too painful. In any case, what recourse do petty minds have but to attempt to degrade those whose voices start to rise and reign in the perpetual Conference of Books!

For comfort, as always, I turn to Abu Hayyan al-Tawhidi (d. 414/1023), whose writings have transformed many nights, like this one, into a carnival of intoxicating thoughts. How ironic that the one whose books have kept me company so many nights got along with no one. He lived and died a social pariah, and he sought revenge. Thinking that people did not deserve his insights, right before his death he burned his books. How foolish could he have been! How could he think that he had a choice in the matter; his books transformed and preserved him nonetheless. I smile despite myself for, ironically, his books are next to the writings of Ibn Daqiq al-'Id (d. 702/1302), who, despite his extensive knowledge, was famous for his good nature and humor. Al-'Id got along with everyone, but he did not write as much.

A Conference of Books is always full of ironies, for here an irony begets an irony. I nearly chuckle when I notice that the famous and wealthy Fakhr al-Din al-Razi (d. 606/1210), the author of the commentary on the Qur'an, has been placed next to the famously impoverished Abu Ishaq al-Shirazi (d. 476/1083). The former enjoyed his wealth as much as the latter enjoyed his poverty. Al-Shirazi was endowed a school, al-Razi was endowed bodyguards, and I was endowed the two of them.

Fajr prayer now becomes due, and dawn breaks in through the windows calling the Conference to an end. As always, I turn to take the last glance at Ibn al-Kutub (the son of books) Jalal al-Din al-Suyuti (d. 911/1505), who acquired his name after being born on top of a pile of books. His fate was sealed from that moment on, and he lived to produce some of the most profound writings. He used to turn down all positions or gifts offered to him, for what possible use could they serve! At forty he isolated himself from all people and spent the rest of his life with his books. Every day he was born and reborn on that same pile of books. "Ibn al-Kutub," what a fitting name for a scholar from the civilization of the Book, the one civilization founded to fulfill the exhortations of a single majestic and divine Book.

Daylight threatens to invade every corner and shelf. The arguments and debates reduce themselves to a never-ending murmur. I must now go and remind some people that "At first, God created the intellect." I apologize to the books that I did not visit this night. It does not really matter because the supplications go on anyway. I clean the room and prepare it for the next session. But why is it that I always find a tear somewhere? I ask myself, "Will I be able to attend the Conference tomorrow and who will attend with me?" I pray and supplicate but then, as always, I wonder, "Until when will the Conference be held at night? Until when will the Islamic Civilization be present, here, every night? Until when will the Islamic Civilization exist in a small, crowded apartment, in a small town, outside Princeton, New Jersey?"

CHAPTER 2

The Night's Visitor

In that small town outside Princeton, New Jersey, in that small crowded apartment, the Islamic Civilization still stands. Despite the delusions of its puritan reformers, despite the ecstatic hallucinations of its self-declared saints, despite the revisionism of prejudiced historians, and despite the utter ignorance of its people, the Islamic Civilization still stands. Embodied in the abandoned schools of Salihiyya, in the deserted student markets of Cairo, in the eroding forts of the Mediterranean, and in the supernal mosques, the Islamic Civilization stands dignified in its reclusion and solitude. But most of all, it is embodied in its books, and tonight it is here, in its full vibrancy and power, present in the Conference of Books.

It is a cold Monday night and all the steaming drinks of the world provide but an illusion of warmth. I think of the Muslims wrapped in blankets accumulated through the centuries. Have they finally found their peace and security? I hear from a corner two simultaneous verses combining in rhythmic tones: "You who is folded in garments, rise by night. . ." (73:1–2), and the second verse joins in, "You who is wrapped in his mantle, arise and deliver. . ." (74:1). The call always comes in the night; you just have to choose to listen. I loosen my garment and allow the cold to invade my limbs.

In this Conference, I sit alone surrounded by you. You are the repository of our wisdom, the meticulous record of our failures and successes, and of our reasons and whims. You connect the past to the present and the present to its genuine self. So, my dear books, why are your guests so few? From that singular divine Book you created a civilization. From an inspiration you created an idea, then a thought, then a system, then a vehicle, then you discovered roads and signs. Why do Muslims insist on re-inventing the wheel at the beginning of every journey? Do any people deny their heritage more than we do? Is there a people more self-effacing than we are? Are there any people who dare limit God's manifestations to a single Golden Age and live enslaved to the illusion of a re-created history as much as we do? Can't we see that every age is God's age and that every age is to be honored, studied, and absorbed but never reproduced?

I lose myself in my spiraling thoughts but the cold awakens me. Tonight, Ibn al-Mulaqqin is between my hands, and it is offensive to indulge my mind while ignoring his. "Read, in the name of your Lord. . ." (96:1) and so it must be. Tonight, his *Tuhfat al-Muhtaj ila Adillat al-Minhaj* (*The Guide for the One Seeking the Proofs of the Minhaj*) will take center stage. But when you visit with one author, the others do not suddenly fall silent, they continue to adorn your mind and soul with the life of knowledge. His book was written to examine the various narrations and authenticity of the *hadiths* cited in a major Shafi'i law book, named *al-Minhaj*, written by al-Nawawi (d. 676/1277). Thus, one scholar's work completes the work of another.

Dear Ibn al-Mulaqqin, I know that this is not your most important work, but most of your books were lost in that infamous fire. What a privileged and tragic life you've led! People called you Ibn al-Mulaqqin, the son of the teacher, and how much you hated that name! Your name was 'Umar Ibn 'Ali Siraj al-Din al-Takruri. Born 723/1323 in Cairo to a Shafi'i family, your real father was a grammarian. He died when you were one year old. Al-Shaykh 'Isa al-Maghribi, a Qur'an teacher and a close friend of your father, married your mother and raised you. He treated you as a son and you used to call him father. He raised you to exceed him in knowledge and fame, and people eventually forgot that you were not his blood, and so you were named after him. Why then did you hate that name so much? Didn't al-Shaykh al-Maghribi not only support you through your youth but even create an endowment that supported you throughout your life? Forgive me, I do not wish to imply that you were ungrateful, but I wish I could reconstruct your life and understand you better than you understood yourself.

When did the Sufi fever hit you my friend? You claimed that you met *al-Khidr* and people say that you used to wear a rough wool garment all the time. Was that because you believed this to be the *Sunna*, as you claimed, or was it because you spent all your money on books? When did the book fever inflict you? You married once. Did she understand your worth? Did she love your books as much as she loved you? Was she, herself, a book?

Your library was legendary; it is reported to have been thousands of volumes. Sometimes historians of your age describe your library more than they describe you. So many historians recorded that incident when a scholar died and his books were being auctioned off but on a cash-only basis. You rushed home, anxious and excited.

"Quick, help me find every *dinar* at home," you called out to your wife. "Here! Go quickly, may Allah be with you!" she yelled as she stood at the doorstep watching you disappear into the crowd. She worried in vain. You made a killing that day. People actually bothered to remember and record the books you bought at the auction. Why is it that people seemed to remember things we could not care less about today?

You studied with thirty-four teachers, some of them quite famous. You traveled from Cairo to Yemen to Hijaz to Damascus and Aleppo—all in the pursuit of knowledge, with your wife and son by your side. What amazes me is that your son attended many of your classes and earned many certificates (*ijaza*s) with you. But eventually, you settled down to teach, and history records 195 of your students—179 were men and 16 were women. You issued *ijaza*s to only thirty-three of your male students, but you issued *ijaza*s to all of your female students. Was this because you only accepted the most qualified female students or was it because only the most talented female students would seek you out in the first place? But even your three grandchildren, two of whom were women, excelled in Islamic sciences and ended up teaching *hadith* and *fiqh*. Forgive me, I know I wonder about too many things, and I ask too many questions, but only by reconstructing the past can I begin to understand the present. Only by reconstructing you can I reconstruct myself.

You collected thousands of books and wrote seventy-five books; how beautiful your life must have been! But no one is left without a *mihna* (a trial and test), my friend, and the most painful *mihna* is betrayal. When Sultan Sayf al-Din Barquq (d. 801/1398) offered you the position of Chief Shafi'i Justice of Cairo, some of those who are at the margins of history forged a piece of paper to prove that you paid a four thousand *dinar* bribe to create that offer. You were promptly thrown in prison until some of your teachers interceded on your behalf. But sometimes betrayal comes from those closest to us. A few of your own students accused you of incompetence and plagiarism. You never bothered to respond. Did it simply hurt too much?

We can never fully understand Allah's ultimate wisdom and design. At the age of eighty, a fire callously devoured your library and most of your works. This was the final blow. Your son said that you sat bewildered, staring into open space, tears constantly dripping. And, in a few days you collapsed and died in 804/1401. But do you realize that the students you left behind went on to produce hundreds of other majestic books? I feel you and read you in all of them.

Soon, the sun will rise and the pattering of people will drown out the sublime murmurings of this Conference. The erratic whims of people will mimic themselves as principled positions, and our present will continue, disjointed from our past. I must continue to decipher your text and somehow find you between the lines. As you know, my friend, books are not just about ideas. Books are about people, real people, through the centuries, counseling and advising other people. Truly, "Say: travel in the lands and see how came the end of those before you. . ." (30:42).

CHAPTER 3

The Pirates of the Intellect

The mundane challenges the spiritual, interlocked in an eternal battle they crave for the peace of balance. Thousands of papers flood this place. Organizational papers, foundational papers, legal papers, literary papers, papers of wisdom, and papers of idiocy, frivolous papers and serious papers, satanic papers and divine papers—they are all here. You sit in a boat of consciousness floating on a sea of papers. How difficult it is to stay afloat! God, how the art of navigation demands every iota of intelligence and skill! The sea is fraught with treachery and delusions. The pirates of intellect can torment the most gentle of beings, and below every surface are lascivious sharks doomed by their pettiness to a life of perversity. Yet, you must persevere.

Tonight the ocean is in an uproar. I extract myself from the midst of thousands of papers drowning my mind in anxieties, and I resuscitate my soul. For here, in this small apartment outside Princeton, New Jersey, towers the Islamic civilization, at once diminishing the frivolous and superficial. Embodied in books, it is rich in its diversity and unified by its coherence. The Conference of Books has begun and the silly demands of life can wait.

The rising sublimations from hundreds of books break through the waves and inundate my soul. I am here present in humble readiness aching for the imperturbability of knowledge and tumultuousness of thought. The Conference has begun but the main speaker has not been announced. We are all bound in this eternal quest to discover the Divine Will, and to discharge the Covenant of Reflection. In creation are the sublime manifestations of Allah, and who will represent them tonight? In anticipation, the murmurs turn into whispers, and I recite the Qur'anic verse, "All sounds humble themselves in the presence of the *Rahman*; nothing will you hear except whispers." (20:108)

"Each circumstance begets its response," al-Jahiz declares as he steps forward, "and tonight I see that I fit the circumstance, for no one has confronted the pirates of intellect as much as I did." 'Amr Ibn Bahr Ibn Mahbub, known as al-Jahiz (the man with the protruding eyes), was an unrelenting Mu'tazili and was as mysterious as the date of his appearance on this earth. Some said he was born in 155 A.H., others said 159, others 160 or 163 or 164 or 165. His thought timeless, his range boundless, and his legends immeasurable, he is fit for most circumstances.

I smile, clear my eyes with delight, and ask, "Is it true that the 'Abbasid *Khalifa*, al-Mutawakkil (d. 247/861), retained you to tutor his children but, having met you, was so repulsed by your looks that he paid you and promptly fired you?"

"Of all my legacy," al-Jahiz exclaimed, "this is what first comes to your mind?"

"I am sorry," embarrassed I say, "but your writings were so full of humor, you yourself related this story about yourself."

"My humor is reserved for those who can understand my reflective introspection and considered retrospection. I see that the pirates of intellect, the sharks that crave the pedantic and thrive on the insignificant, have crippled your judgment. You would have done well to reflect upon my humorous parables."

"You wrote about animals and plants, worlds so familiar but yet so incomprehensible. But my friend, I am puzzled by people and life. I am puzzled by generosity and miserliness, by love, loyalty, and betrayal. I am puzzled by reason."

"I wrote about all of this as well. In every manifestation of life, whether in animals or plants, I saw a lesson, and I detested, how much did I detest, one-dimensional intellects. I lived fighting the pedantic morals of the pirates of intellect, of the traditionalists, and of the bureaucrats. I lived defending the beauty of thought and the art of reason for it is not reason alone that the pirates detest but the aesthetics of reason."

"Yet you wrote an essay in praise of Turkish soldiers which you gave to the minister al-Fath Ibn Khaqqan, killed with al-Mutawakkil in 247/861, who just happened to be of Turkish origins. What did this have to do with the aesthetics of thought?!"

"Oh, that again! Although an Arab from Basra, Iraq, I embraced the enlightened universalism of the 'Abbasids, their defense of rationalist thought and their integration of universal knowledge from all cultures."

"But you lived through the reigns of eleven 'Abbasid Caliphs, starting with al-Mahdi (d.169/785) and ending with al-Mu'tazz (d. 256/869). You were a declared Mu'tazili and yet, you were close to all of them. You always enjoyed the favors of those in power!"

"Not true! I was only respected by all of them. But I was close to al-Ma'mun (d. 218/833), al-Mu'tasim (d. 227/841) and al-Wathiq (d. 232/846), all three were enlightened men of learning and reason. They honored and supported the Mu'tazila. Al-Mutawakkil persecuted the Mu'tazila and Shi'a."

"But al-Ma'mun had persecuted the traditionalists and imprisoned Imam Ahmad Ibn Hanbal (d. 241/855)!"

"Each is accountable for his own deeds! For myself, I rejected the suffocating logic of the traditionalists such as the Hashawiyya and I resisted their intimidations and threats until the end. In my essay on '*Tashbih,*' I unequivocally stated that it is *haram* for any rationalist to yield to intimidation and refrain from speaking his mind. Whosoever feels that he has something to say, must say it!"

The ineffable mysteries of history and life are numerous, and what are books but life made timeless! Yet, the ambiguities are never clarified. The Mu'tazila insisted on rational and free thought, but when in the throes of power, they persecuted their opponents. But perhaps I have been ungenerous to my friend. His age is not mine. Ideas are timeless, but the applications are limited by their age. I should be grateful that the mistakes of the past are the lessons of today.

Didn't al-Jahiz have a conference of his own? Didn't books surround his life, and didn't the Islamic Civilization meet every night hosted, protected, and enriched by him? He was a moralist who tempered the dogmatism of morals with the discipline of reason. He confronted the pirates of intellect who, possessing no intellect of their own, rehabilitated their ignorance with intolerance. He resisted the extremists who confronted the tumultuous sea of life by dreaming of dominating others instead of dominating their own insecurities. What better example of this than his battles with the oppressors of women?

Whether al-Jahiz had an inherent regard for women will always remain debatable. But he rejected the vulgarity of mind and soul that permits a person to disdain half the human beings in the world, the type of vulgarity that utilizes the intellect of women in raising children but then sees nothing of use in that intellect once the children are grown men, and the vulgar morality that secludes women from public life as if women are for the private consumption of men.

In his essay on women al-Jahiz wrote, "We do not say, and any reasonable person cannot say, that women are above men or lower than men by a degree or two or more. But we have seen people who revile [women] the worst of revilements and disdain them and deny them most of their rights. It is true impotence for a man to be incapable of fulfilling the rights of fathers or uncles unless he disparages the rights of mothers and aunts." In his essay on female singers, al-Jahiz argues that the seclusion of women was never a part of Islam. Notable Islamic authorities have clearly permitted conversing and dealing with women, and there is no evidence to support the seclusion of women. The foundational principle, al-Jahiz declares, is that everything is allowed in Islam unless specifically forbidden, and the tastes and distastes of people are immaterial. Zeal in protection of honor is admirable unless it forbids what Allah has made *halal.* Al-Jahiz sums up the problem in the following statement: "This is a matter where the extremists have gone beyond the zeal for honor to the realm of bad

Truth!

manners and the lack of intelligence." The honor of men need not be founded upon the degradation of women.

Many rose in arms disparaging and attacking his integrity. He was accused, among other things, of being an extremist Shi'i. It is no longer possible to distinguish fact from slander. But the power of his words out-lived the gossip and out-lived the flesh. When the Caliph al-Mutawakkil died, al-Jahiz, honored by his struggle and exhaustion, took his beloved books and moved back to Basra. There he spent his last years producing gems of thought and transforming the living flesh into books.

Al-Jahiz, my most honored companion, forgive me, but I judge myself, not you. But what is the difference between the two? I cannot distinguish between the genuine and false about myself or you. Yet, I feel that the truth is not as important as the diligence in seeking the truth. The certain fact is that after years of embracing books, the books finally embraced you. In 255/869, while you were ill and weak, your books collapsed upon you, crushing you to death. In reality, your books honored you by delivering you unto life.

But the night had advanced to the point of retreat, and the morning announces its commanding presence. Al-Jahiz fades away, for every enlightenment will yield to the stagnation of the dark. The morning extinguishes the glittering lights in my soul and mind and heralds the dullness of the mundane. I must now abandon the certainty of the past to the delusions of the present. But the Conference of the Books promises to restore the luminous Islamic Civilization once again to my soul as it did in so many ages and for so many souls. My friend, till we meet again, peace be upon you.

CHAPTER 4

The Terror of Bigotry

In the small crowded apartment outside Princeton, New Jersey, despite the often-silencing agonies of life, the Conference of the Books endures. At times, the delight that some take in crucifixions, the treachery, and the wretchedness becomes too much. At times like this, the Conference starts losing its audience and patrons, and even its keeper nearly despairs. But the Muslim Civilization has endured the obscenities of history and, through its Conferences, it has persevered with dignity throughout the ages. These conferences are the unwavering record of our action and inaction, of our beliefs and dreams, and of our determination and despair. At the end, the record always prevails.

So many people, in a glimpse of a second, were extinguished. Children in a day-care center, happily anticipating the return of their parents, were forever denied that moment. I remember my six-year-old son in school and his smile when he sees me, and the horror baffles the intellect and heart. The world of books seems so remote and distant. The faces, the smiles, and tears of children from Bosnia, Chechnya, Kashmir, Rwanda, and Oklahoma mingle in the mind and the pain becomes overwhelming. My dear books, forgive me. Tonight, I need the time to mourn and grieve. The nationality of a victim is as immaterial as the nationality of a book. If hurt, I mourn and grieve.

The news arrives that the suspects are "Middle Eastern looking." What does that mean? Does that mean they are good looking? Mean looking? Strange looking? I resent the fact that the reverence of mourning is violated by this confusion. The reality sets in that some people are suspecting Muslims. How could that be? I remember past

Conferences. How many books forbade the killing of civilians? There must be a declaration of war, the targets must be military, and the attack must be discriminating and proportional. You may not destroy plants or livestock, or poison streams. So many Conferences have declared that those who attack the defenseless are the *muharibun*, the worst of all criminals. The Qur'an calls this "an act of corruption on earth." How could the perpetrators be Muslim then? But I recall that all civilizations have their murderers, and I mourn and grieve.

But soon the faces of the accused emerge. They do not look good, mean, or strange. They look like people, people accused of a crime. Do all Muslims look like suspects? But those who accused Muslims refuse to apologize. The serenity in which I must mourn and grieve is once again denied me. Some zealots argue that despite the facts of this case, the real threat still comes from Muslims. In other words, Muslims are tried and convicted for a crime that they are not even accused of committing. If Muslims attended the Conferences of history, this shameful bigotry would not be allowed to pass. If Muslims read history, this would become the equivalent of the Dreyfus Affair.

The real danger to the United States still comes from Muslims! When the record prevails, it will be recalled that the most serious threat to the United States has always been posed by racism and bigotry. Is it that ignorance of the record produces bigotry or does bigotry exist independent of any record? In any case, the cost of ignorance is always the denial of dignity. Right now, dignity demands that we be allowed to mourn and grieve—mourn the victims and grieve for the bigotry.

CHAPTER 5

The Civilization of the Book

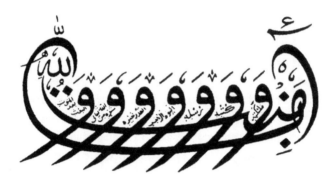

"The *Rahman* taught the Qur'an, created humans, and taught them discernment" (55: 1–4). The Qur'an is the embodiment of this divine ability—the ability to discern, comprehend, judge, and intelligently express that which is believed. Tonight I sit with you in my lap. In your presence I am ashamed to exist. But where can I go? I am not so luminous or so pure as to dissolve into you. So I try to integrate your divinity within my human soul. Do I succeed? Do I ever succeed? My Qur'an, my beloved Reading, The Reading that started all readings, The Reading that preceded all readings and that inspires all readings. What a privilege it is to have you and what a burden! The actual word of the Divine Essence, the tangible presence of The Divine in our midst. What a privilege and what a burden! How can I, with all my weaknesses, anxieties, and fears, understand you? But I love you too much to stop trying to understand. Yet, I love you too much to dare think that I do, in fact, understand.

Imam 'Ali (d. 40/661) once said, "Sleep demolishes the resolutions of the day." So I don't sleep. I never sleep. I spend the nights with you struggling and pleading with each and every one of your words. You say, "Surely in the long wake of the night the soul is receptive and the words more telling" (73:6). So how could I sleep? Perhaps a spark from your enlightenment will search for me in the dark and not find me. Perhaps it will call upon me but my unconscious mind will alienate it. I stay up waiting for the call and praying that you will always find me.

When you do find me, what do you find? You find a reader limited by his abilities, biases, ignorances, and experiences. You find a reader who, in attempting to understand, constructs the text, the author, and himself. Imam 'Ali said, "The Qur'an is but a book between two covers—it is humans who read it, understand it, and implement it." The Qur'an is a text, and a text mediates between the author and the reader. The Divine authorship of the text compels this mediation, and the human readership ensures its dynamism. So throughout history, we debated you—created or uncreated, literal or symbolic, rational or mystical. We debated the principles, the history, the ethics, and the laws. In reality, through you, we were constructing ourselves and we were debating who we are and what we are. Then debates stopped and the dynamism of the process stagnated because we became convinced that the reader is as divine and immutable as the author.

But here, in the Conference of the Books, the debates still rage on and the dynamic discovery ends only to begin again. In the small crowded apartment outside Princeton, New Jersey, the Islamic Civilization, the Qur'anic Civilization, still stands, reproducing itself every night. Has a single text ever played such a pivotal role in any world civilization? Has there ever been a civilization based on a text, a single text, before this one? Weren't we the civilization of the Reading? But how did a civilization founded on reading forget the art of reading? Why is it that the people of the Book came to disdain books? My God, You said that they forgot God, so You caused them to forget themselves. But one forgets himself only if he is no longer able to read himself. Is this how we came to forget You? Is this how we came to forget the art of reading?

Perhaps some fools believed that a single book can replace all other books. Perhaps, in this day and age, these fools came to believe that since we have the Book, we need no other books. But books do not preclude other books, they only generate more books. I remember the verse, "And the Prophet said, O my Lord! My people have taken this Qur'an with utter abandonment" (25:30) and it torments my soul. What greater abandonment is there than to deny the essence? If we abandoned The Text is it any wonder that we abandoned all other texts?

But tonight is a blessed night because this Conference is about you. You said, "*Ta Ha*, We have not sent the book upon you to cause you distress" (20:1–2). So I will not distress or despair. How can I despair when I am in such dazzling company! Ever since Allah has revealed you, how many moments of enlightenment have you generated? How many glimpses of divinity have you permitted? How many sighs, how many tears, how many thoughts? If only I could experience each word as it penetrated every mind. Instead what I do experience are the books you generated. The list of books about you or because of you is bewildering. Thousands of books on your grammar, your style, your history, your philosophy, your purposes, your laws. Some are lost, most are still manuscripts, some are published, and some are here tonight in this Conference.

The early commentaries were short, no more than a single volume. But these were the first expressions of love and nothing can reproduce that honesty. Yet most of them are lost. Sufyan al-Thawri (d. 161/777) and 'Abd al-Rahman al-Saddi (d. 128/745) note their fresh and untamed impressions with timid bashfulness. The much more daring Muqatil Ibn Sulayman (d. 150/767) is not published. Actually, he was published once, but the Egyptian government thought to void 1,400 years of history and banned him. I remember a night like this one when a bookish friend and I managed to get the microfilm of the manuscript. We spent all night printing and copying with such excitement. We were upholding the will of history. Muqatil, don't despair, you are bound to overcome. Many years earlier, some people tried to suppress the writings of Ibn Jarir al-Tabari (d. 310/923), and yet his commentary on the Qur'an is now uncontainable. Al-Tabari tried to record the historical context of the Qur'an. Instead, he reproduced much mythology. Today, most people mistake his mythology for history.

Nothing equals the pristine honesty of Abu al-Hasan al-Mawardi (d. 450/1058). For every verse, he lists four or five opinions as to its meaning and purpose. What a delightful banquet of ideas for those who believe that Allah cannot be contained by a human mind. About a hundred years later, the systematic works of the Mu'tazili al-Zamakhshari (d. 538/1144) and the Shi'i al-Tabarsi (d. 548/1153) emerged. Both men are a testament to the fact that in Allah could be the liberation of the human mind. Yet, while al-Tabarsi would put the sectarians of today to shame, al-Zamakhshari made no secret of his disdain for Sufis and Sufism. As in every Qur'anic conference, Fakhr al-Din al-Razi (d. 606/1280) sits in a world of his own. His commentary is thirty volumes of precise reason conducting the divine symphony into exquisite rhyme. I always place him next to the technical and unimaginative al-Baydawi (d. 685/1286) and Ibn Kathir (d. 774/1372) to balance the ecstasy of reason with the moderation of discipline. How ironic is history! Al-Baydawi, the Iranian from Shiraz, is now predominantly read in Egypt and Syria, and Ibn Kathir, the scholar of *hadith*, is now considered the orthodoxy on the Qur'an.

Hundreds of scholars approached the text of the Qur'an, absorbing it, and becoming absorbed by it. It transformed them, but they transformed it as well. I read none of them for an inherent truth, but for the truth of the transformation, and I search for my own transformation. In a word, when I read you, I read myself. None of the commentaries provide mechanical points of reference for authenticity. They only point the way. They exemplify the method for discovery, but they are not the discovery. The authentic, genuine truth only comes when the self, informed by its heritage, transforms and is transformed by the text.

God, You declared that, "Authority (*al-hukm*) is for none but God. In Him, I trust, and in Him, must trust those who are capable of trust" (12:67). But I struggle with myself to be able to trust and in this is the transformation. God, You said, "It is not possible that a human being to whom is given the Book and Wisdom, and the Prophecy, should say to people: 'Worship me instead of God.' No, to the contrary, he would say: 'Be the people of God by virtue of what you taught from the book, and by virtue of what you have studied'" (3:79). So I refuse to worship another and I refuse to worship any book. Authorized and empowered by You, I teach myself the Book, and I study all other books. In this, I worship and in this I search Your *hukm*.

God, Your *hukm* cannot be in the law books; Your *hukm* is in the minds that understand and study the law books. Many have written on the laws of the Qur'an. Some of them are here in this Conference tonight. The Hanafi al-Jassas (d. 370/980), the Shafi'i al-Kiya al-Harrasi (d. 504/1110), and the Maliki Ibn al-'Arabi (d. 543/1148) are present. Al-Qurtubi (d. 671/1272), the Maliki, and his huge compendium placing the laws in the context of their meanings are here as well. You know how much I cherish them and how often I consult them. But it is pedantic and even pretentious to equate the laws in the books with Your *hukm*. Can Your *hukm* be contained and limited by a law? No, Your *hukm* is embodied in the process that seeks out the meaning of the law, and in the causes and purposes of the law. Laws cannot transform or enlighten. The meanings behind the law will both transform and enlighten.

The hours have passed and the night is subsiding. The Civilization of the Book must now bring its Conference to a close. But the Conference never ends, it only adjourns. As I re-shelve you I pray, God forgive me for taking Your Book with such abandonment. Tomorrow, You willing, I will continue my transformation. God, through a single book You transformed us into a civilization of books. Will we ever remember this transformation? Will the people of this nation once again transform into Your nation, a nation of books?

The Interminable Conference

I read, "O' people, We created you from a male and female, and formed you into nations and tribes so that you may get to know each other. Indeed the most pious among
you has greater honor with God" (49:13), and the Conference began again. It is the same
Conference in a different time and a different place. It is an interminable Conference that
never ends although the attendants come and go. It is the Conference of the Books.

The place has changed. It is no longer held in a small, crowded apartment in
Princeton, New Jersey. It now convenes in a crowded house in Austin, Texas. The time
does not matter, the place does not matter. This Conference is its own time and place.
It defines its own space.

I had stopped reporting on this Conference for a year. It is not that there is nothing to say, but the thunderous oratories of books are silencing. If you listen to every
book, you may never speak. But here the problem is augmented ten-fold. This is an
Islamic Conference for Islamic books. The proceedings of this Conference, the murmurings, the rumblings, are all done in a language not of this place or age. The expressions, phrases, symbols, and discourses have been immortalized by time in a
book. But the book was a product of its age. Immortal yet contextual, textual and si-
multaneously contextual, this is the inevitable dilemma of books.

In this Conference hundreds of books stand and converse—books on *sira, hadith,
fiqh, tafsir, usul, adab,* and much more. Yet, my books, in this context you are so foreign, so marginal. You are an anachronism!

Here, in this time and place, you are fossilized showpieces. The orientalist uses
you to confirm the inferiority of the other, and the oriental uses you to apologize for

being that other. As to the rest, you are incomprehensible, your language archaic and your universe of symbols impenetrable. Your terminology and categories impress that who is tolerant, enchant the patient, assure the alienated, misguide the stupid, and is ignored by the contemporary.

Here in this place and now in this age, they do not care about your categories: the *hasan* or *qabih*, the *'ilal* or *maqasid*, the *'amm* or *muqayyad*, the *zann* or *yaqin*. Here and now, they care about deficits, portfolios, health insurance, gang violence, sexism, proms, drunk driving, date rape, and teenage pregnancies. Yet, I know that you are eternal and immutable because you speak forever. But you are contextual because it is the people who read you who must speak to the age, the people who read you who must transform through you into a book for our new age and new place.

My dear books, you are the living example of a people's irrepressible desire to search for and discover the Divine Will. You are the humble servants of that Will, the living documentation of the search for God's ends and means and purposes. You are the living proof of the submission, so you are the living proof of Islam. You are what made us and we are what must make you.

God said, ". . .We formed you into nations and tribes *li ta'arafu.*" *Li ta'arafu* means to get to know one another. But the word *'arafa* (to know) is quite profound. It connotes kindness, goodness, tolerance, and patience. In its various forms, it could mean to observe and learn, to seek after something, and to recognize that which has become customary and that which is good. All these nuances of meaning are embodied by the process of knowledge. To know is to learn and teach—learn about others and teach about ourselves. To learn and teach, that is *ta'aruf.* And neither learning nor teaching can be accomplished without kindness, tolerance, and patience.

My books, your story and message must become known. In order to learn and teach, we must know ourselves, and that is not possible without you. It is reported that the Prophet said, "Whoever knows himself [or herself] knows his [or her] God." To know God is to know God's creation, and all nations and tribes are a part of that creation. What a magnificent and sublime process of self-knowledge and knowledge of the other, united in the knowledge of the Divine. And it is all realized through you.

If you are outdated or irrelevant to this time and place, it is only because we, ourselves, are outdated and irrelevant. You do not embody the truth—nothing does. But you are a demonstrative proof of the truth—the truth of knowledge, the truth of the process and the method. The process and the truth that is founded on kindness, tolerance, and patience, and this is relevant to every age.

CHAPTER 7

On Betrayal

"She had the seed of a traitor!" This is what he told me when I inquired about his breakup.

"A traitor? Isn't this too harsh?"

"No," he replied, "You know the problem in the Muslim community. I just didn't like the way she talked to men, and then her lack of forthrightness about it."

I felt uncomfortable, and he felt it. "Well, *insha' Allah,* it's all for the better," I muttered and rose from my chair, signaling that it is getting late. "I better get back to my books!" Thank God that they did not get married, I thought, as I closed the door behind him.

It is time for the Conference of the Books to re-convene and I must clear my mind. I must be respectful to my interlocutors and give the books my full attention, but the trials of life are difficult. What is behind my friend's statement, "I did not like the way she talked to men and her lack of forthrightness about it?" Is it the intelligence of anticipating evil or the wisdom of reading the propensities of people? Or is it the sin of suspicion and reckless judgment? Or is it the patriarchy of sexism that allows to men what it will not allow women? What is my friend talking about? Betrayal, the possibility of betrayal.

And what problem in the Muslim community was he referring to? I felt impatient with my impatience. Why didn't I ask him and why was I in such a hurry to get out of an uncomfortable situation? The Muslim community in the United States does have an unreasonably high rate of divorce—higher than the norm. But is divorce, by definition, a form of betrayal? Marriage is built on a promise, that promise is called by God the "heavy covenant." Divorce is a breaking of that promise.

But what is the definition of betrayal? Is it simply the breaking of a promise? I picked up Ibn Hazm's (d. 456/1064) *The Ring of the Dove.* Ibn Hazm, a well-known Zahiri theologian and jurist, wrote this elegant work in Jativa, Andalusia, in 418/1027. In it he expounded his theory of courtly love, a theory that would later have a profound influence on medieval Europe and the Troubadours. I flipped through the book to the chapter on betrayal and the first words were, "As fidelity is a most lofty attribute and a truly noble quality, so betrayal is base and detestable in the extreme." I read through the chapter but did not find a definition of betrayal—only descriptions of the act.

I opened the Qur'an and read: "God advances the example of Noah's wife and the wife of Lot for those who do not believe. They were married to Our two pious servants but they betrayed them and even the apostles could not avail them in the least against God. . ." (66:10) The question then is: How did Noah's wife and Lot's wife betray their husbands? Noah's wife called her husband insane behind his back, and Lot's wife snitched on Abraham's guests. Here, the betrayal is not necessarily the breaking of a promise but the violation of a trust. But is every violation of a trust a betrayal? Someone could trust me when I did not ask to be trusted. For example, a person could expect me to act as a loyal friend when I never accepted the friendship.

I pondered the question further. Betrayal is not just the breaking of a trust, but it is the breaking of a trust that has been accepted. In other words, if one accepts a trust that has been placed in him or her, then one has created the expectation of trustworthiness. Violating this induced expectation is betrayal. In that sense, every breaking of a promise is a betrayal. But then betrayal is at the heart of every major sin, for one betrays himself before betraying others or God. There is no broken home, destitute child, vanquished nation, or forgotten book without some form of betrayal. In fact, betrayal is at the heart of every *fitna*, and *fitna* is worse than murder (2:217).

If betrayal is such a grave offense, then how is it possible that it be committed? What possesses a person to create the expectation of trust but then degrade himself or herself by betraying! I recalled Ibn Hazm's words: "But you must know that uncomely acts such as betrayal never appear as such to those who perform them, therefore their repulsiveness is doubly disgusting to others innocent of them." And I muttered to myself, "God does not like those who are treacherous" (8:58).

Since my friend unwittingly had engaged me with this most distressing topic, I thought "every hardship should beget ease." So I decided to spend the balance of the night with Ibn al-Marzuban (d. 309/921) and his book, *The Superiority of Dogs Over Many of Those Who Wear Clothes.* Dogs are loyal and human beings are capable of treachery. But dogs are loyal without making promises or creating expectations of mutual trust. Truly, in all of God's creation is a lesson for us.

CHAPTER **8**

A Prayer

The pangs of thought, memory, and conscience erupt in the night. There are no restrictions and no escapes. Every night we are put on trial by our past. Our life is a series of convictions, paroles, and suspended sentences. Here we are. The keeper of the Conference of the Books has become a teacher! But when did that happen and why? The position has changed from student to teacher, and the expectations have altered accordingly. The position has changed, but the substance remains the same. Now, a stream of students come with questions, and the keeper is paid to provide answers. Yet, this is a delusional game! If only he could be paid to remain a student, he would not even for a second participate in this game.

Today, a student comes to say that she has done what she will forever regret—not once or twice but many times. She, in utter degradation, attempted to quench a thirst only to feel a greater longing every time. She needed the emotional comfort, the security, and attention more than anything else. No one ever understood her or gave her the comfort she craved. Now, she has found someone who loves her and wishes to marry her, but the past is an ominous presence.

In the mosque they told her that, "A fornicator cannot marry but a fornicator or an idolatrous woman, and a fornicator cannot marry but a fornicator or an idolatrous man. Such conduct is forbidden to the believers" (24:3). Then she asks, "With my past, can he marry me? Should he marry me?"

I remember all the times I have been asked this same question, and I feel my heart being flooded with pain. She then asks the common question: "Not all of them were all the way. Does that make a difference?" Why do people play these games with God?

Yes, it makes a difference for a judge in a criminal court, but as to God? I don't know. Whether it is all-out intercourse or everything but, that is a technical distinction. Law thrives on technical distinctions but morality does not.

I attempt to end this awkward situation, and so I quickly say, "Well, it says in verse five of the same *Sura,* 'Except those who repent and make amends, God is most Forgiving, Ever-Merciful.'" "Yes," she says, "but doesn't that refer to an exemption from the punishment for slandering chaste women?" I think to myself, "Great! She's done her homework!"

At what level should I respond to her? Should I ask her why she did it? Does that make any difference? Will that alter the sad fact that God's trust was abused and the body loaned by God misused? Shall I go on to talk about the complex emotions that are implicated in these situations? The hurt, the memories, the distrust, the disappointment, the doubt, and the feeling of being pursued by your sins wherever you go? 'Umar Ibn al-Khattab (d. 23/644), before Islam, buried his daughter alive. The memory of her wiping the sand off his forehead just before he covered her with dirt tormented him until the end. Sadly, sins do not die, they are only forgiven.

Fortunately, I am not a counselor or religious adviser. I am a professor, and I can hide behind the opinions of books and the cold voice of texts. "Well," I said, "the jurists disagreed about the meaning and application of this verse." According to one report, this verse was revealed when a Muslim man wanted to marry a repentant prostitute named Umm Mahdhul. After the verse was revealed, the Prophet told him not to marry her. Other reports state that the verse was revealed when a Muslim named Marthad wanted to marry a Meccan prostitute named 'Inaq, and the Prophet advised that he not marry her. Yet other reports assert that it was revealed when the Prophet forbade a group of newly converted migrants in Medina called *Ahl al-Suffah* from marrying a group of prostitutes living in Medina.

Some late Shafi'i jurists argued that the verse means that if a fornicator marries someone who is chaste, the contract is void. Other jurists maintained that this verse addresses the honesty of a marriage contract. If a man or woman is a fornicator and conceals this fact upon marrying a chaste person, the chaste person will have the option to void the contract upon finding out about their spouse's dishonesty. Yet, other jurists disagreed and argued that the verse only refers to those who have been criminally punished for fornication. A person punished by a *hadd* (one hundred lashes) for fornication can only marry a person similarly punished. Another group of jurists asserted that the verse means that divorce must follow adultery. If a spouse commits adultery, the marriage is dissolved. A group of jurists examining a variety of precedents argued that the verse means that if a man and woman fornicate, they must marry after the criminal punishment is enforced.

A large number of jurists argued that the verse was abrogated and that if a fornicator repents, they can marry whomever they will. However, the sin must be disclosed to the potential spouse. 'Abdullah Ibn Mas'ud (d. 32/652), the Prophet's Companion, asserted that one should not marry a fornicator unless they are satisfied that they have fully repented and unless they wait a period of time to be assured that there is no pregnancy.

Here it is! The full range of opinions. The evidence cited by each side is overwhelming and I save her the agony of going through it. She stares at me puzzled and annoyed. "So what do I do?" she says. I shift uncomfortably in my chair and hear myself babble, "Well, you must be honest with him; this is a condition to the contract. You must fully repent and then proceed with your marriage and life." "But," she mutters sadly, "even if he forgives, it will never be an equal relationship!"

Later that night, I sit in the midst of the Conference of the Books. I nervously open one book as I close another. What intuitively makes sense to me might not be what God wants. I must make sure. But even if God forgives, is the agony of sin ever really erased from our minds? Sin has this horrid ability to chase one throughout life.

Irritated, I wonder, why are these books so cold? Why aren't the agonies of our feebleness and the pains of our senselessness reflected in them? Why is the complexity of human life infinitely more convoluted than the refinement of books? Even if he forgives her, will he trust her? Will she forgive or trust herself? And if he trusts her, will his imagination manage to forget the presence of those men when he is with her? Exhausted, I pray for them: May God guide them, bless them, and give them serenity and peace. I remind myself that, ultimately, in every case, all thought and all knowledge must reduce itself to a prayer.

Donkeys Carrying Books

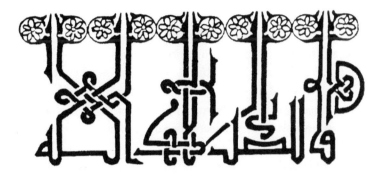

The symbolic world of Islam invokes pain—fear and pain. The verse, "We have not sent the Qur'an upon you to cause you distress" (20:2), does not resound in many hearts. The Qur'an talks of donkeys carrying books (62:5), and these donkeys continue trampling on many minds. "We made some of you the means of trying others. So will you persevere?" (25:20). God, we do try to persevere but the trial of these donkeys is more demanding than any other.

Today's class is about *Surat Yusuf (Joseph)* and there is so much to analyze and ponder. "*Alif Lam Ra*, these are the verses of the immaculate Book. We have sent it as an Arabic Qur'an so that you may understand" (12:1–2). The story told is painfully current and relevant. The saga of hope and despair, of weakness and strength, and of stupidity and wisdom requires careful handling. He struggles to recall every thought and every word heard in the Conference of the Books about this *Sura* and prays, "God, let us not carry a burden we cannot bear" (2:286).

A woman, her mouth open as if in a gasp, sits fixedly staring at the performance. Her white pale face protrudes in front of her blond hair. Excited, she struggles to overcome an obvious exhaustion. He had seen her in previous classes, but many audit his courses, and most faces come and go.

After class, there is an inevitable feeling of let-down. An idea could have been done better justice, and a thought could have been better explained. Expression always uncovers the silent incoherence of many ideas. Invariably, ideas sheltered by silence always seem much more coherent than when expressed. As he stands surrounded by students demanding elucidations and clarifications, he notices the woman standing away from the group talking to his wife. Their faces seem solemn and serious; his wife speaks with intensity, and the woman listens anxiously.

The circle of students starts to dissipate and he notices his wife edging her way toward him with the woman following. They stand close and his wife urges: "Ask him! Ask him!" For some reason the woman hesitates; bashfulness has always been a virtue! His wife finally exclaims with an obvious sense of distress, "She's been wanting to take her *Shahadah* for a year now but the people in the mosque tell her she must first wear the *hijab!*"

The people at the mosque! And who are these people? She has been studying Islam and has read the Qur'an a few times. For a year, she has been on the verge of taking the *Shahadah* and becoming a Muslim, but each time she is dissuaded by a debate on the *hijab*. She is told that the *hijab* must accompany the *Shahadah* or, at least, a declaration that the *hijab*, in due course, will be adopted. Inquiry into the matter is foreclosed by *ijma'* and no further reflection or discussion is warranted. Perhaps, and perhaps not.

The claim of *ijma'* is the very process by which *ijma'* is formed; the claim of *ijma'* always far proceeds its existence. Does the *ijma'* of an age bind every age thereafter, and how does one define a particular age? Does it matter that the jurist al-Razi (d. 606/1210) and many others held that whoever contradicts the *ijma'* is not a *kafir* or *fasiq*? No matter, these are complicated issues that do not yield to polemic debates. The question before us is a basic sense of priorities. No, not even priorities, but a basic sense of decency and respect of rights. If a person wishes to take the *Shahadah*, one must take it from them, advise them, and pray.

The Prophet accepted the *Shahadah* of an untold number of people, and even the *Shahadah* of a soldier in the battlefield was considered valid. After Mecca was conquered, those who gave their *bay'a* to the Prophet promised to uphold the five pillars and refrain from committing any of the *hudud* crimes. Needless to say, a *Shahadah* is not a *bay'a*, and *hijab* does not involve a pillar of Islam or a *hadd* crime.

Does it make any difference that the *hijab* was not decreed until the very end of the Medina period, and that the verse says, "This is nearer to them being recognizable so that no harm will come to them"? (33:59). Must the *'illa* (operative cause) of the law exist for the law to exist? (*al-'illa taduru ma'a al-ma'lul wujudan wa 'adaman*). If harm is the operative cause of the law of *hijab*, what greater harm is there than to desire the *Shahadah* and to be denied it?

Later that night, in the secluded comfort of the *Conference of the Books*, he finds himself reading Ibn al-Qayyim's (d. 751/1350) *I'lam al-Muwaqqi'in*. The *Conference of the Books* gives no comfort to donkeys. The invention of the automobile has made donkeys entirely irrelevant to this Conference.

Whatever causes hardship and misery cannot be a part of *Shari'a* even if people believe it to be so, Ibn al-Qayyim argues in the *I'lam*. Shihab al-Din al-Qarafi (d. 684/1285), al-'Izz Ibn 'Abd al-Salam (d. 661/1262), and Abu Ishaq al-Shatibi (d. 790/1388) speak of the processes by which the *Shari'a* eases hardship and begets facility. The Prophet is reported to have warned us against repulsing others and God declares: "Allah desires ease for you and desires not hardship for you" (2:185). Perhaps all of this is irrelevant. Perhaps there is no greater hardship for the Muslim *Ummah* today than the calamity of women not being properly covered.

CHAPTER 10

To Murder the Soul

رسم الله الوهو الوهم

How does one reclaim a right compromised at a moment of weakness? How does one reclaim what has been forcibly taken away by the compulsion of power? How does one regain the equilibrium of the soul after an imbalance? How does one stop the descent into annihilation after being caught at the edge of a spiraling whirlpool?

If one takes your tangible property, one is taking merely what you own and to forgive is to be generous. But when one usurps your intangible quality, your moral property, your realm of consciousness, or that infinitely vague moral space we call the self, how can you forgive and how can you be generous with the self?

Questions crowd in my bewildered mind every time I encounter the world's ugliness. This ugliness gives me the frame of reference by which I understand the world's beauty . . . but I suffer nonetheless. She confronts me with what I cannot explain. She reproaches me at every encounter without saying a word. Does your dignified and sanctimonious Conference of the Books deal with the extremities of ugliness? Does your Conference console a murdered soul?

After an uncomfortable pause, she tells me that as a child she learned that love is a service. The warmth and love of a parent that you take for granted came to me at the price of my soul. She senses the anxiety on my face and she says: "Yes, I was sexually molested by my father most of my life." Do you have any idea how that feels? I learned early on that my body was not my own—it was simply a price to be paid in return for attention and affection. I learned to hate and sacrifice my body and to cower each time in shame. I was locked into a cycle of degradation and bitter self-hate. The barriers of decency or morality were long ago destroyed. Your dignified Conference cannot endure the degrading details so I will save you the agony. But who talks about me in your dignified world?

Now, I refuse to be a victim. I do not want anyone to die or suffer for my sins or my father's sins. Each is responsible for his own. Every waking moment I try to empower myself, to reclaim myself, and to assert the right to say no. But do you have any idea how it feels when you learn that loving your parents means to service them, and to disassociate from your body, and to experience the death of your soul?

I tried to find what my fellow Muslims have to say about me or to me. I found books written by atheists, Jews, and Christians, but nothing by fellow brethren. Nothing by Muslims about rape, sexual abuse, or child molestation. Do I exist in your world? I tried to talk to my fellow Muslims about my "experiences"—have you ever experienced the shifty eyes, the uncomfortable glances, the change of topic, and the self-assured advice to forget the unforgettable?

If Allah says that, in the case of one who murders a person, it is as if he murdered humanity. How about when your body is stolen and your soul is murdered, and you are left to make sense of it all? I must admit to you, I attend so many lessons that lecture on the sanctity of parental rights and the gravity of severing the ties of blood and I feel lost. The Qur'an says: "Would any of you like to eat the flesh of their dead brother? Surely you loathe such a deed. . ." (49:12). How about those who devour the flesh of their living daughters—are they still to be considered parents?

A sister once told me that the worst of all sins is *shirk* and the Qur'an says: "We have enjoined on people benevolence toward their parents; . . . should they contend with you that you associate with Me that of which you have no knowledge, then do not obey them, but accompany them with kindness in this world, and follow the way of those who turn to Me in humility" (31:15). This sister reasoned that if *shirk* is the worst of sins and even then I must accompany them with kindness, then the response to sexual abuse must still be kindness. But, once again, I must admit to you that when I see my father, I get flashbacks and I frequently vomit or feel intense pain in the violated parts of my body. I do not want answers from you. Your Conference seems to discourse about everything. But does this Conference talk about me?

For a passing moment I wonder why people consume each other in this fashion. Why is it that some people feed their souls by consuming the souls of others? How could the private sanctity of the family become the locked door behind which the most egregious slaughter takes place? I cannot sugarcoat the realities to her, and I cannot pretend not to feel. No, she is not present in my Conference. I open the books of the moralists from Ibn Abi al-Dunya (d. 281/894) to Abu Hamid al-Ghazali (d. 505/1111) to Taqi al-Din Ibn Taymiyya (d. 728/1328), and I find no mention of her or her suffering. The jurists were very reluctant to hold parents liable for offenses committed against their children. Some even cited, out of context, the Qur'anic verse,

"No mother shall be made to suffer on account of her child, and no father shall be made to suffer on account of his child. . ." (2:233), in arguing that a parent cannot be punished for killing his child. No doubt they were wrong. The only place I can find a discourse about her is in the writings of non-Muslim authors. Most bookstores have a section on abuse and self-empowerment. But our books are silent. Unfortunately, my sister, you have not yet entered our consciousness. I know that in some circumstances an apology is an insult. But this whole Conference is an apology for our contemporary reality. I write this in your honor and may future Conferences acknowledge your reality.

A One More Knowing

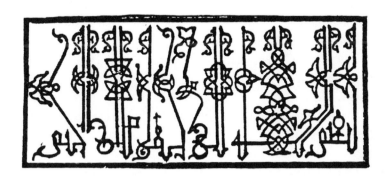

Wa fawqa kulli dhi 'ilmin 'alim—a phrase occurring, after a proclamation, in verse 76 of *Surat Yusuf* (Joseph) that resonates throughout every Conference and every night. "So he searched their saddle-bags before his brother's, then produced the cup from his brother's bag. This is how We planned for Joseph, for he could not take his brother under the law of the king unless God so willed. We raise in status whom We please. And over everyone endowed with knowledge is one/One more knowing."

In the strained hours of nightly reflections, this phrase taunts, torments, and comforts you. The scholars would debate whether it means that over everyone endowed with knowledge is a person more knowing, or that over everyone endowed with knowledge is the One who is All-Knowing. The one does not exclude the other. In either case, the impact upon you is the same. When it comes to knowledge, you are tormented by your status, taunted by the status of others, and comforted by the status of God.

If you could struggle with problems of your own construction, the hours of reflection would not be so strained. You would control the problem and its solution. You would no longer be taunted and, at times baffled, by the way others think of and resolve problems. If only you could filter all the problems through your own unitary and individualistic perceptions, you could escape the long agonizing hours of incoherence. If only you could speak to yourself—if you could be the speaker and the audience, you would make perfect sense.

But every morning as you emerge from your sanctuary, you are taunted and tormented by the endless stream of challenges to your coherence and lucidity. Your convictions remain solid. It is your very lucidity that is challenged. A student tells you that the only way she can afford repaying her father's debts and going to school is to objectify herself every night into an item of consumption on a dance floor. She asks, how is that different from the way men and women are objectified and consumed every day in their corporate jobs? A woman tells you that she feels objectified and consumed in her marriage. She is no longer an individual with feelings and emotions, but she is simply a functional role—a role that she plays without dignity or pride. Doesn't that give her the right to seek after one who does make her feel as an individual and humanizes her dead soul?

A man, after fifteen years of marriage and three children, tells you that he has now found a woman who is "better for his religion." She brings him closer to God than his present wife. He asks, "Don't I have an unequivocal right to divorce, granted to me by God?" Then he adds, "As to the children—children are resilient, and when they grow up they will understand."

A kid has become convinced that the devil has blue eyes and that on the Final Day all the evil ones will be resurrected with blue eyes. Doesn't that tell us something about the worth and nature of races? Another kid has become convinced that the heart of Islam is the *Khilafa* (Caliphate) and until there is a *Khilafa* everything is *haram*. Doesn't that create an unwavering duty upon all of us to focus on the singular goal of re-establishing the *Khilafa* on this earth?

A woman argues that what she does with her body is her business. Her body is her canvas; it is where she asserts and expresses herself. The man arguing with her seems to think that every woman's body is his business, his canvas, and his means to self-expression.

Life confronts you with absurdities. Layers of problems that demand not only clarity of thought but expression. To know what is right needs only conviction, but to be able to communicate what you believe to be right needs lucidity. Yet, lucid expression demands lucid thought, and the clarity of a thought is inseparable from the clarity of the expression that communicates it.

Knowledge belongs to God, and coherence is your duty. You carry the burden of lucidity in understanding and expressing God's knowledge. The infinite ability of human beings to produce absurdities only reminds you of your status. Over everyone endowed with knowledge is The One who is more knowing. The burden of lucidity taunts and torments you. The knowledge of The All-Knowing comforts you. And you pray, "God, ease the burdens of my heart and lift the impediments of my tongue so that they may understand what I say" (20:25–8).

CHAPTER 12

Women as an 'Awra

The Conference of the Books consoles our reality with a dream. The dream is complex and rich but serene. It is the serenity of faith directed by the intellect and disciplined by morality. In this dream, the human soul and mind are uplifted by the Divine. The Divine affirms the innate worth of the human being. A dream might exist at the edge of reality, yet it remains only a dream. By its very nature, a dream urges, teases, and provokes reality, but a dream is not real.

Early in the morning hours you sit engulfed in your dream. The last ten days of *Ramadan* break down your body. Liberated, you further abandon the physical to the metaphysical, and you abandon what you know for what you hope to know.

As the hours pass, a knock on the door announces the end of supplications and the serenity of isolation. If the Conference is a dream, then our reality is a nightmare. Why is it that the victims of this nightmare are most often women, and the victimizers are genderless beings?

Yet another woman attracted to the religion and repulsed by the followers—validated by the Qur'an and voided by Muslims. "When I first visited the mosque, believe me, I was dressed modestly. But a man ran yelling at me," she insists. My first lesson in Islam was that men have bodies, women only have *'awras* (private parts). In fact, I am nothing but an *'awra*. Her eyes fill up with tears. I have become so desensitized to those tears.

The second lesson learned was even more painful. Allah says, "When you are greeted with a greeting, then greet with one fairer or repeat the same greeting" (4:86). Allah also states, "And when you enter houses, greet each other with a greeting from

Allah, pure and blessed. That is how God explains things to you clearly so that you may understand" (24:61).

But I don't understand. I was told that when you enter the house of God, you may not greet men. In fact, when you enter anywhere you may not greet men. I was told that if greeted, I may respond in a low voice. *Al-salamu ʿalaykum* may be answered in an equal *salam* (greeting). Greet only if greeted embodies the same logic of speak only if spoken to.

"I am not a petty person," she says in her typically defensive fashion, "but I don't understand." How could the religion that "liberated" women transform them into an "*ʿawra*?" How could women be liberated, but denied existence? If I am denied the right to greet someone, I am denied the right to assert my existence. If I wait to be greeted before I may respond, then I am awaiting my existence to be acknowledged before I may exist.

On the Final Day, the righteous will be bestowed with an immeasurable favor. They will be greeted by God, and their greeting will be "*salam*" (33:44; 10:10). Their merit will be acknowledged by God—a generous greeting that affirms their worth. But men are not my God, and my worth cannot hinge on their acknowledgment or generosity.

I pull *Fath al-Bari,* the commentary on *al-Bukhari* (d. 256/870), from the bookshelf, and I review the rules with her. I wish I could respond to a moral argument at a moral level. Instead, I review the rules.

The evidence conflicts and the jurists disagree. The Kufan jurists forbade women from greeting men. Other jurists allowed it without restriction. Maliki jurists espoused a subjective standard—both sexes may greet each other if there is no fear of sexual enticement. I wonder what type of person becomes aroused by an act of common courtesy?

She pauses lost in thought. Legalities can stun morality. She asks, "And what do you think?"

What do I think? I think the pedantic indulges the absurd. I think you should say, "Peace be upon you, we do not seek after the ignorant" (28:55).

CHAPTER 13

The Authoritative and the Authoritarian

This Conference thrives on the provocation of complexity. Muslims, nowadays,
are provoked by complexity. This Conference exists, marginalized by obscurity.
Muslims are obscured by their marginality. Meanings and concepts are aggravated by
words and phrases. Ideas are imprisoned by the very words that express them. This
Conference is injected in the midst of clichés, sales pitches, and gross oversimplifica-
tions. Chaos and complexity is the stuff of creation, but order and stability is the craving of life. The authoritative directs the complex and stabilizes the chaotic, but the
authoritarian dooms all to death.

Your book, *The Authoritative and the Authoritarian in Islamic Discourses,* has
been published, and you remember the days when you thought that a single book
could change the world. You remember your short *jalabiyya,* and patchy beard, your
miswak in the upper pocket a re-affirmation of power and triumph. The sparkling
white head cover limited your range of vision and provided you with such unencumbered clarity. Back then a single book, *Riyad al-Salihin* (The Gardens of the
Righteous) symbolized all the world had to say to you and all that you had to say to
others. Parts of *Hayat al-Sahaba* (The Lives of the Companions) would be read in
the mosque and visions of a perfectly ordered, perfectly structured society would relieve the stresses of your mind. When you bought a copy of *Sahih al-Bukhari,* you
believed that all the problems and answers of existence were contained therein. Any
contradiction was a challenge and any challenge was a negation of your existence.
Every time you would assure yourself, "I will commit the whole of *Bukhari* to memory and then. . ."

You remember a world streamlined into self-invented categories—simple and yielding to a perfect causality. You believed that if you do your *du'a'* well on Friday the rest of the week would be perfect, but if you would forget a single verse or phrase, then the order would unfold and collapse. A simple world—an authoritarian world, comfortable with its delusions, submerged in immaturity.

You remember the day you seized your sister's cassette tapes and destroyed them. Music is *haram*, you declared. When your mother punished you, you declared that your mother was living in *haram* as well. Your mother never listened to music either. The only thing she listened to was Qur'an, but you did not get the point. It took you years to get the point.

What a world—a world streamlined and in its dimensions, fed by ignorance and sheltered by arrogance. An authoritarian world where you are the authority. A world where the magnificence of God is represented through the authoritarian voice of a self-righteous self. A world where the Divine voice becomes imprisoned by a human voice and the human voice ascends to the throne. An essentially God-less world.

Now, years later, you publish *The Authoritative and the Authoritarian in Islamic Discourses*. God's Will must be discovered through its evidence and signs. The voices aspiring to comprehend the Divine Will are authoritative indicators, but they never become the embodiment of the Divine. These voices might be authoritative but they must never become authoritarian. *Riyad al-Salihin* and *Sahih al-Bukhari* are raw materials—raw indicators to the Will of the Divine. The materials could be used to construct either the authoritative or the authoritarian. If the authoritarian is constructed, the text is rendered subservient and submerged into its representer and reader. If the authoritative is constructed, the text survives unencumbered and unlimited by its representer and reader.

It was the endless spew of contemporary oral gyrations that once rendered your world uni-dimensional and linear. But the day came when you abandoned the contemporary apologetics and the rot of the modern decay in Islamic discourses and embraced the wonders of a bygone civilization. You read Imam al-Haramayn al-Juwayni (d. 478/1085) explaining that the purpose of a *Shari'a* inquiry is not to reach the right result but the inquiry itself. You read Jalal al-Din al-Suyuti (d. 911/1505) arguing that God's Will is not the ruling reached but the search for the ruling. The result of a search is not the point—the point is the search. A life consumed by the search for the Divine Will is the Divine Will and is the ultimate morality.

In short, you grew up and your conscience grew. You are no longer as threatened, but you are no longer as confident and secure. You realize that while we seek to discover the Divine Will, we never come to embody it. While we search the truth, we are not the truth. From this came the Conference, from this came the book. The child of the Conference, for the sake of the Conference, in the way of Allah—May He accept.

On Obedience

La ta'ata li makhluqin fi ma'siyyat al-khaliq—no obedience is owed to a created if it entails disobeying the Creator. This principle is the spring from which this Conference flows, the very breath of its life and the source of its legitimacy. Its existence empowers this Conference and its implications confound it. The simplicity of the principle complicates our world and the complexity propels the discourse. In its essence, it establishes the authoritative and negates the authoritarian. It refutes the irrationality of despotism and ignites the search for a rational liberty.

This principle is not about the rights of God but the rights of human beings. It is not about the authority of God because the unlimited cannot be defined. Rather, it is about the authority that a human being may exercise over another. The principle limits the authority of human beings and, hence, defines it. Defining the limits and asserting the boundaries for ourselves and others is the very essence of dignity. "We have honored humankind," God declared, and so the grant of dignity was affirmed. What remains is for human beings to find it and assert it, and in the search for the Divine Will and the rejection of human whim, dignity is invariably found and asserted.

To associate partners with God (*shirk*) is the ultimate indignity. How could one worship that which is equal or inferior? Servitude is surrender, and to surrender the self to the self is an impossibility and to surrender the self to others is to descend into degradation. But to surrender to the supernal uplifts you from the sublunary and mundane.

You ponder the questions and reflect upon your own failures. The convoluted challenges of life risk to cast you into muddled confusion, and so you must remind yourself of the fundamental principles. The more basic a principle, and the simpler it is, the more difficult it is to follow it consistently. Simplicity and consistency are a symmetrical incongruity.

A student came to inquire about marriage and recount the long and tortuous story of her parents' opposition. Her parents insist on their right to choose a suitable match for her. The parents wish to assert their own identity through the daughter's marriage. They wish her to marry a man from their culture and their hometown. The mother, disempowered in her own marriage, empowers herself by usurping the daughter's choice. The daughter must prove her love and loyalty by loving the mother's choice. Some parents seem to think that their children are not a trust but an extension of themselves without an identity or a dignity separate from the parents' own.

The struggle is over the power of definition—the power to define the daughter, to define her character and identity. As a part of that struggle, the mother insisted that the daughter remove her *hijab*. She must take off her scarf, exit the house, and enjoy a forced march around the neighborhood. The muse of *fatwas* cannot be resisted and so the mother crafted her own: Between the duty to obey your parents and the duty to be modest, she asserted, obedience to the parents takes priority. Ultimately, if parents have the power to uncover their children's bodies, they also have the power to decide with whom these bodies enter into conjugal relations. But if the home environment denies sons and daughters the power to set their own boundaries and assert their own identities, according to their own understanding of the Divine Will, nothing remains of dignity. If parents do not affirm their children's right to be liberated by the search for the Divine Will, then these children will learn to succumb to human whim—whether their own whim or the whim of others.

I console her and myself by remembering the fundamental principle. Obey no one if it means disobeying God. But she inquires about the famous verse in *Surat Luqman* and asks: "God tells us not to obey parents if they attempt to force us to disbelieve in God and to deal with them kindly. Doesn't that mean that we must obey in all else?" (31:15). I recall the beautiful wonders of this verse. It states, "If they attempt to force you to associate with Me *(tushrika bi)* that of which you have no knowledge, do not obey them, and accompany them kindly in life." *Shirk* encompasses *kufr* but goes well beyond it. *Shirk* is to accept anyone or anything as a master co-equal with God. The issue is not whether one should obey his or her parents, the issue is whether one must obey God if it entails disobeying one's parents. The Qur'an repeatedly berates human beings for blindly following the commands of their forefathers and ignoring the commands of God. I pause to ponder the endless possibilities that abound in the expression "that of which you have no knowledge." Does it refer to the fact that parents can always assert superior knowledge by virtue of their experience? Does it refer to the fact that parents are the gatekeepers of the mysterious knowledge of culture?

No one will dispute the honor and respect that are owed to parents. But respect and blind obedience are not synonymous, and the authoritative and authoritarian are not the same. First and foremost, the worth and dignity of a human being must be demonstrated and taught in the parent-child relationship. Even parents may not replace the Will of God with the authoritarianism of human will.

CHAPTER 15

To Suffer the Children

The hours roll by without a word written. Thoughts crowd your mind and none seem to yield to coherence. The books thunder in their eternal discourse and you listen, frozen in time. Human emotions confound your ability to listen clearly or comprehend fully. A man sits in front of you agonizing over separation from his son and his heart feels empty and vacant. But you know that every separation entails a birth and every birth is a separation. The pains of separation or birth invoke a new life laden with a thousand reflections. The reflections crowd in your mind, none yielding to coherence.

God stated a principle: "No mother will be made to suffer for her child nor a father for his child" (2:233). As a legal principle, it dictates that parents should not be made to suffer because of their children. But parents will always suffer anyway. It is a principle of aspiration that will never be realized because parents suffer for their children by the simple fact of living.

The man sits before me, his hands folded on his lap, his shoulders burdened and broken, and his pale smile struggling to survive. He says, "I can't stand the separation; what can I do but pray for my son?"

I think of the stories that the Conference tells and the verses of the Book roll in my mind. "These are the verses of the illuminating Book. We narrate to you from the history of Moses and Pharaoh in all verity, for those who believe" (28:2–3). How the stories (*qasas*) of those before us comfort, console, and teach us! The stories of those before us crowd in this Conference awaiting to be noticed and told. How he needs to be consoled and comforted! I feel the details of his pain, but there is no need to add to his burden.

The verses continue to flow in my brain: "The Pharaoh had become high and mighty in the land, and divided the people into classes [and factions], oppressing a group of them slaying their children and assaulting their women for he was indeed a tyrant" (28:4). But God wished to favor and liberate those who were oppressed, and to have the Pharaoh and his soldiers suffer what they feared the most. The liberator was a child and the means for liberation was a mother's suffering.

God inspired Moses' mother, "If you are afraid for him, cast him in the river without any fear or regret, for We shall restore him to you and make him an apostle" (28:7). Despite God's assurances, the mother's heart became empty with grief and she almost revealed who he was "had [God] not strengthened her heart so that she will remain a believer" (28:10). Ultimately, God restored the child to his mother "that she may be tranquil and not grieve, and know that the promise of God is true, though most people do not know" (28:13).

I wonder how was Moses' mother inspired? Was it through the directness of revelation or the subtle assurance of faith? How did she spend the night after separation? What supplications and entreaties did she pronounce? And how did God strengthen her heart?

The stories of grief endured by the Prophets give us a sense of relief. If those who are chosen and divinely inspired can suffer because of their children, then our sorrow need not be endlessly augmented by guilt. How did the Prophet feel when he received God's decree: "Muhammad is not the father of any of your men, but a Messenger of God and the Seal of the Prophets" (33:40). In a single revelation, he was informed that none of his sons would survive and I remember the Prophet grieving for the death of Ibrahim. Joseph's father suffered the agonies of separation and his eyes turned white with grief (12:84).

I look at the man sitting before me and I share his sorrow in silence, for none of the thoughts in my mind can be expressed. How apt it is to describe children and wealth as a temptation and test (8:28)! Children and the love we have for them are the ultimate beauty, and how often we are tested by beauty!

Embarrassed by my silence, the man quotes the verse, "God does not withdraw a favor bestowed upon a people unless they change themselves, for God hears all and knows everything" (8:53). He pauses and then adds apologetically, "When is a calamity the just result of what people do, and when is it a test of endurance by God? If only I knew which of these am I enduring." I speak slowly weighing each word, "My friend, the Prophet was survived only by Fatima (d. 10/632), his daughter. All of his other children separated from him in this world. May Allah bless you, and bless your son."

I quietly remember the Muslim scholar and historian 'Abd al-Rahman al-Jabarti (d. 1241/1825). He vehemently criticized Napoleon and the French occupation of Egypt. He attacked the government of Muhammad 'Ali in Egypt, and his writings

THE SEARCH FOR BEAUTY IN ISLAM

were banned for many years. For years, they could not silence him, but when they killed his son Khalil and sent his body through the streets of Cairo on a donkey, he was silenced. Al-Jabarti lived his remaining years in grief and died from his sorrow. Was his love for his son his one weakness?

I recite to myself, "Say, if your fathers and children, and siblings and wives, and families and wealth, or the business you fear may fail, and the mansions that you love, are dearer to you than God, His apostle, and struggling in His cause, then wait until God's command arrives, for God does not show transgressors the way" (9:24). May Allah bless your soul al-Jabarti, how could I be so presumptuous as to judge you! Only Allah knows the extent of the test you have been put through.

As if he heard my inner soul and secret supplications, the man before me says in a soft voice, "What if you are forcibly separated from your child not because of a struggle in the way of God, and without the consolation of a *jihad*, but rather because of the whimsical frenzies of some people? What if you were separated from your child, not in the cause of Allah, but because of a mere senseless accident soon to pass into oblivion?"

I say then, my friend, that patience is the cause and the way of God, and say: "Patience [in adversity] is most beautiful, and God is the One from whom to seek help for what you describe" (12:18).

CHAPTER 16

On Forms of Terror

Terror. Terror paralyzes the senses and numbs the intellect. The reflexes of the body cringe and the intellect races to understand. Like disease, terror is a state of chaos. Like health, peace is vibrant order. But terror is rarely its own purpose or object.

The gripping fear that a terrorist sees in his victim's eyes is not the point. The point is the aftermath of the terror, when the panic dissipates and the horror sets in. Terrorism is a symbolic message communicated through violence. The weak strive to communicate their refusal to surrender, and the strong strive to communicate their demand for surrender. In reality, the weak only communicate their desperate powerlessness, and the strong communicate their unfettered dominance.

The news rolls in about yet another terrorist attack. Terror invades the vibrant order of the Conference and produces a stunned chaos. By its very nature, terror is the suspension of reason, and without the balance of reason, this Conference comes to a halt. In its essence, the ability to reason is the ability to discern and distinguish. Terror seeks neither discernment nor distinction; terror seeks to generalize and stereotype its victims. It denies its victims the worth that comes from the distinction of individuality and transforms the individual into a cause.

The jurists of Islam spoke about the criminal who targets the defenseless and weak, who attacks unexpectedly and indiscriminately, and who uses terror as the primary method for achieving his ends. They called him the *muharib*. Such a criminal was declared to be most vile and deserving of no reprieve. The jurist Ibn Rushd, the grandfather (d. 520/1126), ruled that a criminal who terrorizes people in their homes is a *muharib,* and Ibn al-'Arabi (d. 543/1148), the Maliki jurist, declared that a rapist is a *muharib* as well. The texts of this Conference are full of discourses on the evils of *fitan* (civil discord) and invocations against the states of terror. For in a state of *khawf* (fear) and *rahba* (terror), and in the absence of *amn* (safety), they proclaimed, "Neither prayer nor thought is performed properly and God's *Sunna* on this earth is frustrated."

In today's age, there are many reasons why neither prayer nor thought can be performed properly. So many people live engulfed in layers of fear that eventually numb the senses. Happiness is more a sense of indifferent acceptance than a rational response to reality. People live with fears that are far more real and far more dull than the threat of a terrorist attack. The fear of becoming reduced to a number or statistic, the fear of becoming among the acceptable percentages of the unemployed, bankrupt, or homeless is ever present. Yet Muslim jurists were right. A criminal who targets civilians, and attacks suddenly and indiscriminately, is particularly vile. Those who induce terror as a primary method of communication are despicable.

But it is not only violent terrorists who induce fear as a means of communication. Intellectual terrorists are equally vile. Intellectual terrorists are emotional extortionists. These terrorists, who are often racists, sexists, classists, or religious bigots, employ the language of fear. They generalize and essentialize a people, reducing them to a phenomenon. They incite fear and terror toward their victims and force the victims into a horrified silence.

I listen to the endless flow of words about Arabs and Muslims and the terrorist threat. So many political opportunists, career seekers, gossip hunters, and intellectual terrorists throw around self-righteous verbiage about political Islam, militant Islam, and the dark forces of fundamentalism. The symbolic universe of Islam—the call to prayer, the kneeling positions during prayer, and the scarf—is consistently invoked and associated with the distant and the scary. In the frenzy of coverage on everything Muslim, there is always the hint of the alien, mysterious, and unknown. Some less sophisticated intellectual terrorists do not bother placing a modifier before the word Islam and directly speak of the Islamic threat or Muslim violence. The singular emotion and feeling that is persistently appealed to and invoked in their audience is the emotion of fear and the feeling of terror. The audience is incited to fear and hate Muslims, and Muslims are induced to live frightened and horrified.

I suffer the silence of the Conference and the paralysis of reason. Muslims have become stereotyped and generalized and they suffer a different form of terrorism, the terror of being fired from work, attacked in the street, and harassed and discriminated against. They fear the brutalization of a Bosnia or Kashmir—the executions, the rapes, and the indifference of the world. I pray that the Conference of the Books will speak louder than ever before. The only response and remedy to the terror of ignorance is the serenity of reason.

Dial-a-Fatwa

The knowledge that is God makes all else tentative. The certainty that is God reduces all else to conjecture. The more one learns the more one asks, and the more one asks the more one discovers the Divine. In this Conference the only absolute is God; all else searches for the absolute. If one claims knowledge, humility before The All-Knowing makes the heart shudder. In this Conference, arrogance is the only ignorance and temporal knowledge is but a question.

It is reported that the Maliki jurist Sahnun (d. 240/855) once observed: "The most ready to issue *fatwas* are the most ignorant." It is also said that al-Imam Malik Ibn Anas (d. 179/796) would be asked about fifty issues and he would perhaps respond to one. Through the transmissions of history, it was reported that al-Haytham Ibn Jamil said that al-Imam Malik was asked about forty-eight issues, thirty-two to which he answered, "I don't know." The annals of Islamic history are full of anecdotal stories demanding diligence in researching a *fatwa* and counseling reserve in the issuance of *fatwas*.

Books have been written on the qualifications of a *mufti*, the conditions for seeking a *fatwa*, and the requisites for its issuance. Muslim jurists forbade *al-tasahul fi'l fatwa* (issuing *fatwas* without proper reflection or research). Such a deed was considered to be illegal and a sin. In fact, many jurists argued that one can sue a *mufti*, in malpractice, for negligently issuing a *fatwa*. In other words, negligence in discharging one's *fatwa* duties creates a legal cause of action.

But here in the United States, the comfort of a *fatwa* is right at your fingertips. As definite as a guaranteed-delivery pizza parlor, a *fatwa* is just a phone call away.

With the sound reliability of a vending machine or the immediacy of an order of french fries, a *fatwa* is readily available. Call 1-800-95-FATWA and you will find the *Fatwa* Service. Monday to Thursday from 1 to 3 pm E.S.T. and on alternate days, *fatwas* are available in Arabic and English. Two days ago, I called the *Fatwa* Service and I was greeted with a message informing me that the *Fatwa* Service is out of order until further notice. But the point remains. Muslims in the United States issue *fatwas* left and right without any regard to conditions, rules, traditions, sources, or anything else for that matter. There are hundreds of self-declared *muftis* who, after reading a couple of books on *hadith,* become the viceroys of *fiqh* on this earth.

Every Muslim may be entitled to declare an opinion on whatever he or she wishes. But a *fatwa* is not a point of view; it is a legal opinion. A *fatwa* is not personal advice given in response to a personal problem and it is not simply an answer to a question. A *fatwa* is a non-binding legal opinion issued in response to a legal problem. For instance, if one asks, "How many times a day do Muslims pray?" The answer to this is not a *fatwa.* If one asks: "Do you think it is a good idea to marry someone older than myself?" The response to this is personal advice but not a *fatwa.* However, if one inquires about a problem that is the proper subject of a legal inquiry, then one is asking for a *fatwa.* For example, if one asks, "My father is opposed to my marrying this man, but legally, could I still marry him anyway?" This question solicits a *fatwa.* A *fatwa* assumes a conflict of evidence and a need to weigh and evaluate the evidence. In the language of *fiqh,* a *fatwa* is issued in response to a problematic matter (*amr mushkil*). The point is well-illustrated by the following incident: A man asked al-Imam Malik about a matter. Imam Malik responded by saying, "I don't know." The man retorted, "But this is a simple and easy matter." Irritated, Imam Malik said: "Nothing is easy in knowledge and *fatwa.*"

A dial-a-*fatwa* 800-number implies that the law of God is but a phone call away. God's Will need not be searched or sought; you need not sweat nor pain; you need not reflect nor persevere. Instead, you make a phone call. The least one can ask is that we pay for the phone call.

CHAPTER 18

On Knowledge

The supplication "And say, Lord increase my knowledge" (20:114) pervades every corner of this Conference. In every Conference, and throughout the ages, it has ignited the search and the discourse. God poses the rhetorical question: "Are those who know and those who do not know equal?" (39:9) In the symbolic universe of Islam, ignorance is *kufr*, and a dead intellect is equated with the darkness of a dead soul.

It is reported that the Prophet said, "He who issues forth in a search for knowledge is in a state of struggle in the cause of God until he returns." Countless hours in countless Conferences have been spent in this struggle. The signs of God are manifest in every creature and creation, and the struggle to discover is but a supplication in the name of the Creator.

Our traditions are replete with exhortations of knowledge and warnings against ignorance. It is reported that the Prophet declared scholars to be the inheritors of the prophets and the pursuit of knowledge as the way to paradise. Islamic history and culture responded in a concrete and tangible way: Hundreds of endowments (*waqfs*) were created throughout Islamic history to support universities, scholars, and scholarship. As Muslims searched for God, they discovered the diversity of God's creatures and creation in all its richness and magnificence. They uncovered and enriched the heritage of the Greeks, Persians, Romans, Israelites, and Arabs. Thousands of Conferences sprouted all over Muslim lands as Islam reintroduced the world to the Civilization of the text. For a few hundred years, most of the roads to knowledge went through Islam.

Yet another distressing visit to the bookstore. I compare the size of the Islam section to the Christian and Jewish sections, and the Islam section pales in comparison. The titles of books in the Islam section are the same week after week. Once again, I complain to the managers and, once again, they cite the lack of sales in the Islam section. "There is movement in the Christianity and Judaism sections, but not Islam," I am told. I know from experience that Muslims hardly read—not even the Qur'an for that matter. If Muslims do pick up a book from one Conference or another, they search for a book that affirms what they already know.

Muslim roads to knowledge are blocked by dogma, apologetics, laziness, and simple idiocy. But most of all, Muslim roads are blocked by a near total disregard for the value of the intellect and the role it plays in the pursuit of knowledge. Muslims today prefer to construct buildings rather than minds.

While the world discourses on Islam, Muslims exalt Islam and pretend that the world does not exist. All too often, discourses on Islam engage Muslims as subjects and not participants. In the United States and the West, academic presses such as Oxford, Cambridge, Princeton, Harvard, or Westview publish on Islam and Muslims all the time. The authors of these works are most often not Muslim. Universities and government institutions fund and support research and teach courses. Popular presses, whether in book or journal form, report on Islam and Muslims everyday. Politicians, journalists, legislators, educators, and others base their impressions of Islam on these mainstream discourses. Muslims do not impact the mainstream discourses in any significant sense.

The Muslim response is to build Islamic centers, organize camps and conferences, and pretend that the mainstream does not exist. Although Islamic centers are necessary for generating a basic sense of community and identity, they are rarely a serious avenue for knowledge or discourse on Islam. As to the camps, conventions, and conferences, all too often they are no more than pep rallies or cheerleading events.

In the contemporary age, whoever controls the flow of information controls the discourse. Muslims do not shape or control the discourse on Islam; Muslims are discoursed about but do not discourse back. The flow of information about Islam rarely originates, or even passes through, Muslim avenues.

Attempts have been made to fund Muslim educational institutions and alternative presses. However, these attempts have been marred by two distinct problems. First, the quality, in terms of content and form, is often so substandard to what is produced by the mainstream that it is often ignored. Second, often, such efforts have been supported by Gulf money, which usually promotes a particularly dogmatic and anti-critical view of knowledge.

It is reported that the Prophet said, "A Muslim will not tire of knowledge until he reaches Heaven." The problem occurs when one does not tire of knowledge but tires of the dogma, slogans, and clichéd rhetoric encountered in Islamic centers and conferences all over the United States—where does one go after that? Or when those who wish to pursue knowledge must either live in poverty or accept easy money from those who offer easy solutions. The problem is when every wealthy Muslim prefers to build a building than support a mind, and when Muslims forget the value of a book despite the fact that their religion was founded on a book and is all about the role of books.

NYC Bombing

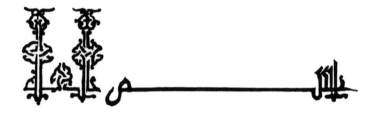

Bigotry and prejudice thrive on constructed images. These images are the product of selective knowledge and complete ignorance. Bigotry and prejudice rely on uncritical judgments and swift conclusions. Those who possess the power to construct an image also possess the power of judgment, and the power to defeat or support bigotry and prejudice.

This Conference is a symbolic construct. It is a symbol for the sanctuary of thought and the repose of knowledge. It is a symbol for the reflective life offered by Islam and the book, and for freedom from the delusions of bigotry and hallucinations of ignorance.

One recent summer, two Palestinians were suspected of planning to bomb the New York City subway. In the process of arresting the suspects, the police shot them. The Muslim fellow who turned in the suspects was placed under deportation proceedings, and Mayor Rudolph Giuliani announced to the world that there was "no question" that the two suspects intended to "attack the United States, to attack Israel, and to attack Jewish interests."

Many writers, commentators, and politicians endlessly spoke about the Islamic threat, political Islam, Islamic fundamentalism, and Islamic terrorism. The Immigration and Naturalization Service (INS) was criticized for admitting the suspects into the United States although Israel had accused one of them of being a member of a terrorist organization. Effectively, the INS was criticized for allowing Palestinians into the country and for not allowing Israel to regulate the ports of the United States.

The incident and the response to the incident fed into the constructed image of Islam and Muslims. Once again, a few individuals were made the representatives of one of the world's main religions and its followers. Terrorists refuse to distinguish between the guilty and innocent. Taking their cue from terrorists, many commentators refused to distinguish between suspicion and guilt and between guilt and innocence.

On August 24, 1997, the *Washington Times* reported that the FBI suspected that the NYC bomb plot was a hoax. FBI and CIA investigations were revealing that the suspects did not have any paramilitary training and did not have any particularly strong religious convictions. The FBI suspected that those involved were motivated by the idea of collecting reward money rather than supporting a political goal. Apparently, the suspects learned of something called the Heroes Program, offered by the State Department, which offered rewards to those providing information about terrorist operations. The suspects evidently came up with a scheme to plant the pipe bombs, report them, and collect up to $2 million in rewards.

Whether these allegations are true or not is beside the point. This version of the incident, which does not comfortably fit within the constructed image of Muslims, was largely ignored by most commentators. Mayor Giuliani made no apologies, and so-called specialists did not endlessly pontificate about what the recent FBI and CIA investigations in the case tell us about Islam and Muslims. No one went blabbing on about how this incident is indicative of the crises of Islam in the age of post modernity, the Muslim rage over the loss of identity, or the long history of confrontations between Islam and the West. There was complete silence. This version of the facts did not fit within the constructed image and, hence, after the euphoria of yammer, there was complete silence. But even all of this is not the point.

The point is that neither in the construction or deconstruction of the popular image do Muslims play a role other than the role of subjects. The subjects of a discourse provide the raw material from which a discourse is formed. The subjects do not themselves engage or direct the discourse. Muslims sit passively as they are accused and exonerated; as they are constructed and deconstructed. The problem is not the lack of Muslim activists or activism. The problem is the absence of those who have the financial and intellectual power to co-opt and reconstruct the discourse and the image.

Most politicians, commentators, educators, and writers are not Muslim, and have no reason to appease Muslims. Most of those who fund politicians, media organizations, schools, and Islamic studies programs are not Muslim and have no reason to cater to Muslim demands. Consequently, Muslims are powerless to direct the discourse or define the issues around which the discourse is to flow. Even more unfortunately, most Muslims do not appreciate or are not interested in the value of the discourse, the construction of an image, or the symbolic significance of a Conference of Books.

CHAPTER **20**

Umm Ahmad and the Judge

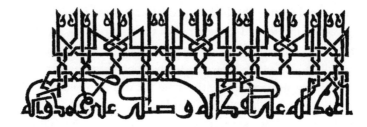

T he distention of the soul crowds the serenity of the mind. The key to justice is
the balance, but the balance is a risky state of repose. For justice to exist, there
must be a claim of right, but claims of right are often the gateway to the despotism
of arrogance. Without people claiming their rights, how could justice exist? But how
does one resist the temptation to arrogantly transform a claim into an entitlement?

She exclaims frantically, "You can tell him I am not the nice, sweet woman he
married. He can't push me around anymore!" He yells, "Tell her I will make her life
miserable. She will regret the day she ever met me!" The ugliness of claims and coun-
terclaims, of accusations and counteraccusations, of threats and counterthreats—the
ugliness of divorce. I explain that I am not the middleman for the negotiation of insults. I assume that I was sought out by the combatants because I am the keeper of
books and the servant of the Conference. However, I quickly discover that this assumption was rather presumptuous.

I explain to them that this Conference offers centuries of reflections and elucidations on such domestic warfares. Their reaction betrays their belief in my insanity and
in the futility of the Conference. "Tell him he is a selfish self-centered jerk," she declares after a long pause. "Tell her she is no better than garbage." Of course, I tell neither him nor her anything.

God commands those overtaken by the trauma of divorce not to "forget the
goodness" that was between them and to remember that God sees what they do
(2:237). The command is to be decent and to be humane, but this injunction is rarely
honored or respected in a divorce. God says, "If you are benevolent toward each other

and mindful of God, God will be fully aware of what you do" (4:128). Yet, in no area of life are people less mindful of God and of the obligation of benevolence.

The worst aggressors are often those who believe that they are only defending themselves, and the worst enemies are often those who used to share a life. The hurt, the disbelief, the justifications, and the self-righteousness are far more intense in these situations. The accumulated resentments manifest themselves in a stream of demands. The self-doubt and guilt are treated with massive dosages of insecure arrogance. Worst of all, the trauma and anxiety express themselves in endless claims of right. The crusade waged against the unholy other leaves the homeland deserted and haunted by demons.

What is needed is not a strict sense of justice but a generous sense of benevolence. God comments about people in this situation, *"Wa uhdirati al-anfusu al-shuh"* (4:128). A remarkable expression! People in these situations tend to become selfish, ungenerous, and ungiving. It is not that such people are necessarily greedy or covetous, but people become afraid, lest, in the process of giving, they give away themselves. I remember the Qur'anic verse, ". . . and We make some of you a means of trial for others, to see whether you are steadfast. And your Lord sees all that you do" (25:20).

The first casualties of a failed marriage are the children. The second casualty is your relationship with God and the third is your relationship with yourself. The disintegration of the bond between one human being and another often heralds the destruction of the bond between a human being and decency.

She awakens me from my deliberate phase-out and proclaims, "Are you listening?" I look at her, mindful of the hour and the creeping exhaustion. I say, "May I tell you a story?

"Once upon a time, in the third century of *Hijra*, there was a man and woman in Kufa. They had gone through an extremely unpleasant divorce. The woman accused the man of everything on the face of the earth and the man accused her of the same. For a full year, the woman would file a new complaint with the judge every week. The man would appear in court and counterclaim. In the second year, the woman showed up in the judge's court. Upon seeing her, the judge knew it was going to be a long day and became restless. With visible annoyance and obvious sternness, he inquired, 'What can we help you with today, Umm Ahmad?' She said, 'Judge, Abu Ahmad will be the reason for my downfall in this earth and in the Hereafter. He is the reason for my misfortunes and sins. Judge, you must order the *Muhtasib* (marketplace police) to forbid Abu Ahmad from entering the marketplace near my home.' The judge, surprised by the request, quickly asked, 'But why, Umm Ahmad?' She said, 'Because when he passes me in the market, I smell his foul odor and I feel compelled to curse him. And as you know judge cursing a fellow Muslim is a very serious sin.'"

CHAPTER 21

The Book Massacres

In 656/1258, Baghdad was drowned in red blood and black ink. Hulagu and his Mongol armies splattered the streets of Baghdad with mutilated corpses and clogged its rivers with thousands of books. As one reads the accounts of history, fact and fiction mix in a complex stream, but the unadulterated pain remains very real. That year, those who could understand no discourse sought to extinguish all discourse. Today, it is substantially the same. Today, those who can barely understand any discourse try to control all discourse (see Qur'an 4:78). The Mongols had no use for thought or people, so they tried to destroy both. Today's tormentors are Mongols of thought. Rather than exterminate people, they exterminate their intellects. A Conference of the books tells the story of the death of so many other Conferences, and the awareness creeps up upon you that in order to kill a people, one must kill off their ideas.

At times, grief numbs the senses and knots the heart and mind. You supplicate with that ever so beautiful prayer: "Lord, lift the burdens of my chest, ease my way, and unravel the knot of my tongue that they may understand my words" (20:25–28). The Mongols were barbarians; they did not censor or distinguish, but destroyed all without discrimination. In doing so, they gave Muslims the benefit of notice—Muslims clamored to hide and protect their sources. Eventually, with Mahmud Ghazzan (who ruled until 704/1304) coming to power in 658/1259, the Mongols converted to Islam and the destruction of texts stopped, although the slaughter of people continued. Today, Muslims are still slaughtered around the world, and it is Muslims themselves who slaughter their texts.

Today's book massacres do not normally take the form of book burnings or mass drownings in a river. Today's massacres are far more insidious and effective. They take the form of quiet editing or banning of texts—texts that had survived the Mongols and many other invaders only to be censored today. No notice is given and the reader has no idea that he or she is reading a "cleansed" text. Somehow, the puny mind of the censor imagines that it is qualified to judge the cumulative discourses of the centuries and define Islamic authenticity. Feeble intellects threatened by complexity tend to censor it.

The *Fatawa* of Ibn Taymiyya (d. 728/1328) has been edited by today's censors and offending text has been removed. The only uncorrupted edition of the *Fatawa Ibn Taymiyya* is the one published in Cairo in the 1960s. All editions published after that have been "cleansed." In a yet-to-be published edition, further "cleansing" has been ordered. Ten pages have been quietly deleted from Ibn Taymiyya's *al-Jawab al-Sahih li Man Baddala Din al-Masih* and when a publisher tried to print the full text, he was arrested and his printing house was burned down. It seems that although Ibn Taymiyya survived the Mongols of yesterday, it is unlikely that he will survive the Thought Mongols of today.

After a four-year search, you find *Bihar al-Anwar* but only without three offending volumes. Furthermore, you realize that only in the past ten years have these three volumes been "cleansed" from the text. The *Tafsirs* of Zamakhshari (d. 538/1144) and Muqatil (d. 150/767) have been banned in some Muslim countries for years. The works of Muhyi al-Din Ibn 'Arabi (d. 638/1240), Ikhwan al-Safa, Abu Hayyan al-Tawhidi (d. 414/1023), and al-Qadi al-Nu'man (d. 363/974), to name a few, are likewise banned in some Muslim countries. The *Fatawa* of Rashid Rida (d. 1935) although printed in the 1970s are now considered un-Islamic and are quite rare. Unless you buy the full text of *al-Manar,* you must be willing to pay a few thousand dollars for a six-volume set. In one Muslim country, the works of the Maliki jurist, Ibn al-'Arabi (d. 543/1148) were banned because he was confused with Ibn 'Arabi (d. 638/1240), the Sufi master. The absurdity has reached the point that even the age-old stories of *A Thousand and One Nights* have been "cleansed."

For centuries, those who tried to destroy Muslims targeted their intellectual heritage. The problem is far worse when those who declare themselves the protectors of Islam seek to destroy their own heritage. For centuries, Muslims, saturated with the morality instilled in them by the Qur'an, preserved both agreeable and offensive texts alike. The Qur'an reminded the Prophet that he is neither a warden nor a guardian over people (4:80 and 88:22). It is baffling that the Thought Mongols of today claim a position higher than the Prophet. The Mongols of medieval times were barbaric and ignorant and so they sought to be vanquishers and conquerors. The Thought Mongols of today are civilized, ignorant, and arrogant, and so they seek to be gods.

CHAPTER 22

To Kill Parenthood

This interminable Conference is founded on the right to testify—a right that is inherent to the relationship between the Creator and created. Once created by its Maker, a right cannot be undone, for like a gift from the Maker, a right can be rejected but it cannot be denied. A right, truth, relationship, or gift created by God may be searched, but whether missed or found, it will always exist. The indefatigable production of books, which fuels this Conference, is an aspiration toward infinity, and infinity is the inseparable quality of God. As such, this Conference is founded on a right to aspire and testify.

The testimonies of these books resonate throughout history with numerous moments of human arrogance. The arrogance of one era judges and mocks the arrogance of another. What human beings once, upon a historical moment, saw as sensible or natural is later judged to be barbaric and absurd. A human relationship, which once might have been deemed inevitable, might be seen in a different age as repugnant or reprehensible. Acknowledgment of the Divine does not eliminate this process, but it limits its vagaries.

Imagine that in our era, a single, underpaid, under-educated, and over-worked bureaucrat may storm into your house and, armed with a court order, may proceed to grab your children from their school or home. The children would be temporarily kept in a state facility and your access and ability to see or talk to your children would become severely restricted. If the bureaucrats decide to do so, they may ask the state to declare that any ties to your children be forever eradicated. After a jury trial and thousands of dollars spent on legal fees, a jury may decide that you no longer belong to your children and your children no longer belong to you. What you thought was the only relationship not artificially constructed by society, you discover, is susceptible to being completely deconstructed by the state.

There will come an age in which people will scoff at our incoherencies and barbarisms, and they will look with disbelief at our logic and structure. One of the absolute absurdities of our age is that we attempt to deny a fundamental right given by God; we attempt to completely erase the relation of a parent to a child and a child to a parent. In our age, we extinguish the right of a child to his or her mother or father and call it the "termination of parental rights." We empower the state to claim that a parent may be severed from his or her child, and upon "clear and convincing evidence," we re-arrange the relationship that was created by God. As incredible as it seems, the state has the power to decide that it is in the best interest of a child to lose his or her parents forever, and be re-assigned to a new set of claimants who forever will pose as the child's parents. To forever deny the right of a child to know, honor, or even denounce his or her parents, I propose, is a moral outrage.

When God states, "Call them [adopted children] by the names of their fathers, that is more just with God" (33:5), a moral principle, not a law, is proclaimed. The moral principle creates an imperative that is more conducive to achieving justice. In a just order, children may be protected and nurtured by those who are not natural parents, but the parent-child tie is sacrosanct. Every time this relationship is tampered with or denied, we move further away from God's justice. In a state in which Muslims live, the state should not be allowed to retain the power to terminate the rights or liabilities of a parent or child.

When God declared Muslims to be the best nation sent to humankind because they enjoin the good and forbid the evil (3:110), God had obligated Muslims to be the pioneers on the moral frontier. They, before anyone else, must identify the barbaric and condemn the unjust. As such, Muslims must be at the forefront of the human rights discourse because, in our day and age, it is largely through that discourse that the barbaric and uncivilized are identified. In the contemporary age there are many human rights which are asserted and claimed. For example, we claim that there is an absolute right not to be tortured or degraded. No limitation, derogation, or reservation is permitted from that right. Yet, what greater torture could there be than the absolute agony and pain of a parent losing his or her child, or a child losing his parent? It is ironic that there is an absolute prohibition against torture but there is no similar prohibition against the absolute torment of losing your child.

There are only a few God-given absolute rights. The right not to be tortured is one of them. But definitely the rights of parenthood are as integral and as absolute. If children are neglected, mistreated, or abused by their parents, Muslims must be the first to demand that the children be protected and the parents be rehabilitated, if possible. But the termination of a parental right or the permanent denial of the right of a child to his or her parent should not be an option. A right or relationship created by God should not be open to the vagaries of human discretion and judgment. As any person who had the displeasure of being involved in this horrendous process will testify, a parent would rather be tortured or lose his or her property, liberty, or even life, but not his or her child.

CHAPTER 23

Killing Flies

This is the time of the month in which the vibrancy of the Conference must surrender itself to the stagnant paper. This interminable timeless Conference must yield to the confines of time and space and become defined within the corners of a piece of paper. Yet, this is all a delusion, for at this time of every month, I neither define nor limit the Conference. I only take a snapshot; it rumbles on and on with or without me. There are those who wish to deny its existence and there are those who imagine themselves a conference all on their own. But they expire without a memory or trace and the Conference lives on.

October 10, 680 (10th of *Muharram* the 61st year of *Hijra*) was a turning point in Islamic history. Al-Husayn (d. 61/680), son of 'Ali and Fatima and the grandson of the Prophet, was surrounded and slaughtered in Karbala by the governor of Iraq, 'Ubayd Allah Ibn Ziyad (d. 67/686). 'Abdullah Ibn 'Umar (d. 73/692) advised al-Husayn not to go to Iraq and to stay in the relative safety of Mecca, but al-Husayn insisted. Al-Husayn's death was nothing short of a moral disaster and the magnitude of grief was enormous.

Shortly after this event, a man went to ask Ibn 'Umar a question. The man wanted to know if killing flies during *ihram* at *hajj* is allowed. Upon hearing the question, Ibn 'Umar became upset and he said: "Have you no shame? The Prophet's grandson was killed in our midst, and you ask me about killing flies?"

The sad reality is that among contemporary Muslims in the United States, many would not understand why Ibn 'Umar became upset. In fact, if this man existed today, he would have become a sterling candidate to head an Islamic center or to direct one of the proliferating Islamic organizations in the United States. The issue is not whether the man had the right to ask about killing flies. Rather, the issue is this man's psychology and his sense of priorities. In light of the problems plaguing the nation, killing flies does not seem to be a particularly pressing issue.

Today, there is news of fresh massacres by Serbian troops in Kosovo. This comes in the wake of threats of new massacres in Iraq. What are the pressing issues in our community? The pressing issues are whether one can marry a Jinn or not and whether witnesses are required for the ceremony. Students at a Christian seminary are visiting the local mosque for the first time, and they are offered *hijabs* as parting gifts. The only serious issue discussed is whether they should be Arab or Indo-Pakistani style *hijabs*.

In every age there are those who are unable to differentiate the fundamentals of Islam from its particulars. In every age there are those who, empowered by a bizarre sense of priorities, confuse their own pedantic and petty selves with the heart of the religion. Shaykh Muhammad al-Ghazali (d. 1998) used to describe them as people who approach Islam from its tail.

But the problem today goes even further. Here and now, the fly-killing man would immediately be recognized as an expert on Islamic law, and praised for his attention to detail. Here, the ignorant guide the ignorant, and the foolish lead the foolish. As God says: "And thus We cause the unjust to lead the unjust because of what they have done" (6:129). Sadly this verse describes the state of affairs in most of the Muslim world, and is particularly relevant to Muslims in the United States.

In the United States, the field of *Shari'a* is flooded with self-declared experts who inundate our discourses with self-indulgent babble and gibberish. These are the self-declared experts on the Will of God who, because they are unwilling or unable to exert themselves in the search, superimpose their ignorance upon the Divine Will. There is no longer a distinction between the demands of their ego and the Will of God. Islam is there to service their national identity or cultural identity or gender identity or, at times, even their need to feel distinguished in a career or to feel popular in a social setting. Their sense of what *Shari'a* is, or what is significant to *Shari'a*, is defined largely by their fragile egos and individual insecurities. The market of Islam is saturated with self-declared experts whose egos are bigger than their knowledge, and whose delusions are far more potent than their realities.

CHAPTER 24

Attending Jum'a

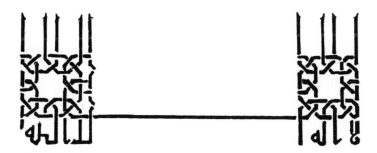

All stories end in the same redundant way. All stories end with the death of all those concerned. Between the wonder of birth and the stupor of death exists the chance for enlightenment. There are those who wish to believe that there is nothing beyond the bridge, but we all cross it anyway. Enlightenment is to know the Creator and created, and to realize that the Conference of the Books is the gateway.

It is *jum'a* and the *imam* rambles on and on. The topic is as unclear as the grammar. A boundless web of familiar terms and phrases are woven, but they all dissipate the second they leave the *khatib's* mouth. The endless rhetoric stupefies the intellect and puts one in a trance-like state. The numbed brain yearns for signs of life but like a drug, rhetoric is addictive. It induces a state of intellectual paralysis that is as ugly and comfortable as death. Once one is accustomed to this state of dullness, any vibrant or critical thought is bound to cause a profound state of disturbance.

Weeks ago, a young man gave a simple but beautiful *khutba*. Someone in town had issued a *fatwa* that it is more important to memorize and learn to recite the Qur'an than it is to understand it. The young man wondered, How is it possible to search the Divine Will and to obey God if one does not understand God's speech? The most surprising aspect, and a rare quality in the culture of sermons, was that he spoke meticulous English and Arabic.

And now you find yourself in this town again. You ask about the young man and you are told that, "There are issues, brother." "What issues?" you inquire. "He does not fulfill the qualifications, brother; his appearance is not Islamic." "How so?" you ask. "He does not wear a beard, he tucks his shirt in, and, in addition, he is not married."

In all the years of studying *fiqh,* you were not aware that these were pre-requisites for leading prayer. A beard, an untucked shirt, and marriage. You remember years ago when every *imam* declared war against the Polo shirt horse and the Lacoste alligator. You wonder, Is intelligence a pre-requisite too? Well, at least these qualifications are novel and original and, after all, we have been calling for the rekindling of *ijtihad*!

The *imam* giving the *khutba* blows his nose and you awaken for a moment. You notice his watch and you wonder if that is part of a proper Islamic appearance. Absurdity begets absurdity and you find yourself wondering: How about buttons on a shirt or socks on feet? How about eyeglasses, underwear, zippers, velcro, tennis shoes, sneakers, jeans, pantyhose, brassieres, ties, raincoats, gloves, or earmuffs? Which of these, if any, is consistent with a proper Islamic appearance? How do we generate a systematic way of distinguishing between an untucked shirt and other items? Well, at least in the case of the brassiere, Shaykh Bin Bazz issued a *fatwa* saying a woman may not wear it if the purpose is to commit fraud. Fraud is never a good thing. But what if a man wears a shirt larger than his size to conceal the fact that he is overweight? Yet the *'ilal* (legal operative causes) of fraud are very different than those that pertain to an Islamic appearance. The analysis must be consistent, systematic, and coherent. I suddenly remembered that a month ago an *imam* in the same mosque led *jum'a* with his shirt tucked in. But he was married. Perhaps married *imams* may tuck their shirts in and unmarried *imams* may not. Perhaps the distinction is that. . .

I felt the intellectual rigor mortis that follows insanity setting in; I felt the Conference distant and fading away. I was dying before reaching the end of the bridge. Blissfully, the call to prayer started, and a breath of life seeped in again.

They got their married *imam* with his beard and untucked shirt. They got their *imam* with the numbing rhetoric and incomprehensible broken English. But what they perpetuated is intellectual death.

CHAPTER 25

Burdens of a Generation

This Conference tells the story of memory. In it, memory is constructed and retained. Allah calls us to the remembrance and so why is it that we forget? And why is it that this Conference exists in a perpetual state of oblivion?

This Conference comes alive in my unfettered dreams. Intoxicated by the power of memory, I am liberated in a dream. Yet, I am fully awake, attentive, and entirely at peace. Does this Conference emanate from my consciousness or does it flow within me and, hence, shape my consciousness? In those strange, bewildered moments, dreams lapse unto reality and just for a few, wonderful seconds I can truly see.

The memories of childhood and adolescence rarely visit my dreams. But when they do, such honored and cherished guests are they. Yesterday, adorned by his dignity he visited me. This beautiful smile that for so long I loved, re-emerged from the midst of book covers, papers, and dust. Delighted by his presence, for a moment the Conference paused in his honor.

In my dream, Dr. Hassan Hathout sat on that same old chair, to the left of the room, in his apartment in Kuwait. I, full of a poetical energy that has now faded away, sat shuffling pages of cryptic verses. When I woke up, I was full of such joy and longing. Back in those days, I would take a deep breath before calling him, back in those days I would count the hours before visiting him, back in those days I was truly alive.

I got out of bed and strolled to my den with a heart weighed with so many memories. At moments of panic, I used to remember his ever so serene smile and it would comfort me. At moments of doubt, his praise was authentic certification of my worth. At moments of vanity, casually mentioning that my family and I were among his guests brought me instant prestige.

I smiled as I remembered the countless, tortuous hours in which I subjected him and his family to my poetry. I would visit accompanied with pages full of words. Out of his kindness, he would listen attentively and praise generously. Now, years later, when I re-read my own poetry I realize how kind and generous he was. His poetry, on the other hand, and use of language, was nothing short of majestic. Whenever he would appear on television, he would insist on speaking classical Arabic. The Arabic teachers in my school would gather to listen to the program and try to catch him committing a grammatical error. They never did catch him. When I left to go to the United States, my father, saddened by my departure, went to visit him. Dr. Hassan comforted my father by telling him "a good bow throws an arrow far away and never retrieves it." Through the years of separation and to this very day, this statement calms and comforts my father and inspires me.

In one of my visits I told him that at Yale I pray in the library, and that I put a sign on my back that reads, "Muslim at prayer." He laughed and laughed. Years later he talked about a friend of his who prays with a sign on his back. He called me a friend! He is such a generous and kind man.

My father would tell me that Hassan Hathout was a companion of Hasan al-Banna (d. 1949), and I would never tire of seeking out the stories. Hassan Hathout would speak of al-Banna with such love and adoration; he would speak of a relationship not guided by politics or law but by a basic sense of human decency. In fact, in every interaction with Hassan Hathout and in every conversation, God and God's religion were not about technical laws, arguments, or disputations, but about a basic decency and fundamental morality. Hassan Hathout became a living embodiment of an Islam that is ever so tolerant, forgiving, loving, and, most of all, humane.

As I thought about the dream and strained to recall the details, I noticed a recent issue of *The Minaret* lying on my desk. "Fighting Cancer With Faith" was the title of his article. The article was a wonderful statement of faith and gratitude, but as I read his acknowledgment of his wife for forty-six years, I cried. Dr. Hassan always chided me for my inclinations toward the tragic and melancholy, but this was different. Here, there was no tragedy or sadness. I recalled God's verse: "There are men among the faithful who have been true to their covenant with God. Some of them fulfilled their vows and some still wait and stand firm" (33:23). I felt happy for him and prayed that Allah would give me the strength to follow in his footsteps.

I realized through the years of struggle and endurance how much he has been an inspiration to me and so many others. But I also realized that now the burden is on me and my generation. Can we discharge the covenant and inspire those who follow us? Do we possess a similar fundamental sense of decency and morality? Part of this decency and morality is that we turn to those who taught and inspired us, to those who permitted us the privilege of finding much that is decent in life, and to those who became the symbolic representation of living human beauty, and say thank you. Thank you.

CHAPTER 26

The Dialectics of an Apology

Arrogance and jealousy, two primordial sins, are fed by the iniquity of entitlement. From the blasphemy of Satan to the obscenity of Cain with Abel, the delusion of entitlement permeates and prevails. The arrogant person feels entitled to what people are not willing to concede, and the jealous person feels entitled to what God did not give. Both persons confuse their wishes with the Divine Will, and wed the two in an unholy bond.

A religious person lives his or her life in search of the Divine Will. But there is always the danger that if one searches for something long enough, one might come to believe that he or she is entitled to find it. The tragedy, however, is when one comes to believe that he or she has in fact found it.

This Conference is my peace and repose. The legacy preserved and sustained in these books constructs and deconstructs me every night a thousand times. When I am constructed, I am taken apart by the majesty of God, and when I am deconstructed, I am inspired by the power of God. The dialectics of the process keep the Conference humbled, but vibrant and alive.

This month, three cases are brought to my attention. Each one of them is saturated with claims of entitlement, arrogance, and jealousy. In the first case, due to jealousy, the *imam* of a mosque is conspired against, accused of misappropriating funds, and fired. The missing funds are later found and the *imam* is vindicated. In the second case, a father forces his daughter into a marriage, which she detests. Later, the husband is found to be a scoundrel who drinks, gambles, and enjoys thrusting obscenities at his wife. In the third case, a wife plans to divorce her husband months before he is even aware of her intentions. In preparation for the divorce, she quietly transfers the family savings to a secret private account in her name. Years later, when her new husband does the same to her and misappropriates her funds, it dawns on her that she has committed the crime of theft against her first husband. In all three cases, the offenders realize that they have wronged their victims. In all three cases, the offenders wish to seek forgiveness from God. But in all three cases, the offenders refuse to seek forgiveness from their victims. Forgiveness, they argue, is a matter between them and God, and, therefore, what difference does it make if the victims forgive or not? The administrators of the mosque refuse to apologize to the *imam*; the father refuses to apologize to his daughter; and the wife refuses to apologize to her first husband.

The only one before me right now is the woman, and as I sit listening to the careful articulation of a philosophy of arrogant repentance, I am reminded of the man who recently awarded me the title of the Great Satan. Realizing that perhaps the title might be a bit of an exaggeration, he decided that an *istighfar* might be in order—an apology, however, is a superfluous gratuity.

In all the cases mentioned above, the individuals concerned received counsel that the forgiveness of a human being is no more than a technical nicety unrelated to the mechanics of *tawba* or repentance. The woman argues with me that since she now has asked God to forgive her what does her ex-husband have to do with anything! I am amazed at the arrogance which permits a person to use the remembrance of God as the tool for forgetting human beings. I am amazed at the fact that the absolution of God becomes the mechanism by which the rights of human beings are derogated and dismissed.

In the discourses of this Conference, the rights of human beings are not a useless marginality. The rights of God are forgiven by God but the rights of human beings must either be redressed or forgiven by the possessor of the right. For example, the Hanafi jurist al-'Ayyini (d. 855/1451) states in *Sharh al-Hidaya* that the usurper of property will not be forgiven for his sin, even if he repents a thousand times, unless he returns the stolen property. Muslim jurists debated at length as to whether even the imposition of the criminal sanction will constitute an immediate forgiveness for one's sins.

I ask the woman for permission to read her a passage from *Ahkam al-Qur'an* by the Maliki jurist Ibn al-'Arabi (d. 543/1148). The passage states: "The rights of human beings are not forgiven by God unless the human being concerned forgives them first, and the claims for such rights are not dismissed [by God] unless they are dismissed by the person concerned. . . The rights of a Muslim cannot be abandoned except by the possessor of the right. Even the *imam* does not have the right to demand [or abandon] such rights. This is because the *imam* is not empowered to act as the agent for a specific set of individuals over their specific rights. Rather, the *imam* only represents people, generally, over their general and unspecified rights."

I am not sure about her response. She asks with a tone that betrays a degree of indignation: "Are you saying that God cannot forgive? Isn't this *shirk*?" But we are not talking about God's Ability or even Will. We are talking about the morality of justice. Forgiveness cannot justly be given for a persistent and continuing sin. It is the dismissal of peoples' rights which permitted the initial infraction—the stealing of the money, the firing of the *imam,* and the forcing of a woman to marry someone she detests—and it is the dismissal of peoples' rights which now makes one refuse to apologize. In other words, it is a continuing, uninterrupted infraction. She exclaims now with open indignation, "And what is this Ibn al-'Arabi saying anyway?"

I take a deep breath, and strain to reach beyond the veils of ignorance and the structures of discourse to the elusive essentials. I smile as if I discovered it. "He is saying it is rude not to apologize."

CHAPTER 27

The Essential Individual

A human being consumes another human being when he or she reduces and essentializes the other into a use or function. The individuality, emotions, feelings, and particulars of the consumed become relevant only to the extent that they facilitate or promote that use. For a person to be thoroughly consumed, they must be packaged and stereotyped into a function. The function must then yield itself to the desires or needs of the consumer. The fact that, in some measure, we all consume each other is undeniable. The fact that we must strive not to do so is a moral imperative.

In this Conference no participant or author is essentialized or consumed. Each demands to be an individual and each demands to be part of the group. Each stands singular and unique, but each is part of the glorious truth of the *jama'a*. As individuals, we stand accountable to God, but as a *jama'a*, we receive the blessed hand of God. As reported, the Prophet said: "The hand of God is with the *jama'a*."

Visitors come seeking the secret of the collective discourse. I meet them as an individual, burdened by weaknesses and limitations of a physical and intellectual space. But the Conference responds with the power of a primordial discourse not set in time or space. She used to be a commodity pretending to be a model; her pictures splattered in magazines and posters around the world selling a delusion. She says, "Before Islam, I was essentialized and packaged for immediate consumption. Like the picture of a juicy hamburger before inducing a sale, I had to be mentally and emotionally consumed. I converted to Islam and changed my world. I enjoyed the anonymity—the fact that I was unrecognizable, and that I was simply a part of the whole. I disappeared in the *jama'a* and enjoyed the fact that my individuality was ignored."

I am curious about the reason for this visit and even more curious about her use of the past tense. I ask, "Are you still at peace?" She hesitates, but then says, "I don't wish to be selfish or individualistic, but what is the balance between the individual and the *jama'a?* The individualism and materialism of the society I grew up in has caused me untold degradation and pain. But sometimes, I miss myself."

I say, "The thoughts I offer you, I offer you as an individual, but I am not individualistic in doing so." Although the thoughts are the thoughts of an individual, they rely on a collectivity of experiences, thoughts, and ideas. There is a difference between individualism and being an individual. Individualism is a creed of selfishness, self-reference, and private truth. Being an individual is an act of self-worth, collective reference, and public truth. You, at one time, used to be packaged for consumption, not because you were an individual. Quite to the contrary, in packaging you for public consumption, your individuality and personhood was streamlined, stereotyped, and ignored. You no longer stood for who you are as an individual, rather you became an image or symbol for something that had nothing to do with you. This could happen when people take a picture of you and publish it, but it also could happen when, in the context of a group, your individuality becomes ignored. There is no qualitative difference between a person consumed by commercialism and a person consumed by authoritarianism.

"And the *jama'a?*" she asks. I search for the collective discourse and then say: It is reported that the blessed Companion of the Prophet, 'Abdullah Ibn Mas'ud (d. 32/652), said that when the majority is in error, then the *jama'a* becomes what you believe to be right before God. Furthermore, the jurist Ibn al-Qayyim (d. 751/1350) said that the command to adhere to the *jama'a* means a command to adhere to the truth. That is why, as Ibn al-Qayyim explained, the *jama'a* could be a single person.

The *jama'a* is not a numbers game, and it is not a prescription for "groupthink." When it comes to the truth before God, you must seek it as an individual and be held accountable for it as an individual. It cannot be an idiosyncrasy or whim, and you must pursue it with diligence and honesty. If you believe that you have found it, you must then bring it to the group. If you are right you will be rewarded twice and if you are wrong you will be rewarded once. My sister, God has said: "Each one of them will come before God on the Final Day as an individual" (19:95). Islam, my sister, cannot be the excuse for the denial of the wonder of the individual or become the excuse for the dictatorship of the majority.

CHAPTER 28

The Search for Beauty

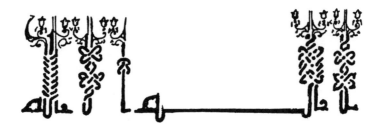

The *Conference of the Books* searches the past for moments of beauty and truth. In this search, the *Shari'a* becomes the method and the way. The mind channels the search through the limitations of the present to the unbound potential of the future. In the past we find the signs of God, and in the future the promise of God; the present is nothing but a transient state. The mind is an imperfect conduit that, by necessity, corrupts the search. For how can we transform the signs of God into the promise of God without imposing ourselves upon the search? The *Shari'a* is the sign of God and the promise of God, and we are the imperfect conduits leading to the way. Knowledge of our imperfections should restrain us, but knowledge of God's perfection should liberate us. In our imperfections and temporality exists the secret of the *Shari'a*'s perfection and immutability.

The *hadith* says, "God is beautiful and God loves all that is beautiful." The temporal manifestations of God's beauty perish, but the perennial truth of God's beauty remains forever (55:26–27). God's beauty is unchanging and objective, but it is pursued, realized, and manifested through the subjective limitations of God's creations. I am, for instance, beautiful; the fact that I am God's creation endows me with this beauty, and this beauty is eternal. But the extent to which I realize and manifest this beauty depends on my subjective limitations, which will most certainly perish. Since the *Shari'a* is the way to God, it is of necessity the way to beauty. Every time I see something beautiful, I suspect that I have found a manifestation of the Divine. But because of the fact that I am aware of my subjective limitations and imperfections, I restrain my zeal with the duty of investigation and reflection. After all, how many people sought to worship God, but ended up only worshipping themselves?

So many of those who have the beautiful spark of youth seek the discourse on Islam and human rights. The images of Islam in their minds are not ones of beauty. Rather, they associate Islam with everything ugly, unpleasant, and inhumane. They come with the ingrained notion that Islam does not have an interest in the beautiful, moral, or ethical, but only looks to the strictly legal and functional. In these popular perceptions, Islam is a legalistic religion whose numerous laws vitiate the need for morality or ethics or for a sense of beauty. The encounter is rendered frustrating when a Muslim jumps up in the midst of discussion and declares, "Beauty is a corruption, and that is why there is no law in *Shari'a* which commands that we should care for beauty." An educator can only search the past and look to the future, and hope that the present will pass.

Shari'a is the search for the beautiful because it is the search for God. There is an innate and intuitive sense of the beautiful which is the *fitra* that God has implanted in all of us. This *fitra* is corrupted not only by arrogance, which often equates human desire and the truth of God, but even more, it is corrupted when people ignore or forget its existence, and forget that they have an intuitive sense of the ethical, the just, and the beautiful. God commands that humans observe *ihsan*, command the *ma'ruf*, and forbid the *munkar*. *Ihsan* means that which is commonly known to be good, *ma'ruf* means that which is commonly known to be right, and *munkar* means that which is commonly known to be reprehensible. In each of these categories, the implicit assumption is that humans possess an intuitive sense of right and wrong. This is why God states that wrong and right have been inspired in every soul. Those who corrupt their soul fail, and those who purify it succeed (91:8–10).

The medieval jurist, Khamis al-Shaqasi, in his *Manhaj al-Talibin* argues that for every place and age there is an appropriate rule. For example, he asserts, in Medina, people forbade their maidens to go out uncovered (*hasirat*), while in Oman, it was considered reprehensible for maidens not to cover. Therefore, he concludes, everything that Muslims consider reprehensible is, in fact, reprehensible. Al-Shaqasi has a point but he is not entirely correct. There is no doubt that laws change with time and place, and that community standards are relevant in identifying the appropriate rule for the right age and place. In other words, community standards are relevant for distinguishing the beautiful from the ugly. Nonetheless, community standards cannot replace the need for the moral inquiry. Put differently, culture cannot replace morality. We search the Divine Will through several avenues of evidence. Among the avenues of evidence are textual sources and cultural practices. However, the Divine Will must also be searched through a moral and ethical inquiry.

In the contemporary Muslim world, the political and cultural often completely override and replace either the moral or textual inquiry. The idea that Islam must be associated with all that is humane, ethical, moral, and beautiful is often alien to the contemporary Muslim context.

Beyond the cultural and legal, there is also the beautiful. There is no doubt that hostility to Islam and prejudice against Muslims play a large role in the way Muslims are treated and perceived. But, perhaps, the ugliness of prejudice has permitted some of us to forget that the Prophet has been sent as a mercy to humankind, and that mercy is beautiful. Most of all, we cannot forget that we seek the beautiful because God is beautiful.

CHAPTER **29**

Hegemony and Terrorism

G od reminds Quraysh of the twin blessings: protection from hunger and safety from fear (106:3–4). In the presence of hunger and fear, life becomes full of anxiety and pain, and the indispensable values of dignity and reflection become exceedingly difficult to achieve. The very soul of life exists in the sublime subtleties of its discourses. But in the absence of dignity and reflection there is only a mindless form of wailing. When human beings no longer feel safe, secure, dignified, or honored, the discourses of life are replaced with the crippling anxiety of alienation and the exasperated cries of desperation.

The Conference of the Books is the beautiful and subtle discourse of life—it thrives in the midst of the beauty of reflection and dignity, and dies in the midst of degradation, fear, and desperation. Pragmatism is but an experience, and idealism is but a dream. If we live solely by the force of experience, we fall captive to our limitations, and if we live solely by the force of dreams we fall captive to delusion. This Conference channels our experiences into a statement for higher ideals. In the existence of fear and desperation, we neither experience the glory of life nor do we dare to dream.

Despotism breeds desperation, for it is a denial of the essential and inherent dignity of the human being, and terror imposes the crippling logic of fear, for it denies the ability of a human being to feel. The most powerful form of despotism in the modern age is the despotism of hegemony, and the most powerful form of terror in today's age is the onslaught of sudden, unpredictable, and indiscriminate violence. Hegemony is the supremacy over the production and control of the images that transmit value and

THE SEARCH FOR BEAUTY IN ISLAM

culture. It is the reproduction and manipulation of the symbolic value by which we understand the good and bad, the ugly and beautiful, and the sound and absurd. Hegemony, through the power of images and symbols, ultimately defines our wants and desires, and controls the way we define the limits and boundaries of our lives, as well as the way we interact and relate to others. Through the production of images and symbols, we learn how to dress, how to speak, how to work, how to rest, how to love, and how to hate. Through the production of images and symbols, we learn how to understand our experiences in life, how to shape our expectations, and even how to relate to our dreams.

The question of who has hegemony today is largely irrelevant. The relevant question is who is perceived to have hegemony? The perception is that hegemony belongs to the agnostic culture of consumerism and materialism, which deconstructs the individuality of each human being and dismantles the richness and the uniqueness of each culture. This hegemonic culture champions an ethic of consumption and, in turn, essentializes and reduces the individual into a basic commodity to be exploited or discarded depending on the individual's functional utility. There is no room in this hegemonic view for individual or unique expressions of identity, or for cultural particularism. The perception is that the United States and Western civilization, as a whole, are the masters and perpetuators of this hegemony. American and Western ideals and values are being projected onto the world, and the nations and cultures of the world must accept or be mercilessly opposed, fought, and cast as pariahs and outlaws.

It is this perception of hegemony which ignites and nourishes the culture of terrorism. Terrorism is a form of resistance to the anxieties and desperation which results from the negation and eradication of one's unique identity and sense of self-worth. However, terrorism is not a constructive or persuasive form of resistance, but a destructive and particularly futile form of opposition. Terrorism is not a counter-culture to hegemony, rather it is the complete lack of culture. Like many expressions of desperation, it is not the assertion of a counter-moral value but the complete lack of moral value. Fundamentally, terrorism is a desperate admission of defeat and an inability to persuade.

By its very nature, terrorism is similar to hegemony. Both are quintessentially repressive; both control and oppress, and both dehumanize and manipulate. One manipulates through the power of prurient enticement and the other through the vulgarity of terror. Both objectify their victims, consume their bodies, and violate their souls. Nonetheless, while the hegemony of images manages to bewitch and mesmerize many hearts and minds and souls, terrorism wins neither mind, nor heart, nor soul.

God does not punish a group of people by the sins of another, and God says: "O, you who believe, stand firmly on the side of God, and be just witnesses. Do not let the injustice of others lead you into injustice. Be just; that is nearer to piety—and fear God" (5:8). Terrorism attacks a perceived injustice by imposing an indiscriminate

74

message of fear. It does not distinguish between the guilty or innocent, and destroys all without regard to culpability or individual responsibility. Human worth and human dignity are sacrificed for the sake of communicating a message of protest or resistance and, therefore, human life becomes not an end, but simply a means. Often, the argument is made that the dispossessed and disempowered do not have a way to resist except by the use of terror. But it is better to die suffering the injustice of others than to survive by inflicting injustice upon others.

In resisting the current agnostic culture of hegemony, one must construct a counter-culture which offers an alternative. As Muslims, we cannot construct an alternative that is opportunistic or pragmatic, or an alternative that is hegemonic or oppressive. As Muslims, the only option open to us is a principled, ethical, and moral alternative. We cannot protest by wailing or terrorizing; we must protest by discoursing and convincing. We cannot achieve a silly, perceived victory over the bodies of some, and lose the hearts and sympathy of most. Our alternative must be the vigorous thundering of the Conference of the Books, and not the terror-filled thundering of bombs.

CHAPTER 30

Longing for Brotherhood

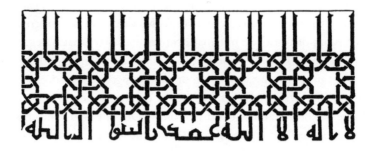

T he wonder of brotherhood cannot be invented by genes or constructed by law. It is a magnificent state which is equal in worth to an escape from Hellfire or a gift of Heaven, for those who were on the brink of Hellfire were saved by brotherhood (3:103), and those who attained Heaven were anointed with brotherhood (15:47). It is equal in status to the wonder of beauty, the nobility of dignity, and the magnificence of decency. But brotherhood is a state, and not a status. As a blessing, it flows, bonding souls and hearts, but it cannot be legislated, quantified, or institutionalized.

Neither theology nor law replaces the need for a fundamental and intuitive sense of decency or beauty. All the institutional structures of the world cannot impart to the obstinate the fundamental sense of decency and beauty that is at the core of brotherhood. And, all the effective mechanisms of activism and intellectualism cannot conceal the ugliness when brotherly love is absent. The Qur'an speaks of those who will come to God on the Final Day with a pure and healthy heart (26:89). But what law or what institutional command can cleanse a tainted soul or mend a fractured heart? What law or command can create the sweet moments that build that majestic bond? What law or command can instill an unwavering fidelity to a beautiful memory? Laws and commands exhort and punish, but if the heart is corrupted, no command or order can replace the intimacy and truthfulness of a lively conscience, beautiful soul, and loving heart.

We sat long hours conversing on an abstract and indefinable concept called "the movement." We dreamt of partners and mates, and of an altered future. There was this vague sense of a destiny, and the desire to invent the exceptional. God's Will was searched at potlucks, in camps, on hikes, through lectures, in debates, and in sleep. God's Will was searched in the midst of midnight coffees, scribbles on notepads, and greasy meals. God's Will was embraced by wishful thoughts and meddling dreams.

There was a feeling of a tie or an exceptional bond which united the participants in this fantastic dream. We imagined the coming of an Islamic movement. We imagined that there would be a diligent and unwavering brotherhood interlocking our emotions and thoughts around the bond of God. There was a pious and silly sense of confidence about the difference between the demonstrative individual legacies that we could see all around us, and what we believed we were going to be. If earlier generations had become distracted by life, well, we were going to be different. We would remain faithful to the ideal.

After years of reflection and distance, I come back to the same place. I visit all the old locations, the houses, the cafes, the streets, and the campuses. The remnants are there, but the effect is gone. Years later, there are marriages and divorces, there are children and schools, there are homes and jobs, but the bond between us and the brotherhood is gone. I do not lament the memories, for the memories are history, and history is a lesson. It is not that we are inactive, because most of us remained as active as one could hope. But the brotherhood that makes the activism of one a way of loving the other is now lost. The Prophet is reported to have said, "You do not become a believer until you love for your brother what you would love for yourself." Such brotherhood is a state by which you love, worry, and crave for your brother. Brotherhood is a state which permits a group to move from the realm of a cooperative effort to the imperative of a shared destiny. It is a standard by which the success of a group is measured by the success of its individuals, and by which the strength of a group is measured by the strength of the bond that unites its members. The success of a group does not depend on its ability to unite over a cause or by its ability to work toward achieving a cause. Rather, the success of a group depends on its ability to transform its own members into a cause.

I do not blame the partners of my youth, for I realize that we were a fiction created by the polemics of the moment. I, like my partners, forgot that brotherhood, like decency or beauty, is a state and not a status. Without diligence and effort, decency degenerates into indifference, beauty degenerates into blandness, and brotherhood degenerates into a habit. The blessing of brotherhood is given by God to those whose piety is channeled into an unwavering sense of fidelity to all that is decent and beautiful. Ultimately, brotherhood is the just reward for those who are truly decent and truly beautiful.

CHAPTER 31

The Culture of the Mamnu'

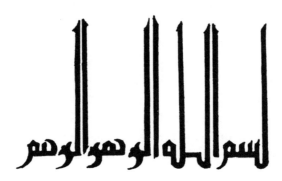

"M*amnu' ya akhi*" (brother, it is forbidden). This chilling phrase travels down your spine, sending trembling memories of fear. You pace up and down the room recalling the endless times in airports, in mail stations, in libraries, in bookstores, in schools, in government bureaucracies, and in Islamic institutions that you heard this phrase. It does not mean that something is prohibited or sinful; it means the blacklist, the forbidden, the banned. Endless times, your heart races, your throat grows dry, your palms sweat, the acid in your stomach battles to invade your throat, and the heat explodes from under the skin covering your face as you wait. You stand in front of the divine imposter awaiting his loathsome declaration. Reading from some mysterious list, he raises his head and spits out, "*Mamnu'*!" A work of thought, a member of the Conference, and a way to God—a book, has been banned.

You stand puzzled by the why and how, but it does not matter, for it has been decreed by the immutable list of the devil that the book has been banned. You may not buy, read, mail, or receive it. It has been banned. Their arrogance and ignorance clashes with your determination and knowledge that you will find a way to salvage the banned and read it. But today is different. The banned is not something you wish to read but something that you wrote. The divine imposter is not sitting in front of you, but you hear about his declaration over the telephone while in the safety of your home, and while the object of the ban lies in front of you on a table. Your book, *The Authoritative and the Authoritarian in Islamic Discourses,* has been banned for the second time in one year by the endless stream of divine imposters in the Middle East.

You pace up and down the room reciting, "And those whose hearts find peace in the remembrance of God, for in the remembrance of God do the hearts find peace" (13:28). There is no lamentation or regret but only determination and trust. "For the scum disappear from the face of the earth, while that which is good for humankind remains. . ." (13:17), and you know that what you wrote will remain and prevail, and the scum will be flushed away by the Conference and by a million unrestrainable Conferences to come throughout this earth. This accursed word *mamnu'* is but the torrent that brings the scum to the surface, but doesn't a torrent invariably wash its own scum out? You wrote *The Authoritative and the Authoritarian* as a protest against the arrogance of the ignorant; you rejected the attempt of some to become the voice of the Divine, and you submitted to the authoritativeness of the Divine, but rebelled against the authoritarianism of those who attempt to speak for the Divine. You developed a methodology by which the authoritative and authoritarian could be set apart. You rejected the oppression of patriarchy and sexism, and you rejected the despotism which makes women nothing better than slaves to men, or which makes men slaves to their own whim, or which enslaves the Divine text to the dogmatics of its reader. God has said, "See what things God has sent down to you as a blessing? Yet, you make some things forbidden and other things lawful? Say, has God permitted you [to do so] or do you invent things and attribute them to God?" (10:59). Among the unique and singular blessings of God is the power of the intellect and the beauty of the discourse. Among the singular blessings of God is this very Conference, and who has the right to make it forbidden or to censor its discourse?

Nonetheless, the authoritarianism of the *mamnu'* fights back, for it rejects the very premise of this Conference and the beauty of the discourse. It wishes to make the lawful forbidden and the forbidden lawful and it wishes to become the embodiment or even the replacement of the Divine Voice. God confronts falsehood with the truth and the froth is always more visible and dazzling, but what remains is the truth (13:17). God has empowered us to command justice and to enjoin the good and forbid the evil. This empowerment becomes a vested right in all of us, and it becomes a part of God's Covenant and what God has commanded to be joined (*yuwsal*). Human beings and God are joined by the rights and duties of the Covenant and joined to each other by God's empowerment to command justice and enjoin the good. The empowerment to command justice and enjoin the good is but a command to engage in the Conference and engage in the discourse. God has given us the right to search and speak. If we speak out of whim or ignorance, we abuse the trust and incur a sin. If we speak out of diligence and discipline, we discharge the trust, and honor the blessing. But no one is empowered to take away our right to search and speak. No one has the right to silence the discourse or void the Covenant. That is why God says, "But those who break the Covenant of God, and cut asunder the things that God has commanded to be joined, and work mischief in the land, on them is the curse, and their fate is miserable" (13:25). What greater mischief could there be than the culture of the *mamnu'* and the arrogance of censorship?

Since its publication, *The Authoritative and the Authoritarian* has been translated to Arabic. Two separate publishers have attempted to print it, and twice it has been banned. In the Middle East, we are used to the culture of the *mamnu'* and the mischief of censorship. But the problem is not limited to the Middle East. In the United States, the book has been banned in several Islamic conferences. Nearly all Muslim book distributors have refused to carry it, and most Islamic magazines have refused to advertise it. Invitations to Islamic conferences have all but dried up, and at least in one mosque and in some correspondence you have been given the ambitious title of the "grand devil." So, you pace the room pondering this whole experience, wondering about the influence that certain Middle Eastern governments and cultures have here in the United States. Perhaps for many Muslims in the United States, their bodies are free and their pockets are full, but their intellects remain enslaved by the poverty of authoritarianism and the misery of the *mamnu'*.

CHAPTER 32

On Being in Love

In the *Conference of the Books*, the physical exists only to testify to the eternal, and the eternal is intellectual and ethereal, unbound by a corporal reality. An ephemeral existence is, by its very nature, contingent and cannot be an absolute reality. But an ephemeral existence can and does testify to a higher and absolute truth that is not contingent upon the existence of the physical reality.

I caught myself engaging in spiraling thoughts which found their way to my strained tongue. What a humbling moment it is when one feels the exhaustion of one's own mouth.

He sat before me in respectful confusion and doubt, and I realized that, since moving to Los Angeles, I have become accustomed to living with my own thoughts. I have forgotten the art of answering a question, and since the marginalization of my book, *The Authoritative and the Authoritarian in Islamic Discourses*, I have become the main audience attending to the ongoings of my mouth.

My first visitor and interlocutor in months asks me about the tribulations and trials of love, and I increase his suffering by subjecting him to the trials and tribulations of my rambling tongue. To my surprise, he did not come to discuss a text or jurist; he came to describe the agonies of love. He explained that he finds himself constantly engaged in torments of doubt and hope. He invents excuses to be in her presence, endlessly chides himself for every word said to her, and finds himself silly and incoherent. He reads the Qur'an for comfort but finds that it only makes him love her more. Remarkably, he even finds her between the lines of *Kitab al-Kharaj* by Abu Yusuf (d. 182/797), and in the romantic lectures on statistics and quantitative analysis. He finally escapes to

Ibn Hazm's (d. 456/1064) *Ring of the Dove*, but finds his torment augmented by Ibn Hazm's description of love as an affliction that overtakes the body and mind. Throughout his description, I listened without interruption; however, my tongue sparked into action when he said that the woman he loves is the most beautiful person he has ever seen. After his initial description, his demoralized silence proved irresistible and useless in attempting to restrain the eruption of thoughts brought about by the topic of love.

You must realize, I declared, that the physical is not only temporal, but it is also flaccid and frail. It is deceptive because it explodes with such arrogance and assertiveness that one can lose sight of its reality. For instance, a beautiful flower erupts with such overwhelming force and power that it might deceive one in admiring it for itself. The arrogance of its beauty conceals the fact that it quickly withers away and is replaced by another. The truth of its beauty, in reality, testifies to a higher truth, a beauty unbound by corporal laws.

This higher existence is the intellect which makes sense of and constructs and reconstructs reality. The resilience of the ethereal intellect contrasts sharply with the frailness of the body. The intellect, in its resilience, is able to construct and justify anything and is able to wish for anything. It is this wishfulness that keeps our minds and spirits lively and resilient, and that allows us the blessing of dreams and hopes. Yet, it is also this wishfulness that threatens to deceive us into arrogant assurance, and that permits us to ignore the reality of our temporality. Hence, most sin and evil is not the result of a deliberate act of corruption, but the result of an arrogant state of wishfulness and blind confidence. Therefore, in the Final Day the hypocrites will be reprimanded for allowing themselves to be deceived by wishfulness (57:14). Isn't it ironic that the intellect produces and understands values, but it is also the reason that values are deconstructed and undermined? Nevertheless, we must use and rely upon our intellects, for without the intellect, all that remain are the cravings of the frail body. Without the intellect, all that remain are the ailments, desires, and demands of the body.

In his typical, understated fashion, he said, "Are you saying I must use my brain and not blindly follow my desires?" Despite my admiration for his succinct simplicity, I could not oblige him. What I am saying is that you obviously suffer a physical attraction, but this physical attraction, despite its powerful arrogance, is nothing more than the craving of physical beings. Like the desire to see a beautiful flower or consume a delicious meal, in itself, it is meaningless unless it testifies to a higher reality and a higher being. This higher reality is the ethereal intellect which is capable of understanding and creating values and meaning. Yet, the intellect, itself, is dependent for its existence on perception, comprehension, and projection. Therefore, the intellect cannot be an ultimate and absolute being. Rather, the intellect obtains its worth and its value from its ability to testify to the ultimate truth, the Supreme Being.

What I am saying is this physical attraction must be evaluated in terms of its effect on your intellect and your intellect's relationship to God. Does that woman empower your intellect? Does she enrich your intellect's ability to reach for God? Instead of thinking about her beauty, ponder whether this beauty brings you closer to God. Perhaps this way you can distinguish between an affliction and blessing, and between a craving for physical consumption and a love bestowed upon you for the wondrous sake of God.

I do not know what my friend decided to do. But my heart was warmed when he smiled such a wonderfully beautiful smile. *Insha' Allah*, a beautiful smile in the sake of God.

CHAPTER 33

Lecturing on the Ugly

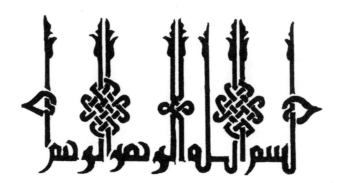

"I eschew politics when it is unlawful and eschew law when it is not moral. To the extent that politics is not subject to law, it is reprehensible, and to the extent that law is not subject to morality, it is reprehensible." So the lecture went. "Reason and compassion, disciplined and guided by the search for the Divine Will, must constitute the essential unity which forms the backbone of politics, law, and morality. Whether in the written text or in the texts of creation, the Divine Will is the most crucial guide and foundation. Politics without law is nothing but opportunism, and law without morality is nothing but despotism, and morality unless guided by the Divine Will risks becoming nothing more than a concession to whim. But the search for the Divine Will, if not anchored in reason and compassion, risks becoming a draconian affirmation of the most base and mundane subjective desire and impulse. At the very core of reason, compassion, and God, is beauty—such unadulterated beauty."

Such is the ranting of an intellect existing in perpetual supplication to an ethereal Conference. The Conference of the Books' incessant longing for beauty, the beauty of creation, the beauty of God, pervades every moment, every emotion, every breath, and every throbbing nerve. A life of morality, reason, and compassion is so pre-eminently beautiful, while a life plagued by opportunism, despotism, and whimsy is invariably ugly. If politics is not beautiful, it is unlawful, and if law is not beautiful, it is immoral, and, most important of all, if religion is not beautiful, it cannot be religion.

I paused to look at the directed stares of my audience. Adorned in their beards and *hijabs*, a few Muslims sat at a dinner table to my left. At the rest of the tables sat

Jews, for it was Chabad and we were at the Hillel. What a magnanimous opportunity for the intellect to engage the intellect and the spirit to embrace the spirit, for two people defeated by fear and intoxicated by arrogance to discover and create. As I entered the building, I was met with a group of Muslims protesting my entry. "We do not want to lose respect for you," some warned. But since when has the desire for approval motivated me. Once someone declared, "I do not respect you." I responded, "But that is most unfortunate for you."

The audience stared at me expecting a discourse on politics and law, on wars, states, and elections, on the similarity of rules and difference in injunctions. But without morality all of this is simply ugly.

Earlier in the evening, a Jewish student asked the Muslim sisters why they wear the *hijab,* and they said for modesty. Because men are weak, women were commanded to cover. What an ugly vision this is—a vision in which men salivate to uncover, and women cower to cover. Yet, this same evening a Jewish student insisted that all women who wear the *hijab* are extremists. What a repulsive logic this is—a logic which condemns people for practicing their conviction. Obsessive visions and whimsical logic create an essentialism that is as simple in structure and as destructive in effect as a lethal virus.

"Existence," I continued with the lecture, "tends to eventually frustrate and embarrass all essentialisms." Existence is too complex, it is diverse and rich, and thus, it does not easily surrender to bipolar visions. In fact, creation constantly changes and evolves in order to confound and bewilder the essentialists. Haven't you noticed that any political doctrine or legal system, or claim of morality, that fails to take account of the complexity, diversity, and individuality of existence finds itself marred in oppression, despotism, and cruelty? Fairness and justice demand that each variable be given consideration, and each consideration be given its due weight. So how can the essentialist individual who does not recognize variables or considerations be fair or just? And how can an unfair or unjust person be of just character? And isn't justness of character at the epitome of beauty?

For instance, consider the world in which we live. Merve Kavakci, a Turkish woman, is elected to the Turkish parliament. Because she wears the *hijab,* she is not permitted to take an oath by which she swears to faithfully serve those whom she represents, and she is ultimately stripped of citizenship. What befell Kavakci is a product of an essentialist and unparticularized understanding of the role of a *muhajjaba* woman. Turkey's democracy is too weak and unjust to revisit one of its most repulsive essentialisms. A woman stands up to confront an unthinking herd of men and demands her right to self-expression, and people do not line up to congratulate her for challenging the traditional role of women, or for deconstructing models of patriarchy, or for reclaiming feminism. She is simply another fundamentalist on a seditious secret mission. Isn't this simply ugly? No edifice of legality can justify such immorality.

Another example: In Israel, religious parties freely practice politics, support and oppose candidates, lobby for laws, clash with secularists, and worship God. But the participation of a Muslim group in politics is branded as political Islam or Islamism, and all political Islam is extremist by definition. The Jewish ultra-orthodox, conservative and reformed, vigorously assert their rights in Israel and the United States, and enrich the political process with their arguments and visions. But the likes of Daniel Pipes, Steve Emerson, and Joseph Bodansky, in the most vile form of essentialism, quickly brand any Muslim group which enters the political process as fundamentalist and fanatical in its very essence. Isn't it bigoted to claim that a devout Jew or Christian is capable of partaking in civil society while a Muslim is necessarily crippled by his or her religion? Isn't this simply ugly?

In Kosovo, people are massacred, raped, and expelled in mass. Yet, some continue to growl incoherent phrases about the risk of a fundamentalist state in the midst of Europe. In these diseased minds, rape, extermination, and expulsion are a necessary evil if done to avoid the bogeyman of Muslim fundamentalism. At the same time, Turkey, the unwavering protector of civil liberties and bare heads, sits contentedly on the sidelines as Russia has epileptic fits in the name of ethnic and religious solidarity. Of course, political Christian Greek Orthodoxy does not pose the slightest danger to world peace or tranquility. While women in Bosnia and Kosovo are stripped and raped, and while a group of protesters stand in front of the Federal Building every day of the week defending the right of Serbian soldiers to rape women with impunity, Muslims babble endlessly about the rights of women in Islam and the dangers of the luscious female figure on world serenity. Isn't this picture utterly ugly?

As I stand lecturing in the Hillel after the Chabad services, I wonder about the protesters who met me earlier. The Hillel invited me to lecture on Islam and I lectured on the beauty that Islam inspires in every fiber of my being. I wondered how often mosques and Islamic centers have invited Jews to lecture on Judaism. Didn't God say that we were created as nations and tribes so that we will come to know each other (49:13) and isn't it beautiful to know the other?

At the end of the lecture, the audience clapped, and then, not to be outdone, the table on my left repeated the three mandatory *takbirs*. I felt no pleasure. God is always great but I recoil at the unfortunate impression that my lecture is somehow sanctified by God's greatness. God's judgment I will face alone, but I can never discern the intensity or depth of a human response from the invented modern dogma of Muslims. I wonder whether it is beautiful for a people to be dogmatic even in their emotive expression of pleasure or displeasure.

CHAPTER 34

A Night With the Qalam

This voice is liberated in this majestic Conference. Realizing its irresolute ignorance, it hopes to be delivered from its resistance. It hopes to be delivered from its impedance and stubborn ignorance. The *Conference of the Books* is the sublime voice of our very existence. It reflects our silly pattering, our sad confusions, our melancholy delusions, and the jubilant moments of perception. The voice of the Conference flows from the voice of God, a voice searching for its originator, its mentor, its most omnipotent guide. When is a person more free than when a person seeks to be free? A person who does not seek is drowning in the morbidity of his meaningless existence. A person who fancies himself to have become absolutely free becomes enslaved to the delusion of a self-proclaimed divinity.

I don't know if he visits me in reality or in a dream. I also don't know if there is a precise divide between what we imagine and what is real. I don't know if these voices, these images, these visions, and what I proclaim to be events, are real. Perhaps he is one of my friends who, long ago, was devoured by savages. Perhaps he is the echo of my defiant father or the impression of my unfailingly upright mother. Perhaps he reverberated from the torment of so many martyrs or he resonated from the supplications of so many believers throughout the years. Could he be the reflection of that most generous smile of Hasan 'Abd al-Ghani who survived the dungeons of Egypt and the war in Palestine, but succumbed to cancer? Perhaps he was there with the *Qurra'* of Medina who were infatuated with the Qur'an, or perhaps he helped inspire the two hundred volumes of *Kitab al-Funun* by Ibn 'Aqil (d. 513/1119). Maybe he was burned to ashes on the first day of December 1499 when Christian soldiers in

Toledo gathered the contents of one hundred and ninety-five Muslim libraries and torched them.

Perhaps he is the truth that remains regardless of the words that are uttered. Perhaps he is the *qalam*—the *qalam* by which God taught humans what they knew not (96:4–5). "*Nun, by the qalam wa ma yasturun;* by the grace of your lord you are not mad*"* (68:1–2). Perhaps *nun* is the ink, the *qalam* is the pen, and *yasturun* is what people write. But perhaps *nun* is God's infinite and unreachable knowledge, the *qalam* is the intellect, and *yasturun* is what people conceive of and construct. While the pen or the intellect is the invariable truth and the unassailable reality, the product of the pen or intellect is a construct—a construct that exists between fact and fiction, a construct that is imagined and real. Everything relative has the status of the in-between.

He appears at those moments of confusion and frustration when I miss the kind, blissful face of my mentor, when the feeling of marginalization and abandonment becomes overwhelming, or when the alienation from my people becomes distinct and profound. He appears when I am exiled from the Conference or when the petty envy of petty people forces an exile upon me. He appears in the aftermath of an immorality or to contain an eruption of ugliness.

My friend, there is an *imam* who destroyed one hundred copies of a book (which happened to be *The Authoritative and the Authoritarian*) with which he disagrees. The *imam,* in a monotone voice of presumptuous piety, declared that the ends justify the means. My friend, a Muslim cab driver, refused to give a blind woman a ride because of her seeing-eye dog. He focused on the desecration of the dog, and ignored the desecration of ignorance and cruelty toward a fellow human being. My friend, can you believe that the misogynistic work entitled *Islamic Fatawa Regarding Women* is a best-seller? Shouldn't it more accurately be called *Fatawa Against Women*?

Self-declared scholars declare the law of God to be whatever they want it to be, dictators are the teachers of democracy, and egoists endlessly preach that God is supreme.

Traveling among Muslims, such are the labors of the day and the burdens of the night. So vast is our plight that the promise of a new dawn is nowhere to be seen. How could Islam co-exist in a Muslim's heart with the ugly and obscene? Where is the *qalam?* What is the manifestation of the *qalam?* What is its essence? What does it mean?

In the hymns of the night, my friend permeates my soul and reminds me that, as long as the question is asked, hope is never lost. "The essence of the *qalam* is in your essence," he says. "You have the *qalam* in you, and this enticement should lead you to think. The manifestation of the *qalam* is the profound declaration, 'You are of an exalted moral character'" (68:4). The true manifestation of the *qalam* is in the proper moral character nurtured by an intuitive sense of decency and right. What did those who are at a far distance from the *qalam* do? They do not hearken to the truth, they falsely promise and pronounce the oath, they slander and malign, they transgress the bounds, and they are harsh and cruel (68:10–13).

What does God command other than *ihsan*? And, *ihsan* is derived from the word *hasan,* which means the good, proper, and beautiful. Those who transgress the bounds and are cruel are marred in arrogance, for they speak without the knowledge of the book, and they presume that a divine covenant or promise has made them favored in the eyes of the Lord (68:37–9). It is spiritual arrogance which corrupts the natural endowments given by God. It is spiritual arrogance which alters the natural balance and the state of justice and beauty inspired by God into human beings. The *qalam,* my friend, is the divinely endowed perception and cognition which guides us to what is decent, beautiful, and gentle.

The delights of the night remind me of so many encounters with writers and their thoughts. My spirit overflows with the ecstasy of the pen and the word. In a moment, I remember the inspired *qalam* of Ibn 'Aqil (d. 513/1119), who once wrote:

> Observe God's gentleness toward God's creatures: how God has endowed them, for their own welfare, with perceptions beyond cognition, with exigencies impelling them to do what is right and to refrain from evil and corruption. For instance, God's creation of carnal appetite, and the excitement of nature to seek sexual intercourse, which is the way of progress and the preservation of the species; of suffering, resulting from the feeling of compassion for animals, so as to refrain from engaging in causing pain to others, and to curb the assailant; and of making joy, resulting from praise—a motive for the performance of good deeds, since praise is given only for the good. To this category belong all things that remove harm and attract good. God does not allow the good to lack the motives inviting to its performance; nor does God allow the performance of evil deeds to go without taunts impeding performance. Glory be to God Whose generosity flows over with beneficence, in the knowledge that it is good and beneficial; Who wards off corruption in the knowledge that it is evil, and God can dispense with it; Who turns God's creatures away from their courses, by various means in the here and now, as well as with God's menaces of punishment in the Hereafter!*

---

* Quoted in George Makdisi, *Ibn 'Aqil* (Edinburgh: Edinburgh University Press, 1997), 235. Translation slightly changed to reflect my understanding of the original.

CHAPTER 35

A Homily for Ibn Rushd

The clocks surrounding this desk count the pages turned. The rustle of pages and the pattering of clocks are the only sounds to be heard. The sound of inhales and exhales seem like an unwarranted intrusion—unwelcome and irreconcilable. An intrusion. The squeaking of the chair is another bodily contribution. It relentlessly intrudes and disturbs the symmetry of the intellect, its timelessness, and its perfect isolation. The aching muscles, the redundant breathing, the stale moisture of sweat, and the deterioration and friction of metal remind us of our agonizing limitations. The grasp of the intellect, the abstractions of thought, and the immateriality of words promise us a glimpse of the universal and eternal. The human intellect is ephemeral and derivative; it only grasps ideas but can it really invent or create them? But to the extent it associates itself with the absolute and non-derivative intellect, it may see the universal, eternal, and divine.

I hear the time pass and threaten me with the eventuality of sleep. I smile at myself as I think that since we have figured out how to count time, we have learned to die before our time.

The self-imposed exile and isolation allows me to defy time as I suffer to grasp the timeless. Confident in the failure of my quest, but in the success of the effort, I try to understand the beginning and the end. I re-read Ibn Rushd's wondrous book, *The Beginning of the Juris-Consul (Bidayat al-Mujtahid)*. The disagreements of the schools are traced to their rational cause, to the first distinguishing premise, or to the lack of a rational premise. The inner coherence of the law is exposed, but the possibilities and implications gradually open and unfold. The law is rendered into an open text, accessible and empowering for open minds. If God is unlimited and powerful, and if God is the absolute and perfect intellect, how could God's law be irrational or closed to the possibilities of the intellect?

My waning and disintegrating body longs for the company of two of his books: *The Essential in Jurisprudence (al-Daruri fi Usul al Fiqh)* and *The Conclusive Word in the Congruence Between Shari'a and Reason (Fasl al-Maqal fi ma bayn al-Shari'a wa al-'Aql min al-Ittisal)*. My invigorated intellect has long absorbed them into my soul, but I long for their touch, for the comfort of the material.

Ibn Rushd believed in the harmony between the *Shari'a* and the intellect. He believed in a sober life in which God's law must make sense. Intoxication induces irrationality, and today, many Muslims intoxicated with arrogance and drunken with perpetual ignorance deny the law of God its sobriety. If the constituent elements of existence are the intellect, soul, and body, how could God's law deny existence to its elements? How could God's law be irrational, soulless, immoral, or impractical? The irrational is ugly, the soulless is ugly, and the oppressive is ugly, as ugly as the odor of rot that emanates from intoxicants. And God's law, like God, can only be sober and beautiful—genuinely and uncompromisingly sober and beautiful. "Praise be to God, the most beautiful of creators." Yet, no one can deny that even among the people of God there are those who are addicted to the putrid and foul in existence.

I realize that as I approached the end of a chapter I can no longer hear my breathing. I stop to restore the balance, and stare at the clock in contemplation. Ibn Rushd died in isolation. This most beautiful mind that unfolds before me on these pages died persecuted and isolated. I wonder if in his last days, the rustle of papers, the intrusion of breathing, and the annoyance of time became his stubborn companions? I wonder if he thanked his persecutors for his isolation?

In this world, my God, how do we react to persecution? What do we do when the created becomes obsessed with dominating the created instead of submitting to the Creator? Persecution, my Lord, is the *fitna* which you described as worse than murder; it is the distorted intellect seeking to spread its diseased aberration; it is the created conspiring to become the Creator.

But I know that those who covet mindless oratory comprehend from words only their oratorical effect. Their world is a redundancy of orations producing impulsive effects. Their arrogance invites them to project their ignorance and deny that there is a place in religion for the intellect. It is little wonder that these closed minds seek a closed world, suffering a stagnant creation and a suffocated intellect. It is little wonder that these types persecuted Ibn Rushd and forced him into isolation.

Ibn Rushd (known in the West as Averroes) was born in November 1126 (520 AH), one month before his famous grandfather died. Ibn Rushd's grandfather was a famous Maliki judge in Cordova who, toward the end of his life, dedicated himself to a conference of the books, reading and writing extensive works. Ibn Rushd's father, who was one of Ibn Rushd's teachers, was also a jurist and, for a brief moment, a judge in Cordova. Ibn Rushd himself had many notable teachers, among them the conservative Maliki jurist al-Qadi 'Iyad (d. 544/1149), who at one point was Ibn Rushd's grandfather's student. One of Ibn Rushd's fellow students, studying under al-Qadi 'Iyad and destined to play an unfortunate role in Ibn Rushd's life, was Muhammad Ibn Zarqun (d. 586/1190).

Ibn Rushd quickly rose in stature first as the judge of Seville and then as the chief judge of Cordova. In an age in which the threat of a Christian invasion of Spain was an ever-present reality, people reacted with a stagnant conservatism. But Ibn Rushd was interested in liberation, not preservation. He wrote several works upholding the role of the intellect, and defending the *Shari'a* against the dishonor of irrationalism.

One wonders, among the vices of jealousy, intolerance, arrogance, and dishonesty, which vice can claim the highest rank in the folds of ugliness? As ever in the annals of human existence, all four conspired to sweep away Ibn Rushd in the dark torrents of an inquisition.

It all culminated in the early 590s/1190s. Ibn Hajjaj, a preacher in Seville; Ibn Jubayr, a poet; and Ibn 'Ayyash, a high-ranking bureaucrat—all dedicated their oratory talents to demoralizing the man of intellect. Ibn Hajjaj and Ibn Jubayr went about howling about bottomless pits of heresy, and Ibn Rushd's former fellow student, Ibn Zarqun, joined the onslaught. Not only did Ibn Zarqun accuse Ibn Rushd of heresy and ignorance, but also of plagiarism. Ibn Zarqun claimed that sometime before he had lent Ibn Rushd a book on the differences between the schools. Not only did Ibn Rushd not return the book, Ibn Zarqun claimed, but he added some minor items to it and re-issued it as *Bidayat al-Mujtahid*—the *Bidayat al-Mujtahid*! In truth, Ibn Zarqun's surviving works are nothing more than mindless compilations from borrowed texts, nothing approximating the intellectual force of Ibn Rushd.

Abu 'Amir Ibn Rabi', another unremarkable jurist who did not leave behind any notable text, made a career out of obscenely insulting Ibn Rushd in public. Ibn Rabi' remained a judge in Cordova until he fled when it was conquered by the Christians in 633/1236. Several of the mediocre jurists, unable to match wit with wit and proof with proof, got together and combed through Ibn Rushd's numerous writings. From Ibn Rushd's works, they collected various excerpts which they considered heretical, compiled them in a single volume, and went to meet the Caliph, Abu Yusuf Ya'qub al-Mansur (r. 580–595/1184–1199), toward the end of 591/1194. "There is the proof of his heresy!" they declared, hoping for Ibn Rushd's end. But, in an open debate held in Cordova, Ibn Rushd held his own and, for the moment, the conspiracy failed. But the venom of jealousy and arrogance is unrelenting. The preacher, Ibn Hajjaj, aided by an entourage of envious jurists, maintained the pressure. One day in particular was an omen of days to come. Ibn Rushd, accompanied by his son 'Abdullah, went to the Cordova mosque to perform their '*Asr* prayers. Ibn Rushd and 'Abdullah had previously co-authored a book entitled, *The Conjunction of the Separate Intellect with Man.* Induced by the staleness of the dull afternoon, the rabble attacked Ibn Rushd and his son and threw them out of the mosque. 'Abdullah, a doctor of medicine, painfully recalled this incident until he died.

In 593/1197, the Caliph finally caved in and banned the study of philosophy and ordered the burning of the works of the philosophers. Ibn 'Ayyash, the bureaucrat, authored the decree. In this decree, he did not mention Ibn Rushd by name but Ibn 'Ayyash referred to a people who plunged in the seas of delusion, and who claimed to use their intellect and claimed to express the truth, but who are destined to hellfire. Ibn Rushd was removed from his judicial position and exiled under house arrest to Lucena, a town near Cordova. There, Ibn Rushd would live in isolation, from one conference to another, resenting the annoyance of time and the intrusion of breathing.

But the *fitna* of life was not through with Ibn Rushd yet. The true quality of a person only appears under the weight of tribulations. 'Abd al-Kabir al-Ghafiqi (d. 617/1220), Ibn Rushd's trusted student and friend, distanced himself from Ibn Rushd and apparently joined the band of slanderers. Other disciples such as Abu Bakr Ibn Jahwar and Abu Muhammad Ibn Haut Allah (d. 612/1215) turned against their teacher. Ibn Haut Allah went as far as to deny that he was Ibn Rushd's student and to omit Ibn Rushd from his chains of authority. Nothing in this world stabs deeper than the betrayal of a student.

But, of course, the world is not made only of cowards, and some, such as the jurist Abu 'Abdullah al-Usuli, stood by Ibn Rushd. During the inquisition, he refused to denounce Ibn Rushd and, as a result, was exiled to Aghmat. Later on, he was pardoned and eventually became the chief judge of Bougie. But the mindless preacher Ibn Hajjaj kept after him until he had him arrested and tortured, and as a result, al-Usuli lost his eyesight. He died shortly thereafter in 612/1216.

As for Ibn Rushd, he was returned from his exile in Lucena and was sent to live in Marrakesh. But that very same year, demoralized and still in isolation, he died in December 595/1198.

Ibn Rushd's intellect lived long after memory buried his persecutors. Ibn Rushd has been recalled in conference after conference and alighted many comatose intellects and stale nights. He survived despite the condemnation of the bishops of Paris, Oxford, and Canterbury in the seventh/thirteenth century and went on to help salvage Western civilization. Life's ironies are but lessons in morality. Even Ibn Zarqun's grandson, Muhammad Ibn Muhammad (d. 621/1224), a loyal student of Ibn Rushd, was imprisoned by the same inquisition that his grandfather helped to start.

When a great man dies, the grounds for jealousy often expire. The same parasites who lived by sucking his blood during his lifetime are the same parasites who now live in the trails of his glory in his death. After-the-fact supporters emerge from cracks and holes to claim that they knew the great man and always loved him. At Ibn Rushd's funeral, among those who emerged to praise his piety and knowledge was none other than the infamous poet Ibn Jubayr, the man who for so long persecuted Ibn Rushd. Truly, from God we come and to God we will return.

CHAPTER 36

The Sunna of the Beloved

If envy is a sin, then I am the incurable sinner, for I envy every eye that ever caught a glimpse of you. I envy the waves that carried your voice and the air that touched your cheeks. I envy even the ground that once served you, and I confess to you that despite my indulgent sins, my shameful whimsies, and my ugly flimsies, I confess to you, "I love you."

My confessions are as silly as my muted words. You have been loved by so many more substantial than I, and what good does my silence or confession possibly do?

So many moments have I sat sheltered by the night in the midst of these books, my mind fulfilled but my heart calling for you. Only my shame restrains my words from filling pages of books and from whimpering into the night, "I long for you."

This Conference of the Books, in countless days and nights, ignited by your memory, calls upon the world to ponder your legacy. Despite the citations, the arguments, and refutations, nothing equals a blissful moment spent engulfed in your adoration. For all the enlightenment of books, the brilliance of beauty, and the purification of light coalesced in the moments of time that hosted your life—Muhammad, Ahmad, Abu al-Qasim, *al-Nabi al-Amin*, the Messenger of God.

Permit me, my Prophet, my own beloved Prophet, to tell you that I do not know you from the majestic debates of this Conference. I do not know you from the lectures of learned teachers, nor from some infatuated delusional dream. No, I do not know you from the books full of sayings you reportedly said, and I even do not know you from all the reports about your life and about your likes and dislikes. I know you from a moment in time in which I fell in love with you.

I know you because God taught you, praised you, and honored you. I know you because God comforted you, consoled you, and empowered you. I know you because God loved you.

My Prophet, I know you through a heart that loves.

I know you through every moment of compassion I extended to another. I know you through every moment of pain I felt for the agony of others. I know you through every moment of dignity and honor. I know you through that day my brother and I walked two miles in the desert heat to bring water to a dying cat. Or, the day we intervened to stop a man from beating his wife only to have her blood mingle with ours. Or, in those days in which we were never cool, current, fashionable, or popular because those values never existed in a household raised in your love. But I also know you through every moment of shame I felt for my weakness, arrogance, anger, and profanity.

I think of you, an orphaned child, with wide pure eyes rejoicing at life. I see you in your youth, quiet and bashful, in your solitude, feeling the longing for God. I feel your tranquility in the arms of your wife, and your trembling body with the advent of truth. I see you sitting bewildered and sad in Ta'if, persevering through the trials of life. I think of you comforting your Companion in the Cave of *Hira'* with your trust in God. I think of you instructing your soldiers away from the ants' nest and mending the broken wing of the injured bird. I feel your beautiful smile tenderizing my world and hear your laughter in the midst of children. I watch you mending your cloth, and then playfully racing your wife. I ponder your poverty, and the agony of your grief over your dying children. I think of your kindness and forgiveness with every hypocrite and fool, and of the way you honored and dignified your followers. I think of the hypocrite 'Abdullah Ibn Salul yelling at you, "You and your donkey stink," and you refusing to hate, punish, or take vengeance. I think of all of this and I feel you in my heart, and I believe I know you.

And yet, my Prophet, there are those who see your *Sunna* only as an endless array of legalistic and pedantic reprimands. They know you only through transmissions and reports, seeing you only through the filter of commands. There are those who understand the *Sunna* as mindless imitation and soulless regurgitation.

But for me, and may God forgive me, your *Sunna* is a moment of unadulterated beauty spent in your love. Your *Sunna* is your beauty, and beauty cannot be mimicked. It must be felt and loved. All the descriptive manuals of the world cannot teach an ugly heart about beauty. And all the reports and transmissions of the world cannot teach the obstinate heart the *Sunna* of the beloved.

CHAPTER 37

Colonizing Women

Could a heart that ignites with truth burn in vain? In the age of madness, could this longing be my bane? My beloved, take this hand and quench this pain. You know me—You know me. Bless me with the insight so that I may rest in Your grace. I am too content in Your love to dream of heaven, and I am too vain to agonize over hell. But I am completely submerged in my aching need to bask in Your glorious face. If this is arrogance, then help me know my place, but if this is glorious, then purify me so that I may reach the exalted place.

In the serenity of the night, the Conference of the Books seeks You. But it never dares to believe that it has reached You. No. It converses, it argues, it dreams, it quivers, and it trembles at the doorstep of Your omniscience. Isn't a complacent love an arrogant disgrace!

At night, I drag the ruptures of the day. I haul its pains, and stand naked probing into every wound and cut sustained that day. Stepping into the Conference of the Books, I struggle to erase and heal the filth and pain. And, then it starts—the immutable sublimation in Your name. Purified, I rid myself of my fears—from the contaminations of my ravenous oppressors. You liberate me from the agony of the inquisition—from the *mihna* of a contaminated life spent in disgrace.

In my mind, when You are here, nothing ugly can co-exist in this space. When You are with me, I transcend myself to the innate. In this fantastic obscurity, I lose myself to find You. My mind is obscured by the unfolding of Your grace, but Your mercy guides me to a transcendent intuition. In my intellect I find that only You—only You are innate. In the innate there is only beauty. Nothing ugly can co-exist in this space.

Could an interpretation overcome the innate? Among those who claim to follow your message there is such a profound alienation. It always stands threatening to drag me to an arid wilderness. The ugliness of a stranger is a self-affirmation, but the ugliness of your brother is a profound alienation.

Covered in false piety, the wealthy successors of Your most sanctified place go to Egypt and India and purchase brides in a contract made in Your name. They pay a dowry to the impoverished family of a helpless girl and marry her for a week or month in a rented place. After fulfilling their desire, they return the girl to her family, perhaps to be recycled, or perhaps to wait until she expires on some future date. The flesh and limbs of powerless girls become part of the attractions generously offered to tourists during their stay. This happens in Muslim lands, this happens in contracts written in Your name. This is done by a group of people who use the garb of religion to hide a mutilated and rotted morality. I ask a group of so-called jurists, and I am told that "as long as the intent to terminate the marriage occurs even a minute after the formation of the contract then it is all valid." What a remarkably legal and remarkably immoral response!

I remember, from years ago, the wailing of a girl being drafted into the service of some over-gorged, over-oiled customer. A day later, we found her bloodied body on the side of the road. Apparently, she preferred the embrace of a truck to the embrace of the *dinar*-wreaking glutton.

At times, legal technicalities are nothing more than a technocratic immorality. If people are objectified and consumed, no law or legal deduction could make the immoral beautiful or the ugly acceptable.

I think of these jurists and reflect on their endless rhetoric about the rights of women in Islam—on the honorable role of women and on the covering-up of women. But I fear that the seclusion of women has taught them that what is secluded is to be possessed and owned. And, all possessions are to be used. Yet, some possessions are forgotten until thrown away, some are recycled or replaced. The fact is that those who ache to regulate women are those who invariably violate them, and those who are obsessed with defining the limits for women are those who observe no limits with women. Colonizers always set borders that affirm their power, and you, my technocrats, are colonizers of women.

The ethical pulse that constitutes our being defines the life of our religion. The sexploitation of any Muslim, and in fact any human being, is a degradation upon our religion. Whether a woman is used and discarded in Egypt, the United States, or any other place, what can one say about a jurist who fails to take a moral stand? Imam Ahmad Ibn Hanbal (d. 241/855) refused to accept the opinion of any jurist who succumbed to al-Ma'mun's (d. 218/833) inquisition (*mihna*). Today's *mihna* is in every drop of oil that greases the conscience. Today's *mihna* is in the language of morality usurped and stolen by immoral technocracy. Hasn't the time come to stop accepting the credibility of jurists who succumb to today's *mihna*?

CHAPTER 38

The Page

The nights slide away, and I always confront this page. I must believe that it is an open page. Despite the grease, scribbles, mistakes, and the offensive nonsense, I must believe it is an open page. If the page is not open, then what is the point of the burning midnight oil and the edged quills, and what is the point of the nights and days?

I close my eyes and think there must be much more that we could say. In a world plagued with screeches and screams, diatribes and sound-bites, sermons and pleas, there must be much more we could say. "Say: If the ocean was ink for the words of my Lord. . ." (18:109). Oceans would expire before the words and wisdom of God, but we, as the agents of God, what do we have to say? No, the book written this century does not even include our miserable page.

I search my heart for a joyful emotion by which to greet the century, but I must not rely on my brain. I must neutralize my agitated rationality with an anesthetic of hopeful faith. Yet, I must confess that I am frustrated by the arbitrary divisions of history, by the spoilation of time, and by our torpid pace.

We entered this century colonized, but are we any freer today? For us, in what way is this a new century? For us, the nineteenth century did not end until the 1940s, and in the 1970s we plunged into an even darker age. In the 1990s, the slaughter, degradation, and humiliation all continue Will the year 2001 suddenly herald a new age?

History compiles the book, and we confront the page. In this century, our page is not full of inquiries, investigations, and vibrant debates. Our page is inscribed with anxious affirmations, defensive proclamations, and arrogant declarations; in this century we confront the risk of a closed page.

We started this century calling for *ijtihad*, dreaming of *shura*, musing over the *Shari'a*, babbling over women's rights, and persistently speaking of a bygone golden age. What is the difference today? What is the difference in our language, themes, or rhetoric? What added knowledge or enlightenment have we attained in the past hundred years? We still adore activism, abhor intellectualism, and happily learn our religion from pamphleteers. We are still impressed by data banks, persuaded by anecdotes, and think that the point of history and law is to affirm our adolescent dreams. *Ma sha' Allah*, we've turned our brains into data processors before they invented PCs, and our intellectualism consists of a fulmination of e-mails.

What progress have we achieved? We advanced by printing gorgeous book covers, by learning that the West is bad, and that instead of clapping we should do *takbir*. What can I say, we started with Muhammad 'Abduh (d. 1905), Mahmud Shaltut (d. 1963) and Rashid Rida (d. 1935) and ended with Bin Bazz (d. 1999) and al-'Uthaymiyyin (b. 1929–).

I chide myself for the pessimism that threatens to descend into misanthropy. It is a sin not to see the wonders and beauty of God in God's human beings. But it is truth that makes me see the fustian age of Muslims as an utter frivolity. I need not go further than three days in last November in order to feel I am slipping into a civilizational breach. Since the beginning of this century we have been meeting in councils, assemblies, and conventions to address what in the old homeland they call issues of destiny (*al-qadaya al-masiriyya*). These are ecclesiastical-like congregations, which attempt to fabricate an enforced orthodoxy. These are councils of fantasized *ijma'*, which ignore the rich legacy of diverse traditions, conflicting opinions, and liberating indeterminacy. Like a medieval Christian council of God's Truth, these congregations produce a liturgy of proclamations and declarations, which seal the discourses of centuries in a matter of days. Instead of our mindless paltering, we respond, not by critical analysis and debate, but by slipping into a paretic state.

At the end of this century and in the United States, an honorable and impressive list of jurists met in Detroit, Michigan. Adorned by a title no less grand than the *Shari'a* Scholars Association of North America, in three days in November, and according to their declaration, after "extensive discussion and debate and commentary on the presentations made," the scholars reached conclusions in the form of a double-spaced, thirteen-page declaration. The matters discussed and resolved were no less than: 1) Custom and its place in Islamic law; 2) Purchasing homes through traditional banking facilities and interest-taking; 3) Divorce, remunerative divorce *(khul')*, and judicially imposed separation; 4) The role of arbitration in divorce proceedings; 5) Dealing with conflicts between Islamic and Civil Laws; 6) Duties and competence of *Imams* in divorce contexts; 7) Political participation; and 8) Sighting the crescent and its relationship to the two *'Ids*.

Half of the thirty-eight or so scholars have never lived in the United States, the vast majority have never stepped foot into an American courtroom, and at least half live under corrupt and oppressive governments, and yet, these issues were discussed and decided in three days. Despite my friendship and high regard for some of them, my alienation feels extreme. When in our history have we had a *Shari'a* association or council? When in our history has the Will of God, instead of being searched, been debated and declared? When have jurists lapsed legal and factual determinations, decided issues with a dogmatic knowledge of context, and crossed oceans to issue dictates? When in our history has *ijma'* been asserted in councils, and when, instead of the schools of thought, juristic discourses, books, and papers, *fatawa* and counter-*fatawa*, preponderance of evidence and preference, have we become a culture of oil-nourished plutocracy?

The sad truth is that, despite the turn of the century, we are not writing a new page. Our well-oiled century began in the 1970s and we are still drowning in fields of easy money, easy conclusions, easy solutions, and pro-forma discussions. And, because the Muslim oil-century is not about to end in the year 2001, and because our papers are greasy, full of stains and scribbles, and devoid of meaning, I will wait to celebrate the new century when I can find a clean new page.

CHAPTER 39

My Friend

I wake up mingled with sweat. The images of the nightmare melt me in my bed. I wake up fighting my breath, and I extract myself from the sheets and covers. I mumble, "I fear Islamic law is dead."

My friend, the last time I saw you, you sat covered by a blanket, your protruded eyes glazing upon your bed. Is he home? I asked your mother. She did not greet me with "itfaddal." She nodded her head and muttered "*ya rabb.*" In your room, as usual, the single light bulb hung from its crooked wire, but on that day, it looked as if it was holding onto life by a thread. The desk lamp, the books, and the chipped grayish walls all looked dead. I sat on the edge and tried to restrain my eyes. I could not tell if you were there, I could not ask about the pain or the screams or what you might have felt. I could not explore the marks on your ankles, on your back, or your armpits. I did not dare look at your fingers. I was too terrified to open the door of horror. What if it became an all-engulfing hell—what if we discover that it has buried us, and that we are now dead. No, I dared not look at you or talk to you. I wished that as in the old days, we could argue about a book. I wished that your mother would bring in the tea—the tea that I never liked, but which always accompanied our debates and dreams. That tea had become the symbol of hospitality in an otherwise profound alienation. But this time, the tea did not come, and you did not speak, and I sat wishing I could break up into pieces and melt.

Finally, my words came out stupid and insolent, " *'izayyak ya. . .* How are you?" Did you think I was an idiot? Perhaps you were silent because you did not hear me, and I am not sure how long I sat there avoiding looking at you and staring at the open doors of your balcony. Finally, a faltering voice, weak like the murmurs of graveyards, called, "Khaled." I looked up with a momentary delusion of hope; it was your beloved voice. What can I say now, I wondered, and turned to look at your slumped head. What have they done to you! I wished I could scream and yell and tear the walls. I wished I could run in the streets screaming at the top of my lungs, "You cowards! You subhuman pieces of . . . What have you done to him!" But instead I sat utterly powerless staring at your slumped head. Finally, words rolled out as if your heart was lodged in your constricted throat, "Khaled, remember when I told you, I fear Islamic law is dead?" I remembered. Of course, I remembered. But I. . . on this particular day sitting there on the edge of your bed, I had no idea what you meant.

Not much else was said that day. I told you I would come back and I never did. I thought of you every day, but I knew that like lamented memories, I had become part of the pain. A few months later, it is as if I knew—I felt it. I wrote you, and when I found a reply envelope in my mailbox, I knew you were dead.

That day, when I saw you in your bedroom, I knew that we had become uprooted. We had become destined to roam in search for a past and future. We had become the nomads of a lost civilization.

The room that once echoed hours of readings and debates had become a tomb. The nights spent arguing about *Shari'a* and about *takhrij, tashih, tanqih* and the uses of *taqlid* had been drained from the darkened walls. All the boisterous noises struggling to re-kindle our muted heritage had become choked up in your pain.

In the time of dreams, we engaged many conferences—conferences of thought, conferences of debate, conferences of books. For us, *Shari'a* was a process, it was a search, it was a structure of authority and preference, and the study of the Divine way was the way. We knew that all the roads seeking God led to God, and we occupied ourselves with the introspection of conscience, with the discipline of diligence, and the collection and absorption of evidence. The *dalil*, that indicator, that piece of evidence that pointed to God, was the singular preoccupation of every night.

My intellect was dull and unsensational. It flourished in the shelter of silence and non-confrontation. You, my friend, your intellect was a fire that ignited with open fury. Your intellect confronted, dazzled, and consumed the weary.

One of those days you insisted on debating one of the insecure and angry fanatic groups, and they displaced upon you their utter misery. That day, with your bruised face and sliced bloody lip, you laughed and joked and insisted that life is but a beating. "At least a physical beating reminds you of your long forgotten body, and rejuvenates the balance in your commitment," you said.

We debated with you the wisdom of debating these fanatic groups, and you looked at us and said, "Don't you realize that I fear that, between the rhetoric of activism and the arrogance of despotism, Islamic law is dead? In the age of modernity, in the age of certainty, in the age of arrogant structuralism, and simplistic codification, in the age of single reliance on isolated *hadith*, in the age where law is expected to be simpler than human beings and is expected, in turn, to simplify human beings, in the age in which pointers to God are not enough because we demand the precision of maps, in the age in which the best certification in Islamic law is an engineering degree, I fear that Islamic law is dead. Islamic law is not the rules, but the process of the rules. Don't you see, hermeneutically, structurally, and epistemologically, I fear that Islamic law in the modern age is dead?" We looked at each other and someone blurted out, "No wonder they beat you up!" We laughed, and when the tea was served we drowned our fears and alienation.

My friend, as long as you remained our aching conscience, I would not believe a word you said.

I don't know what happened that brought upon you the demons of the dawn. After they came, we no longer met. What have the guard dogs of the majesty done to you to erase your body and sap your commitment? They sapped away your life and left us without laughter. They left us with the terrifying realization that our beloved heritage might be dead. The last day I saw you there was the single wire, and the ailing light. There was the pain hidden by your debilitated flesh. There was the silence broken by the proclamation of death. And, there was the seed of my nightmares and fears.

I live in the Conference of the Books in defiance of my fears. As long as the Conference continues, you are my conscience and I will not concede defeat. But, once in a while, when the nightmare visits me and plunders through my head, I wake up melting in my sweat and mutter, "I fear Islamic law is dead."

CHAPTER 40

The Truth of Silence

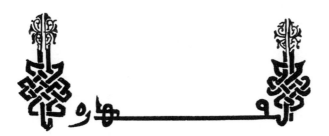

Every night my heart splinters like the dissipation of thought. Every night melts the heart that has become frozen by the indifferent cold. I stand before You burning in the inferno of my soul, confronting what my delusions have allowed me to ignore.

I stand humbled by the silence, a mere beggar at Your door. In the silence, I am banished by reproach, I am rehabilitated by hope, and I confront the turbulence of my soul.

What do I say to the One Who knows the sigh before it leaves the heart? What do I say to the One Who can see the glimmer of light in the midst of the darkness in my mind? What do I say to the One Who indulges the pretenses of my intellect but rekindles the truth in my heart? What do I say to the One Who observes my ostentatious pretext take me to heights of self-deception, but every single time receives me when I fall apart. What do I say to the One Who knows the end before the start?

If I say I love You, I fear that my notion of love is terribly flawed. If I say, forgive me, I fear that my presumptuousness will set us apart. If I say, take me, I know that Your hands only touch the purified. My God, I am in fear of my fear. The filth on my hands yearns to be purified, and before I seek to touch You, have I cleansed the impurities clinging to my heart?

No, I do not say or talk. I sit here stubbornly clinging to this singular spot. Adorned by the silence of this night, I listen to the reproaches of my soul.

God, we are but a luscious cover of skin punctured by holes. We covet to intake and emit through enthralled skin punctures until we eventually rot our very core. Mesmerized by the pandemonium of senseless noise in life, we are oblivious to the corruption of our mind and soul.

In silence I know. I know that I am tired of the discord in my thoughts. I know that I am tired of the clamor of my breath, and the racket of my heart. I am sickened by the clangor of my teeth, and the bedlam gushing from my mouth. I am tired of the bawling of tears and the dissonance of dreams. I know, so I strive to ignore the moaning of my body and its lecherous holes. I strive to escape every single distraction of noise or sound, and in the truth of silence I know what cannot be ignored.

There comes a moment in time when all the voices will fall silent before the Lord. The silence of humility is broken only by the whispers of self-reproach (20:108). I must live this moment now, for he who does not rehearse the inevitable is most certainly a fool.

My God, I live drowned in the noise of words and thoughts. I live drowned in the endless humming of distractions and sounds. Presentations, performances, speeches, and arguments saturate the fibers of life. And, this life is but a harangue of incoherence masking the embarrassments of vice. Even the pretensions of beauty are but a boisterous shroud cast upon our pain and strife. God, I realize that I use every being that emits a voice, I use every distraction of desire or thought, I use every pain or pleasure, I use every bit of disappointment or hope, I use every single moment of noise to avoid listening to my soul.

You swear by the self-reproaching soul (75:2), and I swear by You as to the agonies of the reproaches of the soul. But it is only when I shut off all the noise, close the books, and rein in my thoughts, do I hear the resilient chiding of my soul. Such is the virtue of silence—in silence we are confronted, splintered, and, ultimately, restored.

Our inner prophet speaks and we mute the voice. We emit and inhale odious fumes of talk. We talk in conferences, we talk in programs, we talk in gatherings, we talk in meetings. For every moment of delusion, doubt, or ignorance, we give a talk. We emit and inhale fumes of talk. We talk to cover the anxiety of guilt and torment of fear. We talk because there is so much to conceal. We talk so that the self may not speak.

Between the boisterousness of acts and words, we drown the silent dignity of our being. The noise of frivolity becomes our distorted sense of meaning. If only we would embrace the silence, we would find the Divine voice. We use the pedantry of legalism, the pomposity of activism, the sophistry of scholasticism, and the unmitigated hypocrisy of formalism to mute the voice. We hide in robes and scarves, we hide in beards and *miswaks*, we hide in pamphlets and tapes, we hide in an endless stream of chat groups and oratories from one true fact. The day will come when there will be only the silence, the soul and a Lord Who knows the sigh before it leaves the heart.

CHAPTER 41

On the Beating of Wives

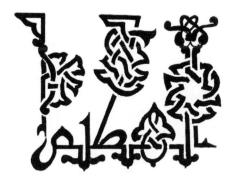

This Conference resonates with visions of the subtle and sublime; it permeates the world with echoes of The Divine. Centuries of discourse coalesce upon a moment to ponder a single emotion in time. The records of existence are reopened and examined as the ideas migrate and rebound. It is not what we know, but what we could know that guides us; aren't the possibilities limitless when exploring the Divine? We search for God in the permutations of the rejuvenating text, in the enticements of beauty, in the revulsions of ugliness, in the restitutions of conscience, and in the wonders of creation.

I ask my God for a guideline, and I always find it in beauty, for my guide is beautiful and sublime. How can The Beautiful demand of us anything but the beautiful? If there is a beauty to life, it is that we derive from the magnanimity of God the urge for the beautiful and the refined. "Blessed be God, the best of creators" (23:14), Who placed in us the desire to transcend in beauty the ravages of time.

She tells me with a face solemn with emotion that her husband struck her and that, although she suffered no pain, she cannot accept aggression. The *imam* in the mosque advised her that her husband is her guardian, and God has decreed that a beating is not in this case a transgression. If she is seeking divorce, this is not a sufficient cause because an opportunity to perfect humility is hardly a loss. If you have disobeyed, the *imam* said, then you are defiant. A *nashiz* in the book of God is an arrogant woman who does not see her husband as her boss.

But she tells me that it is not her desire for a divorce that guides her as much as it is a sense of betrayal. Feeling that her dignity and the dignity of her husband are not treated as of the same nature or worth is treachery of the worst kind.

I ask her, trying to gauge her exposure, "Did the *imam* explain to you why?" She says, "I looked it up myself—an affront to my equanimity and to my belief in the dignity of self-composure. If my husband has to resort to the ugliness of violence, then he is hardly the one to be entrusted with such a right."

I said, "If you believe that God is beauty, I can share with you the murmurings of this Conference. This mind can flow with reflections and thoughts, but do not expect from me any conclusions. It is not what I know, but what I could know which drives my sense of beauty."

It is reported that 'Ali (d. 40/661) had said that before Islam, if a man struck his wife, the shame of the act would plague him and his descendants for many years to come. After all, the man would be known as a wife beater. How could such a shameful act be sanctioned after Islam when Islam is the liberator?

"But the verses. . ." she says. "The *imam* based his opinion on verses and not reason."

I am torn when speaking to my fellow Muslim for I see much beauty in reason. We do not worship an irrational god; all creation testifies to the beauty of His reason.

"Then let us examine the verse," I said, "for the Qur'an is the guide to our reason."

"The Qur'an says: 'As for those women who you fear their *nushuz*, admonish them, abandon their beds, and beat them. If they obey you, do not seek to persecute them for God is high and greater than you all' (4:34).

"'And, if you fear a breach between them, then appoint two arbitrators, one from his family and the other from her family. If they wish for peace, God may facilitate between them for God knows everything (4:35).'

"I proclaim, much turns here on who is being addressed, the context, and what *nushuz* means. Let me first tell you that it is often said that these verses were revealed when Umm Salamah, (d. 62/681), the Prophet's wife, complained about the preferential treatment of men. Shortly thereafter, a man from the Ansar struck his wife. The Prophet decreed that as he struck her, he will be struck. But then the verses were revealed, and the Prophet ruled that there is no retaliation between husband and wife.

"Now, my sister, let us set out the foundations of our reasoning. Do you know of a woman who finds beauty or dignity in a beating? Considering our knowledge of men, do you see a reason for God to entrust husbands with the administration of equitable beatings? God informs us that the purpose of marriage is to find friendship, tranquility, and mercy (30:21; 7:189). Is this consistent with an empowerment to administer a beating? In the Qur'an, men have not been empowered to beat even a servant or child, so what is the secret of their empowerment over their wives? Furthermore, a trustworthy person is one who follows the *Sunna* with his children and his wife. Did you ever hear of a single occasion where the Prophet struck one of his wives? Even more, the Prophet is reported to have said that the worst of you are those who beat their wives. Elsewhere, it is reported that he said that those who beat their wives are not among the best of you. I ask you my sister, and ask the learned *imam*, if a man neither follows the *Sunna*, nor is of the best character, why should he be entrusted with the just administration of violence? As to the reason for the revelation of the verse, I must admit it leaves my heart in painful doubt. One, whether this is the occasion for revelation is disagreed upon. Two, all the report holds is that there is not a right to formal retaliation between husband and wife. Even then, the jurists have held that if there is a physical injury or death, then there should be retaliation between husband and wife. By God, aren't there injuries to dignity that make death preferable to life?

"All that I have said so far is that I need certainty. Before I ascribe to God something that torments the heart, before I admit to men the power of execution, I must weigh the possibilities in my head. If there is the glimmer of beauty to be pursued, then my mind will search the subtleties of what has been said. If I have a shadow of doubt, I will run to the refuge of the beautiful.

"Having properly prefaced what may be said now, notice that God commands that in the case of a breach, two arbitrators will be chosen. The jurists disagreed on whether the arbitration and its judgment are optional or a mandatory delegation to the state. 'Ali, the Companion, ruled that the arbitrators act as judges and if a husband wishes a marriage to continue, he must comply with their adjudication. It is reported that 'Ali told a husband that he is not free to ignore the results of an arbitration. But I fear, my sister, that there is an inconsistency in an arbitration that follows a beating. It seems to me, and God knows best, that to say, "if you fear a breach," after the authorization of beating, is a tension in the text. Wouldn't you say that if there is a beating after being abandoned in bed, a breach has already occurred? If the husband has already abandoned his wife and beat her then what is the point of the arbitration? Isn't this like calling for a trial but assigning the penalty first? Why is the husband entrusted to be the accuser, judge, and enforcer, and after we so entrusted him, we then say, go to arbitration for reconciliation is best! What if the husband believes his wife is a *nashiz*, and then beats her, but the arbitrators decide that he is a cat-torturing scoundrel who is hopelessly disturbed?

"By God, my sister, this is a test. The wife beaters will be content, but all others will want to scrutinize the text. First, I must admit that if someone struck my sister or daughter and I was asked to judge the offender and the offense, I would doubt the equanimity of his and my character—I would doubt him for beating his wife and doubt myself for wanting so badly to slap his head."

She smiled and so I continued, "Now we ask the question: What is *nushuz* and who is the *nashiz* and who is being addressed?

"The jurists, may God bless them, say that *nushuz* is arrogance and defiance, and a *nashiz* is an arrogant and disobedient person. Some jurists, such as Ibn Rushd, the grandfather (d. 520/1126), said that a *nashiz* is a deviant woman who refuses to pray,

109

fast, or cleanse herself from impurities. But there is a problem here. The word *nushuz* is used to describe men as well. For our Lord says:

> If a wife fears from her husband *nushuz* or rejection (*i'rad*), there is no blame on them if they seek an amicable settlement between them. For amicable settlements are best although the souls of people incline toward greed. If you do good and practice self-restraint, God knows all that you do (4:128).

"Some say that this verse was revealed when Sawdah (d.54/674), the Prophet's wife, feared that the Prophet would divorce her so she relinquished some of her rights so that he would keep her. But this report is an abomination, for how do the reporters know what fears plagued Sawdah's heart? And, didn't God give the Prophet's wives a choice and they chose him? No, our Prophet would not single out a wife with the dishonor of a discriminatory separation. Other reporters said that this verse was revealed when a husband and wife constantly fought over the husband's second marriage. They divorced and re-married several times, but eventually they reached a reconciliation. In any case, what the jurists agreed upon is that this verse means that a form of reconciliation between husband and wife is better than a separation.

"The question I ask you, my sister, is what does *nushuz* mean in the second verse (4:128)? Does it mean the disobedience of a husband to his wife? But does this mean that a husband owes a duty of obedience to his wife? Is a husband a *nashiz* if he disobeys his wife? And, why does God distinguish between rejection (*i'rad*) and *nushuz* when it comes to a husband? If *nushuz* means arrogance, defiance, and disobedience in the case of the wife, does it mean the same thing in the case of a husband?

"The jurists, may God bless and forgive them, troubled by this tension, said that *nushuz*, in the case of a wife, means disobedience, and in the case of a husband, means a grave and known sin (*fahisha mubina*)."

The sister curled her lips and adjusted the hair that slipped from the scarf adorning her head. Her eyes glanced at the volumes of books on the crowded shelves. Yes, it is the aches of the pathways of knowledge which distinguish the striver from the dead. After a pause she carefully said, "Does this mean that *nushuz* in the case of wives means a grave and known sin as well? A wife commits *nushuz* if she commits a grave and known sin?"

With a glimmer I said, "It is reported that the Prophet in his final pilgrimage proclaimed, 'O' people, I command you to treat women with kindness for they are your support. You have no other rights over them unless they commit a grave and known sin (*fahisha mubina*). If they do, abandon them in beds and beat them lightly, but if they comply do not transgress against them.'

"It seems to me that the Prophet uses the expression *fahisha mubina* as the equivalent of *nushuz*, and that *nushuz* means a *fahisha mubina* (a grave and known sin). If that is so, then *nushuz* cannot mean disobedience or a case of simple disagreement. If there is a serious disagreement, then the state may compel an arbitration. But this is entirely different from a *fahisha mubina*. A *fahisha mubina* usually means a grave sexual sin. For instance, a *fahisha mubina* is sexual activity short of intercourse, or intercourse that cannot be proven by four witnesses, or, if there are four witnesses, intercourse in which the witnesses did not see the actual insertion of the organ into the organ. A *fahisha mubina* is not disobedience, arrogance, or insolence. It is sexual lewdness."

She then commented, "But all you have argued for thus far is that *nushuz* means a *fahisha mubina*. This could mean that in such a case a husband would have recourse to a beating. Perhaps I did not deserve to be struck by my husband, but that is only because I did not commit a grave and known sin. But why would men be entrusted with alleging, investigating, and penalizing the commission of a grave and known sin? My husband is a suspicious person who thinks a smile or headache is incontrovertible evidence of treason."

I exclaimed with a smile about to explode upon my face, "As to your husband, in God we seek refuge from ignorance and arrogance. As to you, I believe your words are well-reasoned. You should know that Ibn Rushd, the grandfather, was once asked whether a man who caught his wife performing lewd acts with a foreign man in bed could beat his wife and imprison her. Ibn Rushd responded that the husband may forgive his wife or divorce her, but anything beyond that would be a transgression. For it is God Who said, 'Do not hold them despite their will to harm them,' (2:231) and it is God Who also said, 'Either stay with them in kindness or divorce them with kindness' (65:2).

"The Qur'an talks of a marriage full of tranquility and kindness or a divorce restrained by justice and kindness. Where in this do you see a place for abandonment and beatings?

"Recall, my sister, that in the same chapter of al-Nisa' (4:15), God decrees that women guilty of lewdness (*fahisha*), upon the testimony of four witnesses, are to be confined to their houses until repentance. For God in the Qur'an says: 'As to your women who are guilty of lewdness (*fahisha*), take the evidence of four witnesses from among you against them. If the witnesses testify, confine them (the women) to houses until death claims them or until God ordains for them some other way. If men among you are guilty of lewdness, punish them. But if they (the men or women) repent and amend (their behavior), leave them alone, for God is forgiving and merciful' (4:15–16)."

At this point, she quickly interceded, "But it is said that this ruling was abrogated by the punishment for *zina* (fornication). Whipping has been decreed instead of imprisonment."

I responded, "True, that is what is said by those who accept abrogation in the Qur'an, but this is not material to my point. Reading the context as a whole, and not verse-by-verse, new possibilities offer themselves. What if verse 4:34 is a specification or limitation upon verse 4:15? Therefore, what if the one who commits a *fahisha* is a wife, and four witnesses are not available, then the remedy is spelled out in 4:34? Alternatively, what if 4:15 is stating the rule for unmarried women and 4:34 states the rule for married women? If you accept abrogation, then 4:15 and 4:34 would both be abrogated. But if you do not accept abrogation, then 4:15 spells out the punishment for *fahisha*, not *zina*, for unmarried women, and 4:34 spells out the punishment for *fahisha*, not *zina*, of married women. In both cases, you need witnesses and evidence, and in both cases, you need a finding and judgment.

"Consider the possibility, as in the case of banditry (5:33), 4:34 is stating a rule of proportionality. Admonishment is the normal rule, but if a wife resorts to abandonment, she could be abandoned, and if she strikes her husband, she could be struck? But if the parties do not wish to engage in a boxing–match, then the solution is an arbitration blessed by God. Alternatively, 4:34 is not addressed to husbands at all but to the state. Meaning, if there is an allegation of a grave and known sin and it is proven by the resolution of a court, a separation or corporal punishment may be ordered. In case of a disagreement not involving a grave and known sin, an arbitration may be ordered. In other words, the remedy is not left to the discretion of husbands but is given to a court. Nothing in 4:34 necessitates that the remedy be in private hands, for history and creation have shown that when it comes to punishment husbands are hardly the ones to be trusted."

She smiled with the doubt of a skeptic and said, "But how about the *nushuz* of husbands, what becomes of that? What becomes of verse 4:128?"

I rejoiced at the beauty of heuristic arguments, "What about 4:128 my sister? 4:128 and 4:34 are not remedial complements. The *hadith* of the Prophet as to 4:34 equated between *fahisha mubina* and *nushuz*. Does the *hadith* necessarily extend to 4:128? See, many jurists thought that the *nushuz* of 4:34 (for women) means arrogance or aloofness and the *nushuz* of 4:128 (for men) means a lewd sin. I believe that because of the Prophet's *hadith*, if anything, it is exactly the opposite. But, in any case, even if *nushuz* always means a lewd sin, all 4:128 says is that there is no harm in reaching a compromise if it is to avoid a divorce. There is nothing in 4:128 that says husbands may not be punished for lewd acts. In fact, the presumption in pre-Islamic Arabia was that only men are subject to criminal penalties, while women are to be left to the disposition of their families. Criminal punishment for men was assumed. Criminal punishment for women is specified in the Qur'an, but specification does not necessarily mean the exclusivity of a rule; it could mean the extension of the rule to a category otherwise presumed not to be covered. Furthermore, please note that 4:16 does require punishment for men as well. But it does not specify the punishment. Instead, it just says, 'Harm them.' It could be that whether the man is married or unmarried, if there is a *fahisha*, the punishment is the same."

She frowned slightly and said, "But, if I may ask, if 4:15 refers to unmarried women, what does God mean when God says, 'or until God ordains for them some other way'?"

I responded, "I am not sure, nor is anyone else. Those who accept abrogation said that it means the abrogation of the rule by the decreeing of the punishment of *zina.* I tend to think it means marriage. So if the woman is unmarried and she has committed lewdness, she is under a form of house arrest until marriage or repentance. If she is married, then 4:34 applies and it is as we have previously said."

She placed her forehead in her palms, squinted her eyes, and then exclaimed, "So, what you are saying is that 4:34 is not talking about disobedience, it is talking about lewd acts. In the case of a lewd act, known and proven in court, a court may order a separation or corporal punishment for a wife. In the case of a husband, corporal punishment may be ordered, but we are not sure about an order of separation. But, on a separate matter, 4:35 is talking about normal but serious marital disputes. In the case of a rift between husband and wife—a rift unrelated to allegations of lewdness or the like—a court may order an arbitration?" I found myself suddenly pensive and subdued in thought. "My sister," I said, "this seems to me a better and more beautiful interpretation (4:59). Yet, I promised no conclusions, for the flow of thought can only know tentative resolutions. But if I managed to create a shadow of doubt about the permissibility of wife beatings then the pious will stay away from situations of doubt. Only the most arrogant will dare assume the right to inflict a beating, and I hope that no woman will accept a husband who arrogantly takes liberties with her beauty and pride. To beat your family is an ill-manner, and a foul and revolting action, and the Prophet said that he was sent to perfect our character. I am repelled by ugliness, and I take refuge in the gift of the mind capable of interpretation. If I find in my heart revulsion and consternation, I take it to my Lord, and in the bounty of the Conference I extract the beauty of my Lord's creation. For God does not wish an injustice upon people (40:31). It is not God who commits injustice, but it is human beings who transgress against themselves (3:117). It is my Lord who said: 'This is the [most] beautiful way (religion), so do not abuse it so as to wrong yourselves' (9:36). May God forbid that I be among the unjust and ignorant (33:72) who ascribe to God anything but the pure and beautiful. Surely, my sister, if we fail to interpret, we only transgress against ourselves."

CHAPTER 42

The Beating of Wives Revisited

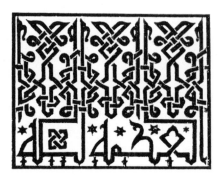

The truth of God ignites my life. The passion overwhelms me with visions of beauty—of light and enlightenment. The passion chases the shadows from the niches of my mind. Illuminated by the light of the heavens and earth, I am like a brilliant star. In this luminous state I discover true love—a light upon light.

Where does the Conference of Books come from? From the mind unrestricted by bounds? From a substance as diffuse as light? From the blessed tree feeding upon streams of light? From a native urge to follow the glimmers of insight? A Conference of light founded upon visions of light.

She sits with her hands folded upon her lap. She is the sister who visited me before with questions about her matrimonial plight. Her husband had beaten her and claimed that he is empowered by a divine right. After we discussed the permutations of meaning in God's text, she had been immersed in study and thought. Now, her lips hold back, but her eyes betray the contentions of her mind. My sister, bring your queries out to the light, for suppression leads to a festering darkness in the heart. Do not worry, it is an honor to be remembered after the lucubration of many nights.

"Last time," she proceeded to say, "we discussed the beating verse in the Qur'an (4:34). You said that 4:34 cannot be understood out of context. You argued that verse 4:15 decreed that women guilty of sexual lewdness, upon the testimony of four witnesses, are to be imprisoned in their homes until repentance or marriage. Men are punished through other means, perhaps by corporal punishment. You then read 4:34 to say that if a woman is married and she commits sexual lewdness, she may be chided, ordered to be separated from her husband for a time, or she may receive corporal punishment. But you insisted that these powers are not delegated to the husband, but to the state. Upon an allegation of lewdness, probably to be proven by four witnesses, the state will choose the remedy. In this context, my brother, you relied on the *hadith* of the Prophet in arguing that *nushuz* does not mean disobedience but, effectively, means *fahisha* (lewdness)."

"Yes, my sister, all of that is part of what I said. And, what did I say about the arbitration verse (4:35)?"

"My brother, you said that *shiqaq* is a breach or rift between husband and wife. You argued that it is illogical for arbitration to follow punishment. It is irrational for us to say, let the husband beat his wife, and then proceed to arbitration. If the husband had beaten his wife, he had already accused, convicted, and punished her. What is the point of arbitration then? My brother, you argued that verse 4:35 is general in scope. It basically says that if there is a fundamental rift, whether the rift arose because of an act of lewdness or otherwise, then a binding arbitration may be ordered. I believe, my brother, this is what you said."

"Yes, my sister, it is what I said."

"Brother, may God bless your Conference and increase its days, I have been living in an intellectual daze. At times my heart is reconciled and my mind rebels. At times it is exactly the opposite, my mind is content and my heart objects. I doubt if I should question, but I question nonetheless. So, I ask my brother, what do you think of what Ahmed 'Ali said in his translation of the Qur'an? Ahmed 'Ali said *daraba* does not mean to beat, but it means to have conjugal relations. Ahmed 'Ali argued that 4:34 instructs that if a wife is rebellious advise her, or separate from her, or have conjugal relations with her according to what the circumstances would dictate."

"Yes, my sister I know of Ahmed 'Ali's interpretation, and I used to incline toward it, but after study I no longer accept it. *Daraba* could very well mean something other than to beat, but the usage in 4:34 does not support what Ahmed 'Ali contends, and God knows best."

She nodded her head quickly and then rushed to speak. "Can you explain to me again what you said about verse 4:128? I have relied on my memory and my memory has failed. I was always told that 4:34 applies if a husband is not pleased with his wife, and 4:128 applies if a wife is not pleased with her husband. That is what all the *imams* in mosques say."

"Sister, what I said is that 4:128 cannot be so read. For 4:128 only speaks of a wife reconciling with her husband. According to what you were taught, the law of God would be truly strange. If a husband is not pleased with his wife, he may chide her, abandon her, and beat her. But if a wife is not pleased with her husband, she may only reconcile with him. This law would be disturbing, if not absurd.

"What I said is that 4:128 is not a general verse, and it sets no normative law. It addresses a specific situation and simply advises that God does not object. What 4:128 says is that if a husband had committed a serious infraction or desertion, but then the couple wishes to reconcile, they may do so and there is no objection. The Qur'an then comments, reconciliation is good, and warns against greed. There is no reason to consider that 4:34 and 4:128 are complementary, or that one verse is for women and one verse is for men. Verse 4:128 assures couples that even after a major infraction, they may forgive and forget. The verse does not address the necessity of punishment and does not involve the state."

She looked at her hands and then raised her head. "All right, I want to tell you but I don't want you to be upset. I recounted your views to a scholar whom I should not name. He said that what you say is against the consensus of opinions, it is a fearful *bid'a* (innovation), and that you are a liberal of questionable fame. I asked others and they said more or less the same."

"Sister, if that is the case, then listen to what I have to say. As to the name of the scholar, I already know his name. As to the consensus, that I will not concede, for I do not accept a consensus that permits an error to prevail. The consensus of one generation does not bind another, and an immoral unanimity is immoral all the same. As to the notion of *bid'a*, the real *bid'a* is when the ignorant speak and pontificate. Didn't Qadi Khan (d. 592/1196) say, 'Know that a man becomes restless and bored, and is overcome by insecurities, ignorance, and a defective brain. This man's affliction only increases when he becomes surrounded by idiots who sing his praise. Then this man fills his mouth with the words of scholars and spews out phrase after phrase. Neither does he understand nor do his followers understand the implications of what he says. It is better for the rational man to guard his mouth for the ignorant only fall flat on their face.'"

Alarmed she interrupted, "Listen, brother, even if they are wrong, remember that God says, 'Let not the injustice of others lead you astray.' You are no longer in the pursuit of knowledge, you are engaged in a tirade."

I felt embarrassed and ashamed; as much as I dislike ignorance, I should respond instead of condemn and blame. "Yes, I am forgetting my place," I said. "A reprehensible *bid'a*, my sister, is based on whim and habit, not on an equitable interpretation of God's words. The best I read on the subject of innovations is the book named *al-I'tisam* by the Maliki jurist, al-Shatibi (d. 790/1388), who argues that what is based on moral insight is not a reprehensible innovation, but is a new insight on God's way. Further, do the people you consulted know what the previous generation of scholars have said? Most of the books of law are not even published yet. And, if we find one or two or ten or more scholars who agree with me, does that affect the quality of what I said?

"As to the last point, for me, infamy and fame is all the same. Liberal or not is but a game of names. I find a delegation to beat one's wife an embarrassing shame. And, if that is liberal, then I sing the praises of this kind of blame."

The sister intervened as if to re-orient the conversation, "But would you agree that your interpretation is not what jumps out from the sources as the most obvious understanding?"

"My sister, this depends entirely on the moral assumptions upon which you approach the problem. May I ask you, is beating your spouse a part of a superior character? Is it a virtue? Is it something beautiful and good? Notice, my sister, that the vast majority of women or men would find being beaten, at the very least, detestable if not intolerable. Intuitively, we know this—we are sure of this. In fact, by our very nature, we cringe at the idea that God empowers any husband to beat his wife, even if she is rebellious, disobedient, or obnoxious. As evidence of this intuition, we are troubled by the idea that verse 4:34 permits this type of behavior, and so verse 4:34 is not what we normally share with friends or strangers. We are troubled by it, and so we say things like, 'Yes, but the beating cannot cause injury or pain' or we say, 'A husband can strike his wife only on the shoulder with a small twig or feathers or the like.' We cite the Prophet's traditions that prohibit striking the face or the traditions that state that men with superior character do not strike their wives. Yet, my sister, we repeat Ibn Majah's (d. 273/887) report that 'Umar Ibn al-Khattab (d. 23/644) struck his wife all the same. But wasn't 'Umar of a superior character?"

"Yes, most certainly, but perhaps he made a mistake," the sister said.

"Sure, perhaps. But the point remains, there is something troubling about the idea of striking a spouse. I am suggesting that much of the material prohibiting corporal punishment that causes injury or pain is a symptom of our intuitive discomfort."

"But," the sister cut in, "suppose the wife is truly a reprehensible person?"

I said, "Okay, let us assume that she is a truly reprehensible person. Let us assume you chide her and then you abandon her in bed. What do you think hitting her with a small twig on the shoulder will accomplish? If she is an insensitive person, she will laugh at the futility of the procedure, and if she is sensitive, she would not deserve to be beaten in the first place.

"Now, we also repeat traditions from the Prophet, which prohibit beating a camel or any other cattle, which prohibit the striking of a maid, and which state that striking a slave is a legal cause for manumission. Our intuitive discomfort with an authorization to beat one's spouse is confirmed by the fact that there are numerous traditions which state that the Prophet never struck a wife, maid, or any other member of his household. This fact is often cited as proof of the Prophet's superior character. Furthermore, we read that 'Ali, the Companion, prohibited the striking of women even if it is in response to an assault of defamation or cursing. All of this confirms our intuitive moral sense that striking your wife is simply wrong. Add to this that there is no reason to trust the equanimity or entrust the discretion of men, and then, my sister, what do we have?"

Surprised by the question the sister hesitated, "I guess we have a troubled heart."

Experiencing a rush of excitement, I quickly said, "And, if we have a troubled heart, we take advantage of the facility of the mind. The facility of the mind manifests itself in interpretation. In other words, we resort to interpretation, and search for the intent of the Divine."

She cut in with a hint of impatience, "But what if the interpretation is unprecedented?"

"Sister, what if it is unprecedented? We do not serve God through a blind obedience to what we think is the law. We serve God through a perceptive examination of our understanding of the presumptions of the law. A precedent is there to guide, not to blind. A precedent points us toward the right direction, but it cannot become an obstruction to God's way.

"There are precedents that confirm an absolute moral value. For instance, there are precedents that confirm the value of life or protect people's honor. Life and honor are moral values. When we find a precedent that portends to promote a certain moral value, the only question is whether the precedent, in fact, furthers or promotes such a value. We examine the precedent in such a light. This can be termed a *maqasid* inquiry. The *maqasid* are the moral values of the *Shari'a*. The *ahkam* (positive laws) of *Shari'a* promote moral values, and it is our duty to ensure that the laws are, in fact, in the service of moral values and not that the moral values are in the service of the law.

"Keep in mind, my sister, that there are absolute moral values. These values are not factually contingent, and they are not historically or contextually dependent either. They do not depend on circumstance or on the level of human understanding or appreciation. For example, the preservation of life or the protection of the mind, which is protected by the prohibition against intoxicants that compromise the mind, or modesty, which is a part of humility and a part of the preservation of dignity, or honor, which is compromised by slander—all of these are absolute moral values. Absolute moral values are established by the divine command through cumulative ways; they are repeatedly affirmed by God and so there can be little doubt that they are in fact necessary and absolute, and that human beings must understand and promote them.

"But there are also derivative moral values. Derivative moral values are subject to historical contingencies and limitations. It is not that these values are contingent in their nature or essence, but they have contingent potentialities. God affirms these values, but affirms them as a higher order of existence. In other words, an order that seeks to establish a superior state of existence would fulfill such values. Put differently, absolute moral values are the minimum required for a moral society. Derivative moral values are necessary for a superior moral order. Perhaps I can explain it this way: A minimally moral society will preserve and protect life or mind. Freedom or dignity are derivative values; they are derived from the necessity of protecting life or mind. Human understanding of what is necessary in order to protect life or mind could be historically contingent. Furthermore, our understanding of what is needed to promote dignity or freedom could develop with our understanding of what is needed for the existence of a superior society."

She looked at me with stern probity and said, "Does this mean that not beating your wife is a derivative moral value?"

Taken somewhat off guard, I responded, "I would not state it that way. I would say preservation of life, honor, and mind are absolute imperatives. Dignity is necessary for the preservation of honor and mind. I then ascend to the understanding that a resort to violence, in this stage of human development, tends to undermine a person's dignity, and this undermines a person's integrity of honor and mind. The fact that beating one's wife was perceived by earlier authorities to be consistent with the absolute moral values of honor and mind does not bind me or you in any way."

"But," she protested, "you seem to be saying that not beating your wife is a part of a superior existence and not what is required minimally for a moral life. Brother, I find this objectionable. My husband, who as you recall did beat me, could say, 'Good enough, I am content with a minimal moral life, I am not a Prophet or saint.'"

"Sister, to this I would say two things: One, a person who is content with the minimal and does not strive to achieve a superior moral existence is not moral at all. Two, and more significant, I am not talking about moral values in the sense of deciding on an individual course of behavior. I am talking about legal interpretation. For instance, take the familiar example of slavery. We ascend to the understanding that slavery is not consistent with a moral life. But why? Because God already told us that a superior person, i.e., a truly moral person, would not own slaves. Because God advised us to manumit slaves in every way possible. As a matter of legal interpretation, we then decide that a moral society which strives to be truly moral will prohibit slavery as a matter of law. This does not mean that an individual may decide that owning slaves is consistent with his own minimal moral standards. In other words, the category of derivative moral values is an evidentiary matter, but it does not affect the imperative nature of the value. As a matter of legal investigation, we suspect that the prohibition of slavery is a moral value necessary for a better society. Does this mean that we can simply decide that we don't want to be a better society? Certainly not. To the extent that a derivative moral value becomes necessary for the fulfillment of an absolute moral value, as far as its obligatory nature is concerned, it, in turn, becomes imperative and unwavering."

With her sternness giving way to a slight smile she said, "And, so what would you say to someone who claims that based on your moral analysis, you would feel at liberty to overrule textual laws?"

"I would say, who am I to overturn any law! All I am saying is that this moral analysis would create a duty in our mind to re-investigate our understanding of the law, and to find an interpretation that is consistent with the morality promoted by the fundamentals of the law. What I am saying is that my intuitive sense seems to indicate that the beating of wives is immoral. It is immoral because it is not consistent with basic *Shari'a* values, such as protection of honor or mind, or derivative *Shari'a* values, such as protection of dignity. This intuitive sense is confirmed by a significant part of the Islamic tradition. As we said, the practice and *Sunna* of the Prophet is not consistent with the use of beating. There are traditions that describe beating as hateful and detestable. There are traditions that say beating must not cause injury or pain. There are traditions that prohibit the striking of the face because striking the face is humiliating and degrading. And, most importantly, the Qur'an tells us that marriage should be based on mercy, compassion, and friendship, and our experience teaches us that physical violence is not consistent with mercy, compassion, or friendship—because of all of this, I feel obligated to investigate and to interpret the Qur'anic verses. I feel obligated to interpret so as to resolve any conflict, and to reach a higher moral order. Sister, what may I ask is unacceptable about this approach?"

I was relieved when I saw a smile break upon her face. She paused, rubbed her hands, and looked at the clock hanging on the wall above my head.

She said as if speaking to herself, "I wonder how far the method of moral inquiry will take us." But then she raised her head and said, "Like any powerful force, it might take us far, but many dangers lurk ahead. I sense that a moral inquiry does not just limit itself to inspiring us to re-investigate the law, but it also calls upon us to apply critical moral insights to the traditions as well."

I understood her concerns, and I wanted to address, but not alleviate, her fears, "Sister, I implore you by God's mercy and enlightened way, what other choice do we have? Either we live as immoral animals and ascribe our immorality to the commands of God. Or, we seek to purify our intellects and hearts to elevate ourselves to God's beautiful and majestic way. God's way is high and beautiful (*'ulya*) and everything else is lowly and not as beautiful (*dunya*). Shouldn't we seek to elevate ourselves to the most exalted way? If we know God through intuition, and if God is exalted and beautiful, don't we then know what is exalted and beautiful by intuition as well? How could our intuition be trusted to know God, but not be trusted to know what is exalted or beautiful or anything else? And, isn't our intellect there to fulfill the beautiful aspirations of a pure intuition? And, isn't the divine text there to aid the intellect in its mission?

"Sister, I implore you, if I read in the sources that the reason verse 4:128 was revealed was that the Prophet wanted to divorce his wife Sawdah, and that, in order to avoid a divorce, Sawdah gave up her marital rights, and so the Prophet kept her, what am I supposed to do? The jurists derived from this that if a wife becomes old and undesirable, and her husband wishes to divorce her, she may pay him money or give him jewelry to avoid such a miserable fate. By a minimal amount of thought you discover that, in effect, what is being asserted is that even if the husband is a scoundrel and an ungrateful greedy buffoon, God has no objection if the poor wife would purchase her husband's mercy and favor. Does this sound moral or beautiful or part of a decent character to you? Sister, I read that 'Aisha (d. 58/678), the Prophet's wife, praised the uprightness and bravery of the women of the Ansar in Medina. These women did not hesitate to stand up for their rights, and did not hesitate to ask any question without embarrassment or shame. Then, I read that 'Umar was critical of the independence of the women of the Ansar, and did not approve of their boldness. Upon hearing that the Prophet's wives argued with him and even raised their voices at times, he confronted the Prophet and protested his tolerance of such behavior, and the Prophet simply smiled. Then, I read that 'Umar complained about the women's defiance and insolence, and the Prophet permitted the men to beat them. Reportedly, the beating verse was revealed to vindicate 'Umar. Afterwards, seventy women protested the beatings to the Prophet, and then he declared that those who beat their women are not among the best of men. In other reports, the Prophet said, 'Those who struck their women are not the best of you.' Now, I implore you, sister, how do we reconcile 'Aisha's praise of the character of the women of the Ansar with 'Umar's protest? Is it believable that our Prophet, who never struck a woman, servant, or slave, would issue a blanket authorization to all men to beat any woman? Is it believable that the Prophet, with his excellence of character, would permit to men what he, himself, considered to be entirely reprehensible? Is it believable that God would side with 'Umar against His own Prophet on an issue of such moral significance? God describes the Prophet as a person of excellent moral character, and we are told that God rejects the judgments of the Prophet's morality. With your knowledge of the Prophet's moral character, is it possible that he would sanction violence against women? Does this sound moral or beautiful or part of a decent character to you?"

"No, no it does not," she lowered her head and whispered.

"Then if it is not beautiful, I cannot accept the reports concerning Sawdah or 'Umar without a heavy and demanding burden of proof. The reports must be of impeccable and resounding authenticity in order for me to accept them, and thus, I do not accept them. My sister, these are chauvinistic traditions injected into Islam by people who lacked understanding. I don't care what the pharmacists of Islam (the scholars of *hadith*) say about their authenticity, I will apply a more demanding and probing standard because these reports are not consistent with what I know about the Prophet's character, or the circumstances of his marriage to Sawdah, or the treatment of his wives, or the nature of his mercy and compassion. Even when the Prophet suffered greatly from his wives, he would not accept any suggestion to divorce any one of them or abandon any of them or leave any of them. Perhaps it is true that Sawdah gave up some of her marital rights because of her age, but that does not mean that she feared divorce or that the Prophet intended to divorce her. How is it possible that the Prophet would refuse to even censure his wives and then permit other men to beat their own wives? We have reports that 'Ali detested and punished physical violence by husbands against their wives. We even have reports that 'Umar never struck a woman after he became a Muslim. Abu Bakr al-Siddiq (d. 22/634) never struck his wife. The Prophet never struck a servant or wife, and insisted that women be treated with dignity and honor. In fact, it is reported that after the victory over Mecca, the Prophet said, 'Do not strike them [women] and do not insult or degrade them.'

"All of this gives me a long moral pause, and troubles my heart. If my heart is troubled, can't I resort to my mind to probe the tradition and precedent? Can't I tell my beloved jurists, I believe you misinterpreted or misunderstood God's exalted way? Shouldn't I investigate before ascribing to God something so disturbing and grave? Can't I tell my esteemed jurists that this is not consistent with the command to perfect our character, and that you, my jurists, misunderstood the superior moral values that are now necessary in order to fulfill God's absolute and fundamental moral values? Don't I have the right to question, investigate, and hope and pray? My sister, I have the right—the right I earned through the Conference, the right of light and enlightenment, the right of the beautiful in the service of The Beautiful, and the Right of Light founded on the Love of Light. Sister, the right of light upon light, and God knows best."

CHAPTER 43

In Praise of the Marginal

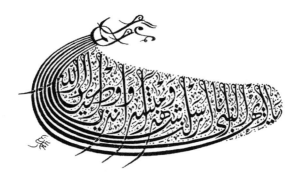

"And from the outskirts came a man running who said, 'Oh, my people, obey the Messengers, obey those who ask you for no reward and who are rightly guided'" (36:20). From the outskirts, from the enormity of marginality, I find meaning.

I call You and You hear my call, and I find meaning. I call unto others, and I am ignored, and in that is all the meaning. My thoughts are like the drizzle of rain before the storm, its generosity is its restraint. These thoughts are like the generosity of the dawn before the searing sun. They are like the generosity of warmth before the scorching of the smoldering heat. Yes, in the restraint of marginality, there we find the full meaning.

Don't you see that in the restraint of virginity, in the restraint of modesty, in the restraint of the whisper in the ear of the beloved, in the restraint of the hesitant gaze, in the restraint of the soft touch, in the restraint of the diminutive kiss, in the restraint of the demurring prayer, in the restraint of the diffident thought, in the restraint of the judicious word, in the restraint of a timorous love, in the self-conscious bashfulness of beauty, you will find the unrestrained and full meaning?

Have you seen the restraint of this Conference, have you noticed its tenacious marginality? Have you heard the marginality of the distant melody? Have you compared the subtlety and tranquility of beauty to the rambunctiousness and restiveness of ugliness? Have you compared the equivocations of life to the decisiveness of death? Have you noticed the resonance of life compared to the finality of death? Have you compared the marginality and richness of life to the utter poverty of death?

My God, in marginality I am alive, and in marginality I find myself. Your centrality and the marginality of all else is but a reminder that through restraint and humility we will find ourselves. Every marginality is but a taste of the truth to come, that the temporal bliss of life is but a glimpse of the eternal ecstasy of the Divine.

God, I have stood before the solemn pleasures of life. All its trappings, all its enticements, all its delusions have defied my sense. If the pleasures of life are meaningless, then I would have found meaning in death. The questions simmer and gurgle in my head. Is the eruption of arrogant pleasures simply a tedious test? Can the marginality of worldly pleasures carry a meaning beyond itself? Are the marvels of creation but a vanity seeking absolution? If the melody from majestic chords is just a test, then why does it console the torrents of the tormented self? If the gaze upon the soul of purity is a delusion, then why does it absolve the agony of sins? If the ecstatic tremor in the presence of a bashful beauty is a sinful omission, then why does it pacify the recalcitrant heart? If the liberation of the soul at the moment of intoxicating union is but a passing vanity, then wouldn't virtue set us apart? If every blissful gift is either a test or an indulgence, then what is the meaning of beauty, and what is the meaning of love?

God, considering Your centrality, what is the meaning of all else? But it is the marginality of this Conference that has interspersed the moments of elucidation in this aching head. The marginality of this Conference is the guarantee of its humility; the insight of this Conference is the taste of the enlightenment to come. God, You promised us the bliss of the heavens of unadulterated enlightenment. But your justice necessitates that we experience the marginal as a taste of the truth to come. In the omens and joys of this earth, in the clouds that warn of the rage of thunder, we experience Your blissful mercy despite our unabashed plunders. Yes, the marginal is but the messenger of grace concealed in the distance between meaning and vanity.

I realize that when we touch, when we gaze, and when we love, it is but a taste of a potential ecstasy. Even the union in marriage is an experience of Your unity. You are all the potentials fully realized and the marginal is but an unfulfilled potentiality. If we experience the pleasures of this earth as a venture into the Divine, then this life is no longer a vanity. What a melody, beauty, or love teaches us is the potentiality only found in the Divine of utter happiness and unfettered ecstasy.

CHAPTER 44

A Love Song

When I open my eyes, I am inflamed by your most wondrous sight, and when I close my eyes, I am at peace but blind. If wisdom is the province of a believer, can you imagine the believer's dominion over beauty? I want nothing from you—neither your resentment nor your love—for when I want, I turn only to God. I pray only for the memory that consoles us in our irrefutable temporality. I wish to denounce all the semblances of our obstinate futility. Don't worry, I do not want from you recompense nor vindication. Didn't Ibn al-'Abbas (d. 68/687), may God preserve his spirit, say, "For one who is slain by love, there is no recourse or compensation?"

My dear, my sister in God, I wish I could imprint my withering image upon the light of your eyesight. I wish I could ignite with a million poems and engrave them upon your heart. I wish I could combust with perception, wrap it in an impeccable vision, and guide your life from the very start. I wish I could leave a trace. When the pestering of sleep breaks my will, I wish I could banish my tired eyes to the ruins of my heart, and then spring back to life dancing before your wondrous face. I wish that God would give me in this world, through your memory, an eternal space.

My sister in God, in my heart there is a tenacious arrogance that wishes to deny temporality its merciless place. But like the leaf that dances with such intrepidity and is then swept by the resolute stream, like the mettled mountain settled in its confidence as the wind withers it away, like the heart that longs to love but only drowns in dreams, like the mind that struggles to know, but is relentlessly brutalized by its fears, like the star that collapses unto itself, and the sky that documents its decay, like the dying leaves when they crunch and break under my oblivious feet, I live in arrogance, and after a delusional repose, I inevitably rot.

But beyond the arrogance and the inevitable decay, it is love which lingers on and reaches out to divinity. It is this love, beyond the lock or knot, beyond the nuptials or vows, beyond communion or troth, beyond the body or lust, it is this love which defeats the mundane. You see, I seek no timorous touch or quivering kiss or tremulous embrace. I seek no torment or frustration, and I seek no relief from my pain. I seek to surpass my life and exceed my own fate. I seek to share with The Divine, a supernal state—a state of bliss, of ambrosial love and paradisiacal taste, an emotion of unadulterated felicity, uncorrupted by need or want—an unremitting emotion of unrequited love that expects no selfish utility in return. That is my love for God, and that is the love of God—a love which, if we mimic, we see the wonder of God on this earth.

My beloved, Ibn Hazm (d. 456/1064), may God grant him peace, had once said that love is not forbidden, it is rather like an affliction that could induce a state of misery or grace. If we suffer love and heal it with the mundane, this affliction will become lechery, boredom, and an abysmal disgrace. But if we rise with the magnanimity of the emotion, we experience something of the divine and ascend to a state of grace. Love me back or not, I am satisfied that I exceeded my body, my temporality, and this telluric earth.

I will close this supplication recounting what Ibn Hazm had said a thousand years ago. I know that there are fanatics in religion who will say, "What made him compose this obscenity? Surely, he has deviated from the path and committed a near scurrility." I will tell them what I tell you, in love there is no sin, but in sin there is lechery and salacity. If you wish to condemn, condemn sin, but to condemn love is a vulgarity and blasphemy. Doesn't the blasphemer deny The Divine, and isn't The Divine beautiful and sublime? And, isn't it vulgar to praise The Divine, but to disdain the elements and attributes which define the sublime? The most sublime love is the love of God, but any other love is a flower in God's garden of immaculate beauty.

CHAPTER 45

Migrating to the Shaykhs

What cures the vacuous heart when its delusion reigns supreme? What restores it when the truth becomes its haunting fear? What cures it when it pours the insignia of piety into the depression of its fears?

When piety becomes an emblem worn by the fatuous mind, does not the light of God dim and disappear?

My Conference, the Conference of Books, fills my heart with the beauty of God. Abolish my emblems, my insignias, my markings, and all my wishful lore. Leave me naked with nothing but the cover of truth. Fill the depressions of my heart with the knowledge of my Lord. Banish my fears to the light of my soul, and restore my memory so that I may never forget. Shake me into consciousness and confound my delusions. Hide me from the inducements of arrogance, but let me live in my own full view.

A life that once contained so much beauty is now scattered at the shores of memory. There is no salvage possible, but you, my Conference, collect the remains, save the truth, and restore its beauty.

The rapturous voice of the Qur'an would always blast from the radio at dawn. My beautiful mother would stand in the kitchen slicing the bread. My *jalabiyya* and white *kufiyya* always hung behind the door. "*Al-salamu alaykum,*" I would call out as I left for the mosque, and when I returned I would find my mother still in prayer. The school uniform never changed its navy colors, and I hated the idiocy of trousers and shirts. By sunrise, the news announces yet another Israeli bombing, and always with the obligatory announcement, "And our armed defenses forced the enemy to retreat." This had become the code phrase confessing our utter degradation and defeat.

The *Shaykhs* said that the heart of the believer is wedded to beauty, and excellence is beautiful. So, at school, failure or mediocrity was not an option; "a believer is adorned by the dignity of *jihad*," they said, "and the pulse of *jihad* is but the struggle for success."

Upon returning home from school, the duality of our existence took full force. The navy skin was replaced with the flowing white, the naked head was covered with the *kufiyya*, the *miswak* was placed in the pocket, and the scrawny beard was mixed with musk. The metamorphosis was a pilgrimage to a dream—a dream to locate ourselves within a historical moment somewhere between the pride of the past and the alienation of the present.

No matter. None of us believed that we were going to change the world with a *miswak* or that our headgear was going to restore our past. Books in hand, I would yell, "*Al-salamu alaykum*," and head to the mosque. We did not spend the time in dogmatic activism or in pretentious pedantry. We studied.

Torn between a present and past, torn between two cultures, between two countries, between two identities, between two schools, between two sets of teachers, between two sets of friends, and between two sets of books, we studied. How easy it was to succumb to the temptation of demonizing one reality and idealizing another. How powerful the temptation to mend ourselves by embracing only one and renouncing the other. But one was not *jahiliyya* and the other Islam, and how could we heal ourselves by the arrogance of commending ourselves and disdaining all others?

With the ruthless reigning of the sun and the sizzle of the desert sand, I would head to the mosque. At the corner were the irresolute, seven, short, and small trees, strangely standing there muttering an endless *tasbih*. Inexplicably in their midst, was the broken stump of a cement pillar. Years ago, it was my companion and the center of so many infatuated dreams. In those years, I dreamt of those majestic and supernal eyes. I would sit on the stump praying to catch a glimpse. Perhaps she will notice the solemn kid cemented on his stump hiding in his headgear. If I squeezed "*al-salamu alaykum*" from the tremor of my lips, and if she answered, I would float with the clouds in pure ecstasy. But the nature of youthfulness is cruel. I loved my cement stump, but it abandoned me.

Often, in the searing heat of the sand, I would remember Bilal Ibn Rabah (d. 17–21/638–642) under the rock. In the past Abu Bakr al-Siddiq (d. 22/634) freed him, but today who can set us free?

God sends reminders and ties the future with the present and past. On the side, after the defiant trees, is the decaying fur partially covering the skeleton of what once was a cat. When the time comes, I pray that I will be covered and comforted by the hands of the Lord. After passing the wire fence separating the neighborhood from the freeway, I would cast my *salams* upon the ant nests. The brothers had cut an entrance into the fence, and with a deep breath and the name of God, we would dash across the road.

At the mosque, we studied and prepared. We chided the failures of memory, lamented the complacent molds of the intellect, and rebelled in debate. In the *masjid* of 'Umar Ibn 'Abd al-Aziz, from *Maghrib* until *'Isha*, it was the daily *halaqa* of Shaykh 'Adil 'Id. On Wednesday and Friday, after *'Isha* was Shaykh al-Wirdani's *halaqa* on *usul* and *qawa'id*. Shaykh Wadi taught the Qur'an for three hours every week. "The *Shaykh* will cover five pages tonight." "No, he will be disappointed that we are still confused about last week's round." "He said *istihsan* is nine-tenths of the law, and he is surely to ask us to elaborate upon this and expound." "No, he will ask us to reconcile conflicting *hadith*, all of which are equally sound."

Every night a Conference embraced us, every subject accosted us, every question defied us, every book dismantled us, and every *Shaykh* restored us. We chased the light until it absorbed us, glowed within our hearts, and set our intellects free. We loved our *Shaykhs* in God and for God, and we exposed our souls to their sincerity. There were no grades or chairs or classes, and we did not live by the conformist standards of some bureaucratic ministry. Nothing but the consciousness of love and piety, and the tests of love and piety are demanding and most severe.

Shaykh 'Id entered shortly before *Maghrib* prayer, and we eagerly arose—our yearning always betrayed our repose. Our adoration was expressed in subtleties—the glass of water, the nervous question, the *barak Allahu fik*. I loved this man as if he were a small glimpse of the Prophet—a longing that rests for a moment in hints of the beloved. Shaykh 'Id, may Allah bless his soul, like most of the other *Shaykhs*, despite his unwavering smile, had seen the depth of the dungeons of Cairo. After Azhar, he enrolled in medical school and was dragged away as he wrote his fifth-year exams. After disappearing in prison for twenty years, he re-emerged. When we would say, "This must have been difficult *ya Shaykh*," he would reply, "Better to remember the brothers who are dead."

I rush to him, "*Kayffa halak ya Shaykh?*" "*Al-hamdullilah*," he smiles, "Are you prepared?"

I am prepared, but it is never sufficient. How can my intellect suffice when it attempts to understand the ways of the Divine? We gather in the left corner of the mosque. Today is Thursday and the center is occupied with the ranting of the *Tabligh*. As their voices are raised, I remember a time when I sat in their midst. At that time, Islam was but the sum total of transmitted *hadith*, and the Qur'an was but a single verse. In the midst of the *Tabligh* we read, "Say, This is my way, I invite to God with a clear vision, I and whoever follows me. Praise be to God and I do not associate partners with my Lord" (12:108).

In those days, we floated knocking at doors, inviting people to our way—a way of clarity, the clarity of the insignias we wore, the short *jilbabs*, the *miswaks*, the beards, the clichés and slogans that we worshipped and adored. A way of clarity—but without a vision.

In those days, I invited everyone, and forgot myself. My exterior defined me, and my insignias were but a condemnation of the world. In those days, my judgments were as quick as a gun. In those days, my clarity was the sheath of my blade, and *takfir* was my fearless sword. It was, and it remained so until one day I awoke. I was in another fit of condemnation against my sister, brother, mother, and father. The issue might have been the beard, or it might have been perfumes, or the absolute necessity of a *bay'a* to an *imam,* or the prohibition against music, or television, or ties, or trousers, or brassieres, or stitched undergarments, or toothpaste, or jello, or jam, or the prohibition against plucking one's nose-hair, or the necessity of removing the pubic hair, or the condemnation of mixed gatherings, or mixed telephone conversations, or the despicability of un-Islamic mathematics, or the evils of art, or the reprehensibility of saying good morning, or the imperative of burning most books, or the innovation of writing and reading novels, or the innovation of wedding rings, or the obligation of praying the five prayers in the mosque, or the heresy of the Shi'a or un-Islamicity of the very air we breath. I don't remember which, and it does not matter. My father usually ignored me as he continued to look in his books. But on that particular day, he closed his book and looked straight at me. "All right, since you seem to have found the law of God that we all have missed, we will all obey you and even give you a *bay'a* if you wish. I have but one request. You go with me and attend a lesson on *Shari'a.* If you comprehend what is said, and answer all the questions just off the top of your head, then you do know all there is to know, and the knowledgeable should be exalted by all."

With utter arrogance, I agreed. Little did I know that I agreed to change my life. I failed to answer a single question or even understand the questions posed. Whether we spoke of *takhrij* or *tarjih,* or we spoke of *tanqih al-manat* or *dabtt al-isnad,* whether we spoke of *dalil al-'aql* or *dalil al-sam',* or the *sunan* or *musnads,* I could not comment or understand. If I cited a single *hadith,* I would be challenged with ten others plus the precedent of the Companions and successors, and a meticulous accounting of the full evidence at hand. In frustration, my eyes swelled with tears, but even back home, I was too arrogant to admit my utter defeat. But I knew I reached the turning point, I knew that the leisure of my clarity came from the facility of idiocy. How easy it is to say, "I see," when you can gaze at the dark and see the shadows and ghosts you most fear.

Hardly a week passed, and I was in the hands of Shaykh 'Id. I was in the hands of many books, and many *Shaykhs.* Many nights were spent in many mosques. We would sit in the circle, and read. The teacher would correct and question; we contested the text, and it became the leverage to our ideas. During the school year, the pace was measured and slow. During the summers in Egypt, there were *halaqas* after *Fajr,* after *'Asr,* and after *'Isha.*

I remember you, my teachers with reverence and respect. Shaykh Wadi, Shaykh al-Wirdani, Shaykh Khalaf, Shaykh al-'Isawi, Shaykh 'Ali al-Zanati, Shaykh Ibrahim al-Fadl, Shaykh Husayn 'Uwidah, Shaykh 'Adil al-Radi, Shaykh al-Digawi, Shaykh al-Baguri, Shaykh Ibrahim 'Abd al-Khaliq, Shaykh Muhammad al-Ghazali, Ustadh Hasan 'Abd al-Ghani, and Ustadh Hossein Modarressi. How can I ever forget?

On another hot and burning and sadly painful day, I made the walk to the mosque for the very last time. I entered the mosque after *'Isha* prayer when the *halaqa* was done. I embraced my *Shaykh's* heart and anesthetized my own. He had forbidden us from kissing his hands, but I disobeyed. "*Shaykh*, I am leaving to the United States tomorrow—I feel that there is nothing else I can do." The insanity of fear was taking over, the rabid disease of violence was taking over, the distortions of Wahhabism were taking over, the oblivious indifference of the Tabligh was taking over, and now perhaps, I will find a new home.

Go with Allah's blessings my son, and keep the learning close to your heart. It doesn't matter where you reside, you have already migrated to the Conference and to God.

CHAPTER 46

On Revising Bigotry

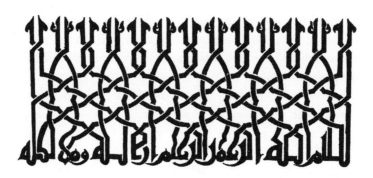

The Conference unfolds to the balanced mind. Its soul is the honor of the search, the equanimity of judgment, and the breath of beauty. Beauty is an intricate state of balance weighed by the scales of the Lord. The essence of beauty is balance, like the equipoise of sight, the restitutions of love, and the harmony in the Divine Word.

I sit unfolding on the pages of the Conference, uncovering the power of beauty to restore the imbalance of the mind. It is love, which I nurture in myself, for it guards the scales. But if love has the power to guard the scales, bigotry is the ugliness colonizing the feeble soul. Bigotry is an infection of fear or hate, pillaging through the immunities of the heart. Bigotry is the quintessential disruption of the magnanimity of the mind.

It was the bigotry of colonialism that once intruded upon our existence and ravished our lives. It severed us from our Conference, and persuaded us that our heritage is but a lie. The disease of colonialism had infected our hearts, our minds, our limbs, and our sight. We saw our history as a corruption and aberration to be apologetically denied. Infected with bigotry, in our imbalance, we idealized the beginning of our history and the rest—we demonized.

Whether it is the bigotry of fear or hate, the bigotry of the colonizer or colonized, the bigotry of friend or foe, the same ugliness corrupts the scales of the Lord.

A new piece of bigotry by Daniel Pipes, and the intrusion disrupts you. It is not that the bigotry is novel or original, but the very fact that you take time to respond is an annoying chore. What can one say to bigotry that could possibly help it restore the imbalance in its soul? What can one say to those who project their ugliness unto existence, and come to believe that history is like a painted whore—it exists for their pleasure, for their whims, and exists to service their political goals.

Pipes's new revelation about Islam and Muslims is that their history is quite possibly a lie. Misery loves misery, and so Pipes teams up with Ibn Warraq, a pitiful figure inviting Muslims to liberate themselves from their religion and their Lord. Earlier on, Ibn Warraq fascinated us with his ranting about why he is not a Muslim. Of course, his title came from Bertrand Russell's *Why I Am Not a Christian*, but while Russell wrote philosophy, what Ibn Warraq wrote is an inanity, and an utter intellectual bore. This time the man with the funny name collected a bunch of articles and published them under the title *The Quest for the Historical Muhammad*. One of the two introductions to the book is written by a fellow with the pathetic pseudonym Ibn Rawandi. Perhaps, our contemporary authors are alluding to the friendship between the historical Ibn Rawandi (d. 298/910) and al-Warraq (d. 247/861), both from the third Islamic century. The Manicheism and heresy of the historical figures is debated, but compared to the originals, our modern authors are unfortunate mutations and intellectual trolls. Perhaps, our two authors could not imagine that a Muslim writer could be named anything except the "Ibn" or "Abu" of something and thought the pseudonyms sounded really cool. Perhaps, our authors simply sought to hide behind their bigotry and sought to create with their pseudonyms their own mysterious lore.

Pseudonyms betray the lack of conviction and the cowardliness of their adopters. In any case, the issue is not the facetious name holders; the issue is our ostentatious long-time friend Daniel Pipes. Pipes, like his jovial friends, contends that Arabic sources on Islam are inherently unreliable, and so what we think we know about Islam is not what we should know. Pipes claims that Arabic sources were written a century and a half after the Prophet's death. Furthermore, non-Muslim sources dramatically contradict the standard Muslim biography of the Prophet Muhammad, and when a Muslim and a non-Muslim speak, of course, we all know whom we should believe. Pipes applauds the efforts of revisionist historians such as John Wansbrough, Yehuda Nevo, Judith Koren, and Patricia Crone. According to Pipes, historical revisionism challenges the idea that Muhammad preached in Mecca, that Arabic was the language of early Arabia, that Arabic was the language of early Muslims, that there were ever such people as the early Muslims, that the Prophet was born in 570 or, for that matter, that Muhammad existed at all. The Qur'an was not the product of the Prophet or even Arabia, but is nothing more than liturgical material stolen from the Judeo-Christian tradition, stitched together at a late point. Islamic history, as found in Muslim sources, is no more than a pious lie, a salvation history, by a rootless people, a soul-less people trying to invent a unique identity of their own.

Discharging the White Man's Burden, Pipes, may God bless his merciful soul, advises Muslims that revisionism is a school that they can no longer afford to ignore. According to Pipes, revisionism is a toothache, and those poor pious Muslims, immersed in their delusions and superstition, think that the toothache will disappear on its own. But Pipes, like my kind mother who taught me oral hygiene and the importance of a daily shower, teaches Muslims that toothaches don't just go away. Toothaches, you silly willy-nilly Muslims, need doctors, need rationalists, need Pipes because, darn it, they just don't go away on their own! Thank God for Pipes, who like his colonial predecessors, guides us to the truth of history, the falsity of our piety, and the fact that the objectivism of science is the cure for our superstitious souls. Without the cant of our masters, how could we have ever figured out what to do with toothaches, headaches, or any other ache or sore?

Revisionism, like all forms of incipient or established bigotry, rests on several peculiar assumptions. Assumption number one is that Muslims invariably lie. Perhaps the genetic pool of Muslims is the culprit, or perhaps it is that Muslims are prone to conspiratorial delusions and can hardly distinguish fiction from fact. According to Pipes and his revisionists, Muslims have no qualms about inventing, lying, or cheating as long as it serves their salvation goals. The second assumption follows from the first. A non-Muslim source is inherently more reliable because non-Muslims have a notion of historical objectivism. Therefore, if, for instance, a hundred Muslim sources say one thing and one Syriac source says another, it is an open and shut case. The Syriac source is inherently more reliable because those pesky Muslims cannot help but lie. The third assumption is no less interesting. Muslim history is "salvation history" written by the self-serving, unreliable faithful. Muslims are the biased religious refugees who are persistent in their search for their ever-elusive identity. Non-Muslims, on the other hand, are fair-minded even if they have their own set of interests because, after all, non-Muslims have no need for salvation; their Lord has already salvaged their blessed souls. So, the methodology of revisionism is simple: Ignore what Muslims say about themselves or others, and believe what non-Muslims say about themselves or Muslims. The fourth assumption of revisionism is the one least confessed, but is unmistakable in methodology and conclusion. Muslims are a barbaric people; whatever good they might have produced, they must have conveniently borrowed from Judaism, Christianity, or some other more civilized source. Whatever barbarism Muslims might have produced naturally comes from the depth of their hearts and souls, but whatever beauty they may have possessed, they simply stole.

But revisionists will say, "No, you misguided emotional Muslim friend. You simply don't realize that Islamic history was composed in the context of intense partisan quarrels. Knowing how emotional Muslims can be, Muslims simply wrote their history to affirm their beliefs."

But if there was no Prophet or Qur'an or even history, what was the cause of the partisan quarrels? Well, perhaps nothing more than the well-known Arab hunger for money and wealth, or the Arabs' inability to transcend their ethnic divisions and pedantic tribal lusts. The fact that Syriac or Jewish sources had their own partisan interests and biases is immaterial, of course, because non-Muslims invariably speak the truth. Furthermore, the fact that a Greek source might be reporting on rumors or on corrupted transmissions received from Muslims themselves does not at all impeach their reliability. We can never forget; Muslims lie and non-Muslims speak the truth.

Of course, Pipes, and his funny-named friends, conveniently ignore that accounts of the Prophet's life were written in the first century after his death. While they love to claim the authoritativeness of papyri and coinage to their side, they never explain what coinage or papyri they are talking about. Are papyri or coinage reliable evidence regardless of the source? Even more, they ignore papyri written in the first century documenting traditions about the Prophet, and Umayyad and 'Abbasid coinage supporting Muslim historical accounts. They also ignore papyri documented by Sezgin and others demonstrating the existence of the Qur'an in the first century of Islam in its current form. Furthermore, they ignore that the Qur'an does not reflect the historical context of the second or third Islamic centuries, but shows an overwhelming pre-occupation with the affairs of Quraysh, Mecca, Medina, the hypocrites, and the Prophet. According to the revisionists, in the time of the 'Abbasids, in the second and third centuries, Muslims fabricated the Qur'an. But apparently, they did not find a better way to reflect their historical context than to talk about Quraysh or Mecca, concepts which the revisionists believe were invented and which, if one accepts the revisionist logic, no one understood or cared about. Not only that, but even more, those lying, cheating Muslims, instead of relying on their own poetry or mythology, they could not find something better than the Judeo-Christian liturgy. In short, such are the sad affairs of Muslims, they lie and eventually believe their own lies.

But Pipes and his friends will surely say, "Muslims don't have a history and so Muslims cannot understand history. You poor, ahistorical Muslim, here you go again with your emotions getting out of hand. Don't you realize that historical revisionism assaulted Christianity and Judaism as well? Don't you realize that both religions survived, but profoundly changed, as Islam surely will?"

"Well, of course, I thank you for assuring me that Islam will survive. But revisionism in the case of non-Muslim history is a critical skepticism as to institutional and official histories, but in the case of Islam it is outright bigotry. What school of historical revisionism has ever claimed that all Jewish, Christian, British, or French sources cannot be believed? What school of revisionism has branded an entire people as compulsive liars?"

The truth is that revisionists dealing with Islamic history are ideologues without the critical integrity of scholars. We can take one example of Pipes's methodology and ponder his style. Pipes claims that an unspecified inscription and a Greek account lead Lawrence Conrad to fix the Prophet's birth at 522 not 570. Apparently, Pipes did not bother reading Conrad's study. Conrad heavily relies on debates in Muslim sources concerning the dating of the Year of the Elephant. He also relies on debates in Muslim sources regarding whether the Prophet was born in the Year of the Elephant or on an earlier date. Conrad analyzes the claim that the Prophet received revelation at age forty, and simply points out that age forty was considered a literary *topoi* for maturity in Arabic and non-Arabic literature. Therefore, the argument that the Prophet was forty when he started his mission could possibly be a symbolic usage signifying that the Prophet had reached an age of maturity. Significantly, Conrad does not reach a conclusion about the date of the Prophet's birth. Rather, he argues that Beeston's and Kister's conclusion that the Year of the Elephant was in 522 is supported by strong evidence. He then, appropriately, emphasizes the complexity of establishing the Prophet's date of birth. This is a far cry from Pipes's misrepresentation of Conrad. But Conrad is a scholar and Pipes is an ideologue.

Many of Pipes's delusions are fed by the infamous book, *Hagarism.* Yet, very few people in the scholarly community take that book seriously. Even later works by the authors of *Hagarism* demonstrate a greater degree of fair-mindedness and scholarly integrity. If *Hagarism* was written in a fit of indulgent fantasy, the same cannot be said about works that followed in its footsteps. Much of the work of revisionism was spearheaded by scholars with a regrettable political agenda. Like vulgar forms of Orientalism, revisionists sought to de-legitimate and deconstruct the tradition of their perceived enemies. The bigotry of the Israeli scholars Koren and Nevo is evident. They contend that any Arabic source must be corroborated by a non-Arabic source, and if the two sources conflict, as a matter of course, the non-Arab is to be believed. Wellhausen and Wansbrough were biblical scholars, and their circumspect methodology with Jewish and biblical studies contrasts sharply with their speculative fancies with Islamic history.

The truth is that the fanaticism of revisionism in doubting Islamic history is the opposite side of the coin of the fanaticism of pietistic sanctifications of Islamic history. Each is an imbalance, each is extreme, and each is ugly. But the distinguishing feature of revisionism is its bigotry. Imagine if European history was written only by reliance on Muslim sources. Imagine if the Jewish history of the Second Temple was written only by reliance on Roman sources. Imagine if Christian history was written only by reliance on Jewish sources. Imagine if the history of the American Revolution was written only by reliance on British sources. Imagine if Israeli history was written only through the eyes of Palestinians. But it is impossible to write these histories in this fashion because no respectable historian would claim the inherent inaccuracy of all European, American, Jewish, Christian, and Israeli sources. What would Pipes think of revisionist historians who claim that the Exodus of Jews from Egypt is a myth, and that the First or Second Temple never existed because Jews never lived in Palestine at any point in their history? The truth is that the bigotry of revisionists is like the anti-Semitism of Holocaust-deniers who write the history of Jews by relying on the sources of their German enemies.

No, revisionism is not a toothache; it is an insolent attempt to deny a people their very identity, it is the ugliness of colonialism, and the imbalance of fear and insecurity. Revisionism is the heartache of simple bigotry.

CHAPTER 47

An Encounter With the Shaykh
(On the Delusions of the Fog)

"You lived in oblivion, and now we remove your blindfold. . ."

The Conference comes alive with the repose of sight, with the scrupulous record of our virtues and faults. The Conference embraces the resilience of memory—embraces our conscience, tucked in the folds of history. This conscience often eludes us, but the Conference is the sentinel of memory. It is not only the meticulous record of what we saw and thought, but much more—it is the promise of what we could know.

I still remember you, *Shaykh*, the calm clarity in your eyes, the protrusion of your lips between your cheeks, the wrinkles settled in the whiteness of your face, the veins in your hands, and the complicated gray beard. I remember the salty white cheese mixed with tomatoes you ate every day, and I certainly remember who, for a while, as a lesson in humility, prepared it for you. I remember the old-yellow, cheaply printed books, scattered around your half-empty stationery store. You said the deluxe Lebanese prints, with glossy white pages hurt your eyes, but when we gave you expensive editions, I remember, how you rejoiced. Forgive me, but I suspect that the Halabi editions were all you could afford. I remember your long-suffering taped-up radio of some long forgotten brand. And, the tremble of the yellow books in your blessed aged hand. They would tell you about the Azhari *Shaykhs* who received sabbaticals in Arabia, and you would say, "Sure, *insha' Allah*, when we finish educating the people of Egypt first."

I studied with you only for two summers, and read with you some texts, but the lessons you taught me have become the sentinels of my memory, and the anchor of my soul.

I always perched myself on your kind indulgence. And, on a trying day, overcome by a persistent sense of anxiety, I remember tarrying around in your 'Abbasiyya store. When all the students had departed, I fidgeted around, uttering senseless words. Prompted by your *tahmid* and announcement that the day is coming to its conclusion, I finally said, "*Shaykh*, may I say, I know that the Final Day will come, and I will see with an unfailing vision, but that is exactly what I fear. On that day, my record will be set in front of me, and I will lament all my earthly delusions. At times, when I sit in the mosque or when I sit shrouded in seclusion, I can see what's right and wrong, I can see beyond my obtuseness. But again, as I dwell in life, many times I am overcome by something like a fog—anxiety and confusion. It is not that I doubt my God. Rather, I undo what once in my heart was rectified. I overcome my sense of right and drown in torrents of irresolution."

He gazed at his hands, nodded his head and then said, "Yes, yes my friend I know the fog—I know what you are talking about, but I claim no knowledge except my trust in God. Yes, the fog—the fog could lead us blind. It is as when we hear the call of God, glimpse the way, and feel the tranquility, but soon thereafter, we are stunned by irresolution. It is the *hujub*—the clouds, the fog—my son, that confounds our insight, but who does not suffer the fog is not human. Suffering the fog is not the main problem; the main problem is when we decide to befriend the fog and walk into it hoping to stumble upon some comfort or a solution.

"Listen my son, truthful is the word of our Lord, for God has said: 'And We created human beings, and We know the enticements of their minds, for We are nearer to them than their jugular vein. They are surrounded to the left and right, guarded by the angelic souls. Not a word can they utter without the unyielding overseer recording their every word. And, the stupor of death comes with the truth before their eyes. Now, this is what you sought to avoid. And, the Trumpet will be blown; this is the day promised by your Lord. Driven and witnessed, there will come forth every soul. You lived in oblivion, but now we remove your blindfold. Today, your eyesight is impeccable, and your exacting record will be brought' (50:16–23).

"God's record is the divine truth—the truth without our explanations, justifications, obtrusions, or delusions. The truth of words and deeds in their pure, unmediated form. God's truth is without a fog.

"In the *hujub* of arrogance, in the *hujub* of ignorance, in the *hujub* of occlusion lurk the ghosts of our fears and the demons of our confusion. The ghosts and demons dance and taunt, and entice us to follow the shades of the dark. Anxiety overcomes us and so we pause. But we are seduced by the promise of insight and comfort, and so wishfully we walk. Soon, in the misery of the darkness, the ghosts and demons laugh and pounce, and ride us until we can't tell our footsteps and their footsteps apart. We stumble, and walk, and fall for we have become the dwellers of the fog.

"To suffer the fog is human, but the person with *taqwa*, with the precaution of piety, will immediately pause and steady his feet in the way of God. The wise person will arm himself with patience until the fog dissipates with the light of God. Only then will you reclaim your repose and once again you can walk."

"But *Shaykh*," I said, "please elaborate. What is the nature of this fog? How do I know when I am in it? And, how do I know if I am traveling in the light of God?"

"My son, let me ask you, have you ever felt a compelling urge to rise and pray? Have you ever felt the desire to study the Book? Have you ever been ashamed because you simply felt insensate? Have you ever felt embarrassed by your ingratitude toward God? Have you ever sensed your ignorance and told yourself, 'I must make a better use of my life?' Have you ever felt you don't give enough, or that you don't study enough, or that you don't supplicate enough? Have you been asked to do something or enticed to do something and you immediately felt, 'That's not right?' Have you ever, in an instant, felt a deep longing for God?"

"Of course *Shaykh*, I felt all of these things at some time."

"My son, these moments of lucidity, these moments of clarity are gifts from God. They are glimpses of the straight path—of the truth of God, if seen, seized, and developed they become the gateways to the possibility of a transparent life—the transparency of purity and insight, of a life lived in the full view of a probing conscience, and in the full view of the light of God. But my son, the moments are rarely seized, and often we waste the gift of God. We experience these moments, but we hesitate. We experience these moments, but then listen to the voice saying: 'Perhaps what you thought is justice, really is not all that just, perhaps what you sensed is wrong, really is not all that wrong. Perhaps what you felt in your heart is undignified, really is not all that bad. Perhaps what you sensed is ugly, really is not all that ugly.' The voice asks you to doubt the call of your conscience, and, my son, that is the fog—that is the anxious confusion. Now, a wise person does not feel the storm and set sail anyway—a wise person does not walk in confusion. As I said, it is normal to suffer the assaults, and to combat the confusion. But the wise person pauses, anchors himself, and prays until the *hujub* give way. Know that the *hujub* will break, and there will be another opportunity to step through the Divine gateway. The problem, my son, is that the more we stroll in the *hujub*, the more we are lost, and the more we inhabit the fog, the more we stray."

To this very day I don't know why upon hearing this my eyes swelled with tears. I felt both burdened and relieved. I was quiet for a moment as I looked at his warm smile, and thought to myself, "I would be honored to prepare your tomatoes and cheese until the end of my life."

"*Shaykh*," I said, "can we read texts on this? I feel I want to study—I feel this is my innate reaction, and perhaps this is a step through the gateway."

The *Shaykh* smiled, paused and nodded his head. "Yes," he said, "there is much to read on this. This matter has engaged some of the brightest brains."

Sensing that I was at risk of taxing the limits of politeness, I said, "*Shaykh*, I know that you must head home before *Maghrib*, but, if you allow me, I have one more question. How do I measure the extent of my self-deception, how do I know if I strayed?"

"My son," he softly said, "first you should know there is much to read on this issue, and *insha' Allah*, we will learn together. But you should also know that other than God, no one can judge the extent of the fog under which you labor. No human, other than you, can really know the clouds in your heart. So the question is: What is the disparity between your self-perception and the way God perceives you? God's record is the unadulterated truth, but your conscience and memory keeps a record too. So the issue is: What is the disparity between your knowledge of your own record and the record of truth? To the extent that there is a gap between God's irrefutable record, and your understanding of your record, will be the extent of the delusion and fog. Reflect upon yourself, and ask yourself: How do you look in the eyes of God's record? The more you reflect, the more you will know the truth. Recall that the Prophet said, 'The discomforts of this earth are nothing like the embarrassments of the Hereafter.' It is a true shame if one waits until the Final Day to ponder his confusion."

Shaykh al-Digawi is now in the company of his Lord, and I struggle to understand my *hujub* and persistent confusions. But every time I ponder the gap between my record in the hands of God and my tenacious fog, I utter a prayer for the *Shaykh*. May God bless his beautiful soul. I pray that he will find his record what I perceive it to be—a pure, untainted record without *hujub* or fog—without delusions.

CHAPTER 48

Finding the Shaykh

God is the ultimate, the consummate, the final, and the end. But the magnets of self-indulgence and arrogance hide in our moral fog and lead the compass of our soul astray. Without our inner compass, we are lost in the fog, but our merciful Lord places indicators along the way. The indicators point toward God, leading us back from where we came. The indicators become like signs on the foggy trail, consoling and warning the anxious traveler that the throne of God is where all the roads will eventually converge. The indicators are all around us, in nature, in the text, and even in people who cross our way.

God, You are my sustainer and guide in this fog—the call of my intuition and the certain fate. My heart endures in Your beauty even as my body withers and disintegrates. You are the unwavering and immutable vision in an erratic world that can hardly make a promise that it does not betray. My soul and heart cling to You even as my organs and limbs fade away. What possible use do I have for this flesh when this flesh is incapable of offering a moment of pleasure without a reciprocal moment of decay—when its gifts, wrapped in pleasure, conceal unfailing pain.

Wrapped in fog, wrapped in flesh, and in this world, we often lose our way. We aimlessly float, stumbling in our layers of wrapping and suffering the pain. We ignore the anxiety of being lost by telling ourselves it is just a phase. But the pain is God's alarm, and the clock that calls upon us to awake. When we thoroughly adapt and no longer feel any painful restraint, this is when we have settled in the fog, and this is when God's alarm fades away.

There, in that apartment in the Agouza part of Cairo, I would sit in the barren room, the walls decorated only by cracks. There was a table serving as a desk, and a dining chair with its plastic cover aging, but still intact. Directly facing the door was the bed with the metal frame and pallet of Egyptian cotton. This bed once nursed a bout of typhoid and a host of asthma attacks. Yellow books and dreams were this bed's only romance. In this room, books sat in piles on the floor, on the table, on the chair, and on the bed, while some cuddled in my hands. So many books rested there, catalogued only in my head—delegates from generations of Conferences in our past. Two windows with green wooden doors were to the left of the bed. One window looked into the neighbor's living room, and so it was screened by sentinels of books. The other window looked upon a sad building condemned by corruption to desertion and desolation. I remember when the security forces forcibly evacuated that building as the residents screamed in despair. Some yelled, "*ya Sadat, ta' ala ilha'na* (Sadat, come save us)." This was like calling the wolf to save the sheep—Sadat did not come, and the building became empty, but remained, and it probably still remains today.

I sat on my bed trying to commit to memory the full text of Bukhari. Shaykh Husayn had advised against it, but I decided to do it anyway. I don't know if I wanted to do it as supplication and worship, or if my ego coveted the pomposity and vainglory of the type that the people of *hadith* often display. The mission was never accomplished, but those were rather ostentatious and pretentious days. When the majestic call for noon prayer sounded, I closed the book and performed my ablutions. I put on the musk and made sure my white garment sparkled, for I was about to meet Shaykh Husayn.

As I walked down the four flights of stairs, I smiled to myself remembering one of the famous episodes of Shaykh Husayn. He lived on the fifth floor in an apartment building on the same street as mine. On the fourth floor, right below him, in three apartments joined as one, was an infamous place. Customers, mostly from the Gulf, came and went most of the night and day. Sometimes we would notice young college-aged women going in, but most of the girls were clearly underage. A remarkably ugly and fat madam would often stand, in her nightgown, greeting the customers in the doorway. She was well-connected, and no policeman dared cross her way. One day, after arguing with one of the drunk customers as he stood in front of the apartments in his underwear, some friends had had enough, and ten of them went to demand that the brothel be removed to some other place. A fight ensued, and the friends invaded the brothel, and beat and smashed everything that crossed their way. Of course, the police reciprocated their kindness after they dragged them away. Upon hearing of this heroism, Shaykh Husayn was simply enraged. Violence is easy, he said, but often what is easy is also wrong. Instead of this, why don't you stand close by and invite every customer who enters that God-forsaken place to the mosque to pray? Did you offer the women relief or protection instead of this bombastic display? The *Shaykh,* with remarkable vigilance, led his students in a frenzied campaign. Three of the women became guests of the mosque, and the brothel did eventually relocate. May Allah bless the compassionate and loving soul of Shaykh Husayn.

After prayer, I sat beside him waiting, but I did not wish to rush him, so I avoided looking at his face and stared at my lap instead. I had been attending the *Shaykh's halaqa*, but I only had the *Shaykh* for the summer, so I wanted to read some additional text. He had asked me to think of possibilities, and I relished his company, and so there I sat. The *Shaykh* was often quiet, and seemed to enjoy the company of his own mind. When he spoke, it was as if his words drizzled, but before long, his words would develop into a tempestuous storm.

The *Shaykh* eventually looked my way, and said, "So, have you chosen your text?"

"A book of *ahkam* (positive law)—*Shaykh*, a book of *ahkam*, I think." After a short pause, I feared what he might suspect, so I added, "I want to study all of *Shari'a* so perhaps *al-Hidaya* by al-Marghinani or as much of *al-Muhalla* by Ibn Hazm as you see fit."

He smiled as if possessing a secret, "You want to study *Shari'a*," he repeated, but then asked, "but what is *Shari'a*?"

I was puzzled by the question, fearing that this was the beginning of a test. "*Shaykh*," I said, "*Shari'a* is the way to God—the truth of the Divine Will."

"Yes, yes," he exclaimed, "but what is its nature? What is the vision?"

Puzzled, again I commented, "Well, the purpose of *Shari'a* is to achieve the welfare of the people (*tahqiq masalih al-'ibad*)."

"Yes, yes, that is what the sources state, but the nature of something is not its function. For example, I have many functions in life, but are these functions the essence of my nature? Furthermore, if I give you a pound, I have promoted your welfare, but have I necessarily brought out the essence of *Shari'a*?"

I must have looked confused because he looked at me with anticipation, but then continued, "If we are confused about something, we start with the book of God. So, how many times does God use the word or a variant of the word *Shari'a*?"

I felt my mouth dry up, and the eczema on my fingers become irritated by my sweat, "Four times, *Shaykh*—twice as nouns and twice as verbs?"

"Yes, that is correct, and how does God use the word?"

I struggled with my memory, but finally responded, "I believe God uses the word to indicate something like a blessing and gift—like a right way—the source of goodness." I stopped, but then thought that I might as well throw everything in, so I added, "And, the linguists say *Shari'a* means a water spring."

The *Shaykh* smiled, "You want to study the *ahkam*—the positive laws, the legal enactments, the rules that tell you, do this or don't do that—but are the *ahkam* the extent of God's gift?"

I felt that whatever comment I made would lack the necessary depth. But I also knew that Shaykh Husayn had once said that the issue is always the right question.

As to the right answer, only God knows best. I paused again, and thought to myself, "At least I am not the one posing the questions." I gathered my strength and offered, "Well, the law is most certainly God's gift. It is what guides us to God's pleasure."

"Most certainly, yes, but that is not what I asked. Let me ask you this, Is it possible for someone to follow the law, but not gain God's pleasure?"

"Yes," I responded, "the person could be insincere or imbalanced or sacrifice a major law for a minor law."

"Okay, good, but then we ask, is it possible for someone to ignore the law and gain God's pleasure?"

"No," I said, "to ignore the law is offensive. It is as if saying to God, I don't care about Your will."

"Okay, and so we ask, is it possible for two people to disagree about the law, while each practices what he believes to be correct, and yet, for their disagreements and respective practices to be blessed?"

"Yes," I said, "And, each will gain God's pleasure if they are diligent and sincere."

"Okay, so we must ask, what is the basis for that?"

Once again, I did not see it, and so I simply stated, "*Shaykh*, I don't understand."

"Khaled, before we get to the law, what do we consider first? What do we engage before we can say we know the law?"

"*Shaykh*," I said, "I believe it is the *dalil* or *dala'il*, the indicators and pointers to God's Will. The evidence that creates a reasonable belief that God wants such or such—the signs that flag the Divine Will."

"All right my son, so far so good. What if a person honestly and sincerely follows the *dalil* and does not reach the law?"

"Their effort is blessed," I said, "and God is pleased."

"All right, what if a person whimsically or blindly follows the law, but cares little for the evidence or *dalil*?"

"I don't believe that blind imitation is blessed." I responded, "There must at least be a reasonable basis for believing that the law is, in fact, what it is. To just follow the law without some evidence seems to be whimsical, ignorant, and arrogant."

"So then, if you live a life consumed by the search for the Divine Will, are you living your life in the light of *Shari'a*?"

"It seems to me to be so," I answered.

"What if you live a life adhering to the laws? Is that, by itself, sufficient for you to say you lived your life pursuant to *Shari'a*?"

I was confused because I could not locate the direction of the argument. But I knew that the *Shaykh* did not speak in vain, so I was silent. The *Shaykh* looked intently at me as I rubbed my eczema-plagued fingers.

Sensing my hesitation, he said, "*Shari'a*, my son, is not just the *ahkam* or positive commands, *Shari'a* is a way of life. It is the full process of the law—the positive command is simply the by-product of the process. *Shari'a* is the way with its signs and posts, with its evidence and indicators, and with its purposes and ends. The positive commands are like the rules of the road, and the rules are part of the Divine way, but the rules, by themselves, are not the way. The positive laws, the *ahkam*, are the bare minimum for staying on the road; they set the outer limits. But it is possible to follow all the rules and still lose your way. The law does not define justice, it simply sets some of the outer-limits of justice. The law does not define morality, it sets some of the outer limits of morality. And the law does not define beauty, it sets some of the outer limits of beauty. Hence, it is possible to follow the outer limits and still be unjust, immoral, and ugly. On the other hand, if you have no regard, even for the outer limits, then you are not just, moral, or beautiful."

"Shaykh Husayn," I asked, "are you saying I should study beauty and morality in addition to the law, or are you saying that I should study the process of the law?"

Shaykh Husayn smiled at my impatience for the bottom line. "Khaled, my son, I am saying this is the age of *ahkam*. Every one of your brothers and sisters is interested only in positive commands, but very few are interested in the process of searching for God and God's Will."

I felt that I was disappointing him and so I defensively said, "*Shaykh*, you mean *usul* (jurisprudence)? I have taken *halaqas* with. . ."

"I know, I know," he cut in, "but I want you to know that the *adilla* [indicators] are like the words of a language, and the *usul* is its grammar. The *ahkam* are like the full sentences of a language. If you memorize full sentences but do not comprehend the grammar, you will not be able to use a language. The reality is that you simply don't know a language if you memorize the sentences and ignore the vocabulary and grammar.

"I will put it to you in a different way. The *ahkam* are like the medicine and the *usul* its doctor. How could you study the medicine but have no idea how or when to apply it? Could you memorize the types of medicines but ignore the art of prognosis or diagnosis? Importantly, medicine and doctors cannot be equated with a state of good health. You could follow the advice of doctors and take their prescribed medicines, but still be in poor health. To be in good health, you will need to do more than see doctors and take medicines. You need to eat right, exercise, rest, and perhaps do other things as well.

"Now, we have to remember that the outer limits of goodness—or the *ahkam*—have an intricate system of proof, cause, and purpose. You cannot claim to know the law if you do not understand the proof, and cause, and purpose of the law. And, you cannot equate the law to the full and total Divine way; the law is but the boundaries of that way.

"My son, what I am saying is, we must live a life of total service to God. But we should not serve the law just with our bodies and will, but serve the law with our conscience and intellect as well. Compliance requires the submission of the body, but the process demands the engagement of the intellect. However, the engagement of the body and intellect should not mislead you into thinking that the conscience can now rest. The mind can navigate the road, and the body can walk the road, but it is the conscience, my son, that can tell you if the Divine Will has been fulfilled."

I realized that the *Shaykh* was not talking to me, but talking to the generations to come, and so I rested in his company, and listened. I did not fully absorb his meaning, but I did not wish to waste these precious moments with my senseless prattle, and so I held my tongue, and alerted my memory to imprint the words onto my mind. We parted after *'Asr* prayer, for the *Shaykh* had to rest. For the weeks to come, we met every day after *fajr*, and I read with the *Shaykh* texts on *usul*. At a month's end, we barely got beyond *husn* and *qubh* (ugliness and beauty) in the first chapters of *usul al-fiqh*. Yet, I struggled to keep up with his pace. My mind suffered and doubted itself at length, and I confess, I enjoyed a certain wrongful satisfaction when several students joined us and suffered as well.

When Shaykh Husayn passed away, I was already in the States. I missed him terribly, but by then I was struggling to absorb what my memory retained. There is no doubt that at many points in life I lost my indicators, and lost Shaykh Husayn. I struggled to learn that law is an investigation, a discourse, and a process that leads to a rule (*hukm*). I struggled to learn that the rule is the very last step, and perhaps the least important step, in a beautiful search that should never end. I struggled to understand the despotism of rules and the beauty of the process. I strove to understand that, when our conscience wanes, the rule begins where beauty ends. But it is when I understood that in this age we had come to rely on the law to give piety its beauty when, in truth, it is piety that makes the law beautiful, and when I understood that the law cannot find piety, but piety can find the law, and when I understood that the way of God is illuminated by beauty, and not just law, then I realized that the *Shaykh* was my indicator, and I finally found the *Shaykh*.

The Book of Suspended Judgment

Tonight, as I concluded my teaching and prepared to surrender to the investigations of the Conference, I was reminded of my long-forgotten notebook. At times, teaching the *Sira* of the Prophet and reaching the intended goal of the lecture is like walking a minefield. My sparkling students interject with investigations and queries and I am humbled before their zeal for learning. The *Sira* of the Prophet is like the garden of a lover—you can pick its flowers and inhale the magnanimous fragrance, but you must be willing to suffer the thorns prickling your intellect. God has decreed a law that pervades throughout this universe: you can uncover the secrets of beauty, love, and knowledge, but the cost is fortitude, suffering, and patience. "[God] will cause you to suffer so that God will know those who [are willing] to struggle and know the patient" (47:31). But ultimately, the promise of God is, "and bring good tidings to the patient" (2:155). Patience is the demonstrative and definitive proof of non-entitlement and the lack of arrogance, and so, in every time and age, those who are blessed are those who persevere for the sake of the truth, and remind themselves, and others, of the virtue of patience and constancy (103:3).

My students flood me with queries and questions and I am reminded of the by-gone days of my *Shaykhs*. I witness their impatience for conclusions and I recall my suffering green notebook. In those blessed days, I used to keep a notebook with a white tag, and on the tag was scribbled, "The Book of Suspended Judgment (*Kitab al-Irja'*)." At one time, it used to be called "The Book of Ignorance (*Kitab al-Jahl*)," but I soon changed the title after pondering the impossibility of documenting the vastness of my oblivion. Once upon a time, this notebook was my inseparable and trusted companion, for it guarded all the secrets of my heart and listened to all the puzzlements of my mind.

The "Book of Suspended Judgment" was the repository of my doubts and the anesthetic applied to my adolescent impatience. In those days, the pursuit of knowledge was like a racecourse, but I could not run without stumbling over its obstacles. If I thought I had mastered an item of knowledge, I would hold it tightly within the embrace of my mind. I would revisit all the details time and again to make sure that all the pieces were in place and intact. But before too long, a teacher, a book, or even a single overlooked thought would reveal the insignificance of what I believed I knew, and the whole edifice of security would come apart.

In those blessed days, among other subjects, I was studying the *Sira* of the Prophet and the complexity of the data was perplexing. How do you construct the life of such a grand and beautiful person when the reports are often conflicting? How do you recall all the variant reports concerning the same incident? How do you learn who transmitted what from whom, and what were the characteristics of each transmitter? What were the merits and faults of each single source who documented the life of the Prophet and the life of his Companions? How do you differentiate and distinguish what was real from the fanciful projections? In the midst of the imperative need for diligence and authentication, how do you keep the essence of the Prophet's beauty in balanced perspective?

I traversed the roads of knowledge and settled myself in the mosque, and settled myself with the books and *Shaykhs*. We prayed *Zuhr* in the mosque, and then I approached Shaykh 'Id. I told him I would be grateful if we could speak, and my heart danced when he invited me to his home. With a smile, he said, "You have not been to my home yet, and I believe this is contrary to all the *sunan* and laws." I had constructed the home of this blessed man in my mind many times, and wondered what books adorned his shelves, but I never dreamt I would be granted the honor of a visit. As we walked to his home, I asked about his health and heart condition, and he turned the topic around to inquire about my annoying allergies. His home was a garden of books—the garden sprawled upon the floors and the furniture, and I chuckled when I saw that the books had ejected his robes from the closet to the kitchen. I offered to organize the books for him in the summer, but he smiled and said, "Why? Has God given you the power to perform miracles?"

The *Shaykh* insisted that we speak over a meal saying, "My *ful* is world famous, but I am a talent waiting to be discovered." The *Shaykh's* wife said, "Yes, he does a wonderful job opening the can and pouring the contents onto a plate. I tell him '*ya Shaykh* add tomatoes and cheese,' and he says, 'Why compromise the *ful's* integrity?'"

The *Shaykh's* wife asked about my mother and father and sister and brother, and entrusted me to give them her *salams*. Seeing her concern, I wondered if she had ever met them, but she only said, "*inta ibn nas tayyibin* (you are the son of kind people). I am ashamed to admit that I do not remember the *Shaykh's* wife's name.

When the food was served, Shaykh 'Id did not ask what was preoccupying me. As we ate, he only spoke of what was of interest to his wife, and I did not fail to notice this beautiful gesture of Islamic beauty. When she brought out the tea, Shaykh 'Id said, "Khaled wants to discuss his studies," and I hastened to add, "I am just confused about issues related to methodology." She smiled as she poured the tea, and surprised me with a statement that has plagued my heart ever since, "*minkum nastafid ya shuyukh* (perhaps, we can learn from you O' *Shaykhs*)." This was the first time anyone had called me a *Shaykh*, and I hardly qualified as a religious scholar.

Without delay, I confessed, "It is just that I am studying the life of the Prophet and the Companions, and I often struggle with what I learn. I read reports that are contradicted by other reports; I read reports of incidents that seem implausible, or I read that the Prophet proclaimed a sweeping general law about something but only one or two people seem to have heard it. I read sources that say such and such transmitters of *hadith* were reliable and others that contradict this assessment. I guess the issue I am struggling with is one of credibility—how do I know when I am dealing with something that truly describes the Prophet, and when am I dealing with a reporter or transmitter who is projecting his or her weaknesses upon the Prophet? I guess all of this has created suspicions (*wiswas*) in my heart."

The *Shaykh's* wife surprised me when she proclaimed, "*Tilka mahd al-iman* (this is the true nature of faith, or such is the real faith)."

I looked confused, but Shaykh 'Id smiled and explained, "Umm . . . is referring to the *hadith* reported in Muslim from 'Abdullah Ibn Mas'ud (d. 32/652) that the Prophet was asked about *waswasa* (doubt and suspicion), and the Prophet said, *Tilka mahd al-iman* (this is the true nature of faith). It was also reported by Abu Hurayra (d. 58/678) that some people came to the Prophet and explained that sometimes they are gripped by doubts—the kinds of doubts that they are ashamed to confess in public. The Prophet is reported to have said, '*Dhaka sarih al-iman* (this is the nature of sound faith).' There is disagreement among the scholars about what this really means."

The *Shaykh* paused, and perhaps I cut in too soon, "But *Shaykh*, you see? This is exactly what I mean. The first report may indicate that doubt is healthy and good. The second report may indicate that not confessing the doubt in public is what is healthy and good. Or, perhaps, it is good to have doubts, but not good to confess them in public? Does it make a difference that Ibn Mas'ud was an early convert to Islam and a very close Companion, while Abu Hurayra was a very late convert to Islam and was in the company of the Prophet only for four years? How do I evaluate all of this? This is the nature of my confusion."

The *Shaykh* smiled again and said, "May Allah bless you, Khaled; this is exactly why I have high hopes for you. You found the question, and that is what is important. You will have a lifetime to seek the answer. Whether the second report means that it is good not to confess your doubts in public, or whether it means that it is healthy to have doubts, turns on a point of grammar. Of course, the identity of the transmitters and their closeness to the Prophet is relevant. But, resolve these problems at your own pace—why grow before your time?"

"But *Shaykh*," I protested, "When I read about the *Satanic Verses*, for instance. . ."

The *Shaykh's* wife cut in, "*The Satanic Verses*? This whole event is utter nonsense. It never happened!"

Shaykh 'Id laughed, "You see? My wife resolved this matter for herself. Ibn Taymiyya, on the other hand, believed in the authenticity of the event, and even believed it proved the divinity of the Prophet's message."

Shaykh 'Id laughed again when his wife curled her lips in disapproval and proclaimed, "Nonsense, Ibn Taymiyya was wrong!"

"Yes," Shaykh 'Id exclaimed, "my wife never forgave Ibn Taymiyya for this!"

"But *Shaykh*," I continued, "I read the conflicting reports about the Prophet's relationship with his wife Mariyah the Copt (d. 16/637), or the conflicting reports about the circumstances of his marriage to Zaynab Bint Jahsh (d. 20/641) after Zayd Ibn Haritha (d. 8/629), his adopted son, divorced her. I also read the offensive reports about the incident of 'Urayna, and I study the conflicting reports about the Prophet's relationship with Sawdah, his first wife after Khadijah (d. 3 years before *hijra*/619). I read reports that the Prophet never struck, cursed, or insulted anyone, and then I find these reports that claim he permitted men to beat their wives, or something equally immoral."

The *Shaykh's* wife did not share my confusion about these incidents because she quickly interjected, "There are a million reports that the Prophet never struck or insulted anyone, and any self-respecting Muslim woman would not stay a single day with her husband if he dared strike her! So what is the confusion! Do we go fishing in a swamp and then complain about the mud?"

I worried that I was offending her. Embarrassed, I smiled, but the *Shaykh* came to my aid. "Umm. . ., Khaled is just talking about the conflicting evidence. He is not fishing in the swamp, he is worrying about how to avoid the swamp in the first place."

My heart alighted when she smiled and agreed, "Yes, to avoid the swamp, you must first come to know it."

The *Shaykh* turned to me and continued, "Khaled, the Prophet is reported to have said that after his death, there will be many reports about him, and many of these reports will be pure inventions. The Prophet instructed that we must examine these reports in light of the Qur'an. In the Qur'an, God describes the Prophet as a man of great character (68:4). God also says that the Prophet was sent as an agent of mercy and compassion to humanity (21:107), and teaches us that the Prophet was not a man of harsh or gruff character (3:159). Furthermore, God tells us that the Prophet was a caring, compassionate, and merciful person (9:128). A Muslim would know these descriptions to be truthful, and our knowledge as to their veracity reaches the point of certainty *(bi'l qat')*. A Muslim would know these descriptions to be truthful because they are directly from God. We also look in the traditions of the *Sunna* and we find cumulative reports that confirm the Qur'an's assessment of the Prophet's character. Anas Ibn Malik (d. 93/711), his close Companion, tells us that he never insulted or hurt anyone. 'Aisha (d. 58/678), his wife, tells us that he was constantly in his family's service. 'Ali and Ibn al-'Abbas, the close Companions, tell us that he was a gentle soul—loving with children, compassionate, generous, and sensitive with adults. He did not like to criticize or embarrass people. He was the most forgiving and patient person, with a smile adorning his face. Now, in the midst of these numerous and cumulative reports that describe a beautiful human being, we suddenly find an odd report. This odd report says something about him that is inconsistent with our understanding of his general demeanor, so what do we do?"

I did not notice that I threw the question back at him when I asked, "*Shaykh,* what do we do?"

He paused, examining my face, and then inquired, "Khaled, are these problematic reports sufficient to trouble your heart? You love someone because you hear from the most reliable authorities that this person is a wonderful human being, but then you encounter someone of lesser reliability who tells you a troubling story. What do you do?"

"I dismiss it," I exclaimed with a certain degree of immaturity.

"No," Shaykh 'Id said, "We do not dismiss it. A problematic report should not be sufficient to trouble us, but it should give us a serious pause. We might not have the proper perspective on it. What we do instead is that we suspend judgment."

"Suspend judgment?" I muttered, as if to myself.

"Yes, the report might be unreliable, it might be an outright lie, or it might be a fabrication by a misguided friend or vengeful enemy. Different people reported different things from or about the Prophet. Some people reported what they heard or saw, some people reported what they thought they heard and saw, and some people projected their own identities and morality upon what they heard or saw. Other people simply invented and fabricated stories, and some people did not fabricate, but their reports were corrupted and exaggerated by later generations of transmitters. At this point in your life, you do not know—you do not know because you are not equipped to make that judgment. So what do you do? You stay with what you do know. As a Muslim, you know that he was a beautiful man, and you know that because God told you so and you also know because everyone who was close to the Prophet concurred. As to variations and disputations and other types of problems, you remember them, but suspend your judgment. As your knowledge increases, you revisit them, and scrutinize them with your intellect."

"But *Shaykh,*" I interrupted, "when will I know? When will I be able to know?"

"Son," he said, "with diligence and knowledge, you will have the tools. If you persevere and study, you will reach the point in time when you can give knowledge its due. Some reports you will discard as unreliable, with other reports, you will discover their peculiar circumstance, and with yet other reports, you will die before being able to reach a judgment, and you will leave the matter to your students to continue the journey."

"*Shaykh*," I said in a solemn voice, "you know I do not agree with that sect in Islam known as the Murji'a."

"Khaled, this is an entirely different matter. The Murji'a is a sect that believed that, on some matters, you adopt a neutral position and leave it up to God to solve the problem on the Final Day. The Murji'a did not aspire or attempt to resolve the troubling issues—they simply ignored them. I am not telling you to ignore anything. What I am saying is that you suspend judgment about what you do not know, but you work hard to equip yourself with the tools that would enable you to know."

The *Shaykh's* wife had remained silent for a while, but she was listening attentively. She stood up and picked up the empty glasses of tea as she said, "You men do what you want. My tool is my heart—I feel the Prophet in my bones. When I read something, I know if I am in the company of the Prophet or some devil."

The *Shaykh* smiled and touched her hand while proclaiming, "May Allah bless you Umm. . . If all of us had a heart like yours, we would not have a problem. But when the heart wanes, the intellect must come to its aid."

She smiled as she prepared to leave the room and said, "*Ya* Shaykh 'Id, when the intellect wanes, the heart must come to its aid."

I knew that both of them were right. Both the heart and the intellect needed to be developed and strengthened, and both the heart and intellect needed to become allies. I also knew that both my heart and intellect were not sufficiently developed or strong. So I went home and picked up a green notebook, and called it the "Book of Ignorance." I would diligently write in it all the things I wanted to know but could not know. In two days, I was writing too frequently and so I changed the title to "The Book of Suspended Judgment." I recorded every report or thought or piece of information I puzzled over but did not feel equipped to properly evaluate. I resolved in my mind and heart to return to all the listed issues and scrutinize them as the *Shaykh* had said. Over the years, I found that I would go to the notebook and scratch off an item as resolved, only to come back to rewrite it in again in the following week. That poor notebook had become plagued by pencil and ink marks on nearly every page. Eventually, I learned that to suspend judgment about what you do not know is the earmark of patience, and that patience is the earmark of piety and humility. Now, I write my judgments in my mind, and suspend judgment in my heart, or perhaps I write my judgments in my heart and suspend them in my mind. It did not matter, and does not matter, as long as my heart and intellect are balanced and allied, I aid one with the other, and I live in a state of equanimity. I patiently endure the thorns, but I invariably enjoy the flowers.

CHAPTER 50

Dreaming of the Prophet

Prophet of God, Muhammad, may peace and blessings be upon you. Peace and blessings from the heart of this pitiful delinquent, and if you turn me away, I have no grounds to complain. I know that I am a man who is frivolous, malevolent, and trivial; I deem myself entirely contemptible. So if you ignore me, I understand; in fact, perhaps that is exactly what you should do. Yet, you never turned a single soul away especially when this soul, with your love, is entirely at peace. Truly, God and God's angels extol their blessings upon you. "O ye who believe, invoke blessings upon him, and give him greetings of peace" (33:56).

The visions and dreams ravage this sorry mind with images of what was, but to me, they are the only truth that remains worthwhile. I see the images in my wake and sleep, I see them in the Conference and in the books I read. I see them in every instant of the struggle of life. I see them in embarrassment, I see them, and I am invigorated despite my shame.

I see you in your last illness ravaged by the unrelenting fever, and your beloved standing frozen at your feet. I see you dipping your hand in water and wiping your blessed face. It is as if I can hear the rupturing of the breaking hearts and the very echo of the falling tears. I can feel the agony of the earth, and the embarrassments of nature at the illness overcoming your body, and I even feel their embarrassment at the searing heat. But the earth and nature confess their servility to God and their inability to waver before God's decree. I can see it, and I see you overcoming your pain to rise and confront the burdens of fate. You face your people and say, "Whoever has erred and fears his fate, let him come forward so that I may pray for him." Among those who rise is a man who tells you, "I am a liar and a hypocrite and there is no sin that I did not commit." 'Umar Ibn al-Khattab, may God bless his soul, looks at the remorseful fellow and in pity exclaims, "My fellow, you have embarrassed and shamed yourself." But you, and blessed be you, you say, "'Umar, the embarrassments of the Hereafter are worse than the embarrassments of this earth. Allah, give [this fellow] truthfulness, and faith and lead him to the good."

In embarrassment, I confess my love, and, yet, my longing draws me near. I should absorb my shame in silence, but I feel that I will combust if I do not speak. What I want is impossible and even preposterous, but since childhood this has been my singular dream. I want the laws of nature to break, I want history to revert, and I want to spend a single day in your company. I want to hug your hand, kiss your head, feel your heart, and implore you to pray for me. I want to study your movements, your gestures, the blink of your eye, and memorize your every step. I want to imbue every cell in my brain and every nerve in my body with a sense of your balance and dignity. I want to mend my heart by fully absorbing your beauty, and then rebuild my faith in humanity. Yet, I know that if the earth and nature could not pause to grant you relief, history will not revert, and I will have to go on living in my visions and dreams.

In the mind of my dreams, I can see Thawban (d. 54/674), your charge and friend, his face darkened with dismay. You noticed, and thus you asked, "Thawban, what disturbs you?" Thawban gave the answer that lives in my heart, "Prophet, I am not ill or in pain. It is just that when I am not with you, I miss you terribly until I see you. Then, when you mention the Hereafter, I fear that I will no longer see you because you will be in the highest levels of heaven, and if I enter heaven, I fear I will be at a lower rung. But if I do not enter heaven, I will not see you at all. "My Prophet, Thawban deserved a revelation (4:69), but I—what do I deserve when I see you with the eye of my mind, and the love of my heart? I console myself, for in Bukhari it is reported that you said, "A person [in the Hereafter] will be with whom he loves." But what possible claim do I have when I am such an insignificant newcomer at the tail of so many great others?

I confess my love to you, my Prophet, but my love is not a eulogy of enchantment and idolization. It is the love of the assiduous engagement; the love of conviction, of reflection, of study and examination. I want to study your trials and tribulations, your strength, your power and patience, your intricate balance, and unfathomable beauty.

You are but a human—a beautiful human—and a blessed example for all the nations. I see no merit in the love of selfishness and simple sensations. I see no merit in the love that is simply a form of indulgent self-affirmation. I want to absorb your example, transform myself, and learn the road to our salvation. I want to explore the meaning, the subtleties, the implications, and permutations. If I study your *hadith*

154

and *Sunna*, I find but a complex mixture of data. It is the heart and mind that places this matrix of data on a bed of beauty. It is the heart and mind that weaves its morality. It is my vigilant heart and probing mind that engage you in my dreams, and guide my sensations.

I see you after your migration with your camel leading the way. It picks the spot where the mosque in Medina is destined to be. But the land belongs to two young men, and they insist that the land is a gift. But you insist on paying them just and full compensation.

You did not take the rights of people for granted; you did not pretend that the ends justify the means. You treated your people with dignity, and with dignity they learned to live free of fear.

After the hardship and homesickness of migration came the affliction of disease. Both Abu Bakr al-Siddiq (d. 22/634) and Bilal Ibn Rabah (d. 17–21/638–642) fell ill with malaria, and when ʿAisha (d. 58/678) would nurse them they would lament their homesickness in poetry. I see you praying that God would replace the hardships with ease. I see you imploring God that Medina would become the land of the free. It came true my Prophet, but today, we continue our migrations chased by our fears. Our loss of dignity has become an unrelenting moral disease.

I see you, my Prophet, your gaze to the ground is longer than the sky, ever reflecting, adorned by humility. I see you in your dignity. If a newcomer arrives, you move quickly to give them a seat. I see you quick to smile, quick to greet, neither harsh nor offensive, rarely angry. If you did become angry, you simply turn your face away in silence. I see you generous with praise, never castigating or disparaging, averse to conflict, and averse to comfort—always rising to the challenges of history.

I see you in the day of Badr with ʿAli and Abu Lubaba by your side alternating the ride on one camel on the way to battle. ʿAli and Abu Lubaba offer you their turn on the camel, and you exclaim, "You are not more capable of walking than I, and I need God's blessings no less than you."

At the end of the battle, in the midst of your happiness at God's victory, you learn that your beloved daughter Ruqayya (d. 2/624) died, succumbing to disease. And so, victory mingles with calamity, and the blessings and tests of God never cease. So many tests and so many blessings, and I reflect upon your remarkable balance. After the Battle of Khaybar and during the ecstasy with God's victory, your daughter Zaynab (d. 7/628) takes her last breath as you sit close by. You comfort your son-in-law and now motherless granddaughter, and bury your daughter with your own hands. After the expedition of Tabuk, you returned home to find that Umm Kulthum (d. 9/630), your daughter, had died. You console her husband, bury her, and dry your tears. Truly, the tests of God never cease. Then, honored with the Lord's victories and the approach of the Farewell Pilgrimage, a calamity befalls your son Ibrahim (d. 10/632). He falls ill and takes his last breath at your side. He was a vivacious and lively child; your arms embraced him with the delight of love, but now you hold his lifeless body, as your love bleeds in tears. When the sun eclipsed, the mourners said it eclipsed in bereavement, but you stood up and said, "The sun and moon are the signs of God. They do not eclipse for the death of any human being." Earlier during the life of your beloved wife Khadijah Bint Khuwaylid (d. 3 years before *hijra*/619), you witnessed death taking your baby boys al-Qasim and 'Abdullah from her arms. My Prophet, you know that people witness the death of a single child and their sense of balance forever dissipates. I beg of you, teach me your sense of balance in confronting the trials of my fate.

In Uhud, I see you proceed to battle outnumbered by your enemies. At the approach of battle, 'Abdullah Ibn Ubayy Ibn Salul (d. 9/631) withdraws with one-third of the Muslim army and leaves you and the believers to your fates. Despite the defeat in Uhud, you seek no slaughter or vengeance against Ibn Ubayy and his army of cowards. 'Umar offers to kill the traitor, and you declare Muhammad does not kill his people. 'Abdullah Ibn 'Abdullah, Ibn Ubayy's son, offers to kill his father for his persistent sedition, and you, my Prophet, state, "No, we will have mercy, and treat him kindly as long as he remains with us." And, when Ibn Ubayy dies after the Battle of Tabuk, you stand and pray at his grave. In a tradition, 'Umar protests the bestowal, upon this long-time hypocrite, of such a grace. You look at 'Umar, smile, and say, "'Umar, pray behind me for I have the choice, and I chose to pray."

When Hatib Ibn Balta'a betrayed you by sending a message to Mecca informing them of your preparations against them, you hold the message in your hand and say, "What is this, Hatib?" His response is as shameful as his actions, but you accept it with forgiveness and remarkable grace. When Mecca is defeated, you grant all an unqualified amnesty, but Fadallah Ibn 'Umayr conspires to have you killed. Fadallah approaches you, looking for his opportunity to plunge his knife in your chest, but you meet him with calm and a smiling face. You say, "What were you thinking of Fadallah?" Nervous, he lies, "Nothing, I was just thinking of God." You laugh kindly, and say, "Fadallah, seek God's forgiveness, and abandon what you intended to achieve." You speak kindly to him and place your blessed hand on his chest to cool his rankling heat. Fadallah lived the rest of his life saying, "I came to kill him, and I left with no man more beloved and dear to me." On another occasion, Ghawrath Ibn al-Harith stealthily comes up to kill you as you sit alone under a tree. Holding his sword, Ghawrath says, "Who can protect you now, Muhammad?" You calmly look at him and say, "God." Perturbed by your calm and his overwhelming guilt, Ghawrath drops the sword. You rush to grab the sword and say, "Who will protect you now Ghawrath?" Then you throw the sword away and forgive him. Ghawrath returned to his masters in Mecca proclaiming, "I have returned to you [from the land of] the best man." Such is your character—your pain and hurt humbly succumb to your faith. Even when your Companions tell you that they have suffered at the hands of their enemy, and ask you to pray against them, you respond with, "May God guide the people of Thaqif." In Uhud, with your blood mingled with the blood of your Companions, you are told, "If you would pray to God to curse the people of Mecca [God would answer your prayers]." You wipe your blood and proclaim, "I was not sent to curse people. I was sent as an inviter to the truth and as a mercy for the people. May God guide my people [the people of Mecca] for they do not know."

I see you in these glimpses that are as if revelations into your personality. If only my resolve could match my education. In the Battle of Hunayn, once again you confront a major defection, and most of the *Tulaqa'* run in retreat. But the believers persevere and the battle ends in victory. Once again, you seek no punishment, and you accept their contrived apologies. Meanwhile, Abu Talha (d. 34/654), the Companion, runs into his wife Umm Salim wielding a knife angrily—the same courageous Umm Salim who fought in several battles along your side. "What is this Umm Salim?" Abu Talha asks her, and she snaps back, "A knife to fight the enemy, and after that, I will fight those who deserted you in the midst of battle." Abu Talha looks at you and complains, "Prophet do you hear what Umm Salim is saying?" You gently laugh and say, "God has been kind to us Umm Salim, and sustained us from such a deed." For the generations to come, you proclaim that the lives and the honor of Muslims is greater than or the same as the Ka'ba in its sanctity. Despite the pending dangers, you built a society free of subjugation, excoriation, excommunication, and free of fear.

Prophet of God, I long for a life free of humiliation—for a life of beautiful dignity. And, when I long, I visualize you in my dreams. I visualize the moment that Asma Bint 'Amis returned after her migration to Abyssinia. Like most of the emigrants to Abyssinia, she returned after the Battle of Khaybar—after missing most of the early struggle, both its bitter and sweet. Asma was visiting your wife Hafsa Bint 'Umar Ibn al-Khattab (d. 45/665) when 'Umar arrived and saw her. Perhaps he was jesting when he said to Asma, "We migrated with the Prophet and so we have more right to him than you." Jesting or not, Asma became incensed and proclaimed, "By God, I will not eat or drink until I tell the Prophet what you just said, and I will not lie, embellish, or exaggerate." She ran to you complaining and, upon hearing her, you said, "No, he has no right to me more than you. 'Umar and his companions migrated in the way of God once. You [emigrants of Abyssinia] migrated in the way of God twice [the first time to Abyssinia and the second to Medina]." Asma' was a resolute and spirited woman, and such a woman had every right to you. She impressed Abu Bakr al-Siddiq (d. 22/634) and so he married her and, after Abu Bakr died, she married 'Ali your cousin and Companion. Yes, such a woman could claim her rightful position. But what right do we have to you?

When the women of Medina complained that the men manage to outspeak them in meetings, you smiled and gave them their own day. In Bukhari, it is reported that Anas Ibn Malik (d. 93/711) said that any women in Medina could grab you by the hand and lead you to where she wished, and you would follow her until you fulfilled her need or request. In fact, again, it was Anas Ibn Malik who reported that a senile woman in Medina came and said, "Prophet, I need something from you." My Prophet, you replied, "Umm so and so, choose any place in Medina, and I will sit with you until I get you what you need." Both of you, woman and Prophet, sat down in the place she chose, while she talked and you listened. And, you did not leave until you fulfilled her need. Truly, as God has said, "If you had been harsh and hard-hearted, they would have dispersed from around you" (3:159). But my Prophet, today we care about *fitna* more than we care about need. So if a woman in need would grab a man's hand today, the man would probably look at her and growl, "Let go of my hand, woman!"

When 'Umar heard that your wives argue with you and lose their balance, he came protesting that women are bound to learn to defy their men. Your response was a beautiful smile—a response more telling and more eloquent than a thousand words. Your smile, your magnanimous smile—your smile was the earmark of your balance, your dignity, and the blissful essence of your soul. Your smile melted hearts and was more effective than any possible *bay'a* (oath of allegiance) that could be given. Jarir Ibn 'Abdullah said, "Since I became a Muslim I never felt neglected by the Prophet, and whenever he would see me, he would smile at me." When a man attempted to kiss your hand, you smiled and pulled away while saying, "Do not do that, I am one of you."

When someone in your household would call upon you, you would smile and respond, "At your service." In fact, you did serve your family—you deloused your cloth, mended your sandals, served yourself, cleaned the house, kneaded the bread, and hobbled the camels. You would take the camels to graze, you would eat with the servants, and you would carry your own goods from the market. When 'Aisha (d. 58/678) was asked, "How did the Prophet behave at home?" She responded, "He was in the constant service of his family." Anas Ibn Malik served you in your household for ten years, you never chided him or castigated him, and whenever you would see him you would smile.

You owed money to Zayd Ibn Sa'nah. Zayd approached you as you walked with 'Umar and grabbed you by the collar of your garb yelling, "You, the people of 'Abd al-Muttalib, do not pay back your debts!" 'Umar defended you by yelling and pushing Zayd back. You, my Prophet, smiled, and said, "There is no need for this 'Umar. 'Umar, we wanted more than this from you. You should advise me to pay back my debts, and advise Zayd to be kind in the way he demands his rights." You paid the debt back and more, and Zayd, humbled by your kindness, became a Muslim. I also see you walking with Anas Ibn Malik when a Bedouin comes up from behind you, and grabs the neck of your robe. The ring of the collar leaves a red mark on your blessed neck, and you turn around to look at the brute. He yells, "Give me some of the money that God has given you!" You smile, and you grant what he asked for. I find my mind wandering to your solemn robe—this robe that seems to have accompanied you for a good portion of your life without the company of a similar robe. I see you standing in Hunayn with the same old garb. You are distributing God's wealth when a group of louts descend upon you. They clamor and fight over the delusional ornaments of this earth until they force you against a tree and snatch even your very robe. You call upon those louts to return your lonely garb, and gently remind them that, other than the clothes on your shoulders, there is not a single thing of value or item of wealth that you intend to reserve for yourself or to keep. There is no wonder in this, for Anas Ibn Malik had said that in your life you never tasted soft bread. There is no wonder when I hear 'Aisha say that three months would pass in your home without a cooking fire being lit. There is no wonder, when upon your death, the only food found in your home was a small batch of edible grain. Even more, you died with your shield pawned with a Jewish merchant.

Yet, my beloved Prophet, at the end, despite the searing fever and pain, you fight your illness and rise to declare, "People, rancor and enmity is not in my character or quality. The most beloved to me are those who have a right over me, and demand it. If this right is justly theirs, then they will unburden me, and I can meet my God in peace." You prayed *Zuhr* sitting down, and afterwards, repeated your request. Finally, a man stood up and said that he had lent you three dirhams, and you gave it to him promptly. Whoever asked for a supplication or prayer you kindly obliged. The end of your burdens and the beginning of ours were now painfully clear.

Your last words were not about property, dominance, or kingdoms. Your last testament was to maintain our prayers and protect the weak. You repeated the testament until your lips stammered, but the voice had retreated to a whisper. Beautiful in life, and beautiful in death—and so your last act of beauty was to clean your teeth. Then, you put the *miswak* down, and closed your eyes. Your head rested on 'Aisha's lap as she stroked your hair and consoled her tears. When your head grew heavy in her lap, she knew that the Prophet of God had now been set free.

Thus, my Prophet, I engage you, and such is the nature of my visions and dreams. Yes, I confess to you that I wish I could break the law of history and live in the beauty of your comfort. But I know that there is no virtue in the idolatry of love or in the pure indulgence of sensation. We worship only God. You were but a human being. It is just that my heart longs for beauty, and you were such a beautiful human being. So I do what I must do with beauty—I engage it and absorb it in the pulse of my heart, in the folds of my mind, and in every fiber of my being. Beauty, my Prophet, becomes my vision of life and my singular dream.

CHAPTER 51

Women as a Colony

The Conference is the *sakan* and *sakina* of the mind. "It is God Who has made the night your tranquil repose so that you may rest in it; and the day, as that in which you could see" (40:61).

But it is in the night that the Conference comes alive with the repose of sight and the tranquility of insight, as it ponders the beauty and ugliness that the morning had revealed. In the heart of the night, the Conference explodes before our eyes with the meticulous record of what we saw, and the promise of what we might be able to see.

Sakina is the marvelous gift of God—the blessing of God-inspired serenity. *Sakan* is the abode of balance where we find our tranquility. God's gift is but a potentiality, that we may fulfill or utterly fail. In sin and piety, there are no inevitabilities—only the promise of God's damnation and grace. To honor God's gift is the heart of piety, and to debase it is nothing but a disgrace, and an utter treachery. God has given us the night and day as a source of peace and tranquility (28:73), so why do we respond by violence, conflict, and hostility? God has given us homes as a source of serenity (16:80), so why do we respond with anxiety, discord, and agony? God has made peace in prayer and piety, so why do we respond with self-righteous enmity? God made our husbands and wives the source of our *sakina* (30:21) (7:189), and we respond with subjugation, betrayal, and treachery.

I sit in the Conference confounded by a sense of disbelief, muttering to myself, "*Alaysa minkum rajulun rashid*" (Isn't there a reasonable person among you!) (11:78). Our affairs have left me consoling my heart and challenging my mind to restore the fragments of my tranquility. I know that without the balance, disillusionment will push me into a corner of isolation and despondency. Despite the comforts of the marginal corner, living in oblivion is a state of self-absorption—not beauty. But of all the engagements of life nothing is more distasteful to me than to combat other Muslims over our moral identity.

My profession is to teach law, but as a Muslim, I am but a student of morality. As a lawyer, I am a combatant for equity. If the law is just, I honor it. If the law is unjust, I criticize it, and if I am wrong, I plead with God to judge the assiduity of my research and the diligence of my inquiry. But in all, I am but a believer in the beauty of God, and I believe that existence longs for divinity, and that at the heart of the beautiful is God's serenity and human dignity.

And so I ponder the number of times I arbitrated, testified, or worked at divorce cases that lacked even the semblance of dignity. One case involves a man divorcing his wife after thirty years of marriage because it is time for him to consume another spouse. He brings in his handsome *imam* to tell me that God has decreed discretion in divorce for the man, and it is nothing short of *haram* to interfere with this liberty. After thirty years of marriage, the wife is not entitled to the marital home but for three months. As to the *nafaqa* (alimony), it is for three months as well, and perhaps a year—if we allow for some flexibility. This is the law of God, the *imam* says, and don't you dare rule according to some personal idiosyncrasy. For her thirty years of service and marriage, God's law permits the woman the clothes on her back and, of course, let's not forget her jewelry. In this, I am told, is the woman's liberation and true sense of dignity.

In another case, among many, is another woman who, after six years of marriage and three children, protests her husband's polygamy. To keep her as his wife, the husband divorces her civilly, but not Islamically, and marries the new woman civilly and Islamically. When she refuses her husband conjugal relations, he moves in with his new wife and refuses to give her or her children any support. He brings yet another *imam* to tell me that the woman remains her husband's wife despite her objections to polygamy. Support is in return for conjugal relations and, of course, this is not a form of lechery. If the woman does not like it, she can request a divorce, but she should turn the kids over to his and his new wife's custody. But whatever you do, the *imam* tells me, don't you dare go to American courts, for in the courts of the devil, there is no morality.

In a case of this type, which challenges every vestige of morality, a husband degrades his wife sexually. Blissfully, no one claims that the degradation is justifiable Islamically. But the woman's parents pressure their daughter to remain in the marriage and its degradations because a divorced daughter is an embarrassing liability. In the arguments and protestations, the parents proclaim that the law of God dictates obedience to the parents, and if the parents command degradation, how can anyone say differently? When I say that God commanded respect and not obedience, for God did not decree that a person would surrender their reason and the dignity of their autonomy, I am met with a chorus of protestations condemning my insolent blasphemy.

In yet another case, and the cases are many, a man beats his wife and children regularly. In court, an *imam* testifies that the man was acting pursuant to an honest and well-supported belief that this was his Islamic responsibility. In another, a man beat his wife and so she took her children and left. She wants a divorce, but the *imam*, and the *imams* are many, tells her that the *'isma* (power of divorce) is in the hands of her husband. If she wants, she can return her dowry and receive a *khul'* (a quit-claim divorce initiated by the wife), but only if her husband agrees. Her husband owes her no support because she is a *nashiz* (rebellious wife) and, Islamically, she is the abuser's wife unless he divorces her or gives her a *tafwid* (a delegation to divorce herself). In the case of divorce, the nine-year old boy belongs in the custody of the father, and evidence of abuse is not admissible in court—of course, speaking Islamically.

In another case of beating, and the cases are more than anyone is willing to believe, the husband comes to my home with a smiling *imam*. This smiling chap is a college dropout who read some Islamic books with a *Shaykh* in Syria, and, of course, this qualifies him to be the speaking Godhead for all eternity. He meets me with a million *salams*, and even hugs me and places a kiss on my beardless face with such exuberant gaiety. The wife sits in the marginal corner drowning in tears, and the husband sits next to the smiling *imam* rubbing his hands, nervous and rather giddy. "Brother," the *imam* says, "my other brother tells me that you are counseling our brothers against the right of *ta'dib* (reprimand). A brother is commanded by God to reprimand the sister, and I am here as a brother to a brother enjoining the good to my Muslim brother, for the love of a brother to a brother will equal the brotherhood of all humanity. Yes, brother, don't incite the sisters to *fitna* (sedition and discord) and rebellion against the brothers, for 'Umar, with him may Allah be pleased, cursed the one who ignites the *fitna*, breaks the bonds of brotherhood and incites the sisters to evil, evil deeds."

I stared at him then exhaled, "Oh brother! *Alaysa minkum rajulun rashid*? If you would get your tongue out of rhetoric for a second, perhaps we could speak. As to the right of *ta'dib*, a wife is not a child, and so there is no right to *ta'dib*. The traditions on reprimanding a wife contradict the Qur'anic imperatives of *ma'ruf* (goodness) and *ihsan* (equity and kindness), and the *qiwama* mentioned in the Qur'an means service and protection, not *ta'dib*. As for those who accept the authenticity of the traditions regarding beating—don't they say that a beating should not cause suffering or pain? Please tell me, how does a beating with a twig on the shoulder result in *ta'dib*? No, I think such a beating would be considered a joke, if not simply silly. As to *fitna*, there is no *fitna* worse than ascribing to God what is immoral and ugly. . ."

At this point, the smiling fellow knotted his eyebrows, and as his smile disappeared, he cut me off. "*Subhan Allah* at the *dalal al-mudillin* (misguidance of the misguided)," he exclaimed. "Okay, fine, let me tell you quite simply. I know you well, *shaytanhum al-akbar int* (the grand devil), I know all your ranting about morality, reason, and beauty. All this stuff is nonsense—a Western *bid'a* (innovation) from the devil; there is only the *sirat al-mustaqim* (straight path). There is no reason in Islam— the use of reason is *haram, haram.* And, all this stuff about beauty and I don't know what, is how Uncle-Tom-loving Western sell-outs speak. Morality and beauty are what God commands and God commanded the right of *ta'dib.*"

In a near whisper I said, "I didn't know that in Islam morality and beauty is just stuff. And, I did not know that God's law has made our brain a superfluity."

I looked at the wife in the corner, and said, "Sister, do you concede to your husband a right to *ta'dib.* Do you believe your husband has a right to reprimand and beat you?"

She said in a strong and constant voice, "My husband is not smarter, more pious, or more balanced than I. From where does he then get this right of *ta'dib?* The Prophet, may God bless him, never laid a finger on his wives—never insulted, never degraded, and never even yelled, and such was his *sira* (way of the Prophet) in *ta'dib.* The Prophet mended his sandals, washed the clothes, swept the house, and was at his family's service without a hint of arrogance or conceit. These men speak of this and that, and what about following the *Sunna* of the beloved? I believe in the beauty of the Prophet, and if my husband cannot understand this, then I want the liberty to find a husband who does believe. More than this I will not speak."

Frankly, I found my eyes filling with tears, and then I exclaimed, "Truly, *ja'a al-haqqu wa zahaqa al-batilu inna al-batila kana zahuqa*" (17:81) (The truth has appeared and falsity has disappeared. Verily, falsity will disappear). My sister, you have the right to a dissolution, if nothing else, then on the grounds of *'adam al-kafa'a* (un-suitability of the marital partner)."

Yes, there are many cases that could fill a million pages of asinine insanity. But the essential point is that God made our wives our *sakina,* and we respond with subjugation, betrayal, and treachery. God equates the *sakina* of a spouse to the home, to the night, and to prayer in its essentiality. The fundamental truth is that when we degrade our wives, we deny the essence of existence. We like to speak of Islam and liberation, but we close women behind curtains and walls and call it modesty. What modesty is there in men who cannot control their desires and who project upon women their subjugation fantasies? Every time we tell a woman not to speak or act or appear or breathe, we only affirm our own immodesty. What modesty is there in resisting temptation, not by sanitizing our hearts, but by purging women and turning our sisters and wives into a subjugated colony?

The more I ponder the affairs of our nation, the more I realize the distortion that has crept into our psychology. Our gallant men were colonized by other men and were demeaned and humiliated for centuries. In our chauvinism—oppressed,

163

demoralized, and emasculated—we associated defeat with femininity. In the same fashion that the abused becomes an abuser, the colonized became the colonizer, and we displaced our loss of masculinity, pride, and dignity upon our women, and made women a subjugated colony. The real shame is that we denounced the blessings of God and justified our ugliness through religious sophistry.

CHAPTER 52

In the Footsteps of the Beloved

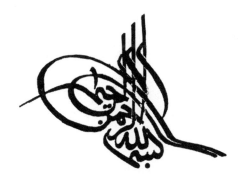

Can we trace the footsteps of the beloved when the beloved has walked away? Can we find the scent, the fragrance, the redolence of his trace? Can we seek the fragments of memory, the smiles, the laughs, and the kind gestures? Can we locate the beauty over fourteen hundred years too late? I agonize over these questions, struggle with the promises, and I refuse to despair.

I agonize over the questions, and so I run to the Conference—I run to the books. I run to the papers and the ink. I run to the transmissions and reports—to so and so reported from so and so. I pursue the evidence in the books, in the testimonials and quotes, and in the layers of words. I pursue it with the relish of reverence, with the fervor of zeal, and the rapture of love. What I want is not to find him, for the Prophet is dead, but to find the perfume of his soul, the radiance of his beautiful face, and the magnanimous bliss of his hands. Yes, I search the *hadith*, the *sunan*, and the *masanid*, I even search the imagination and dreams. Those who love him will understand, and the others will only be interested in the archeology of his footprints in the sand. But the perfume of the beloved travels in the soul—not in the burdened winds or the antiquities of the land.

I search, and what I find are sightings and descriptions of time and place—the reports that say what the beloved said or did, the beloved once occupied this certain space. But I do not want to stare at the scatter of remains, or simply retrace his footsteps, or collect the relics on the trail. What I want is to inhale the perfume, sprinkle it on my soul, wash my heart, and reshape every single cell in my brain. You see, I do not want to commemorate or memorialize, and I do not want to reminisce or build a shrine. I am not searching for graphs or illustrations, I am not searching for plats or delineations. The *Sunna* of the beloved, my friends, is not a map; it lives in our soul not our hand.

I do not want to retrace his steps and then walk along his trail. I want to walk my own trail and route, for in life, no two paths are exactly the same. But I want to walk the road of life with his heart, not mine.

To mimic the Prophet is nothing but an impersonation, for his sublimity cannot be simulated. The instant his majesty is animated, it is reduced and degraded. The replication of his *Sunna* becomes a grotesque parody of images and sounds—a demeaning forgery and an insolent falsification. The authenticity of the Prophet does not mean imitation, but personification.

Beauty is not to counterfeit what cannot be copied, but beauty is to bring to life the truth of the Prophet. And, the truth cannot be placed within the idiosyncrasies of limits. We cannot follow the *Sunna* of the beloved, we must live it—as if inhaling the fragrance only to emit it.

So, I stand in the road of my life confronting my own fate, but I confront it with his fragrance, his truth, and his beauty. I stand in dignity, steady, somber, and staid, for I sit in judgment over myself before God seals my case. When presented with a problem or an argument, I exercise diligent self-restraint. For I ask myself the fundamental question that transcends time, place, or any limitations, "What would the Prophet have done in this situation?"

In whatever life gives or takes, in whatever the liabilities or stakes, in whatever the pains or aches, in whatever pleasures or gratifications, I inhale the fragrance of the Prophet and ask, "What would the Prophet have done in this situation?"

Who would the Prophet have married? How would the Prophet have made love or acted with his neighbors? How would the Prophet have acted in his home, shared the happiness, or reacted to any consternation? How would the Prophet have dealt with an extended hand or acted toward this poverty or privation? How would the Prophet have driven a car, managed a job, or even responded to any small sensation?

The response to the question is mine and yours, not the Prophet's, for the truth, that is the Prophet, is not susceptible to relative individualization. But to ask the question will unlock the heart to the Prophet's beautiful authenticity, and the heart's own moral self-realization.

"What would the Prophet have done in this situation?" A society built on this solemn inquiry is a society permeated with his blessed fragrance, and his miraculous beauty becomes its salvation. His *Sunna* would not be pursued in malformed and contorted imitations, but a fundamental state of transformation.

• • •

Ibn 'Abdullah, Abu al-Qasim, my Prophet, my beloved, you are among God's most wondrous manifestations. My heart is wedded to beauty, and, my Prophet, you

166

are the beautiful marvel of all creation. But the truth is, I have no use for my heart, I want to live through yours.

My Prophet, what words can I find to describe my utter and unrelenting infatuation? "I love you," just won't do, and there are no words, no expressions—language is just a system of bounded significations. When the words leave my heart, they are formalized, interpreted, and corrupted by my own mind. So I absorb the silence, stand in place, and look all around. When I glimpse your footprints or hear the echo of your footsteps, I run to where I know your perfume will be found. I inhale the fragrance, sprinkle it on my soul, wash my heart, and reshape every single cell in my mind. Then I walk on my own road carrying my own burdens and chores. But I confront the blessings, trials, and tribulations not by acting out a parody or attempting an impersonation, but by the authenticity of a personification. And, in every point, and at every sensation, I pause and ask myself, "What would the Prophet have done in this situation?"

CHAPTER 53

The State Between Two States
(A Partnership With God)

In the *Conference of the Books,* each comes with their books in hand, from every time, place, and land. They proceed as if in a procession, presenting visions of God's sovereignty and undeniable command. It is as if they are ejected-souls—ejected by their flesh to become unbounded words. Souls transformed by truth and time to transcend their human form, and to wed our present to our past. Now, they are papers and words, partly material and partly ethereal—a state between two states. Like the esthetics of beauty, its truth is its indomitable fate. Souls carrying books, books carrying books—an illimitable procession of wisdom and folly invigorated by the promise of words. I greet my nightly company, and wonder when will I transform? When shall my flesh eject me, and when will I become an ethereal form—a state between two states—a book of papers and words?

My God, it is not that I am hurrying my fate, but I must admit, I am restless in my present state. I exist in this ephemeral world agitated by what it gives and takes. I am flustered when it gives, and restive when it takes. But this world is like a journey in a dream; it carries you through emotions, but it delivers little that is real. Struggling with this world is like struggling with a dream, only when you deny its visions can you see what was obscured in your sleep.

When I open my eyes and renounce my present shape, I know I am about to awake. I rise and close my eyes to find You, my God, to find the Conference, and the promise of words. I find You, and I know I will transform. Often, at these moments of enlightenment, I combust with such uncontrollable power, I am tormented by my heart's overwhelming fire. I burn to join the ethereal state, and ignite with ecstatic vi-

168

sions while I am fully awake. I ache to become a supernal vision on my own and to become one of Your seraphic servants and mates. Yet, I know my status and limitations more than any other. I know that if I become a book whose wisdom outweighs its follies, I will be satisfied with my contribution, for to be wedded to the truth of the word is to share in the beauty of the Lord. To share in the truth is an ethereal transformation.

• • •

I was lost in hope when the knock at the door pillaged my thoughts. Every visitor honors me, but also tests my transformation. From her anxious and tentative demeanor, I suspected that the issue must relate to marriage. Of all the offerings of this world, nothing is more mystifying than this institution. It commences with a covenant with God, but it is often lived in a deluge of pathetic delusions.

Like many before her, she asks her questions with stern facial control as if to conceal torrents of restless confusion.

"I am Pakistani," she informs me, "and my parents are, sort of, pressuring me to get married. I love and respect my parents very much, and I trust them with my life. They, sort of, introduced me to a Pakistani medical student, and they are confident he would make a good husband. They say marriage is half of religion, and God would want me to marry. My parents are, sort of, religious, and I respect and love my parents very much, and I would trust them with my life. I am an observant Muslim, and it would mean a lot to my parents if my husband is a Pakistani and a doctor. So I want to know what are the rules for marriage in Islam—what are the rules for a good husband?"

Her question threatened to throw me in a spiraling harangue of endless orations, but I held my tongue. Why is it that we always speak in terms of rules instead of what would be beautiful? Do we worship a God of rules or a God of beauty? I understand the beauty of marriage or the truth of marriage, but the rules of marriage I cannot absorb. And, is a husband who is a Pakistani and a doctor part of the rules or part of the beauty or part of the truth? And, how can we approach such a fundamental decision while saying "sort of," instead of with equanimity and resolution.

Instead of a harangue, I said with a stoic face, "Sister, I searched the Qur'an and *Sunna*. I am sure that a husband who is a Pakistani doctor is not to be found anywhere."

Understandably, this annoyed her, and so she protested, "But my parents want me to have a stable and happy life."

"My sister," I said, "I am sure they do, and they are advising you according to what they know. But it is not a husband who will provide you with a stable and happy life—it is God."

This did not persuade her, and so she argued, "But God expects us to take care of ourselves before He will take care of us."

169

I thought to myself now is the time to test my transformation; now is the time to awake. "Sister," I said, "that is true. God changes what is inside a people only when they change what is inside themselves (13:11). But what are the criteria? What are the criteria for God's care? Does God's care mean a secure financial life? Does God's care mean a blissful equanimity of the soul? Isn't it strange when we say that marriage is half of one's religion, and yet we evaluate this half on purely mundane grounds?"

She looked at me as if searching what I said for a common theme. The test of transformation is often one of coherence, and so I adjusted my tone, "Sister, many scholars have criticized the authenticity of the traditions that claim that marriage is half of religion, and I don't believe that it is a reliable *hadith*. Nevertheless, it comes from a culture permeated with Islamic morality. As individuals, we live this life seeking to build a partnership with God, and in marriage the members of this partnership become three. God is a full partner in a marriage that is why the commencement, the pursuit, and the termination of a marriage must be conducted according to the standards of beauty suitable for a partner such as God."

She seemed to have been surprised by my tone because she softened her voice, "But does God enter a partnership with every marriage?"

I thought of the ugliness of many marriages, and I know that the wedding of ugliness with God is a simple impossibility. "Sister, you know the *hadith* that whoever migrates to marry a woman or conduct business, such is the moral value of their migration, and, whoever migrates to God and His Messenger, then to God is their migration?"

She nodded her head and so I continued, "If we marry to affect a divine unity, such becomes the state of our marriage, and if we marry for financial stability or security, such is the mundane state of our marriage as well. We enter every marriage by articulating a covenant with God. But either this covenant is a mere formality or it has actual meaning. Doesn't God say in reference to marriage, 'And, we have taken from you a weighty covenant'? (4:21). God uses this same language when talking about a covenant with Israel (4:154) and a covenant with the prophets (33:7). So is the covenant of marriage as serious as a covenant with the prophets, or does God speak in jest?

"But what is the point of this covenant? What is the purpose of marriage? What is it supposed to achieve? Copulation is one of its purposes, but God emphasizes repeatedly that marriage is a *sakan* and *sakina* (serenity and tranquility), and uses the same expression to describe the blessings of a restful night and the gift of the Prophet's prayers. Serenity and tranquility, my sister, are not entitlements of life, they are a divine blessing and gift.

"But how do we attain this gift? How do we deserve it? We attain it when we enter into a partnership with God, when God is a part of the marital relationship, and when we uphold covenantal obligations. When we do so, God bestows upon us the blessing of serenity and tranquility in marriage. So, yes, God is a part of every marital relationship entered into in God's name, but the quality of the partnership depends on the conduct of the parties. If we start our marital life, for instance, with a lavish display of material wealth in a wedding, one can hardly say that we are off to a blessed start. If we consistently discharge the obligations of the covenant, God bestows His blessings upon us."

She surprised me when she quickly focused the enquiry on her parents, "But my parents would like me to have a serene and tranquil life. Why couldn't that happen with the person they chose?"

I felt disappointed. I talk of a partnership with God, and she is interested in vindicating her parents. I said with an annoyed tone, fully restored, "Listen sister, we do not just happen to stumble upon a divine relationship. This is a matter that takes intent, diligence, and perseverance. I don't know your parents, and I don't know their focus. If we enter a marriage while adopting a mundane frame of reference or material criteria of evaluation, we are entering the marriage wishfully hoping for God's pleasure while entirely focusing on our own delusions. With all due respect to your parents, they are not the ones who will have to sleep with this man every night. They are not the ones who will discharge the obligations of the Divine covenant, and they are not the ones who will have to answer for your marital decisions in the Final Day. You cannot stand before God in the Hereafter and say, 'My parents told me so.' You may consider the advice of your parents for all its worth, but it is your decision, your responsibility, your obligation, and your covenant. Furthermore, and with all due respect to your parents, many parents in this society focus on purely cultural criteria in evaluating the appropriate spouse. Many parents treat marriage as a purely mundane institution. But we must recognize that the emphasis on cultural and social considerations does not equip us to discharge our covenantal obligations or equip us to afford the Divine partner just consideration. Sister, this whole matter is not about your parents, this is about you, your God, and whether you will be able to discharge your covenantal obligations. This is also about whether your partner can help you build a partnership with God."

"But," she seemed to protest, "aren't my parents the most able to identify a suitable partner?"

Perhaps I was wasting my words on what seemed like a parental fixation, but I continued anyway. "This depends on the parents. This depends on their conception of a proper marriage. Ironically, the parents who have been plagued by the most problems in their own marriage are often the most insistent on directing the marriage of their children. It is as if they attempt to compensate for their failures. As I said, I don't know your parents, but if we are not permitted to blindly follow the most learned scholar, and the scholars are the inheritors of the prophets, I don't know how we can blindly follow any parent! As I already emphasized, it is your direct and personal charge and responsibility. The direct and personal nature of this charge is emphasized in the well-known story of Mughith and Barira—do you know that story?"

"Mughith and Barira? No, I don't know it."

"Well, there was a woman named Barira who was married to a man who loved her madly, named Mughith. But Barira did not love Mughith and divorced him. Mughith would follow Barira around crying—with his tears flowing down his beard. The Prophet felt sorry for the love-struck fellow and asked Barira if she would take him back. Barira asked the Prophet if this was a Divine command, and the Prophet said no, it was simply a personal appeal. Consequently, Barira refused to take Mughith back."

She smiled, and so I continued, "There are many reports that emphasize this point. For example, a woman from the family of Ja'far worried that her father would force her to marry someone she did not like. She met with 'Abd al-Rahman and Majma' Ibn Jariya, both companions of the Ansar, and shared with them her concerns. They told her not to fear because Khansa' Bint Khudam was forced by her father to marry someone she did not want, and the Prophet annulled the marriage when Khansa' complained to him. Furthermore, Thabit Ibn Qays's (d. 12/633) wife came to the Prophet and demanded a divorce from her husband. She explained that she had no specific cause for wanting a divorce, other than she did not love her husband, and she feared that her feelings were bound to force her to treat him unjustly. She said, 'I fear *kufr*—meaning, I fear the injustice and inequity. The Prophet asked her to return to Thabit his garden and gave her the divorce. All of this emphasizes the point that marriage is a direct and personal charge and responsibility."

"Okay," she rubbed her hands and inhaled, "but how do I know who to marry? How do I know?"

Encouraged by this friendly pause, I said, "First, know yourself. Marriage requires equanimity and balance, and without balance we transgress upon the rights of others. Without balance we are not just toward God or any other. Often in marriage, or any other relationship, we consume the other, we project our insecurities, fears, and anxieties upon the other. Without self-knowledge, it is impossible to know the other. Without self-knowledge, we cannot know if we are seeing the truth of the other person or seeing the projection of ourselves upon others. We do not know if we are seeing the true nature of the other person or simply the construct we invented and forced upon such a person. Of course, self-knowledge is a long and difficult process, but even the simple awareness of the necessity of self-knowledge will educate your choice, and commence the process of establishing a just and blessed partnership."

"And, other than self-knowledge?" she asked rather amicably.

"You try your best to select a partner who understands the meaning of a partnership with God. I do not mean selecting someone who is simply a practicing Muslim, but someone who is committed to honoring his partnership with God—someone who is committed to a marriage that can ascend from the mundane to the divine, someone who will strive to ascend from suffering the tribulations of life to earning the gift of serenity from the divine." I paused for a moment then said teasingly, "And, if that person happens to be a Pakistani doctor that is fine—we can't count that against the man."

She smiled, and my heart danced in response. Encouraged, I continued, "Now, let me ask you, who is the guide in our life? Which human being should be the example in our life?"

"The Prophet, peace and blessings upon him?"

"Sure," I said, "We follow the *Sunna* of the Prophet, the *Sunna* of the beloved. Therefore, I always try to ask myself, 'What would the Prophet have done in this situation? Who would the Prophet have married?' When we marry, we should select the partner who loves the *Sunna* of the Prophet—the partner who would make the Prophet his model. Your effort is best spent on the person who resembles the Prophet's morality and beauty or on the person who takes after the Prophet. This does not mean marrying someone who pretends to be the Prophet or someone who impersonates the Prophet, but someone who strives to personify the Prophet. I am not talking about someone who thinks that the Prophet was about external appearances or that the *Sunna* is a fashion show. I am talking about someone who struggles to model his heart after the Prophet's heart."

This remark elicited nothing short of an exclamation. "But," she protested, "by that standard, I would never get married. There aren't many who personify the Prophet."

"*Al-afdal fa al-afdal,*" I exclaimed, "The best, then the second best. You search for the best, then the second best. I should say that if you purify and balance yourself, you will only fall in love with the person who reminds you of what you love. And, if you love the Prophet, you will fall in love with a person who loves the Prophet. Of course, loving the Prophet comes in degrees and measures—my sister, loving the Prophet is a journey through ascending levels. If you strive to know yourself, and work to purify yourself, you will sense the presence even of a fraction of the Prophet's demeanor. Furthermore, we should remember that our choices affect the choices of society. If people want to marry doctors, you will find that the number of doctors will increase in society. If people want to marry those who personify the Prophet, you will find that a social incentive is created to study the Prophet, and the more we study the Prophet the more we personify him."

She asked rather deliberately, "What if I find such a person, and he does not propose to me?"

I said without hesitation, "You propose to him! Culturally, men propose to women. Islamically, this cultural practice is a form of vanity. We have the precedent of Khadijah (d. 3 years before *hijra*/619) and other women who either proposed to the Prophet or one of the Companions. No doubt, to do what is culturally uncommon tests our sense of dignity. But you must weigh your sense of dignity against your belief in the beauty of the person you are considering. It is true, the dignity of modesty is beautiful, but the dignity and modesty of seeking the truth is even more beautiful. For instance, a woman once proposed to the Prophet in the presence of Anas Ibn Malik (d. 93/711) and his daughter. Anas' daughter remarked that this woman lacked shame and dignity. The Prophet promptly corrected her, and praised the uprightness of this woman. Therefore, the jurists al-Bukhari, Ibn al-Munir (d. 733/1333), Ibn Hajar (d. 852/1449), and Ibn Daqiq al-'Id, among many others, held that there is no sin or shame in a woman proposing in marriage to a man."

She appeared to be getting tired, but she smiled, and nearly whispered, "But do we have to get married?"

Puzzled, I inquired, "What do you mean?"

"I mean do people have to get married? Is it a religious obligation? My parents always tell me that it is a sin not to get married, and to be married is always better than not being married. Is that true?"

"Sister, the Prophet is reported to have said that whoever is able to marry should do so. But the emphasis here is on the ability, the readiness, and the capacity to be married. Marriage is a basic building block in society and so it is strongly recommended, and in some cases, even required. But this obligation is not absolute. We cannot for example marry a mass murderer, and say God told us to do so. We cannot marry if we are not equipped to fulfill our obligations toward our partner and family, and then claim that God commanded us to do so. Marriage is an institution entered into within the context of obligations and rights, and we must be ready and willing to discharge those obligations and rights. Marriage must become a means to obtain God's blessings—not a means to violate the rights of others, and earn God's displeasure. So, for instance, there are pious and learned jurists such as the Hanbali Ibn Taymiyya or the Shafi'i al-Imam al-Nawawi who never married. I am sure they did not marry because they felt that they could not do justice to their partners, and so they chose the lesser harm. To stay unmarried and not commit injustice against other people is better than to marry and treat your family unjustly. In fact, Ibn Taymiyya insistently rejected his mother's attempts to find him a bride saying that the circumstances of his life would not permit him to treat his spouse justly. So if the question is: Is any marriage better than no marriage? The answer is clearly, no. If the question is: Is marriage a *Sunna* of the Prophet and one should exert an effort to qualify himself or herself to enter into such a blessed institution? The answer is clearly, yes. The *Sunna* of the Prophet should never become an excuse to commit spiritual or intellectual suicide, and the *Sunna* of the Prophet should never be used as an excuse to enter into just any partnership even if this partnership will not be equitable toward God."

She smiled again and was quiet for a long time to the point that I thought she was getting ready to leave. Instead, she suddenly said, "Okay, but I must admit that I am not sure what a partnership with God really means."

"The Arabic expression," I explained, "is *tu'amilu Allah fi ma ta'mal,* which means that you deal with God in whatever you do. As married partners, you ask yourselves, 'What would God think of the way you spend your time or money?' You ask yourselves, 'How would God want you to expend your energies? What would God think of your conversations, your debates, and your arguments? How would God want you to love each other?' We know that if you smile at each other, you earn God's blessings, if you make love, you earn God's blessings, if you joke and laugh together, you earn God's blessings. If there is care, compassion, and mercy toward each other, you earn God's blessings. If you help each other, you earn God's blessings. If you even greet each other, you earn God's blessings. In other words, you live your lives fully engaged with God in whatever you do. You constantly strive to create beauty in your life—the kind of beauty that acknowledges God as a full partner in the marriage—the kind of beauty that deserves the gift of serenity."

Shortly after this statement the sister left. She inhaled, thanked me, and prayed to God to bless me and left. I prayed that my wisdom outweighed my follies. I don't know what impact my words had on her. I don't know what decisions she made. I don't know if she heard me while awake or asleep. I don't know if she thought that the words she heard were a truthful vision or a delusional dream. What I do know, as a matter of certainty, is that we choose our own reality. We choose to descend into the mundane or elevate to the ethereal. We choose our partners and company in our journey.

I prayed for insight and forgiveness as I turned off the light and prepared to leave. But I felt weighed and heavy in my seat as I remembered the burdens of the transformation. God, I know we are human beings. But I also know that when we partner with You, we undergo the transformation. We become neither purified angels nor a decrepit temporality, but we share the ethereal and become a state between two states. God, I beg of You, accept my partnership, aid my transformation, and help me reach for Your heavenly essence.

CHAPTER 54

The Pearls of Beauty
(On Re-Finding Our Lost Civilization)

What have the shelters of ignorance offered us but the delusions of comfort and the derangements of fear? We stand gazing at the immensity of God and life, and tremble at the thought of where this enormity could lead. We close our eyes and seal our lips and quiver in fear of our fears. When we believe that life and God could be tethered to the radius of our intolerance, we banish all richness and thought to the abandoned extremities. But what we've tethered are only benighted demons feeding on our insecurities. In the desolation, the shelters of ignorance beckon us, hissing in our ears, "In my embrace there is comfort, there is the clarity of dismissiveness and the relief from all your fears. If you hold steadfast to the comforts, and seek to learn what you already know, then you already know everything you would want to know. Instead of being marginalized by knowledge, marginalize knowledge, for what you don't have you don't need. If your mind troubles you, then simply put your mind to sleep."

We suffer confusion and so we seek the libations of comfort. Befuddled with ignorance, we crave the intemperance of self-indulgence. In our drunkenness we imagine that we overcame our fears. But every moment of regained sobriety reminds us and terrifies us, and so we dwell further and further into the shelters of ignorance. Until the time comes when the stench of rotted minds mingles with the sweat of addictive fear. Then we discover that what we thought were comforting shelters have become impenetrable dungeons tethering us to ignoble triviality.

I stand frozen and apprehensive at the banks of knowledge, pondering the expanse of its magnitude and the richness of its sublimity. Somewhere in this remarkable vastness are the pearls of transcendence and insight into the Truth—pearls of insight without the corruptions of comfort and distractions of self-indulgence. Somewhere in the vast oceans of knowledge are the pearls of beauty unadulterated by the flaws of experience. Somewhere out there are the pearls of perception into the intricate balance of our existence. But God has decreed that the seeker must dive into the tumultuous sea, fight the waves, and suffer the harshness of the reefs, for those who deserve the pearls of life are those willing to surrender all comfort in the pursuit of beauty.

I ponder this vastness and feel the cringe of apprehension gripping my brain. Do I search the floors of all the oceans, but what if I am lost or overcome by exhaustion and pain? Should I swallow every single drop of their water, but what if I burst or drown in vain? Should I salvage every single shell I find or should I fear that it might conceal the venom of a satanic snake? Should I dive and search with strength and confidence, or should I doubt and suspect every novelty that comes my way? But if I shunned the shelters of ignorance because I refused the slavery of despair, how can I delve into the oceans of knowledge and still be shackled by my fears? If I burst or drown or succumb to some venomous snake, then I die the martyr of the search for beauty, and I pray to God to fill my coming life with the pearls of repose and equanimity in a heavenly state.

The nomads of the lost Civilization live frozen in fear—the fear of gazing at the corpse, confronting their loss, and relinquishing their grip over the fossils of antiquity. The chains of their once-glorious memories have condemned them to the mortifications of an unrelenting redundancy. Old words and thoughts are uttered like chants in a sanctuary of hallowed memories. They supplicate in the name of a bygone oasis and every mirage becomes their prophecy. Finally, the nomads either settle in the makeshift shelters of ignorance or, if they search the oceans, they dare not open a single shell lest the pearls of perception reveal to them the full extent of their ignoble destitution and agonizing reality.

Yes, we are the displaced children of the civilization of the word, pariahs in the world of thought and literacy. We are the outcasts of the unthinkables and unmentionables subsisting on the scraps of hardened ideas. We've forgone the pearls of knowledge in fear of being distracted from our sanctimonious memories. Even the word of God is preserved as a memory and not as a thought to be engaged, in search of the pearls it conceals and then reveals. But the life of a word is measured by the pearls that mark its development, not by the shrines that honor its memory.

I am here in the Conference nursing the anxieties and the nostalgia of the orphans of history. Is it possible that the day would come when ours will be designated "a vanished civilization," remembered only in fables, epics, and pietistic mythology? Can the folds of this wrinkled brain help unfold the truth about our plight or help to restore our extirpated relevance or ravished sense of dignity?

• • •

Such were the exorcisms of this haunted mind when the learned woman revisited me. In her presence, the Conference seems to speak with a hint of jubilance, and I am comforted by her strength and sense of dignity. After the usual greetings, she started speaking as if continuing after a short pause in an ongoing conversation.

"Brother, there is a sister who suffers degradation and beatings," she explained. "There are police and medical reports documenting some of the incidents, but when charges are brought, the sister refuses to cooperate. She filed for a no-fault civil divorce in American courts, but she has been advised that an Islamically created marriage must be terminated Islamically. Her husband refuses to grant her the *talaq* (divorce), and he remains in the marital home demanding that she return. Brother, I advised her that she might obtain an Islamic no-cause divorce by returning her dowry to her husband. But others advised her that this procedure requires her husband's consent, and in any case, her dowry was worth $5,000 and it has now all been spent. I then told her to go to a religious scholar, plead her case, and obtain a for-cause divorce on the basis of cruelty and ill treatment, but no *imam* has dared to oblige her in such a thing. Now, she is like what the Qur'an describes as a *mu'allaqa* (a suspended person), neither here nor there."

She paused and so I spoke, "Sister, this raises an interesting question: If there is no recourse to a judge because of the lack of qualified individuals or the lack of jurisdiction, what happens in such a case? In essence, this is a question of what is the default position—marriage or divorce? If we do not have the means to reach a clear decision, what do we presume to exist, the marriage or a divorce? The legal presumption of continuity (*istishab*) would seem to indicate that despite the lack of recourse, the marriage continues until explicitly dissolved. But the legal presumption that hardship in all cases must be alleviated (*raf' al-haraj* or *daf' al-darar*) would seem to point exactly the opposite way. The question, though, is what are the proper limits and appropriate balance between the two legal maxims? How long before we might be able to say that the physical fact of separation has now dissolved the marriage? God says, 'You either keep [stay with] your wives in kindness and dignity, or you divorce them in kindness and dignity' (5:2)(2:229). But the question is: If this prescription is violated and the woman is left suspended, to what extent should the law re-structure its established rules and precedents to address the moral imperative? Do we perform a *qiyas* (extension of the law by reliance on analogy) on the basis of *ila'* (vow of countenance or abstention from sex with one's wife), and therefore rule that after four months of separation, the woman is automatically divorced, or do we perform a *qiyas* on the *'idda,* and say after three months of separation, the marriage is dissolved, or do we not rely on *qiyas* at all and rely on the first formative principles instead?"

Reining in my musings, the sister cut in, "Brother, but why not rely on the civil divorce? Why not say that when the American civil divorce takes place, the Islamic marriage is dissolved as well?"

"I don't know," I wondered as I scratched my head, "I guess it depends on how you define the marital obligation in the first place. What I mean is if the marital contract is just like any other civil contract, then it is formed and dissolved by the laws of the jurisdiction in which one lives. So, for instance, if I buy a car, the contract is governed by the laws of the land in which the contract was formed. If two Muslims enter into a contract to sell or buy a car, a judicial dissolution of the contract ends the contractual obligation. There is no requirement that the parties re-adjudicate the matter according to Islamic law because the law of the land is considered dispositive of all purely civil contractual obligations. In fact, the parties' contractual obligations, although governed by the laws of a non-Muslim territory, will be enforceable in Muslim lands as long as the contract is not in violation of Islamic public policy. But on the other hand, if the Islamic marriage contract is not considered merely a civil contract but also a religious contract, then the analysis becomes quite different. If the Islamic marriage contract is a form of *mu'amalat* and also *'ibadat*, i.e., a form of civil obligation and religious covenant as well, then a civil dissolution is not sufficient and the Islamic marriage contract should be dissolved Islamically. At least, this is my opinion, and since I believe that marriage is one of those acts that occupies a position between the purely civil and purely ritual (between *mu'amalat* and *'ibadat*), I believe that both a civil and Islamic dissolution is necessary. In fact, I believe that before the eyes of God, the only relevant question is whether people have married or divorced Islamically. The civil component is done to protect the financial interests of the parties. If one pronounces the word of *talaq*, in the eyes of God, the marriage ends from that moment onwards although the civil divorce may be finalized several months later. In the same vein, if two people commit to a marriage before witnesses and exchange the dowry (*mahr*), in the eyes of God, they are married from that moment on. The civil marriage does not improve their status before God. If we fail to distinguish between the civil, secular marriage and the Islamic marriage, we will end up with rather curious results. People may exchange their Islamic vows before witnesses and consummate their marriage, but they would be considered fornicators until they obtain the civil certificate. Alternatively, people may pronounce the *talaq* a million times and yet they would remain married and may have conjugal relations until they obtain a state divorce decree. If an Islamic marriage involves a Divine covenant, I don't know why God would defer to the secular state and submit His judgment to a secular state's decree."

She asked without pause, "But if the purpose of documenting marriages and divorces is to protect legal rights, why can't the acts even of a non-Muslim state be sufficient?"

I remarked, "I would agree if the purpose of the Islamic marriage and divorce rituals are largely organizational in nature. But God describes marriage as a weighty covenant taken by God from people. This leads me to believe that the rituals are not simply organizational but also sacramental—as I said, partly *'ibadat* and partly *mu'amalat*—and, therefore, organizational state acts are insufficient for religious purposes."

"But then," she protested, "this leaves my friend in a real bind. The secular state does not have the power to dissolve her Islamic marriage, her husband will not divorce her, and no Muslim scholar dares to claim jurisdiction to resolve the matter."

"Yes," I commented, "that is a serious problem. But it is not true that no one dares to accept jurisdiction. Until there is an institutional solution, I have accepted jurisdiction in many cases and issued Islamic divorce decrees. As to marriages entered into in the United States, my persistent inclination is that if a woman becomes a *mu'allaqa* (suspended), unable to live with her husband and unable to persuade him to pronounce the *talaq*, if there is sufficient cause, I believe she is entitled to a divorce. If there is no cause, and her husband refuses to accept a *khul'* (a return of the dowry in return for a no cause divorce), I believe fair opportunity has been given, and I pronounce the divorce decree anyway. I believe this is necessary until we can find an institutional solution to this problem."

"But then," my sister inquired, "why not concede to the wife the power to divorce herself?"

Intrigued but puzzled, I commented, "I am sorry, I don't follow."

The sister explained, "If you concede to yourself the power to divorce the wife from her husband, and if you claim Islamic jurisdiction over the disposition of the case, why not simply confess that a woman, any woman, has jurisdiction over her own affairs?"

I nodded my head, "Yes, I see what you are saying. The husband may never admit that I have Islamic jurisdiction over his marriage to this woman. Yet, I am stepping in and claiming jurisdiction any way. If I can, so to speak, usurp jurisdiction, why can't the wife usurp the decision-making power herself?"

"Exactly," she exclaimed.

"Well," I continued, "this raises a most troubling question. As you know, the jurists have always given men the power of *talaq* (*'isma*)—a man may pronounce the *talaq* with or without reason, at any time, and the marriage is dissolved. This seems to rely on a presumption that men are the rightful bearers of this formidable power, the power of divorce. All things being equal, as a matter of law, women should not be given the power to divorce men. But then consider the following complications. One, women are trusted to make their own marital decisions, they may not be forced or compelled, and their marital decision are entirely in their hands. Two, the dowry is a woman's to keep and she may control and dispose of her property as she sees fit. Three, women may insert a condition in the marital contract that delegates to them the power to divorce themselves upon the occurrence of certain events. So, for example, a woman may write in the marital contract, 'If you take a second wife, you [my husband] will delegate to me the power to divorce myself from you, or even divorce this second wife on your behalf.' A woman may even put in her marriage contract the following: 'In return for a reduction in the dowry, you [the husband] delegate to me the power to divorce myself from you with or without reason.' In the opinion of a large number of jurists, this delegated power could be irrevocable, especially if there was consideration exchanged between the parties. In the opinion of the majority of jurists, this could take the form of an oath—for instance, the husband would write in the marital contract, 'I take a solemn oath not to move my wife from her town or to prevent my wife from seeing her parents, and if I violate this oath my wife is divorced from me.' Furthermore, in the opinion of a large number of jurists, including Ibn Taymiyya, a woman may place a condition in the marriage contract that provides the following: 'If you ever strike me for a reason, or no reason, the marriage is automatically and irrevocably dissolved.' All these formulas, whether in the category of *shurut* (conditions) in the *'aqd* (contract), *tafwid* (delegation), *takhyir* (grant of choice), or *tamlik* (transference of the power of divorce), are devices recognized in Islamic law by which a wife is entrusted to control her own divorce. They are all devices by which a woman may control her own fate.

"Sister, in addition to these three considerations, there are three more. The fourth matter to consider is that the wife, herself, may proclaim an oath—for instance, she may say, 'From now and until the end of days you are like a brother to me.' If the wife refuses to expatiate her oath, she and her husband cannot have conjugal relations. Effectively, by swearing in such a fashion, the wife derails the marital relationship. Five, consider that a large number of jurists allowed a wife to be a judge in matters of family and divorce, and so in effect, confessed that a woman can have competence over such important decisions. Six, social experience has shown that men often abuse the power of divorce. Anyone who has lived in a Muslim country will have seen that men often unjustly swear by divorce for every little thing, and often do divorce their wives for entirely unjust reasons."

"Okay," the sister commented, "we have six elements to consider: One, the wife decides whether and whom to marry; second, she controls her property; three, she may, through a variety of legal device, obtain the power to divorce her husband; four, the wife may obstruct her marital obligations by swearing and then refusing to expatiate her oath; five, many jurists decided that a woman may serve as a judge on family law matters; and six, men have mishandled the power to divorce. I understand all six considerations, but I don't see your point. I may add that it is hardly surprising that men abuse the power of divorce, for as the cliché goes, absolute power corrupts absolutely."

Impressed by her remarkable intellectual retention, I smiled, "But sister, if we consider all six points, and perhaps we can add to them several others, doesn't this pose the question: Why are men assumed to have the power of divorce in a marriage unless otherwise arranged? Why is the legal presumption in favor of the power of dissolution in the hands of men? Why do we labor women with the added burden of providing for this power in the contract rather than assume they simply have it?"

The sister smiled and said, "I think the answer to this one is rather clear. It is because the law of God so decreed. God specifically delegated to men the power of divorce and imposed upon women added controls."

"But why?" I asked.

She responded, "Because God gave men a degree over women and made men the maintainers of women. That is what the Qur'an says."

"Yes and no," I said. "As to the issue of men having a degree over women, as you will recall this is mentioned in the very specific context of talking about the waiting period imposed upon women to verify pregnancy and to leave open the opportunity for reconciliation (2:228). There is no question that pregnancy and motherhood is an added burden upon women, and saying that men have 'a degree' over women is not necessarily normative, but could be descriptive, empathetic, or even apologetic. Furthermore, if men have a degree over women by the virtue of physiology, a woman may acquire a hundred degrees over a man by virtue of her intellect or piety. In fact, I will tell you a nice story. A learned and pious woman once complained to a jurist that her husband taunts her by saying, 'I have a degree over you.' The jurist told the woman, 'As to his lonely degree, concede it to him, but by virtue of your superior piety and knowledge, over him, you can claim a thousand degrees.'"

I paused for a moment to see the effect on her face, and when she smiled I continued, "As to the issue of qiwama (guardianship of men over women or men being the sustainers of women) mentioned in 4:34, you will recall that we discussed it before. The verse expressly conditions the status of qiwama to a very particular operative cause ('illa), and the operative cause is the ability to earn and spend. In other words, this is not an unqualified status that men enjoy, or suffer, just by the virtue of being men. It is something hinged on certain conditions precedent that need to be fulfilled. If they are not fulfilled, either because the man is not supporting the family, or because the woman is contributing financially to an equal extent, or perhaps because the woman has an equal earning potential that she chose to forgo, then a man's qiwama cannot exist."

"All right," she retorted, "let's assume for the moment that the issue of men having a degree over women or the issue of qiwama does not pose a problem. There is still the Qur'anic prescription giving men the power of divorce, and there is still the established practice of Muslims over the centuries."

"My sister, you pose a most interesting issue. Which verses in the Qur'an expressly grant men the power of divorce?"

She smiled at me as if she has been anticipating this inquiry. "Verse 2:230 says, if a man divorces a woman irrevocably, the man cannot remarry her until after she marries another. Verse 2:237 says, if you men divorce women before consummation then give them half of the dower. Verse 65:1 says, O Prophet, if you men divorce women then allow the women to reside in the marital home during the waiting period. In all these verses, God addresses men and says, 'If you men divorce women then such and such should take place.' This clearly means men have the power to divorce women, and so the *'isma* (power of divorce) is the hands of the man."

I could not help but be impressed, and I softly said, "May God bless you sister for your knowledge of God's book, but if you will permit me, I want to direct your attention to three significant points. The first point is that none of the verses you cited explicitly grant men the power to divorce women. Rather, they seem to assume it. These verses seem to assume a state of affairs that is already in existence. When we say that the verses grant men the power of divorce, in effect, we are saying this is the clear implication of the text (*mafhum al-nass*). But sister, even if this is the case, does this mean the opposite of the implication is forbidden?"

"I don't follow," she softly commented.

"What I am saying is: If the text assumes that 'X' is the normal course of events, does that mean that the text is forbidding anything but 'X,' so that if we want to introduce 'Y,' one can say this is not allowed? For example, the Qur'an often speaks while assuming the existence of slavery. Does this mean that slavery must always exist? The Qur'an permits sexual relations with spouses and those whom our right hands possess, does this mean that there is an affirmative prescription necessitating the existence of a category known as those whom your right hands possess? The Qur'an relies on the specific historical context of the revelation, and this context recognized slavery and gave men the power of divorce. But the Qur'an does not expressly sanction slavery and does not expressly sanction men's unilateral power to divorce."

"Yes," she cut in, "but the Qur'an mitigates the effects of slavery. . ."

"Yes," I interrupted in turn, "and the Qur'an mitigates the unilateral power of men to divorce women. Look at the verses you just cited. In every single case, the point of the verse is not to empower men, but to mitigate their discretion. In every single case, the whole point is to grant additional rights to women either by saying, 'Don't take back the dowry you gave them,' or saying, 'Don't throw them out of their marital homes,' or prescribing spousal support, or mandating the kind treatment of women in divorce. In every single case, the point is not to empower men, but to protect women from the power men already possess—powers men already possessed by virtue of the customs and practices of the society in which Islam was revealed. In addition to the verses you cited, I might add 65:6, 58:2, and 2:229, all supporting this point. Now, sister, this brings me to the second significant point I think we should consider. The Qur'an often refers to divorce or reconciliation as if it is a collective decision—as if it is a decision that belongs to both the husband and wife. For instance, 2:227 says, 'And, if they [both husband and wife] are firm in their intention to divorce. . .' Verse 2:230 says, 'There is no blame on them [husband and wife] if they wish to reunite. . .' Verse 4:35 says, 'If they [husband and wife] wish to reconcile, God will aid their efforts. . .' These incremental empowerments might be indicative of a normative moral trajectory.

The Qur'an consistently talks about marriage as a source of repose and tranquility, and counsels kindness and honor in divorce. This is not consistent with the notion of a unilateral right given to men that could be subject to widespread abuse. We have the same type of situation with slavery. While the institution of slavery is assumed in the Qur'anic discourse, there is an incremental recognition of the rights of slaves, and a clear moral trajectory that encourages the freeing of slaves.

"Sister, the third point I think we should consider is to look at some stylistic aspects from a comparative point. Please notice that the Qur'an often addresses men in saying, 'Men, if you marry women, do such and such.' For instance, examine 33:49, which, in part, says, 'O you who believe! If you marry believing women and then divorce them before touching them, you do not need to count a waiting period.' Although the Qur'an speaks in terms of men marrying women, no one dares say that marriage is the man's decision. Put differently, the Qur'an assumes that men will marry women, but this does not mean the marriage is the unilateral decision of the man. This does not mean that women need not consent, and this does not mean that women are forbidden from initiating the marriage, or even proposing marriage to a man. Why can't we argue that the consent of women is necessary for a divorce to take place as well? Or, why can't we argue that women have an equal power to divorce as long as they share with men the obligation of *qiwama*?"

She was silent for a moment, and then pensively asked, "But brother, what do you do with the long-established practice of Muslims?"

"Sister, I respect it and honor it—it is a formidable precedent to be considered and studied. But if it no longer persuades me, I will respectfully disagree with it. Many jurists such as al-Razi (d. 606/1210) and al-Amidi (d. 631/1233) persuasively argued that a person who disagrees with an established *ijma'* (consensus) is not an infidel (*kafir*) or even a sinner (*fasiq*). I will believe in my opinion, and I will argue it and try to persuade others of its correctness. But as a matter of legal practice, I will abide with the precedent until I can persuade a critical mass of jurists that the precedent should be overruled. Sister, I also want to add that the established practice is not as clear as you might think. If you look at the *fatawa* of Ibn Taymiyya (d. 728/1328) or al-Wansharisi (d. 914/1508–9), you most certainly get the distinct impression that there was an established social practice of women reserving the power to divorce themselves by the means of a condition inserted in the marriage contract."

The sister was quiet for a moment before exclaiming, "What do I tell my friend? Are you actually saying that women should automatically be granted an equal power to divorce their husbands without even having to state it as a condition in the contract?"

"What I am saying is that the evidence in favor of the presumption that men have an unfettered power to divorce is not as strong as it might seem. The Qur'an simply assumes the continuation of a pre-existing social practice. What I am saying is that men have grossly abused this power of divorce and that I see evidence of this every

184

single day. I know that the guiding principle of *Shari'a* is that hardship must be removed and public welfare must be promoted. Therefore, the guiding principles of *Shari'a* and the empirical evidence cause me to pause and reconsider the whole matter. In other words, it is as if a red flag has been raised, and as a jurist, I must reinvestigate the situation. I find that the level of education, awareness, and social mobility of women has dramatically increased. I also find that the social and financial network that used to secure and support women has disintegrated in all Muslim societies. All of this causes me to look at the text again with a fresh eye, and ask myself some tough and honest questions. As a result, I, in turn, raise my own red flag and call upon my fellow Muslims to help me re-examine this situation."

She smiled again and said somewhat tauntingly, "And, what happens when your fellow Muslims say that you are just a Westernized Uncle Tom trying to gratify the CIA?"

A laugh escaped from my throat, "I would say, may God protect us from the evils of the neurosis of fear and ignorance. I would say that it is not the CIA or the West that beat on your friend and then left her suspended without an Islamic recourse. I would say, do not impose your neurosis, ugliness, and fears upon God's text and deface its pearls of justice. I would say, shame on you for surrendering our rightful claim to humanity, justice, and equity, to the paranoia of fear and the demons of ignorance. I would say that God has prescribed justice and entrusted the meaning of the text to us so that we may search and find beauty."

The sister nodded her head and assuredly said, "Brother, perhaps you can tell them we should respect the Book of God enough to engage it, and search for the pearls it conceals and then reveals. We respect it too much to imprison it in a memorial of shrines constructed from the derangements of our fears."

CHAPTER 55

The Intellectual Refugee

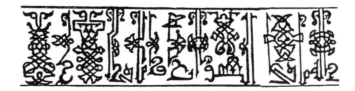

Sometimes, the world unfolds and spills all over me as if in a dream. I try to handle a flood of visions and sights, noises, and sounds, and a million incoherent thoughts pouring out all in a single moment of time, overcoming my sanity. All the words erupt from gaping mouths fumbling with sentences incoherently. All the souls drag their thoughts, and push their bodies ahead, and struggle to find a space until I am shoved out of my head and into insanity. My eyes strain, my ears ache, and my brain throbs as I try to fight the displacement of my mind, and this maniacal lunacy. I drown my fingers in my hair as I plead with my mind to stay its ground and maintain some semblance of ordered rationality. I cannot stem the pain rumbling inside, but I struggle to resist the pillaging of my mind, and pray that, among my people, I do not become an intellectual refugee.

Some twenty years ago, I left a home where thought had to be registered and licensed by mindless androids. Everything in my homeland revolved around the chair of the majesty, and of all the country's brains, only one had the right to speak. Any unauthorized thinking was chased and confiscated, and the word was arrested, tortured and murdered, and buried in a graveyard of mutilated thoughts. And yet, in my homeland, the ghosts of words escaped their graves, and haunted the persecutors with the fear of thought. Perhaps we censored ourselves and suppressed our speech, but we always embraced the promise and beauty of words. Surely our reality was oppressive and painful, but it was also predictable and coherent because both the oppressor and the oppressed understood their well-defined roles. I suffered an unrelenting flood of fear, but I understood my world, and I understood its infamy.

In the United States, and among the Muslim community, I suffer confusion, and fear becoming an intellectual refugee. Here, there is a wealth of words because everyone speaks, but between the thought and speech there is an appalling lack of proportionality. Muslims in the United States eject words like fireworks—they dissipate the minute they explode. Knowledge is considered unnecessary for words, and thought is an optional superfluity. In fact, in our Muslim community, the preachers are considered the teachers, and *Shari'a* is their monopoly. The qualification of a jurist is not the knowledge of jurisprudence, for the pursuit of evidence and proof is an unnecessary luxury. In the world of preachers, books, study, and methodology are entirely unnecessary, and analytical and critical insight, and the use of reason have all been declared a heresy. In our Muslim community, the experts are dieticians, nurses, medical doctors, herbalists, computer scientists, and countless engineers who mutate the *Shari'a* into a faddish curiosity. The anthropologists and sociologists will say this is just a synthesis and a synchronistic tradition, but when does synchronism become an outright deformity?

I move from mosque to mosque counting the absurdities. Our men work in every wake of life and encounter half-naked women in every scene and sight and, yet, insist that praying with Muslim women in the same room in a mosque is contrary to modesty.

The Prophet, in his mosque, never put up a curtain to hide women and never tried to exclude any human being. Women would come to the Prophet, and take him by the hand to address their needs. Men and women freely mingled in the time of the Prophet inside and outside the mosque. When the Prophet gave the *khutba* on 'Id, women complained that they could not hear him well, so he repeated the *Khutba* to them. The Prophet, Abu Bakr al-Siddiq (d. 22/634), and others would visit women like Umm Ayman and Umm Hani in their homes. In the mosques of Mecca and Medina, there have never been partitions nor curtains, and even the Wahhabis, in their rabid fear of women, could not alter this reality. However, in the United States, the thicker the barrier built to cleanse our space of women, the stronger the claim to our Islamicity. This despite the fact that a very large number of jurists held that if there is an obstruction or barrier that separates the men from women in prayer and obstructs the visibility of the women, the women's prayer is not valid.

As I roam between mosques, I encounter a self-declared expert who insists that Muslim women are the source of unwavering *fitna* (enticement and seduction), and demands that Muslim men and women cannot be in each other's company. I ask who is this man and what is his field of study, and I am told he is a gynecologist in town, and most of the Muslim women—the source of his *fitna*—are his patients. I think to myself, may God protect us from the grips of insanity—a man who makes a living from the goodwill and need of women, and their exclusion and domination is his source of validity. It is lawful for him to spend his weekdays between the legs of women, but to engage their brains on weekends is contrary to modesty? What breaks the heart and bleeds the mind is that no one else seemed to notice this shameful travesty. I am reminded of Umayyad Caliph Hisham Ibn 'Abd al-Malik (r. 105–125/724–743) when he forbade the women to circumambulate the Ka'ba in the presence of men, 'Ata' Ibn Abi Rabah (d.114/732), and other Meccan jurists, arose in protest proclaiming, "How could he forbid women from doing so when the Prophet circumambulated the Ka'ba in the company of women?" Hisham regretted his decision and relented, but we refuse to relent—our fidelity to our ego is unprecedented. It is sad to see the state we have reached. In *Mudawwanat* Sahnun it is reported that the jurist Ibn al-Qasim (d. 191/806) asked al-Imam Malik Ibn Anas (d. 179/796) about the validity of men's prayer behind women. Men came late to the mosque of Medina at the time of prayer to find that the mosque had become full with women. These men then humbly prayed behind the women's lines, and al-Imam Malik ruled that the prayer was correct and should not be repeated. May Allah guide us and forgive us for our ignorance.

I move throughout the Muslim community and suffer a million rambling speeches. We have excelled in conferences, symposiums, and retreats handsomely staffed by cheerleaders. The cheerleaders raise the banners, claim our superiority, and assert our manifest destiny. They aim to praise and adulate our intellectual defeat by singing, "Who needs an intellect, all we need is a handsome and luscious beard!" The cheerleaders live on euphoria and are as pretty as can be. But they have no knowledge of the score, nor the rules, and they seem to have forgotten that there is no game and no team. They seem to have forgotten that cheerleading is a brainless idiocy. Cheerleading is not a form of testimony before God—it is tribalism and perjury. What a sad state when a people come to rely on cheerleaders to lead their search for God's beauty, and for their measure of honesty.

It is ironic that Muslims in the United States are probably the only people who do not clap or applaud any speaker or speech. Instead, someone yells out *"takbir!"* and the rest respond in a chorus of shameful monotony. Regardless of how profound or silly a lecture, the response is always the same, exactly three *takbirs*. The Prophet prohibited clapping when circumambulating the Ka'ba. How did this become a prohibition against ovations or acclaim or merriment or festivity? Clapping around the Ka'ba was an expression of idol worship, but did the Prophet ban the expression of sincere gaiety? If women can clap in prayer, then when did clapping become considered an obscenity? I have often wondered, if clapping is reprehensible, what prevents people from yelling out praise and prayers instead of following the herd leaders, and their automated perversity?

I move from mosque to mosque, and I encounter Muslims who seem to think that the harsher and the more perverse the law, the more its Islamic authenticity. God and the Prophet commanded that the mark of Islam is ease and felicity, and Muslims make impossibility the mark of piety. It is not study or knowledge or evidence that determines the merit of a scholar in our community, but the rank is defined in direct proportion to how far the pretending scholar can push the limits of absurdity. In one example, and the examples are many, a pretender advised a Muslim that she should repeat all her prayers of the past thirteen years—she should repeat the obligatory five prayers and all the mandatory *sunan* (*al-sunan al-wajiba*) as well. The reason for this is that she has been erroneously performing her ablutions in all these past years, and the pretender tells her that repetition is closer to piety. She informs me that she can no longer attend my classes and seek knowledge because the obligations of prayer are keeping her very busy. Any contrary evidence I might offer will not be considered because Islam demands this utter absurdity, and the imposition of hardship is the earmark of a true *faqih*. Does it matter that the Prophet said, "One hour in the pursuit of knowledge is better than a thousand prayers!" Does it matter that technical errors in ablutions do not invalidate prayers? Does it matter that even if one must repeat the obligatory five prayers, no jurist had ever said that the *sunan* must be repeated? No, it does not matter because by imposing hardship the pretender has become certified as the real *faqih*.

Others live in this land condemning everything in this culture, and even the very air they breathe. Everywhere, these individuals preach about the evils of the infidel, and demand isolation from society. But then you discover that the same individuals make their living serving the military industry. Others disavow any influence of American culture on their psychology, and yet they speak in platitudes sliced from apple pie. "Whatever rocks your boat," or "Look out for number one" are pronounced as if rooted in Islamicity. Religion is rendered a private affair, a personal emotion, a feel-good sensation, and a cultural or racial identity. Islam is no longer the submission to the Divine Will, but the subjugation of God to the vagaries of our personalities. If you present the evidence, and rational and textual proofs of the search, many respond, "You must earn my respect" or "You don't know me," as if the scholar and his search must be packaged and marketed to the patrons of piety. It is as if an individual may stand arrogantly in his place, and distribute to people portions of respectability. It is as if age, knowledge, experience, wisdom, beauty, and God's law are placed on display to be priced by the consumers of Divinity.

Such are the affairs of our Muslim community. We are not defined by law, principle, theology, or morality. We are not defined by our relationship to God or by truth or beauty. We are defined only by a ferocious sense of insecurity. We are not an innovative synchronism—we are a scary deformity. And, all those who testify against the ugliness are expelled and become intellectual refugees.

When the Devil Speaks

God praises the nation that speaks without fear. The only chosen people are those who command the good and condemn the evil (3:110). Such is the true covenant of God, that the chosen are a people of principle, not the by-product of lineage or the inheritors of some past glory. The covenant is a covenant of words—discharged through words. To paraphrase the Prophet, whoever is silent before an injustice becomes as if a demon. The beauty of God is pure goodness, and the abyss of ugliness is fear, for what other than fear can silence the soul and give the word to Satan? God commands that we speak the truth even against those we hold most dear. Lineage, blood, or love is not supreme—supremacy is to the word that must be spoken truthfully.

Our Exalted and Merciful God has set the unwavering word for all those who believe. The Lord has commanded that we stand firmly for justice as witnesses for God. If others will testify on behalf of blood or tribe, the chosen will testify only on behalf of God. "Bear witness for God, even as against yourselves, or your parents or your kin, and whether it be against rich or poor, for [whomever it may be] God has a greater entitlement over you. Follow not the whims of your hearts, lest you swerve. If you distort justice or fail to testify, beware that God knows all that you do" (4:135).

How can we testify if the walls of dungeons are all we can see? How can we testify if we are not free? How can the believers testify if they live in fear? Are they supposed to sacrifice themselves on the altars of freedom when the altars are now in the control of demons? What truly breaks the heart and chokes the throat is that today, the demons are humans who call themselves Muslim believers. Yet, it does not matter what they call themselves, a name never discharged a covenant or commended anyone to the Lord. What matters is the truth of the word, and that when the pious fall silent only the devil speaks.

I sit in the Conference, testifying to the truth of the word. In my hand is *Risalat Iblis ila Ikhwanihi al-Manahis* (*Satan's Epistle to His Miserable Brothers*) by al-Hakim al-Jishumiyya al-Bayhaqi (d. 494/1100–1). The author was a Hanafi Mu'tazili jurist most of his life, and then the burdens of testimony called upon him to become a Zaydi. He was killed and silenced in Mecca because of his book, and now he joined the Conference, and now he speaks freely. His book, *Satan's Epistle*, was buried among the millions of manuscripts suppressed by the persecutors of the word until my mentor and teacher Hossein Modarressi published and liberated the work. Al-Bayhaqi asked in his book, if Satan on the Final Day would speak, what and whom would he praise? Satan ends up praising and thanking every Muslim who adopted a creed that attributed to God things that are irrational, unjust, or ugly. All those who make Islam the religion of the ugly and stupid lead themselves and others astray, and Satan feels nothing but gratitude and elation for this miserable company.

I start to wonder if Satan would speak about us today, what would he say? Which of our numerous vanities would he choose to praise? I think Satan would have to express his profuse gratitude for our emotions, whims, and fears that induce us to submit to ourselves rather than to our Lord. Satan would be jubilant that our Lord told us to "read," and instead, we excelled in the hysteria of activism and irrationality. In the eyes of the devil, is there a better nation than that which celebrates stupidity, and declares the use of reason to be sophistry and heresy? Is there a better gift to depravity than a nation that treats knowledge as if it is an ornament or decoration, and not the gateway to the truth of our being? Isn't Satan ecstatic when he finds a nation that refuses to learn from its past and constantly tries to reinvent wisdom's wheel? Is there a greater evil than a people who testify against a knowledge they don't know, and excel at testifying on the basis of hearsay? Isn't speaking and testifying without knowledge an act of lying and an act of deceit and perjury? What would the devil say about a people who stuff their pulpits with despots and nominate the most ignorant to lead? How would the devil praise a people who treat their religion as an extra-curricular activity and a "feel-good" hobby? Isn't the devil simply elated with our esteemed sages, puerile kids who think that Islam is a fashion show, and whose egos are their reference points? They have no need for books or knowledge—they simply act the role of the wise and pious as soon as they grow the sprucely beard and find the dapper wardrobe.

What can bring Satan a greater pleasure than a nation that censors its own testimony—a nation that cleanses and bans texts and calls lying piety? Isn't it ironic that the same people who are supposed to be the protectors of the two Holy Shrines are also those who are the corrupters of the Islamic intellectual legacy? What could be more revolting than the fact that those who are the self-declared protectors of piety are also Islam's intellectual thieves? What could be uglier than a nation that bans the thought, suffocates the conscience, strangles the word, and mutilates its scholars, and then calls it religious integrity? What could be uglier than a nation that says, "Fear God, but live in terror of other human beings?" I can nearly hear the bragging of the devil that in the land of the Prophet ugliness reigns supreme. The dungeons are full, and the rights of God are degraded before the rights of human beings. What do we tell our Lord about the thousands of women raped in the Prophet's land, and the Muslims who dare not testify or speak? Thousands of migrant workers are abused and raped, and the offenders escape in the name of national dignity. I can only imagine the devil's celebration of a nation that responds to a man carrying an amulet with a prompt execution rather than with education, discussion, and debate.

Doesn't the devil rejoice at pain, degradation, humiliation, and every moment of indignity? What would the devil say about a nation that covers up and shuts up and excludes the testimony of half of its population, and all in the name of modesty? What would the devil say about the women wrapped in black, placed behind curtains, and then ordered not to speak? Some of us claim that we are seduced by the mere sight or sound of a woman even without the devil's cajolery. Isn't it ironic how we've told the devil that not very much effort is needed to keep him content and happy?

The truth is that the devil often works through the cover of piety. Often if you peel the shell of piety, you will find the devil grinning contently. Ibn Taymiyya once remarked, "How similar is cowardliness to piety, for each of them is based on refrain and restraint!" But the refrain of piety could also conceal itself as a contentment with ignorance and stupidity. Piety could become the vehicle for self-indulgent repression against anything that provokes our insecurities. How many evils in life are anchored on a bed of pretentious piety?

If the devil would speak, how I worry what he would say. Ugliness has spread among us to the point of rot, and our rancid air is full of fear. We do not witness and if we witness we do not testify, but when the silence falls, the devil will speak.

CHAPTER 57

Corrupting God's Book

This Conference was founded on the beauty of the Book, and our Civilization was the civilization of books. Our way to God is guided by the Book, and we found our worth only in books. Our God manifested through the Book, and our identity was defined by books. So how can we become the corrupters of the Book and the betrayers of books?

What type of arrogance permits a people to name themselves God's soldiers and then usurp His authority? What type of arrogance empowers a people to inject their insecurities and hatred into the Book of God, and then fancy themselves the divine protectors? Of all the sins of this world, what can be more revolting than usurping God's Word, and then misrepresenting God's meticulous Speech?

God has promised those who alter God's Word unmitigated enmity and inevitable destruction (4:46, 5:13, 5:41, 10:64, 18:27). Those who say about God what they do not know or what they are not authorized to say are held by God in utter contempt (2:80, 7:28, 10:68). Yet, we live in an age and place where the word of God can be altered and corrupted, and all the fancy Islamic centers and bombastic leaders and preachers could not be bothered to care. We live in an age and place where the so-called protectors of the Holy Sites, Mecca and Medina, have become the corrupters of God's Word.

Their arrogance has convinced them that they are authorized to cleanse Islamic texts of their contents, and become the guardians of the Muslim mind. Even the commentaries on the Qur'an have been cleansed, and Muslims remain largely oblivious to this grave sin. For instance, the commentary known as *Hashiyat al-Sawi* on *Tafsir al-Jalalayn* has been cleansed of passages that describe the Wahhabis as the agents of the devil. Even if one believes that the Maliki jurist Ahmad al-Sawi (d. 1241/1825) has exceeded the proper bounds, this does not give one a license to commit fraud and forgery by misrepresenting al-Sawi's text. Abu Hayyan al-Andalusi's (d. 754/1353) commentary on the Qur'an known as *al-Nahr al-Madd* has been cleansed of passages that refer to Ibn Taymiyya's views regarding God's throne. The cleansing of the printed text is made without any indication or reference alluding to the deletions—as if some barely literate bureaucrat sitting on the cushions supplied by some prince or king is remotely qualified to validate or authenticate the work of such esteemed jurists. But beyond editing the work of jurists, now the corruptions have been extended to the translation of the Qur'an in English and even the *hadith* of the Companions.

For five years or more now, a beautifully printed English translation of the Qur'an has been distributed for free in nearly every Islamic center in the United States. This Trojan-horse translation is found in every Muslim bookstore and in every English-speaking Islamic center. The authors of the translation are professors at the University of Medina, and the book is printed, no expenses spared, in Saudi Arabia. On the very first page of the printed text is a certificate of authentication and approval by the late 'Abd al-'Aziz Bin Bazz, the "Head of the Ministry for Islamic Research, Legal Opinions, Preaching and Guidance" (*Idarat al-Buhuth al-'Ilmiyya wa al-Ifta' wa al-da'wa wa al-Irshad*). Interestingly enough, Bin Bazz did not know a word of English, but he authenticated the text nonetheless. To be fair, however, the translation is a faithful reproduction of Bin Bazz's views with all their idiosyncrasies. On the cover of the book is printed the title: *Interpretation of the Meanings of the Noble Qur'an in the English Language: A Summarized Version of at-Tabari* [sic], *al-Qurtubi and Ibn Kathir With Comments from Sahih al-Bukhari Summarized in One Volume.*

The impression created by this translation is that the reader is not only receiving the insights of the authors as to the meaning of the Qur'an, but is also receiving the insights and implicit endorsement of the text by the esteemed classical scholars al-Tabari, al-Qurtubi, Ibn Kathir, and Bukhari. In the text, the original Arabic is printed in one column, and on the opposite column is an attempt at a verse-to-verse English rendition of the Arabic text. At the bottom of the page, there are *hadith*-reports purporting to explain and elucidate upon the text. But the liberties taken with the so-called interpretation of the Arabic is nothing short of frightening.

The English text has all the appearances of a translation. This appearance is only confirmed by the fact that the regular English text is full of interjections placed within parenthesis, and these parenthetical interjections purport to be elaborations clarifying the meaning of the translated text. A reader who does not know Arabic is left with the unmistakable impression that what is within parenthesis is a natural elaboration upon the intended meaning of the Divine text.

To demonstrate the corruptions of the text, we will consider a few examples. The authors translated *Surat al-Ahzab* (33), verse 59, in the following way:

O Prophet! Tell your wives and your daughters and the women of the believers to draw their cloaks (veils) all over their bodies (i.e. screen themselves completely except the eyes or one eye to see the way). That will be better, that they should be known (as free respectable women) so as not to be annoyed. And Allah is Ever Oft-Forgiving, Most Merciful.

In the above translation, the authors assert that God's command is that women should cloak themselves in a large veil, and cover everything except one or two eyes. The authors liberally equate a cloak to a veil and, according to the authors, God explicitly mandates that the cloaks or veils be drawn over a woman's entire body. The authors' assertions are indefensible in light of what the Arabic actually says. A conservative and literal translation of the first quoted verse (33:59) would read:

O' Prophet tell your wives, daughters, and the women of the believers to lower (or possibly, draw upon themselves) their garments. This is better so that they will not be known and molested. And, God is forgiving and merciful.

The operative words in the Arabic text are *yudnina 'alayhinna min jalabibihinna*. This could mean either "lower their garments" or "draw their garments closer to their bodies." *Jalabibihinna* literally means "their garments." A *jilbab*, singular form of *jalabib*, is a garment worn on the body, and not a veil. A *jilbab* is a garment, like a dress or Arab robe, which has stitches and threads. A single piece of cloth like a *chador* or *'abaya*, which some women wrap around their bodies in the modern age, would not normally be called a *jilbab*. *Yudnina*, literally, means to bring closer or to lower something, in this case a garb. Therefore, one can interpret this verse to require the covering of the legs, or a more vigilant covering of the torso or, simply, modesty, but the original text does not support the authors' rendition into English.

Muslim jurists have disagreed on the meaning of this verse. Some argued that it mandates the covering of the legs or bosom. The majority asserted that it requires the covering of the full body except the face, hands, and feet. A minority view held by 'Ubayda al-Salmani and Ibn 'Abbas maintained that the verse exhorts women to cover their faces. Importantly, however, the reports about Ibn 'Abbas's views are not consistent. Some reports claim that he did not believe the face or hands should be covered. A number of the jurists who held the minority view argued that women are asked to cover their faces and hands not because it is a religious obligation but because of the advisability of distinguishing between free and slave women. This point about the distinction between free and slave women raises a very important issue about the way this verse should be understood. Nearly all the commentators agreed that this verse was revealed to protect women from molestation. These commentators state that there was a group of young and corrupt men in Medina who harassed and sometimes molested women at night. Apparently, these men targeted only slaves and not free women. They distinguished a slave from a free woman by the cloth they wore; if the woman wore a *jilbab*, they assumed she was free and left her alone, and if she did not, they assumed she was a slave and harassed her. The commentators state that in response to this problem, these verses were revealed with the specific purpose of responding to this particular problem. Consequently, many jurists argued that the *'illa* (operative cause) for the *jilbab* is to address this specific type of problem. Therefore, many of those who claim that the *jilbab* should cover the face also hinge the analysis on the operative cause of the law, and argue that this law is relevant only if there is an issue involving the distinction between slave and free women, and a problem involving harassment and molestation. If this particular type of problem does not exist, the exhortations of the verse are not pertinent.

It is quite possible to distill from this analysis a general moral call for modesty and a principle of safe conduct. It is possible to argue that these particular verses are establishing social norms of modesty and self-restraint. Relying partly on this verse, the majority of premodern jurists argued that the *'awra* (private parts that must be covered) of a slave girl is different from the *'awra* of a free woman. They maintained that the *'awra* of a free woman is her whole body except her face and hands, and many jurists added the feet. This means that a free woman should cover everything except the face and hands and, perhaps, the feet. But the jurists asserted that a slave-girl does not have to cover her hair, neck, arms, and some even added the chest. This, of course, raises the question: What is the basis for this distinction? Is the hair, arms, or chest of a slave-girl less capable of inducing seduction than that of a free woman? The response cannot be in the affirmative; the body parts of a slave-girl are no less enticing than their counterparts in a free woman. The response largely depends on social norms. The social norms of the time did not consider it immodest for slave-girls to leave their hair uncovered, while it was considered shameful for a free woman not to have a *jilbab* that would cover her body and perhaps a part of the hair. This raises the larger questions: To what extent is this Qur'anic verse addressing a particular social institution, and to what extent can this verse be generalized beyond its specific social assumptions. One way to generalize the verse is to extract or distill the fundamental moral and normative values that are affirmed by this verse, and, in essence, these values seem to emphasize modesty and safety of conduct. This point is open to debate. For our purposes, however, the most significant point is that this verse raises some rather complex issues that merit reflection and study. But by forcing a single and quite specific narrow minority view upon the verse is, without a doubt, a corruption of God's word. The authors quite intentionally limit the text to a singular meaning that is designed to cater to whatever prejudices they have toward women.

In a similar example and on the same subject of veiling and women, the authors translate *Surat al-Nur* (24), verse 31, as follows:

> ...And tell the believing women to lower their gaze (from looking at forbidden things), and protect their private parts (from illegal sexual acts, etc.) and not to show off their adornment except only that which is apparent (like palms of hands or one eye or both eyes for necessity to see the way, or outer dress like veil, gloves, head-cover, apron, etc.) and to draw their veils all over juyubihinna (i.e. their bodies, faces, necks and bosoms etc.) and not to reveal their adornment except to their husbands, their fathers. . .

196

But a literal and more honest translation of the above quoted text would read:

> And say to the believing women to lower their gaze, and guard their private parts, and that they should not display their adornments except what would ordinarily appear. And, that they should draw their veils over their bosoms and that they should not display their beauty except to their husbands. . .

The Qur'anic Arabic instructs that women should take their *khimars* and cover their *jayb* (pl. *juyub*). The Arabic is *wal yadribna bi khumurihinna 'ala juyubihinna*, which means that women should take their *khimars* and strike with it or place it upon their bosoms. According to the authoritative lexicon of *Lisan al-'Arab* by Ibn Manzur (d. 711/1311), a *khimar* is a piece of cloth that is worn on the head. A man's turban may be called a *khimar* as well, and a man wearing a turban may be called a *mukhtamir*. A *jayb* is the bosom of a human being. It could also be where the neck and chest meet or the beginning of the cleavage area on a woman's chest. Furthermore, a shirt, garment, or pocket may be called *jayb* as well. The jurists add that the *khimar* was a cloth worn by women in pre-Islamic times on the neck and that it was normally thrown toward the back leaving the head and chest exposed. The verse apparently instructs that the piece of cloth normally worn on the head (the *khimar*) or neck be made to cover the bosom or to descend down to the point of touching the cloth. Commentators on the Qur'an repeatedly emphasize that women in Mecca and Medina were in the habit of exposing all or most their chests, even if their hair was covered. Consequently, it is quite possible that the point of the revelation was to call upon women to cover their chests. But whatever the case may be, nothing in the verse indicates that the *khimar* is to cover the face or hands. If the verse intended that the face be covered, it would have stated *wal yadribna bi khumurihinna 'ala wujuhihinna* (instruct them to place the *khimar* on their faces). But the verse does not allude or refer to the face in any way. In fact, what partially covers the face is usually referred to as *niqab*, and what covers the head is normally referred to as *khimar*. But the Qur'anic verse does not use the word *niqab* anywhere. Although the verse does not explicitly require the covering of the hair, it is possible to argue that the verse assumes it. But to extract more than that from this verse requires an incredulous degree of creative reconstructionism at best, or arrogant and malicious misogyny at worst.

One should also note that the verse states that women should not display their adornments except what would normally appear. The Arabic is *illa ma dhahara minha*, which is an ambiguous phrase. The closest rendering in English of this phrase is: "that which appears," or "that which would normally appear." This phrasing leaves open the question of whether customs or social standards may influence notions of propriety and modesty. The vast majority of Muslim jurists asserted that the phrase "what would normally appear" refers to two distinct elements, the first is *'urf* or *'ada* (custom and established practice) and the second is *haraj* (hardship). Meaning, this phrase refers to what are admittedly adornments, and perhaps objects of enticement, but they are adornments that do not have to be covered because they "normally appear" either as a matter of custom or because they need to appear to avoid and alleviate potential hardship. Therefore, jurists such as Abu Hayyan al-Andalusi (d. 754/1353) and al-Razi (d. 606/1210) explain that the operative legal inquiry is: What normally appears as a matter of practice, what needs to appear so that the law will not impose undue hardship, and how can these two elements be accommodated within the bounds of modesty? Modesty does not mean removing all forms of adornments or enticements. One, that is not possible without excluding women entirely from society, and two, the Qur'an acknowledges that certain adornments (*zinah*) are permitted to appear. Modesty, at a minimum, does mean lowering one's garment and covering the bosom area. Most Muslim jurists concluded, from this discussion, that the face and hands are adornments that do not have to be covered because it would create hardship to ask that they be covered, and because established social practices do not necessitate that they be covered. Some jurists evaluating these same types of considerations allowed the appearance of the ears, the forearms, the neck, the feet, or anything one-half of an arm's length below the knee. Other jurists argued that since the *'awra* of a woman in prayer or *ihram* is the face, hands, and feet, in all circumstances, only these body parts may appear. A significant number of jurists thought that the comparison to *'ibadat* is not relevant to the issue of determining which adornments may appear. The rules of modesty in *'ibadat* involve a very different set of issues than those involved in determining established social practice and hardship. Some jurists such as Sa'id Ibn Jubayr (d. 95/714) disfavored exposing the hair although they did not consider the hair to be part of a woman's *'awra*. The majority of jurists argued that the hair is part of the *'awra* of a free woman but not a slave-girl.

As mentioned above, the distinction between the rules of modesty for slave-girls and free women is rather significant. Perhaps because slave-girls lived active social and economic lives, the vast majority of jurists concluded that slaves did not need to cover their hair, arms or anything below the knees. Some went as far as saying the chest of a slave-girl did not need to be covered, but this seems to be in direct contradiction with the Qur'anic verse discussed above. Much of the distinction in the case of slave-girls seems to rely on the appraisal of the twin elements of established social practice and hardship. Relying on their evaluation of these two elements, the jurists concluded that the adornments of slave-girls that could appear were very different than those of free women. Interestingly, a rather small minority of jurists argued that the rules for poor women who need to lead economically active lives were the same as those for slave-girls.

Today, the distinction between free women and slave-girls, to say the least, is spurious, and the whole issue needs to be re-analyzed. Established social practices and hardship connote moral imperatives, but the factual identification of either of these elements is an empirical, not just a textual, matter. In other words, if the law incorporates two distinct normative values, the first of which is the established social practice and the second of which is the removal of hardship, these two normative values need to be balanced against the requirement of modesty. But determining what is, in fact, an established social practice or a source of hardship is an empirical factual question that is subject to re-evaluation and re-examination as the circumstances dictate in different times and places. The input and testimony of women as to what constitutes hardship in today's environment is crucial. Put differently, men cannot simply assume to know what should "normally appear" of a woman's adornment. This is a matter where those most concerned (i.e., women) must have a clear and decisive voice. There is no question that various textual sources establish the outer parameters of this negotiative process—for instance, the chest or anything above the knee may not appear. However, within the outer parameters there is room for negotiation, re-evaluation, and analysis. Most importantly, the Qur'an does not demand or expect that all sources of *fitna* (enticement) be eradicated in society. The Qur'an balances the various interests and rights, and unlike our dismissive friends, the Qur'an does not expect women to bear the full burden of modesty. The weakness of men cannot be the source of hardship and suffering for women, and any approach that does not acknowledge this fact, in my view, is not true to the spirit or letter of the Qur'an.

The authors of the translation, however, seem to be working under a very different set of assumptions. They seem to be under the misimpression that the Qur'an aims to eradicate all sources of enticement in society, and that women should bear the brunt of the burden in this process. Hence, women should be covered from head to toe except perhaps for one roaming eye, and men may happily prance around undisturbed by delectable female parts. Worst of all, this fundamentally male-indulgent view is presented as God's unquestionable truth. The only truth here is that the authors simply forced the idiosyncrasies of their own culture upon God's text. Consequently, none of the richness and equanimity of the text is reflected in their translation. Rather, the text is made to represent and embody their authoritarian and despotic constructions.

The text of the translation does not give any indication that the absurd renderings of the Divine Text are a result of the idiosyncrasies of the Wahhabi authors. In fact, the authors attempt to confirm the impression of the immutability of their renderings by twice quoting a tradition as a footnote to the above quoted verses. The footnote says:

> Narrated Safiya bint Shaiba [sic.]: 'Aisha used to say: "When (the verse): 'They should draw their veils over their bodies, faces, necks and bosoms,' was revealed, (the ladies) cut their waist sheets at the edges and covered their faces with the cut pieces." (*Sahih Al-Bukhari*, Vol. 6, *Hadith* No. 282)

The truly shocking realization for anyone with a command of the Arabic language is the shameless dishonesty and the remarkable liberties taken with translating this *hadith*. The authors' translation of the statement attributed to 'Aisha (d. 58/678), the Prophet's wife, and reported by Bukhari is nothing short of an outright misrepresentation. The original in Bukhari states that when verse 24:31 was revealed, 'Aisha said: "[The women] took their garments and tore pieces of cloth from the edges and *yaakhtamarna biha.*" *Yaakhtamarna biha* means that the women took the pieces torn from their garments and wore them as a *khimar*, and, as mentioned above, a *khimar* could be a piece of cloth worn on the head. So, presumably, the women wore the pieces torn from their garments on their heads. Another version of the same report, also in Bukhari, provides that only the women of the migrants from Mecca (*al-muhajirin*) were quick to comply. Other versions of the same tradition, reported elsewhere, state that the women of the Ansar were the ones who promptly complied. In either case, the original Arabic does not in any way indicate that the veils were worn on the face. The most one can understand from 'Aisha's tradition is that women covered their heads. But one cannot help but wonder, if the women cut a big enough piece from the edges of their skirts to cover their heads and faces, did this mean that these women left their legs exposed? In any case, the authenticity of this tradition, with its many versions, has been questioned, and some versions indicate that the response of the women in Medina was to cover their bosoms.

In yet another example, and there are many examples, of corrupting the text, verse 4:34 was translated in the following fashion:

> Men are the maintainers of women, because Allah has made the one of them to excel the other, and because they spend (to support them) from their means. Therefore the righteous women are devoutly obedient (to Allah and to their husbands), and guard in the husband's absence what Allah orders them to guard (e.g. their chastity, their husband's property, etc). As to those women on whose part you see ill-conduct, admonish them (first), (next), refuse to share their beds, (and last) beat them (lightly, if it is useful). . .

The original in Arabic does not refer to husbands as the recipient of women's obedience. The original talks about women who are pious, humble before God, and observant of God's commands. The corrupted text not only inserts a reference to husbands, but also equates obedience to husbands with obedience to God. Furthermore, the translation leaves the reader with the distinct impression that husbands may punish their wives for what, in the husband's judgment, constitutes "ill-conduct." This leads to a separate discussion all together. Why are husbands, as a category, given full authority to act as judge, jury, and executioner against women for what they alone deem as "ill-conduct"? What if a husband is less pious than the wife? Furthermore, the word used in the original is *nushuz*, which means a serious deviation or gross misconduct and, in either case, the verse does not authorize husbands to beat their wives. The word *azwaj* (husbands) is not mentioned in God's text and, as explained earlier in the *Conference*, the verse is talking about gross sexual misconduct, which is distinct from other types of "ill-conduct," particularly from the purview of Islamic law.

The Noble Qur'an translation/interpretation of the Qur'an is widely distributed in the United States. According to this translation, God commanded that women cover their faces, necks, bosoms, arms, legs, and hands. Furthermore, the reader is informed that God commanded devout obedience to God's self, and then mandated the same type of obedience for husbands. From the gross liberties taken in translating the text, apparently the translators believe that God wishes women to be like housebroken dogs—loyal, timid, sweet, and obedient. One can only ponder, what type of rotted and foul soul imagines that God wishes to imprison women in a sewer of squalid male egos, and suffer because men cannot control their libidos? What an ugly picture they have created of God's compassion and mercy.

According to the translators, God ordered the veil, and the veil must cover the face, except one or two eyes, and only the palms of the hands may appear. The eyes are not supposed to be covered, apparently as a concession to women, so that they may be able to walk. What if a woman had a seeing-eye dog—would she need to cover her eyes as well? But, of course, dogs are devilish abominations in Wahhabi thought, and so perhaps a woman could hire a slave to guide her through the streets. So in this nightmarish and macabre world, a slave would guide another slave to the altar of male divinity.

Furthermore, I cannot help but wonder how does a woman cover the back of her hands, but still show her palms? The translation mentions the wearing of gloves, but again, I wonder, since gloves, as they exist today, were probably unknown to the Prophet, why aren't gloves considered a heretical innovation (*bid'a*)? There is a tradition attributed to the Prophet in which he reportedly forbids women from wearing a *quffaz* (hand cover) or *niqab* while in a state of *ihram* (a state of ritual consecration during pilgrimage). Scholars, however, have doubted the authenticity of this tradition. The scholars asserted that this was simply the opinion of Ibn 'Umar, and it was wrongfully attributed to the Prophet. In any case, *quffaz*, as used in that tradition, meant either a decoration made of cloth worn on the hand as a form of beautification or a loose piece of cloth stuffed with cotton and having buttons on the side worn as protection from the cold. These hand covers were loose, dark, and large. Isn't the tightness of today's gloves a *fitna* (enticement), and shouldn't women wear loose black bags on their hands so that no one may be enticed by the attractive contours of the hand? Truly, ugliness can only beget utter absurdity.

The reader is left with the impression that the idiosyncratic understandings of the authors of the translation are supported by the traditions of Bukhari and the Qur'anic commentaries of al-Tabari, al-Qurtubi, and Ibn Kathir. But Bukhari's reports are grossly corrupted, and the commentaries of al-Tabari, al-Qurtubi, and Ibn Kathir do not support the authors' understandings. In fact, these Qur'anic commentators report a variety of views and conclude that women may show their faces, hands, and feet. In other words, the authors of *The Noble Qur'an* translation usurped the authority of these distinguished scholars, but apparently did not bother to read or correctly represent what these scholars actually said. This translation is nothing more than a faithful reproduction of Bin Bazz's extremely conservative and intolerant views, and the views of the scholars serving in the Saudi *dar al-Ifta*.

It is clear that the authors of the translation and their supporters do not like women, and that they projected their inadequacies and deformities upon God's text and the whole Islamic intellectual tradition. Truly, the agony of the Muslim plight in the modern world cannot be expressed either in words or tears. What can one say about those people who seem to have declared an unmitigated war against women and who brandish the weapons of grotesque misogyny? What can one say about those people who, in their utter ignorance and maniacal arrogance, subjugate even the word of God to their ugliness and deformities? "Who is more unjust than those who suppress the testimony they received from God, and God is not oblivious as to what they do" (2:140). Truly, "These folks, the cult they are in, is destined to ruin, and false is what they practice" (7:139).

The Remembrance

Those overwhelmed by the weight of their legacy will disown it, but those without a history will invent it, and both are doomed to repeat all their past mistakes. One lives in the consolation of a lie, and the other, if confronted by the truth, waives it away. Uprooted by oblivion and dispossessed of an identity, we settle in fictions of relativity where our boundaries blur and fade. Don't you see that those without a homeland in history are branded as aliens wherever they are invited to stay? Without the anchor of history, we live from thought to thought, pulled and shoved by every trend and wave. Some will ground themselves in the rigor of philosophy, but most will live from sight to mind, nursing their fluctuating identity with a whimsical sense of faith.

My visit with this glorious Conference is coming to an end, and I pray that I will be deemed worthy enough to be permitted to transform or, at least, that I will be invited again. This Conference had become the bridge to many repressed memories, and the rediscovery of my sense of balance and dignity. Now, I pounce in the streets with a smile on my face telling everyone who finds me:

I have foundations, I have roots, I have a history, I have a homeland on this earth, I have my own intellectual space. I have delved into the depth of my brain, cleansed the dust and cobwebs of forgetfulness, and chased so many ghosts away. I now know who I am, and my attention is turned to who I want to be. If it hadn't been for a sense of humility and a bashful nature, I would yell, "Embrace me, for my roots and anchor can perhaps offer you a repose of stability."

As I rummaged through the files of memories, I recalled an incident nestled in silence, but now it spoke again. An old sheet of paper reminded me of a time when my young age blessed me with remarkable energy fueled by gleeful hopefulness. I spoke my mind in a way that, at times, bordered on insolence.

Years ago, I was in a conference organized by the Islamic Society of North America with the usual list of speakers and with the customary fanfare. I sat in the audience listening to a panel on "Conflict Resolutions in Mosques." There were a couple of speakers who waltzed with words, and since I don't dance, I was utterly bored. A bearded young fellow with green eyes and Egyptian skin was the last to speak. His bashfulness intrigued me in such a bombastic atmosphere. He talked about a mosque in his hometown that had been plagued by disputes and in-fighting between Wahhabis and Sufis and some other factions as well. The dispute disintegrated into fist-fights with lawsuits and legal injunctions flying all over the place. The judge assigned to the case appointed our Egyptian-colored friend to act as an arbitrator in the case. I am not sure what the procedural posture was, or what were the rules by which everyone had to play, but our friend explained that he sought to arbitrate the matter according to the dictates of Islamic law, and that all the parties to the conflict agreed that Islamic law should be dispositive in this case. In his presentation, our friend quoted the Qur'anic verse: "All the mosques belong to God, so do not call upon anyone else but God" (72:18). He then proceeded to talk about the unprecedented nature of this case, after which he addressed the by-laws of the mosque, the deed of trust, the wishes of the fighting parties, and other similarly fascinating things. I listened attentively, engaged by the approach rather than the substance of what was said. I searched what he said for what would resound in me with a sense of authenticity and legitimacy. Instead, I felt abandoned in a syncretistic world where holes are plugged and covered by patches drawn from scraps and pieces from here and there. There was no synchronism or synthesis or sense of symmetry or proportionality between the conservatism of legitimacy and the excitements of creativity—between the respect for precedents and the irreverence of originality.

After the lecture, I arranged to meet with the fellow and he kindly indulged me. After the kind salutations, I jumped on the subject with great zeal.

"Brother," I said, "you spoke of arbitrating a conflict within a mosque, and if I understood you correctly, you sought the guidance of Islamic law on the matter, but I did not fully understand how you phrased the issue or the problem you had to deal with?"

"The issue," he stated, "is how to resolve the conflict between the brothers in the mosque. The Wahhabis could not live with the Sufis, and the Sufis could not live with the Wahhabis. The situation quickly disintegrated to the point of fistfights in the mosque and, as you know, the mosque is the house of God, and such behavior cannot be tolerated."

"Yes, yes," I agreed. "This is a common problem in the United States. Many mosques seem to suffer from discord whether on theological or ethnic grounds. But

I guess I am wondering about some of your premises. For example, how do we know that a mosque is the house of God?"

He looked surprised and spoke somewhat condescendingly, "Well, brother, you should know that the Qur'an clearly says that mosques belong to God, and that no one should be worshipped other than God in God's abode. Furthermore, the *Sunna* of the Prophet is clear on this point, mosques belong to God."

"Ah, yes, I see," I nodded. "So what was the issue with which you had to deal?"

"The issue, my brother, was how to resolve the conflict between the fighting parties in the mosque."

"But brother," I exclaimed, "I fear that the issue is rather vaguely stated. We can resolve a conflict by the application of rational thought. We can also resolve a conflict by following customary practices or probing contractual expectations. We can even resolve a conflict by an entirely irrational process like tossing a coin, or perhaps we can apply a principle of utility, and count votes, or we can hold an auction and surrender the mosque to the highest bidder. I guess my problem is that I was not clear as to the method you chose to pursue."

He was becoming impatient with my intellectual dullness, "As I explained to you brother," he said, "mosques belong to God, and so the only standard is the law of God, and that is what I enforced."

"All right," I stated. "I will concede that mosques are the houses of God. But should we apply the law of God to God's property because it is capable of producing the best rational results, or because God wants us to do so, or because the parties to the dispute agree that the law of God should be applied? I want to know why we apply God's law to God's mosques."

"First," he commented with an air of credulity, "it stands to reason that if mosques belong to God, then God can and does set the rules for His home. Second, the parties agreed that God's law is controlling, and third, if you are a Muslim, you must believe that God's law will produce the best results—this is a matter of faith. If you don't believe in the wisdom of God's law, you are not a Muslim."

I asked, "What if the parties do not want the law of God to apply?"

"The parties do not want the law of God to apply!" he exclaimed. "Then I would say they usurped God's home—they are like guests in a home who refuse to respect the will of the host."

"So having accepted the argument that a mosque belongs to God, it would make sense for them to follow God's rules in God's home?"

"Yes, absolutely."

"Could there be a mosque that does not belong to God?" I inquired.

"If all mosques belong to God," he responded, "then what does not belong to God is not a mosque. Don't you know that God said in his glorious Book, 'Say, my Lord has commanded justice and [commanded] that you [should] set your whole selves to God at every mosque, and that you pray to God with sincere devotion. Such as God created you in the beginning so shall you return' (7:29). The point is that God lays claim to every mosque."

I continued in his line of thinking, "And, so whatever is so-called owned privately is not a mosque?"

"I would say it is a prayer area, not a mosque."

"Okay, brother, what if I disagree with you and say, the earth is God's mosque, and that the construction of walls to close off a particular area is irrelevant? How do we resolve this conflict? By the use of reason? By the best rational argument? By reference to accepted social practices, or what? By evaluating different types of evidence?"

"As I keep telling you, if you are a Muslim, you resolve the dispute by referring to the Will of God as manifested in God's law—this is an article of faith, not something that I am willing to debate with you. It is like believing that God is good or just or eternal; it is an article of faith, not something that I am willing to prove."

It was clear that he was becoming impatient, and so I decided I better move my point along. "Yes, yes," I said, "what is an article of faith is like a *faith-based foundation* upon which you build other things. It is the starting point and the premise. It is an assumption that you make before you commence your analysis. It is like assuming democracy is good, or torture is bad, or oppression is wrong.

"Fine, I am willing to concede that mosques belong to God and that the definition of a mosque is a matter of Divine Decree. It is like God saying, 'If you want to build Me a home, here are my rules, and if you do not follow the rules, I will not take title to the home.' I will also concede that the rules of conduct in that home are to be set by the owner of the home. God decides what is appropriate conduct in God's home. We are guests who must abide by the host's rules; otherwise we are not welcome. I will concede all of this not because I agree with the structure of your argument, but because I can make a different argument that would lead to the same results. Do you want to hear my argument?"

"No," he curtly responded.

"Brother," I said, "bear with me. I am just trying to understand why we do things the way we do and what is the point of what we do. It seems to me that everything you said indicates the primacy of the Divine Will. It seems that we know what we know either by the use of faith or reason, and I would include a systematic sense of intuition as part of the use of reason. We know, by the use of faith or reason, that God does not need a home. But we also know, by the use of faith or reason, that God owns everything in existence. Why are mosques in particular described as the houses of God (*buyut Allah*)? We are willing to assume this should be accepted as a matter of faith—it is so because God says so. This is the same, for instance, when we consider whether a mosque must be clean and pure. We know that a mosque should be kept clean and pure because we find evidence that this is what God wants. This is what I want to call a *faith-based argument*. A *faith-based argument* asserts that one should do this or that, not because it is good or just or efficient, but because God wants it so. A *reason-based argument* asserts that we should do this or that because it is good, just, or efficient. What I mean by a *faith-based argument* is an argument that is premised on a *faith-based foundation*. The foundation of the argument is not rational proof or considerations of efficiency, but a basic belief and conviction. This argument is accountable and accessible only in a limited way and only to a limited audience. So, for instance, if I say mosques should be pure, and you say, why? My justification might ultimately rest on the Divine Will. You might say, well, I can show you that it is not a good or reasonable idea to keep mosques pure. I will say that I don't care; you can only persuade me by showing me that God wants mosques to be impure. I would say this is a *faith-based argument* because one can be held accountable for holding this belief only to the extent the *faith-based argument* is related to the *faith-based foundation*. What I mean by 'holding someone accountable' is to demand that someone provide the details of their evidence and processes of analysis. A *faith-based argument* is accessible only to those who hold the same belief.

"If establishing that a mosque should be pure is based on evidence of the Divine Will, then it is a *faith-based argument* premised on a *faith-based foundation*. A *faith-based foundation* is not accessible or accountable—it is a belief that could be based on idiosyncratic experience or no experience at all. It could be the result of a dream or a vision or a sense of tranquility. A *faith-based argument* is accessible and accountable only to the extent that it is dependent on the *faith-based foundation*. So, for instance, if I start with the assumption that I believe in God and that I am a Muslim, that is a *faith-based foundation*. I also start with the assumption that the Qur'an is the literal, immutable, and unerring Word of God—that is a *faith-based foundation* as well. If I say, since the Qur'an is the Word of God, I believe it contains the commands of God—this is a *faith-based argument* that flows from a *faith-based foundation*. From the point of view of reason, it is possible for a Divine book to exist that *does not* contain the commands of God. But, to me, this does not matter, I don't care about this possibility because I believe that the Qur'an does, in fact, contain the commands of God, and that is why my belief is a *faith-based foundation*.

"Now, I read in the Qur'an that mosques are the houses of God, and also read that these houses must be kept pure. If I say, 'I will accept this at face value,' it is reasonable to say that the belief in the status of a mosque as God's home, and the necessity of keeping mosques pure is related to my *faith-based foundations*. However, and this is an important point, the process by which I search for the Divine Will and evaluate the evidence is a *reason-based process*. For instance, the search for the definition of purity, or the factual adjudication as to whether a specific structure is a mosque, is a part of a *reason-based process*.

"Here, it is important to distinguish between a reason-based process and a faith-based process, and between a faith-based argument and a faith-based process. I understand the faith-based argument to be basically a justification or explanation. The argument does not explore or discover anything; it simply demonstrates the way that the conclusions are consistent with the foundations. I arrived at the belief that a mosque should be pure, not by non-justifiable means, but by a justifiable process of analyzing evidence. I arrived at the conclusion that mosques should be pure by a rational-based process because the process relies on the collection and evaluation of evidence. But it is a rational-based process only if one accepts my assumptions (foundations). A faith-based process is very different—it does not rely on rational process, evaluations, or evidence. A faith-based process relies on entirely irrational steps to reach a conclusion. The irrational steps are entirely nonaccountable and inaccessible. The irrational steps are like revelation, visions, or dreams. The faith-based process could be consistent or inconsistent with my faith-based foundations. For instance, if my faith-based foundations assert that only the Prophet receives Divine Revelation, it would not be consistent if I claim that I know the law because I received revelation. If I make that type of claim, one would say, 'okay, but you need to revise your faith-based foundations.'

"Now, more to the point: The issue you were lecturing about concerned the rules of conduct in a mosque. Well, we can make rational deductions from the premises that we accept as God's Will. So, for instance, if God says, not to have conjugal relations in a mosque (2:187), we will probably accept the fact that we should not have conjugal relations in the mosque as a matter of faith—as God's Will. We are not going to evaluate the wisdom of the command or whether the command is consistent with the function of the mosque. But we can explore, by the use of reason, the finding of, the meaning of, or the implications of the command. So there is an irrational component to our inquiry, which is the Divine Will. It is irrational in the sense that whatever is ascertained to be the Divine Will is accepted as mandatory as a matter of faith. It is rational only to the extent that it is consistent with my *faith-based foundations*. There is also another rational component, and that is the finding of, the deductions from, and consequences of the Divine Will. So even if we accept that we should not have conjugal relations, we might still ask what is having conjugal relations? Is it intercourse only or does it include lesser sexual acts? Is it limited to sexual acts alone, or does it include non-sexual acts as well? Can we kiss or hug or dance or eat in a mosque? The answer will follow from a rational process of analysis. The rational process of analysis will first ascertain whether God has a Will as to these specific acts. Does God perceive these acts in one way or another? If God has a Will as to these acts, we will eventually need to ask whether the Divine Will trumps the human will because of the possibility that the human will might be inconsistent with the Divine Will. I am willing to concede because of my *faith-based foundation* that the

Divine Will should trump the human will, so this point need not detain us. But then the next question is, assuming that God does have a specific Will as to acts such as hugging, kissing, dancing, or eating in a mosque, we must ask, does God want us to observe or obey His will on the matter? If we conclude that God does want us to comply with God's Will, the next question is, how do we discover this Divine Will?"

As I explained, in my view, the process of collecting and evaluating the evidence is a rational process—the foundations or premises are a matter of faith, but the process of collecting and evaluating the evidence is a matter of reason. The *reason-based process* will be premised on a *faith-based foundation*. For instance, if we have a tradition that says, Do not do impure acts in the mosque. Then, accepting the wisdom or truth of this injunction might be a matter of faith that rationally flows from the *faith-based foundation*. Importantly, deciding on the relevance of this injunction to the problem at hand or any specific fact pattern is a matter of reason. I could evaluate different pieces of evidence that seem to be relevant to the issue. Deciding on what is relevant is a matter of reason, or deciding what the totality of the evidence would seem to require of us, is a matter of reason. For example, asserting that the totality of the evidence seems to prohibit kissing in the mosque is the product of a process of reasoning, and deciding that the specific act involved in a specific case is all the result of reason. But deciding that I must comply with the law, whatever I think it is, is justifiable by faith.

He shuffled and shifted and glanced at me and then snapped, "All this faith-based this and faith-based that—what is your point? Get to the point. What do you want to say? What is the use of all this slicing and dicing—you remind me of the picklers in Egypt who sit in the street slicing vegetables and then dumping it in a big barrel of confusion."

I felt hurt, but I was intrigued by the image of the picklers—I used to watch them in Egypt with great fascination. My intrigue only ignited my determination, for these were the days of hope and zeal. With a new burst of energy I said, "Brother, I am simply trying to establish simple rules for accessibility and accountability. I want us to agree that a faith-based foundation is not subject to accountability and is not accessible to someone who does not share the foundation. I also want us to agree that a reason-based foundation is subject to accountability and is accessible to anyone who will investigate with reasoning behind the foundation. I want to establish that a *faith-based argument*, unlike a *reason-based argument*, is an argument that relies on elements that can only be shared by particular group of people. I want us to agree that a *faith-based process* is also not accountable and not accessible. For example, saying I know what God wants because I had a vision or dream, or I know what God wants because God speaks to me, is a *faith-based process*. The only thing a listener can do is either believe the claim, or not believe it. It cannot be verified or rationally evaluated. But a *faith-based foundation* does not preclude the use of a *reason-based process*. If I am

THE SEARCH FOR BEAUTY IN ISLAM

weighing and evaluating evidence, this is a *reason-based process*. For instance, I can start out by saying, I believe in Islamic law, and I believe that Islamic law should guide my life. This foundation is accepted as a matter of faith. But the process of searching for and evaluating what is Islamic law is a *reason-based process* because it depends on gathering and reasoning through the various pieces of evidence. But I want to go further and make another claim. I claim that if one pursues a *faith-based process* that is not consistent with the Divine Will (or one's *faith-based foundation*), one is committing a grave sin. Why? Because pursuing a *faith-based process* involves the act of exercising legislative sovereignty. But in the case of Islam, an act of sovereignty gains its legitimacy only from the Divine Will, or at least, this is what we seem to agree upon. Using a *faith-based process* to reach a *faith-based foundation* runs the real risk of usurping God's legislative sovereignty. Suppose, for example, that one day I say, 'Part of my *faith-based foundation* is that all Muslims must not eat apples.' You come to me and say, 'This prohibition of apples is very strange, and I will show you by a careful analysis of the evidence that eating apples is allowed in Islam.' To this I respond, 'I have pursued a *faith-based process* and adopted this belief as a *faith-based foundation*, and, therefore, I am not interested in your evidence. Regardless of the weight of evidence or any process of evaluation, this is my firm belief.' Now, either my belief that apples are prohibited is dependent and derivative from the Divine Will or it is not. If it is not derivative from the Divine Will, then it is an act of legislation without authorization, and a Muslim who believes in the supremacy of the Divine Will will think that my claim is without legitimacy. If my belief that apples are prohibited is, in fact, derived from the Divine Will, then there are two options. Either this belief is based on a *faith-based process* (I had a vision or I received revelation), or this belief is based on a *reason-based process* (I looked at the evidence). If the argument is based on a vision or some other idiosyncratic experience, I would need to know why this individual vision is relevant to me. Even if I believe that your vision is relevant to me, I must recognize that there is a *privity* between you and God—God chose to reveal to you what God did not choose to reveal to others. But then we have a problem because it is a tenet of belief in Islam that all revelation ceased with the death of the Prophet. So how can we justify the idea of privity between you and God without reevaluating other *faith-based foundations* of the religion?

"Now, I want to make another claim that is even more aggressive than what I said so far. I think that a *reason-based process* cannot create a *faith-based foundation*. Earlier, I might have intimated that one can start by evaluating and weighing the evidence as to an issue (i.e., *using a reason-based process*) and then reach a *faith-based foundation*. But, in truth, I don't think this is possible. If one starts by rationally evaluating the evidence on a matter, then the conclusions reached are always subject to evaluation and criticism on the basis of the evidence. On any legal or theological point, if you rationally evaluated the evidence then you have used a method that is both accessible and accountable to someone who shares your premises or assumptions. If, after evaluating the evidence, you declare that your conclusions are not open to reevaluation or criticism because they have become a *faith-based foundation*, I would say that the *rational-based process* has become entirely irrelevant to your belief and you cannot cite it in support of your beliefs. You can only cite a *faith-based process*. This would throw us back to evaluating your *faith-based process* vis-à-vis God's sovereignty. *In a nutshell, what this means is that any point of theology or law that was reached on the basis of the evaluation of the evidence can and should be criticized and evaluated on the basis of the evidence.* From my perspective, if you make a point about Islamic law or theology and you are not willing to discuss the evidence, that means you are saying your belief is not accessible or accountable, and, therefore, I may safely ignore you."

When I stopped talking, I noticed he was looking around, apparently trying to find an escape from the pleasure of my company. When his efforts proved in vain, he turned to me and proclaimed, "Brother, all I have to say to you is you are engaging in the forbidden *kalam* [theological disputations] and in the cursed language of philosophers. Both are prohibited because God has forbidden the use of reason in all matters."

I quickly retorted, "You are wrong on all counts. One, let me be very clear about this: I am not a philosopher, and I have not mastered philosophy. I am making distinctions that seem sensible to me. If you think my distinctions are flawed, then advise me of which distinctions should be made instead. Two, I would like you to know that I like picklers and I take offense to what you said about them. Three, what is your evidence that God prohibited the use of reason? Is this a rational conclusion that you somehow reached, or is this your own sovereign legislation on God's behalf? If so, show me evidence that there is privity between you and God. I should add that in the Qur'an, God condemns *hawa* (whim) but endorses reason. In fact, God uses reason to refute the whimsical irrationality of the unbelievers. Furthermore, what you just said does not make much sense to me. Isn't it the rational workings of the brain that weigh the authenticity of the Qur'an versus the authenticity of the *Sunna*? Isn't it the rational workings of the brain that determine the authenticity or relevance or weight of the evidence? If God says no conjugal relations in the mosque, isn't it the rational workings of the brain that identify the meaning of conjugal relations in this context or evaluate the criteria to determine whether a specific structure is, in fact, a mosque? Faith is like certain assumptions one makes for the sake of argument, but reason does all the rest. Faith is what determines that the Qur'an is the word of God, or that Muslims should take what the Qur'an says to heart, or that the Prophet should be obeyed. But reason determines the understanding of the full meaning and implications of something that is accepted as a matter of faith. Reason determines the deductions we can make from something that is accepted as a matter of faith. Finally, *kalam* is not a dirty word. It is a part of our heritage, and we should consider it for whatever it is worth. And, for your information, what I am saying has nothing to do with *kalam*, it is the same type of discourse you will find in books of *usul al-fiqh* (Islamic jurisprudence)."

"Okay, fine," he proclaimed, "but I don't know what you are getting at. What does all of this have to do with resolving the conflict in the mosque?"

"My basic question is: When you resolved the conflict in the mosque, were you implementing your own will, the will of the parties, or the Will of God?"

"As I keep telling you, the mosque is *baytu Allah* (the house of God), and I was implementing the Will of God."

"That is profound," I rather maniacally exclaimed, "that is truly a weighty trust! And did you gain this position as a matter of faith or reason? Did God tell you that you will represent God's Will, or did certain rational processes tell us that it makes sense to accept your decision as a binding representation of God's Will?"

He dryly remarked, "The court appointed me, and the parties accepted me."

I responded, "Then it seems that a rational process, induced by convenience or the logic of consent or the logic of institutional organizations, appointed and entrusted you."

"Fine, what is your point?"

"Do we know what God thinks about your appointment?"

"We can only guess," he said.

"But you assumed, as a matter of faith, that a mosque is the house of God, and proceeded to apply God's rules in God's house."

"Exactly!"

"Your appointment did not come from God. It was the result of a process based on reason. But you were not appointed to apply your own reason, you were appointed to apply something else. In this particular case, that something else is the law of God."

"Sure, fine."

"But how did you find God's rules? Did you use a *faith-based process* or a *reason-based process*?"

"Brother," he yelled, "are you insane! Are you seriously suggesting that I was somehow dreaming up the law or receiving Divine Revelation? This is getting ridiculous."

"Brother, in your presentation you made no reference to any evidence other than the Qur'anic verse you quoted. But, even more, you did not engage in a *reason-based process* that is premised on the Qur'anic verse quoted. It seemed to me that you arbitrated by reference to what the parties were willing to live with or by reference to the by-laws or by reference to conversations you had with some members of the congregation. These are entirely reasonable methods of resolving the conflict, but only if we make very different assumptions than the ones you made. It seems to me that the logic of your argument went something like this: 'I will assume that this is God's house, I will also assume that God has rules for His house and that these rules, as a matter of faith, must be obeyed. I will assume that God has a Will as to conflicts in mosques, and that God wants me to give effect to this Will.' Yet, you proceeded to use common sense, yours and others, to establish God's rules. This is not consistent with your premises or foundations unless you also claim that God's rules are coextensive with your common sense or that God, in effect, told you that God's rules can be located, evaluated, and implemented by the use of common sense. But you did not make such an argument, and, in fact, you explicitly rejected this idea. But then what was your methodology? You seemed to be saying, I know because I know. This could not have been a *reason-based process*, so it must have been a *faith-based process*. In effect, God's Will turns out to be your will—God's rules are what you decided the rules should be. This requires that I believe that you were chosen by God and given the power to articulate the rules, that there is privity between you and God, and not that you have been chosen by a rational process and given the burden of searching for God's rules."

Understandably, he was angry and he raised his voice again, "So, you are saying that I enforced my whim and the whim of others instead of God's law."

"What I am saying is that your methodology confused me. You started out saying that the law of God applies, and I took it that you made this claim as a matter of faith. Then, you proceeded to cite largely sociological evidence and your own intuitions. This seems to me entirely acceptable as long as you acknowledge that the law of God turns on sociology and on your intuitions. Alternatively, you could claim, and perhaps we can then accept, that you effectively speak for God. If you are not willing to make either of these arguments, then I think you need to cite relevant evidence— you need to use a *reason-based process* that is consistent with your *faith-based foundations*. You need to tell us whether we should accept this evidence as a matter of reason or faith, and if you conclude that the evidence points to specific results, you need to make this argument in rational terms. You also need to rationally prove that the evidence applies to the set of facts before you in a particular way. If you are making a *faith-based process*, then your argument is neither accessible nor accountable, and if we don't believe that you have some privity with God, we can all proceed with our lives."

"Well," he protested, "I could have rationally proven everything, but it would have taken forever."

"No," I quickly responded, "I don't believe this is an excuse. You see, I think there is a short-cut to doing this if you are unwilling to do it yourself."

"What short-cut?"

"The opinions, research, and deductive processes of those before you. I noticed that you did not cite a single authority other than yourself. In Islamic juristic discourses, there is a whole field named *ahkam al-masajid* (the rules that apply to mosques). Al-Zarakshi (d. 794/1392) has a multivolume work on the subject of mosques, their ownership, and how they may be run. There are a large number of *responsa* issued on these matters throughout the Islamic centuries that you could have researched and discussed.

There are even legal judgments and opinions written by the Anglo-Muhammadan courts in India that directly relate to the issues that you were discussing. But you did not refer to a single juristic source."

"Oh, I see," he said with some relief, "this again! You are one of those people! This is all about citing authorities. No, brother, we Salafis believe that there is only the word of God, the words of the Prophet and us. As the saying goes, 'They were men and we are men (*humm rijalun wa nahnu rijal*).' We read the Divine text and we apply it, and we do not accept any mediators between us and the text. We do not worship schools or heads of schools, we do not care about what so and so said, or what this or that school of thought held. We only care about what God and the Prophet said."

"Brother," I replied, "I don't know who are the 'those' to whom you refer. But I have several responses to you. First, I already demonstrated to you that your approach to the problem relies on contradictory assumptions. You say, 'No, they are not contradictory, and I am not acting on whim.' I say fine, tell me what you are asserting as a matter of faith and Divine Will, and what you are asserting as a matter of reason, or the product of your own rational appraisal. I am asking you to do that so that I can evaluate your argument and decide whether I can share your faith or agree with your reason. You respond to me by saying, 'Well, I don't have time.' So I say, there is another way—you may search the sources that preserve the efforts of those before you. Find the approaches that you agree with and find the approaches that you disagree with. You can explain the approaches to me and critique them, and this way I can better fill in the gaps that you failed to make clear. For example, suppose that a mathematician has proven a certain theorem, and you come today and make a mathematical argument that is on the same exact point. But you do not have time to go through all the steps and prove to me what needs to be proven. So then a sensible starting point is to incorporate by reference the work of the mathematician, and then explain to me what you agree or disagree with. This is my first point.

"My second point is the following: People before you have made the same search for evidence that you claim to have made. I find that they cited and analyzed more evidence than you did. They discuss Qur'anic versus, analyze the practice of the Prophet, refer to the precedent of the Companions, refer to overarching principles of *Shari'a*, and then evaluate the implications of these overarching principles. You, on the other hand, did not do any of this, and I am not sure if you abstained from doing this because of a lack of diligence, or because you disagree with the efforts of these scholars, or because you think that what these scholars considered to be authoritative sources are not authoritative at all. I am left puzzled, and the only way I can evaluate your claim that you did not find relevant evidence, is to compare your claim to the product of other scholars.

"My third point is this: You claimed to implement Islamic law. This begs the question: What do you mean by Islamic law? Do you mean the Qur'an and *Sunna* as

214

revealed to you? Do you mean the Qur'an and *Sunna* as interpreted by you? Or, do you mean the Qur'an and *Sunna* as interpreted by you and others? Or, do you mean what other scholars at some unspecified point in time and place said is Islamic law? It is not clear to me which, if any of these, you mean. To the extent that your statement does not clarify this point, it leaves me confused. When I am listening to your talk, am I listening to your own school of thought and your own *reason-based process?* Am I listening to your school of thought and the other schools of thought as well? Is every school of thought in agreement with you? If they are not, should I ignore them and listen to you? But why? Is it because a *reason-based process* will prove you more correct and worthy? Or, is it because a *faith-based process* will prove you more representative of the Divine? All of this leaves me confused.

"The fourth point closely follows from the third. To the extent you claim to speak for Islamic law, you could reasonably anticipate that you are creating the impression in the minds of your audience that you are speaking for the full tradition of Islamic jurisprudence. When I say, for example, I am explaining American law, a reasonable listener will assume that I am representing more than my own unique and idiosyncratic individual reading of American legal sources. It is reasonable to assume that I am representing the totality of the American legal tradition on a certain point, and that I will explain the ways in which my own opinions agree or disagree with this totality. Consider a different example. If I talk about the rules of chess, communities of meaning will assume that I am talking about the rules of chess as it evolved through the ages. But if I am using the expression 'rules of chess' to mean an individualistic re-interpretation of the game of chess, I am duty-bound to clarify this point. I think one can reasonably contend that religious communities create communities of meaning and communities of symbolism. In Islam, when one invokes the symbol of Islamic law, Muslims will reasonably assume that you are talking about the Qur'an, the *Sunna,* and the juristic opinions, old and new. But you are excluding juristic opinions from the symbol of Islamic law. Don't you think you are duty-bound to clarify this point?

"My fifth point is a point of wisdom. Let us assume that I am confronting a difficult technical problem in my work. I am told that such and such person had already faced this exact problem or a similar problem, and they managed to resolve it. What would you think if I proclaim that I don't need anyone's help and refuse to ask for anyone's guidance? Wouldn't you think this is rather arrogant, wasteful, and stupid? Ironically, you are refusing to use others as a reference point, but you are expecting others to use you as a reference point. If there are legal precedents on a certain point because previous jurists dealt with a similar problem, what is the justification for refusing to consult with those jurists, by consulting their books, and, yet, claim that your own treatment of the same or similar problem is a precedent for others? If you say, 'Listen, I am not expecting others to follow my precedent,' then why are you telling us about your experience with resolving this conflict? You are telling us because you think that your treatment is somehow relevant to future situations that might arise. Yet, you refuse to acknowledge the counsel of anyone who preceded you. This is a serious problem especially when I consider that the jurists who dealt with this problem before you were more learned and more aware of the relevant pieces of evidence.

"My sixth and final point has to do with the evaluation of evidence. I believe, and perhaps you believe as well, that God instructs us to consult the learned when we confront challenging problems (16:43)(21:7). I also believe, and perhaps you believe as well, that God instructs us to conduct all affairs through a constant process of consultation (3:159)(42:38). I read what I would argue are rather clear Qur'anic commands, to consult the learned and to consult one another, as commands that include consulting with learned jurists, dead or alive. I reach this understanding through a *reason-based process*. Your methodology seems to exclude consulting with learned jurists, dead or alive, on points relating to God's law, and I am at a loss to understand why. You seem to have consulted with the parties involved in the conflict, you consulted with the American judge involved, you consulted with friends and families, and you consulted with engineers and medical doctors in the community. Perhaps you think the duty to consult only applies to those people, or you think that those are the learned people that the Qur'an is talking about. But are you then claiming that the rules of exclusion and inclusion are left to your individual discretion—is it up to you to include or exclude whomever you want? Are you claiming that God is the One who wants jurists, dead and alive excluded, and engineers, doctors, and friends and family included? If so, explain the *reason-based process* that enabled you to reach this conclusion. If not, then claim that God revealed to you the details of the rules of inclusion and exclusion. I assume you have a methodology, but I cannot understand it."

He gazed at me for a long time with simmering rancor, "So, you are basically saying that I should go to the books of some jurist and follow it."

"No, you have not been listening. I am saying you consult the jurists of the past. You study their efforts and methodologies and solutions and then, if you feel that you can discharge your obligation with fairness and diligence, you decide what to follow and what to leave. But unless your belief in yourself is a matter of faith, and unless you are asking us to believe in you as a matter of faith, you must rationally persuade us that you are in fact giving effect to the Will of God. The best way to do that is to explain to us why the efforts of others before you are not on point or are wrong or are incomplete. But to simply ignore them strikes me as inefficient, arrogant, unkind, and rather ugly."

"All I am getting from this," he said, "is that you are in love with intellectualism, and intellectualism is prohibited and condemned in Islam. Brother, instead of this nonsense, follow the guidance of the Qur'an and *Sunna*—this is the straight path, not this twisting and twirling around that people like you are so good at."

"As to your point about intellectualism," I protested, "again, I don't understand. Are you saying God did not give you an intellect, or are you saying that God gave you an intellect but prohibited you from using it? Are you claiming intellectualism is prohibited as a matter of belief and faith because God revealed this to you? Did God communicate the prohibition to you directly, or did you wake up one day with this conviction firm in your heart? But how am I able to share this faith with you if I have no access to your spirit, and you are unable to give me an accounting that would transplant the same emotional conviction into my heart? Perhaps, you are saying that through a *reason-based process,* you arrived at the belief that intellectualism is prohibited. Perhaps you used your intellect to conclude that you may not use your intellect. But then, what is the legitimacy of the intellectual process that you used in the beginning to reach the *reason-based* conclusion that intellectualism is banned? This is like using the democratic process to ban the democratic process—is this legitimate, consistent, or honest? In any case, if you used a *reason-based process* to ban intellectualism, then surely you would be able to share with us your evidence, and if you can't, then why should I be persuaded by your claim? As to the point about the straight path, I believe that the straight path exists and that it is good as a matter of faith. But I search for the straight path, and evaluate the evidence, and ponder whether I have fulfilled my obligations toward it as a matter of reason, not faith. As to my intentions and the nature of my behavior, all I am asking of you is to tell us whether we should accept your role and conclusions about Islamic law as a matter of reason or faith—is the acceptance of your authoritativeness an act of reason or an act of faith?"

"Okay, brother," he proclaimed, "I patiently listened to you. But you persist in using *kalam* and philosophical nonsense. This is Uncle-Tom Americanism, and I pray that God will guide you some day. *Al-salamu alaykum.*"

With that, he turned and walked away. But life reserves surprises stranger than fiction. A few years later, I received the following e-mail from my Egyptian-looking friend:

Dear Brother Abul Fadl:

Al-salamu alaykum. I don't know if you would remember me. We met in New York State many years ago. I gave a talk on resolving a conflict in a mosque and you slammed me. Much has happened since then. I went to law school, and I am now in my third year. After we talked, I did not give the same lecture again because I worried I would find someone like you in the audience. I also did some thinking. I felt bad because, using a faith-based argument (or is it a reason-based process), I felt I was sinning. I said I was applying the law of God because I believed that this is what God wants. But I started thinking that although I believe in the idea of the law of God as a matter of faith, and I accept its wisdom as a matter of faith, the law of God is found and evaluated through a reason-based process. Also, using a reason-based process, I felt I was being ungrateful, arrogant, and dismissive toward the Islamic tradition. The truth is that I tried to look in the old books of Islamic law and could not understand what they were saying. These jurists seemed to be speaking a private language. Is this what you meant when you said communities of meaning or symbolism? What are we supposed to do if we can't understand our tradition?

One more question, if you will allow me—the feeling or desire to be rooted in a tradition, the desire to be a continuation rather than an aberration, to be an evolvement rather than an invention—is this longing for one's roots and origins based on faith or reason?

Your brother in Islam. . .

I wrote him back the following sentence.

Dear Brother:

In response to your question, like the longing for beauty and God, this would be the remembrance—the '*dhikra li'l dhakirin*' (the remembrance for those who remember) (11:114). *Wa al-salamu alaykum.*

CHAPTER 59

The Scholar's Road*

W *a alzamahum kalimata al-taqwa*—the words of your Lord nurse your soul. Let this aching body do what it wants, I am migrating to the word. Let the world play its games and compete for meaningless scores, I live by the word. Let them display their ornaments, flaunt their adornments, worship their senses, bid for the meaningless, exult, gloat, and boast, I am leaving this world. "So leave them to their babble and play, until they face their promised day" (43:83). When all is said and done, nothing remains except for the word.

Yes, babble and play—but when I see the fervor and vehemence by which some babble and play, I never cease to be amazed. The ignorant pursue their ignorance with fury and rage, and they see fear and enemies everywhere. The people of the word are bound by the word, and say, "Peace upon you, we feel no petulance, but we do pity your fate." *Wa alzamahum kalimata al-taqwa*—God has made the believers bound by the "word of self-restraint" (48:26). Those who do not believe burn with the heat and cant of ignorance, but the believers are given the bliss of tranquility, and stand steadfast with the word of self-restraint (48:26). "The word of self-restraint"—what a subtle expression! The word is the testament, and its truth is self-restraint. Regardless of the rage of chauvinism, the arrogance of vanities and the fury of arrogance, the ardor

---

* For this *Conference* I relied on a variety of biographical dictionaries and historical sources such as *al-Muntazam* by Ibn al-Jawzi (d. 597/1201) and *al-Siyar* by al-Dhahabi (d. 748/1348). However, I am especially indebted to George Makdisi's valuable study on Ibn 'Aqil, *Ibn 'Aqil: Religion and Culture in Classical Islam* (Edinburgh: Edinburgh University Press, 1997). The quotes reproduced here are, for the most part, Makdisi's. However, I have changed some of the translations to reflect my understanding of the original sources.

of ignorance, and pestilence of prejudice, God's charge to those who know is principled self-restraint.

> The life of this world is play and jest, but if you believe and practice self-restraint, God will grant you recompense. God does not ask that you surrender all of your possessions. If God would ask that of you, and press [that upon] you, you would covetously withhold, and [asking you to do that] would evoke your hate (47:36–7).

"Evoke our hate!"—such is our pitiful state. If pressured to let go of our possessions, our play and games, and our indulgences and delusions, and if asked to embrace the full meaning of the word, it only provokes in us defiance, anger, and hate. Such is our truly sad state. If confronted with our arrogance, ignorance, self-indulgence, and lack of fair and just self-restraint, we react with stubborn arguments, anger, and hate.

I seek solace in the lessons of the past—in those who held steadfast to the restraint of the word. I seek comfort in those who gave the word its worth, and paid the price in pain and hurt. I find comfort in their suffering, as my suffering is bound to comfort someone else. The road of knowledge is lonely, but the traveler is assured when he finds someone else's footsteps.

There is no need to deny the pain I suffer from the insolence of students, the treachery of friends, and the slander of foes. There is no need to deny that acts of kindness and care are answered with ingratitude and disdain. There is no need to deny that the equanimity of the word is persistently attacked by those who are severely allergic to thought. There is no need to deny that for every thoughtful word, jealousy spews out a thousand scornful words. Jealousy wears the garb of piety and lurks in ignorance, waiting to pounce on any gallant thought. There is no need to deny because my suffering will be the footsteps that comfort another traveler on the road. Those who worship their emotions and live for self-promotion will always torment the servants of reason and the upholders of the word. But, regardless of the pain, we are bound by the truth of piety, and the truth of piety is found in a word. Our history is full of heroes and persecutors. The only question is, whom do we choose to honor and whom do we choose to ignore.

There are so many footsteps telling us the stories of those who agonized and suffered as they walked this road. Our civilization was not built on the comforts of indolence and asininity—our civilization was built on the suffering of the martyrs of the word. When I think of my own pains, I am quickly humbled by the long list of sufferers on the way. I see the footsteps of Abu Hayyan al-Tawhidi (d. 414/1023) who died marginalized and poor. Before his death, he reportedly declared, "People don't deserve my thought!" and burned his own books out of spite against those who tormented him throughout his life. I see the footsteps of the Hanbali jurist, Sayf al-Din al-Amidi (d. 631/1233), who became famous in Egypt, but due to the heathenness of jealousy, he was accused of heresy. Dismayed and broken-hearted, he escaped to Hama in Syria and then Damascus. In Damascus, his fame quickly spread, but the ignorant and jealous chased him again, and after he was accused of rationalism and of having, God forbid, a brain, he was dismissed from his professorial chair in the 'Aziziyya school. I see the footsteps of al-Baydawi (d. 685/1286), the Shafi'i Chief Justice of Shiraz, who was accused of being a Shi'i, and who suffered enormously from slander and jealousy. I see the footsteps of the scholar of *hadith*, al-Bukhari (d. 256/870), who was accused of being a Rationalist and was expelled and exiled until he died a ward of his relatives without a home or money. I see the footsteps of the great Maliki jurist and judge, Ibn al-'Arabi (d. 543/1148), who was dismissed, imprisoned, and exiled, and who withstood his torment with remarkable bravery. I walk in the footsteps of Ibn al-Qayyim (d. 751/1350), and his teacher Ibn Taymiyya (d. 728/1328), who were both tortured and imprisoned for their insistence on honoring the integrity of the word. Ibn Taymiyya, in particular, lived and died a martyr of the word. He was imprisoned and exiled from Egypt and Syria because of his writings, and, after issuing a *fatwa* that offended those in power, he was left to die in prison. I always find comfort in the footsteps of the great Hanafi jurist, al-Sarakhsi (d. 483/1090), who was also tortured and imprisoned because of his juristic integrity. He refused the comforts of a political appointment, was persecuted for his legal opinions, and wrote some of his most famous works in prison. I can never forget the footsteps of the Maliki jurist and judge, Ibn Rushd (d. 595/1198), who was beaten and exiled because of his rationalism, and who died with a broken heart—a heart broken by treacherous jealousy. I see the footsteps of the Shafi'i jurist, 'Izz al-Din Ibn 'Abd al-Salam (d. 661/1262), who was imprisoned and exiled when he denounced the ruler's alliance with the Christian crusading enemy. The Shafi'i jurist, al-Kiya al-Harrasi (d. 504/1110–1), was accused of having heretical tendencies by envious clowns. As a result, he greatly suffered, and was even in danger of being killed, but his life was spared when some colleagues in Baghdad collected signatures on a petition attesting to his integrity. Al-Nisa'i (d. 303/915), the scholar of *hadith*, whose collection is considered one of the six authoritative works on the *Sunna*, was tormented in Egypt by those who were jealous of him, and so he moved to Palestine. In Palestine, he refused to be politically correct and so was beaten, and died from his injuries. The historian and jurist, al-Tabari (d. 310/923), refused all honors and positions, and was the model of sincerity and integrity. This earned him the spite of the ignorant, and he lived a good part of his life persecuted by fanatic Hanbalis. Eventually, no one dared to deal with him or visit him, his books were burned, and even his grave was desecrated by his ignorant enemies. The famous Maliki Qadi 'Iyad (d. 544/1149) suffered numerous obstacles on the road, was eventually dismissed from the judiciary, and died in exile. The grand Shafi'i jurist, al-Suyuti (d. 911/1505), known as the Son of Books, struggled with unrelenting petty jealousies. Frustrated, he eventually removed himself from public life and lived in isolation except for the company of his books. I stare at the footsteps of the Shafi'i jurist al-Nawawi (d. 676/1277), who stood up against a ruler's unjust taxes, was fired from his teaching post, and banished from Damascus. He went to Egypt where he became a chief judge only to be fired again, arrested, and imprisoned. He died poor and lonely in his father's home in Nawa south of Damascus. Ibn Kathir (d. 774/1373) refused to issue a *fatwa* supporting the rulers and was imprisoned and savagely tortured. I glare at the long-suffering footsteps of the Shafi'i jurist and historian al-Subki (d. 771/1370). He was the Chief Justice in Syria but fell victim to ignorance and jealousy. He was accused of sin, corruption, and heresy, and he was eventually removed from his position. Subki's agony and suffering became mythical. In fact, it was said that he suffered a level of persecution that no judge had ever suffered before him in Islamic history. The hardest footsteps to look at are those of the Hanafi historian and jurist al-Jabarti (d. 1237/1822). In response to his bravery and honesty, his writings were banned, his son was killed, and his son's body was displayed on a donkey.

There are so many footsteps, and so many sufferers, that when I think of one example, I immediately think of ten others. But perhaps my closest and dearest friend and companion on the road is the remarkable jurist, 'Ali Ibn Muhammad Abu al-Wafa' Ibn 'Aqil, one of the most gifted intellects in human history. Ibn 'Aqil, the author of books on jurisprudence, theology, and Sufism, was the true incarnation of the majestic word. His *Kitab al-Funun* is a 200-volume work that represents the glory of Islamic humanism, and the beauty that results when the supernal is aided by rationalism. Ibn 'Aqil is the Hanbali jurist who studied with Hanbalis, Hanafis, Shafi'is, Mu'tazilis, and Sufis, and was described by Taqi al-Din Ibn Taymiyya (d. 728/1328) as more knowledgeable than Abu Hamid al-Ghazali (d. 505/1111). The jurist al-Silafi (d. 576/1180) said, "I have never seen anyone like the jurist Abu al-Wafa' Ibn 'Aqil. No one could debate him because of the extent of his learning, the beauty of his presentation, the eloquence of his speech, and the power of his arguments." Other scholars described him as a beautiful man, kind, and generous—a man of sparkling intelligence. I feel invigorated, liberated, and ashamed as I hear Ibn 'Aqil say:

> God protected me in my youth from sin and put in my heart only the love of knowledge. I never cared for play or games, and I only mixed with students of knowledge like myself. Now, that I am eighty years old, I find that my zeal for knowledge is stronger than when I was twenty years old. Despite my age, I do not notice any weakness in my intuition, thought, or memory, and I am no less able to investigate the hidden proofs and evidence, but my physical endurance has waned. . . Yet, it is not lawful for me to waste a single moment of my life. If my tongue is not engaged in study or debate, and my eyes are not engaged in reading, I work my intellect while I am resting or lying down so that when I rise, I rush to write down a thought that had occurred to me. Yes, I find that my zeal for knowledge, now that I am eighty years old, is more vigorous than when I was twenty.

This learned and beautiful man was the one who also said, "I have not abandoned the seeking of knowledge except on two nights: my wedding night and the night my parents died." Yet, this beautiful man was persecuted by those who are ugly and who are, intellectually, his inferiors.

Ibn ʿAqil was born in Baghdad in 431/1039, a descendant from a Hanafi-Muʿtazili line of jurists. From his mother's side of the family, he was related to the famous Hanafi-Muʿtazili jurist, al-Zuhri. Ibn ʿAqil's father was a jurist of some repute who guided Ibn ʿAqil toward the pursuit of knowledge at an early age. Ibn ʿAqil studied with an array of jurists from a variety of intellectual orientations including traditionalists, rationalists, and Sufis. His early teachers included three women scholars: al-Huraniyya, Bint al-Junayyid, and Bint al-Gharrad. At the age of fifteen, after memorizing the Qurʾan and studying grammar and *hadith*, Ibn ʿAqil was ready to commence the study of law at the undergraduate level. He enrolled in the Hanafi school of law, but after successfully completing the first year, his studies were interrupted by disaster.

In 447/1055, when the Saljuqs sacked Baghdad and slaughtered his family, and Ibn ʿAqil became an orphan. Destitute and lonely, he was reduced to poverty. He worked as a copyist for wages, and what little money he made, he spent on learning. But God sent a kind and generous merchant named Abu Mansur Ibn Yusuf (d. 460/1067), who cared for and supported Ibn ʿAqil, and Ibn ʿAqil became Abu Mansur's ward. Ibn ʿAqil re-enrolled to resume his law studies, but this time as a Hanbali student. He quickly stood out as the most distinguished student of al-Qadi Abu Yaʿla (d. 458/1065), the chief jurist of the Hanbalis in Baghdad at the time. Ibn ʿAqil described his relationship to Abu Yaʿla in the following passage:

> Until his (Abu Yaʿla's) death, I never missed attending his classes or accompanying him in his retreats. During these retreats, he allowed me to be with him, keeping him company, be it during walks or while walking beside his stirrup, when he was on his mount. In spite of my youth, I had access to his private moments more than any other of his disciples.

But Ibn ʿAqil's thirst for knowledge was unquenchable, and he continued to pursue many other classes and teachers. The list of Ibn ʿAqil's teachers is remarkable. It includes Abu al-Tayyib al-Tabari (d. 450/1058), al-Khatib al-Baghdadi (d. 463/1071), Abu Ishaq al-Shirazi (d. 476/1083), and Abu Muhammad al-Tamimi (d. 488/1095). It is clear that the teacher's intellectual orientation or his formal association with a particular school of thought did not matter. What did matter was the quality of knowledge and its usefulness. Ibn ʿAqil's attitude toward knowledge, and his zealous pursuit of learning were bound to irritate those who could not understand the value of the word.

During the time he studied with al-Qadi Abu Yaʿla, Ibn ʿAqil continued to attend the classes of several rationalist (Muʿtazili) teachers. Some of Ibn ʿAqil's fellow Hanbali students could not believe that Abu Ya'la's star-student would continue to study with rationalist scholars. Some of these students, probably incited by al-Sharif Abu Ja'far (d. 470/1077), confronted Ibn 'Aqil and demanded that he stop studying with the rationalist scholars. Abu Ja'far was Abu Ya'la's long-time graduate student and assistant, who despite his loyalty and service to Abu Ya'la, was being outshined by Ibn 'Aqil. Abu Ya'la did not demand that Ibn 'Aqil stop attending the classes of the rationalists and, in fact, Abu Ya'la continued to be very close to Ibn 'Aqil, but Abu Ja'far was burning with jealousy. It is unlikely that Abu Ja'far could have declared his open hostility to Ibn 'Aqil during Abu Ya'la's lifetime. All the historical evidence indicates that Abu Ya'la continued to cherish Ibn 'Aqil and even encouraged him to study with the rationalist scholars. It is likely, however, that Abu Ja'far was the hidden force working against Ibn 'Aqil. In any case, Ibn 'Aqil's response to the Hanbali students was simple and straightforward; Ibn 'Aqil argued that he found those classes very useful, and that it was his right to pursue knowledge wherever it may be found. The Hanbali students insisted, while Ibn 'Aqil persisted, and finally, the Hanbalis ambushed Ibn 'Aqil and beat him severely until his blood flowed on the ground.

After the beating, Ibn 'Aqil was undeterred. He continued to study and compose with remarkable vigor and insight, and equally mastered the discourses of the traditionalists and rationalists. He distanced himself from the petty competitions for position or recognition, and remained loyal to the integrity of the word. Ibn 'Aqil, remembering this period, stated:

> My fellow (Hanbalis) insisted that I terminate my studies with a certain group of intellectuals, and they wanted to prevent me from acquiring useful knowledge. . . I endured poverty and hardship and endured working as a copyist with continence and the pious fear of God. I did not vie with any jurist for the chair of a *halaqa* (position of teaching), and I did not aspire to any scholarly post that could have prevented me from pursuing knowledge.

Integrity is not divisible, and that is why you find that those who have the true love of the word are also the people who love the truth. The love of truth requires pious self-restraint so that each and every fact and consideration may be given its fair and just share. Ibn 'Aqil's integrity pervaded every corner of his mind, and guided him through the tribulations of life. When Ibn 'Aqil was about twenty-two years of age, he had a serious dispute with Abu Sa'd al-Mustawfi (d. 494/1101), the Saljuq Minister of Finance, over the reconstruction of Abu Hanifa's Mausoleum. Al-Mustawfi was a fanatic Hanafi politician and, like most fanatics, was not incredibly bright. A mosque was built around Abu Hanifa's (d. 150/767) grave in 436/1044–5, but several disciples and scholars were also buried in the near vicinity of the same grave. In 453/1061, al-Mustawfi decided to tear down the mosque and build a new dome and shrine in honor of Abu Hanifa. The new construction necessitated the excavation of the mosque's foundations, and while digging, the workers unearthed many human bones, which they re-buried in a nearby field. Furthermore, in building the shrine, the Minister misappropriated teakwood and huge doors from churches and synagogues in Samarra. While most people remained silent, Ibn 'Aqil was outraged. He pointed out to the Minister that it was unlawful to build anything by misappropriating the properties of others. He also pointed out that by excavating the bones of those buried in the shrine, there was a good possibility that the workers excavated Abu Hanifa's bones. If, in fact, Abu Hanifa's bones had been excavated and re-buried elsewhere, what was the point of having the shrine in the first place? In addition, Ibn 'Aqil vigorously protested the very idea of disturbing the burial place of the great jurist Abu Hanifa, and others. Although Ibn 'Aqil was no longer a Hanafi, he could not accept this careless disrespect toward a great man of knowledge.

Of course, instead of listening to reason, al-Mustawfi insisted on his conduct and complained to Ibn 'Aqil's benefactor, Abu Mansur, and insisted that Ibn 'Aqil be punished. When asked to refrain from criticizing al-Mustawfi, Ibn 'Aqil replied, "I have witnessed gross and reprehensible acts. My piety and religious feelings induce repulsion in me [against such behavior], and I cannot contain the aversion I feel. . . These people [al-Mustawfi and his supporters] live in total ignorance of the true religion."

At times, acts of integrity might be rewarded in the most unexpected way. For instance, when Ibn 'Aqil was in Mecca, he found a valuable red necklace. Ibn 'Aqil searched for the necklace's owner and found that it belonged to the *imam* of a mosque. Upon returning the necklace to the *imam*, the *imam* insisted on offering a reward to Ibn 'Aqil, and Ibn 'Aqil refused. Years later, after the *imam* died, Ibn 'Aqil married his daughter, who was drawn to him because of his piety and honesty.

The altercations with his fellow Hanbali students and the Minister were just the beginning of Ibn 'Aqil's troubles. In 458/1065, Abu Ya'la, the venerated teacher of both Ibn 'Aqil and Abu Ja'far, died. With his death, Abu Ya'la's professorial chair at the Mosque of the Caliph al-Mansur became vacant. This was the most prestigious chair in Hanbali law at the time, and there were two obvious candidates. Abu Ja'far had studied with and assisted Abu Ya'la for twenty years, but did not seem to be a particularly gifted student. Ibn 'Aqil had completed five years of undergraduate study and seven years of graduate study in law, but at that time, for a candidate to qualify for a professorial position in law, he normally needed fifteen years of graduate level study in jurisprudence. Ibn 'Aqil only had seven years—he was simply too young. Nevertheless, it was possible for graduate students of exceptional abilities to be appointed to a professorial position even before the completion of their studies. Such was the case, for example, with Imam al-Haramayn al-Juwayni (d. 478/1085) and Taqi al-Din Ibn Taymiyya. Ibn 'Aqil, despite being younger than all the other professorial candidates, was selected to occupy the chair, and with this, Ibn 'Aqil became the head of the Hanbali school in Baghdad.

Abu Ja'far was livid. If Abu Ya'la would have nominated Abu Ja'far to succeed him to the chair, without a doubt, Abu Ja'far would have been confirmed as the occupant of the chair. But Abu Ya'la died without nominating anyone to the chair. Abu Ja'far resented Ibn 'Aqil's diligence and attitude toward knowledge, and he hated Ibn 'Aqil's tolerance toward the rationalists. Furthermore, Abu Ja'far was quite simply jealous of Ibn 'Aqil's learning and insight. Interestingly, after becoming a professor, Ibn 'Aqil would teach his classes and leave immediately to study with other scholars. In Ibn 'Aqil's words, "After teaching my own courses, I used to leave my *halaqa* in order to pursue, without respite, the *halaqas* of the religious intellectuals. . ." This could have only further enraged Abu Ja'far, and ignited his hate.

Only two years after Ibn 'Aqil occupied his prestigious position, Abu Mansur, Ibn 'Aqil's benefactor and protector, died. With Abu Mansur's death, Ibn 'Aqil was made vulnerable, save for the protection of God. Abu Ja'far did not waste time; he met with Abu al-Qasim Ibn Ridwan, the Caliph's son-in-law, in 461/1068, and they both made a pact to destroy Ibn 'Aqil.

Abu Ja'far and Ibn Ridwan started a concerted smear campaign. Supported by their students and an army burning with ignorance and jealousy, they accused Ibn 'Aqil of being a Mu'tazili, a rationalist, and a heretic. They spread unsubstantiated rumors that Abu Ya'la secretly hated Ibn 'Aqil, and confided in some that Ibn 'Aqil was a heretic. They even circulated a story accusing Ibn 'Aqil of being a false-prophet and an infidel. If being a rationalist meant having the power of thought, reason, and critical insight, this accusation, thrown at Ibn 'Aqil, was most certainly true. All the other accusations were nonsensical, but envy will make people believe anything. Abu Ja'far and his supporters were intellectual midgets. They could not debate Ibn 'Aqil because of his superior knowledge, so they turned this knowledge against him. They claimed that Ibn 'Aqil used his superior knowledge to excite young men to unsteadiness, causing them to go astray. He confuses young men with his many questions and queries. He makes young men question their faith and emboldens them against the traditions and customs of their elders. Even if Ibn 'Aqil is knowledgeable, they contended, he lacks piety, and if he is pious, he lacks wisdom. If Ibn 'Aqil is not stopped, he will even embolden the people against their leaders.

Ibn 'Aqil's students tried to defend him, but jealousy is one of the strongest forces in the world of games and delusions. People who knew Ibn 'Aqil for many years, scared of being accused, pretended not to know him. Even the few notables who invited Ibn 'Aqil to dinner at their homes during the crisis were attacked and accused of being heretics. Most people distanced themselves. Ibn 'Aqil was forcibly prevented from lecturing in his classes and was not permitted to defend himself. Even publishers, agents, scholars, and students were warned not to accept any written materials from Ibn 'Aqil, and not to deliver any messages or letters on his behalf. Eventually, Ibn 'Aqil lost his professorial chair and, suffering from the treachery of friend and foe, he fell gravely ill. Fearing for the safety of his works, Ibn 'Aqil entrusted some of his writings to one of his friends and students, but this friend and student took Ibn 'Aqil's writings and handed them over to none other than Abu Ja'far himself. Ibn 'Aqil's fate was sealed.

Abu Ja'far and his camp exploited an oppressive edict that was passed during the reign of the Caliph al-Qadir (r. 381–422/991–1031). Al-Qadir was a follower of the Qadiri Creed, and he passed an edict pursuant to which any Shi'i or Mu'tazili could be executed unless he retracted his beliefs. The Caliph in Ibn 'Aqil's time was al-Qa'im (r. 422–67/1031–75), al-Qadir's son. Al-Qa'im was not particularly keen about enforcing his father's unjust edict, but in response to the persistent efforts of Abu Ja'far and his camp, Ibn 'Aqil was arrested, imprisoned and then exiled, and kept secluded. Ibn 'Aqil was reduced to abject poverty again. However, Abu Ja'far and his party were not yet done. After an effort that lasted three years, in 465/1072, they managed to bring legal proceedings against Ibn 'Aqil for heresy, and pursuant to al-Qadir's edict, Ibn 'Aqil was to be executed. But Abu Ja'far did not want Ibn 'Aqil to become a martyr. Instead, Abu Ja'far wanted Ibn 'Aqil to sign and read a retraction in return for a pardon. And, in that same year, on September 24 (8 *Muharram*), Ibn 'Aqil stood in the mosque-college of his accuser, al-Sharif Abu Ja'far, to read aloud the retraction before a great assembly of people. The retraction read in part:

> I [Ibn 'Aqil] purify myself, before God, of the doctrines of the heretical innovators, Mu'tazilis and others; of frequenting the masters of this doctrinal system; of venerating its partisans; of invoking the mercy of God on their predecessors; and of emulating them. What I have written, and what has been found written in my hand concerning their doctrines and their errors, I repent to God for having written. It is not permitted to write those things, nor to say them, nor to believe them. . .
>
> With this, I ask God's forgiveness, and I turn to Him in penitence for having frequented the heretical innovators, Mu'tazilis, and others; for having sought to emulate them; for having invoked God's mercy on them; and for having venerated them. For all of that is prohibited; a Muslim is not permitted to do this, because of what the Prophet has said—the blessings and peace of God be upon him! "He who venerates the author of a condemnable innovation helps in bringing about the ruin of Islam."
>
> The Sharif Abu Ja'far, and his companions, masters and partisans, my superiors, and my colleagues—May God the Exalted protect them—rightly blame me, seeing what they have witnessed written in my hand of works from which I purify myself before God. I am certain that I was wrong, that I was not right. . .
>
> I call on God, on His angels, and on the men of religious learning, to witness what I have just said voluntarily and without constraint. The sentiments of my heart are in complete accord with the expressions of my mouth—May God the Exalted be the Judge! God has said, "God will exact a penalty from whoever repeats an offense. For God is Exalted, and Lord of retribution" (5:95).

One can only imagine Ibn 'Aqil's pain and agony while reading this shameful retraction—the politics of convenience mixed with the spite of jealousy and the insolence of ignorance to degrade a great intellect. And, with this retraction, Abu Ja'far thought that he had finally won. Ibn 'Aqil lived in exile and seclusion until Abu Ja'far's death in 470/1077. Ironically, Abu Ja'far never obtained the prestigious professorial chair he so badly coveted, and he died following a painful and long illness after being poisoned by one of his many rivals. Most importantly, Abu Ja'far left behind no worthwhile work or thought.

During his exile, Ibn 'Aqil met his beloved wife and had several children. Two of his sons died, and he persevered with faith and strength. After Abu Ja'far's death, Ibn 'Aqil resumed teaching in a mosque-college of his own, and eventually became the head of the Hanbali guild. He composed numerous works, and taught some of the most prominent students. Reflecting on this painful period of his life, he said:

> I have seen dynasties come and go, but no power of a sultan, nor that of a crowd, was capable of dissuading me from what I believed to be the truth. My fellow (Hanbalis) subjected me to physical suffering to the point of drawing blood; and I was tormented during the administration of al-Nizam* with legal prosecutions and imprisonment. [And, all I say is] O You for whom I have sacrificed all, do not disappoint my hopes. . .

Of course, God did not disappoint Ibn 'Aqil's hopes. Ibn 'Aqil outlived his persecutors, and died, in body, in 513/1119. In intellect, he lives on, and will live until the very end. When he died, he left behind nothing of this world of play and games. The only things found in his home were his books, and a few garments of cloth. But thousands marched in his funeral, and, according to one source, those who paid their respects were close to three-hundred thousand souls. Ibn 'Aqil honored the word, and was honored by the word. Despite the distractions of games and the noise of babble, he held firmly to the word of self-restraint. For, the key to piety and knowledge is to restrain yourself from drifting into the fogs of this world and to maintain your footsteps along the truthful way.

Ibn 'Aqil, may God bless your beautiful soul, your footsteps are firmly embedded on the road of knowledge and, through the centuries, you have been the enlightenment, consolation, and companion to so many travelers on that arduous road. As for your persecutors, and mine, I only have the words of our Lord: "Turn away from them, and say, 'Peace,' for, in time, they will come to know" (43:89).

---

* Nizam al-Mulk was the effective ruler of the Saljuk Empire from 465/1072 until his assassination in 485/1092. Nizam al-Mulk endowed professorial chairs for distinguished jurists such as *Imam al-Haramayn* al-Juwayni (d. 478/1085) and Abu Ishaq al-Shirazi (d. 476/1083).

CHAPTER 60

Muhammad, the Child

I call upon the Conference and I hear agonized wailing answer my calls. Where are you my Conference—where is the sanguine voice of reason and the flirtatious melody of beauty? Where is the resonance of your words and the power of your belief in humanity? I implore you talk to me, my Conference. I am God's slave—I am your faithful son and the lover of beauty. Don't leave me gasping, frightened, and mummified by this merciless doubt.

I want to devour words and thoughts and pretend that they matter. I want to stroll in the gardens of love and pretend that it matters. I want to inhale the fragrance of beauty and pretend that you matter.

Talk to me my Conference! Talk to me. Don't you see how much I want to reach out for the heavenly song concealed in her blissful eyes, distill the sweetness of her smile, and build a supernal shrine for the truth of beauty? Don't you see that every night I enter the shrine, wrap myself in dreams, and only then can I sleep?

But I call upon you, and I find you sitting by the walls of the shrine, frozen by the agonized wailing, drowning in the screams of a father and child—unable to speak. We witness the scene in horror and disbelief; how do we reach the father and child, how do we nurse their screams with persuasion and speech, how do we heal the terror in their eyes with gifts of gentle beauty?

Muhammad al-Durrah, a 12-year-old child, cowers behind his father screaming, "*Aba ilha'ni* (Dad, save me)!" His little hands cling to the back of his father's shirt, wishfully praying that the soldiers' binoculars and riflescopes can see his tears. For 45 minutes, father and child scream for help, pleading to be spared this utter insanity.

Just an hour earlier, the father decided to visit the used car market and the son, excited by the prospect of a new car, begged to join him. Muhammad wore his colored turtleneck shirt, sneakers, and Uncle Sam's blue jeans, but now, Muhammad and his father cower next to a wall for 45 minutes, screaming and pleading.

An Israeli sniper moves into position and shoots Muhammad four times and his father eight times. Muhammad first curls in his father's lap, then slumps to the ground, covers his face with those little hands, and dies. An ambulance that attempts to reach Muhammad and his father is shot at as well, a paramedic is seriously wounded, and the driver is killed.

The father is crippled for life, the mother struggles to make sense of hell, and so she calls it a sacrifice. But I sit with folded hands, on my moronic chair, with my idiotic papers, my revolting coffee, my abandoned books, and stupid, stupid dreams.

You see, if the Conference would speak, Muhammad can no longer hear.

Muhammad, my child, in the embrace of the grave, there is no beauty, only the waste of the life left behind, and the abominations of decay.

I refuse to take you as a symbol for the Palestinian tragedy or Israeli belligerency. I refuse to take you as a sacrifice for Jerusalem or the Mosque's sanctity. I refuse to take you as a symbol of our utter uselessness and futility. I refuse to take you as a sacrifice, cause, or symbol for anything. I refuse to sugarcoat a rotted, foul, and bitter reality. My son, the truth is that you were not sacrificed for anything; the truth is that after living through an agonizing terror, you were pointlessly slaughtered.

I look at my 11-year-old boy and shudder. I want him to grow and to reach out for the heavenly song concealed in blissful eyes, distill the sweetness of a smile, and build a supernal shrine for the truth of beauty. I want him to be touched by the breath of life, I want him to have the chance to listen and speak, I want him to grow, and when he does, he can decide whether he wants to become a symbol or cause.

Muhammad, I know that now you are among the beauties of Heaven, and this knowledge consoles my heart. My belief in God's justice empowers me to continue calling upon the Conference to come back to me. But what tortures me is the ugliness of human beings who can politicize the death of a child. What tortures me is that I know that right at this moment some ravished heart is swirling in the torrents of hate, plotting to retaliate by killing another child. What tortures me is that people dare to grant terrorism citizenship, a religion, or a race, and then declare it a diplomatic mission entitled to full moral immunity. In what hellish treatise of immorality has it been written that the death of a Muslim child can make the death of a Jewish child just, or that the death of a Jewish child can make the death of a Muslim child just?

Despite the bizarreness of the logic exploited by humans, my faith in God and in God's beauty tells me that the murdered children, Jews and Muslims alike, will rest in Heaven side by side.

CHAPTER 61

The Revelation

Aword suspended in thought is caught in an endless redundancy. Unable to break its bonds, it remains trapped in the idea. For a word to break its bond, it must transcend its form, but in doing so it inevitably transforms into an idea.

Welcome blessed souls to this home. All that you see here is a distraction from the truth of being. All you see is the pretense of shape and form, but we are all the playthings of a mass delusion. If you seek the genuine and real, you will find it in a thought. Existence is but an expression of an idea. All the tangibles are wondrous ostentations simulated in the form of nightmares and dreams. The truth is that all the dissembled facts of form are overpowering abstractions of the mind. There is a wisdom that flows through all perception, but it invents differences without any real distinctions. When I abandon the speculations of my eyes to the discernments of my mind, when I transcend the perceptions of sight to the probities of insight, I see God's wisdom flow through all of existence.

Welcome blessed souls to your home, here are thoughts unencumbered by words—here every essence is stripped to the wisdom at the core. I feel you but I cannot see you. Yet, this is neither a distinction nor a difference; the ethereal is the only proof of existence. Are you angels or the spirits of memory? Are you intellects freed from the delusions of form? Are you translucent texts inscribed on the conscience? Or, are you the nascent wisdom breaking through the bastions of deception? Perhaps you are luminous lodestars in the midst of the despondencies of the fog. The temporal is locked in a specter of redundant projections—of blustering flesh and bones, but in the Conference there is nothing but the ethereal diffidence of ghosts.

I am a fiction constructed by the vanities of want. What a curious state of suspension that feigns existence only to evaporate like the cravings of a sigh. I have seen the Domain of truth, and I have discovered it is but a thought. The difference between a flower and a thorn, between a human and a log is in the idea. The idea is the abstraction in the mind of God, and this abstraction is the essence of being. So I inject my lungs with air and try to justify my body's redundancies. Aren't we, after all, a consciousness positioned within space, defined by belief? But my freedom is in my Divinity.

Come blessed souls, place yourself in any time or place you wish. Be a thought, a dream, a muse, a vision—it does not matter. You are my reality. Be the memory of the body you want—the words of my vanished masters, the cause of my martyred friends, the hope of my buried ancestors, the love I never found, the smiles of liberation that withered into frowns, the dignity entrenched in life but compromised by fear—be the books I read, the books I write, the conscience of the past, the heart of the future, or the lips that defines my want. In every, and all forms, you are the proof of beauty. In the shelter of the night, we will be one in the Conference, our common bond the belief that every word, although the captive of form, is a hint of Divinity.

CHAPTER 62

Shades of Divine Light

As the flowers awaken at the touch of the morning dew, I pace the skies. If it hadn't been for the muddied soil, these flowers would not reach for the Heavens, and if it hadn't been for this broken body, I would not have craved the embrace of the sky. My wings are entrenched in folds of the mind; there is no pain or pleasure; there is no past or present. In fact, there is no space or time, and there is no life or death. There is only this mind. This mind humors my brain, and endures its frivolity, and intemperance. But in the end, and after all is said and done, it is this brain that has been the mind's throne and shelter—the brain returns to the mud from where it came, and the mind returns to God.

This pitiful brain struggles to embrace the visions of the mind. The mind in a translucent moment sees the whole, illimitable truth, while this brain struggles with the acrimony of proofs. The mind absorbs the essence of beauty in a single glimpse, but this brain struggles with perceptions and belief.

I live the hours of the night in the service of the Conference, the money and body spent in honor of the mind. In the early morning hours, I feel the weight of the brain upon my burning eyes, and the neck enthroning the skull threatens to topple its head. I lie down, shut my eyes, and wonder, "When all of this returns to the mud, what will remain of the memory of this pain?" If only this brain could merge with the primordial mind, the ecstasies of insight would demolish all these physical bounds.

Yet, like the mountains, I can reach for the sky only if anchored in the ground. And, it is the primordial wisdom that teaches the roots of the tree to penetrate deeply in the mud so the branches can reach for God. I know that to the extent of my temporal labor and exertion will be the attainments of ethereal insight. Such is the soul of life, through the pains of the physical, we come to uncover that existence is but shades of Divine light. So I walk this earth knowing that the secular is a state of mind. I tread softly on this earth for the future home of this body is in this same ground. But it is at the moments of the utmost fatigue and exhaustion that I feel the closest to God. Isn't our longing for the comfort of God's embrace during our suffering the most profound? Eventually, drained and worn out, this body, and its brain, will surrender to the dimness of a grave, and the mind will be reunited with the blissful light.

CHAPTER 63

The Restorations of the Night

Like a fading image from an eroded glory clinched on a dissolving wall, like the reverberations of youthful fantasies and the resignations of mortal thought, like the cravings of love surrendering to the abatements of forgetfulness, I sit in this Conference.

At times, I am a part of a fading picture of majesty thrust on a canvas of memories. At times, I am but a sentence in an unrelenting eulogy read at the end of dreams. At times, I doubt my existence, and like the ruins of life, I become contested history.

My God, in the late hours of the night, upon the sublimation of words I unfold, and the covers of these books give me my form.

My God, when this body decomposes and the soul retreats to its secret, how will You judge these words? Will you forgive my indiscretions and intemperance, my defiance and rebellion, and the dejections of this aching mind? At times, I stumble into the fissures of my contradictions—at times, I am splintered by the dissensions of my soul. I feel that I exist in this world as a Muslim, but in this world as a Muslim, I don't exist at all.

The night brings me the consolations of limitless promises. My features are set out on the pages of the Conference, I am vindicated in the grapplings of the conscience, and my memories and history are fully restored. In the morning, I am a projection from the past—a misplaced history—as a Muslim, I never belong. Nothing that surrounds me is grounded in my identity—not the streets, the buildings, the schools, the stores, the cars, the computers, the clothes and fashions, the food, the conversations, the symbolisms, the order of nature, the air I breath—not even the seductions and cravings, nor the intonations of words. In non-Muslim countries, I travel packaged in instructions, and in Muslim countries, I am contraband, on the blacklist of silence—my very existence is a violation of the law.

As Muslims, we have become an enigma saddled on the back of history. The nomads of lost memories, our pastures dried up, we have become the grimy merchants of black gold.

My God, which of our maladies do I lament—which do I deplore? Do I mourn the absence of beauty and the displacement of moral insight unto the evasions of law? Do I bemoan the fact that the dignity and honor of a Muslim is denigrated nowhere more than in the Muslim world? Do I complain that in every Muslim country, the prisons are full and the torture and mutilation of human beings are as common as hypocrisy and the prostitution of words? Do I gripe and cry that from the Holy lands to the land of the Nile to the schools of Qum, not an hour passes without blood and screams being flung against prison walls? What grief, when a psychotic murderer defiles Your name by writing Allahu Akbar on his monstrous flag—what blasphemy when Your name is written in the blood of countless innocent souls! What is a Muslim to feel when the flag that bears Your name and the name of the Prophet becomes the banner concealing the profanity of cruelty and the desecrations of tyranny? In the Muslim world, the most compelling and decisive books are those full of confessions written on the flesh of victims, and the most earnest prayers are the entreats for mercy screamed in pain and anguish at the tormentors of flesh and thought. God, You are not worshipped in the lands of torment, for the deity is fear, and terror is the holy order and the final word.

I grieve that in the midst of this ugliness and blasphemy, our proclaimed victories are hideous and deformed. What the collective wisdom of Muslims preserved through the ages, in our fits of insanity, we destroyed. Muslims are dying and so we slaughter statues, and when we assert our presence, we erase history. We brand non-Muslims like animals, and then hypocritically demand justice for our own. In truth, in the squalor of ugliness, we only degrade our existence. How can those who dwell in destruction hope not to be destroyed?

If the Taliban and others do not represent us as Muslims, hasn't God commanded us to bear witness, and to help our brothers by preventing injustice and testifying for the truth? If Islam is a message to humanity, what message do we convey when the record of our teachings becomes a tally of despotism, destruction, and indignities of fear? What is the point of political victories if the price is our moral defeat?

My God, what is the use of this lament and denunciation when Your beauty fills my life with pure exhilaration? If the morning has become my persecutor, I am grateful for the sanctuary of the night. For when the stillness quells the mania of movement and sound, I am pervaded by the purity of Your light. God, my Lord, my comfort and beauty, I implore You to forgive my pertness and perturbations. Despite the confusions and dissensions of the frantic Sun, invariably the Conference lights up the night, and I see You clear and bright. And, in this is the perfect beauty of restoration.

CHAPTER 64

The Exorcisms of the Night

Every night, I splatter myself on the pages of books searching for You. I have frittered so many moments in my life retrieving myself from the squanders of doubt. Badgered by detractors hurling their jealousies and resentments at me, I once guarded myself with defensive justifications and labels of identity. I packaged myself into a fortified shelter well guarded by a spirited ego, but inhabited by demons of doubt.

Now, in this Conference, I dispel myself so that I can find the truth. The fog that comes to consciousness and haunts the night brings the specters that plague this soul. At every corner of this home, I confront the wraith of these books as they seize this heart in an unrelenting hold. As I struggle to breath, I stare into the transparency of their eyes, and quiver at the shrill of their voice. "You silly boy, you escape from one day to the next, but you are a fiction terrified of a lie. What do you care about the threats and risks, when the end has been foretold? Do your delusions convince you that you are alive and that we are ghosts?"

I purge the demons of fear by opening my wounds, embracing the agony, and exorcising the defilements of the soul. God, I am vapor sparked by consciousness attesting to Your beauty. Through the diffusements of the mind, I can discern the sublimity of my role, and by dissipating the cravings and want I can see that beauty is the only true and invariable law. God, the alienations of ignorance desiccate my heart, and I thirst to be filled. But the irony of my existence is that although I seek the nourishment of the mind, I feed on the dead. I am planted in flesh and blood, and yet my consciousness craves the light.

God, I tire of the desires, indulgences, and cravings—of the yearnings, anger, and fear. I tire of the need to be comforted, admired, or understood—of the disappointments and celebrations. I tire of the touch, the embrace, the frown, and smile. I tire of the fables—of the imitation of creation—of the lunge at beauty through cosmetic sensuality, of clinging to life through the blaze of lust, and of the strain to reach eternity through love. I tire of the pretensions of this structured and coherent self, and I find that all that remains is You.

Such are my ranting sublimations—such are the battles of the night. My longings are like a virulent wind blowing through an ever-fleeting reality. Reality is nothing more than a swarm of images constructed by greed and fear, but my longings are anchored only in God.

In the morning, seeing that my face is under siege my pupils without fail ask me if I am all right. I say, "I am a warrior who misses the battles of the night; my mornings are but distractions. In them I long for everything that I should not have, and feign happiness with getting what I do not want."

The pupils ask, "Have you heard those who say that your students have become members in a idiosyncratic club—a sort of apprentices in an eccentric cult?" I say, "What a remarkable cult this is! A cult of books and Conferences—the cult of the exorcisms of the night. I accept no pledges of loyalty, and I dislike the company of obedient sheep. Tell them I am a reader, not some fancy sheikh. We are the cult of the critical mind honored by its eccentricity."

The pupils say, "we offer our *bay'a* (pledge of allegiance)," and I respond, "The *bay'a* is a burden of guidance. While I seek guidance, most of the time I am most certainly lost. There are all types of peacocks across this free land that collect *bay'a* like trophies for their egos. Go seek them out if you wish! If you wish for a leader then know that you have one nestled in your head. If you betray your intellect, you betray yourself, and if you pledge yourself to it, you find God."

"But," they say, "hasn't the Prophet said give your pledge to an *imam?*"

I say, "And, the Prophet also taught that whoever fancies himself a leader should not be so recognized. I am a person whose allegiance is to the Conference and in the Conference leadership does not exist. We are all the nomads of wisdom—travelers in the Way of God. I will confide in you that I wonder if those who crave a leader are precisely the ones that ought not be led. I fear that such people crave to surrender their intellect and will, and to become dull members in a herd of sheep. I wonder if a person who aches to pledge himself to a human being could not find something worthier that merits their loyalty?"

But the pupils pursue me with their doubts and continue to ask, "Have you heard those who say that you are nothing but an academic animating life through thoughts but you hardly exist? You spend your time in academic pursuits—a form of idleness shrouded in aloof futility. Some claim that the real world is about existence and survival—ideas in a world where principles are dead are an indulgent luxury."

"You see," I respond, "academics do not exist. There are those who are paid to teach and write. But often I feel that their salaries are atonements of ignorance—a social penance for the abandonments and frivolities that plague our heads. But note that power without principle is like a missile that celebrates its action with senseless destruction. I submit to you that those who survive for the mere sake of survival are already dead. Those who live without principle are long dead although their energies frantically persist. As for those searching for labels allow me to describe myself, I am the simple keeper of the Conference, a seeker of beauty, and wherever I find my Lord I cease to exist."

CHAPTER **65**

The Unity of Strangers

Surrounded by the humming of ceiling fans, we sit shrouded by books and dust. The incessant protests of car horns from the adjacent streets invade the space, as the history resting in the ancient bookshelves and tables peer at us in silence. Cairo was the city of my dreams and nightmares—the city where repose and terror clinched to the same alleys and streets. I lived, read, and thought in fear, but loved, and believed with undaunted intrepidity. There the worn out books and ancient streets, the insularity of our present and the magnanimity of our history, the savage noise and benign poetry, the cruelty of the rulers and the suffering of the ruled, all was imprinted upon my body, intellect, and identity. Despite the strife and dissensions in my soul, I was home.

On this day, we sit in the care of our books, chasing the words. She is a few feet away, her eyes cast upon the pages. We sit opposite each other melting in a single mind, but share no thoughts. A few strands of her soft brown hair escape from the white scarf that adorns her face, and she holds a white tissue that she raises from time to time to her nose. Only once do I look at her and when her eyes catch mine, we quickly look away. Not once does she speak to me, and I feel no desire to talk. I feel her breathing inside my chest, and listen to our silence speak. What is the use of the intrusive sounds that bang on the eardrums when the orations of silence are so much more profound?

I do not raise my eyes again for I do not want to see the cover of skin concealing her. We sit and read and turn a page and read right into eternity. We do not touch

240

and we never will, for we will never acknowledge our flesh and boundaries. There, on this day, there are no words, no looks, no touch, but a perfect unity in a single mind—we unite in a truth that is neither me nor her. If our bodies touch that would be fatal for the embrace of our souls. This was not love—this was a perfect unity between two complete strangers.

CHAPTER 66

The Testimony

"Do you swear that the testimony you are about to give is the whole truth?"

I hear myself say in a muted voice, "I do," but I know that I don't. I hear the words of God murmur in my heart, "O you who believe, be custodians of justice and bear witness before God even though against yourselves or your parents or your relatives" (4:135).

But, your honor, the truth is that I struggle with the truth. The truth is that our laws have replaced our history, and fear has displaced our morality.

Your honor, forgive me, I cannot tell you the whole truth for I would have to unfold myself upon your bench, and before long I will break into a long wail echoing the centuries of dreams transformed into nightmares. You see, before coming into your courtroom this woman sitting there grabbed my hand and kissed it. Overwhelmed, I cried on her shoulders and her veil is still glistening with my tears. The truth is that as Muslims, sometimes it feels that our only remaining rational recourse is to embrace the tears. Even at this very moment, I want to leave the stand, and to rap myself in a flowing thick garb and to cry myself to sleep. If you wish to understand, you should know that as I shouldered the weight of our history and collapsed in this woman's arms, the one compulsive thought that plagued this pedantic mind is that my fellow Muslims are bound to see the two of us, and proclaim that we have fallen in the *fitnah* of the embrace.

If I begin from the start, I should say that this is a familiar story—so mundane that it hardly elicits a pause. This woman before you was raised for marriage. She discovered on her wedding night that her body, and her function in life, has become commodified, and that the dowry was the price. That first night she aged to the point of senility and the rape decomposed her brain and rotted her heart.

In the United States she raised her children, and dutifully served shifts at Wal-mart. Occasionally, and every now and then, her husband would despair of her comatose heart and attempt to awaken it with a firm slap on the face or with a resounding bark.

The truth is that any law could become the shelter of ugliness and could become the narcotic of the conscience—the truth is that the escape into law is a wonderful narcotic that numbs the heart.

So after twenty years of marriage, her husband escaped to legalities, exercising his God given right to lust, and hoping to marry a young native girl, he divorced his wife.

These are course of events that are hardly the cause for much surprise. All forms of ugliness are premised on self-absorptions, and founded on constructs of self-vindication. There is hardly an aggressor who is not a victim in his own mind, and every injustice is built on a mythology of concessions and self-sacrifice.

Our fellow armed with his undeniable rights, returns from his homeland—in one hand a divorce decree and on the other a new wife—a new girl, a new commodity to be dismantled and undone, lawfully.

Now, we sit in your courtroom seeking my "expert" testimony. The husband contends that since the marriage was commenced and terminated in Muslim lands, Islamic law should govern the divorce. In the alternative, the dowry paid to the woman's family should be read as prenuptial agreement limiting the husband's responsibility. In all cases, the termination ought to be governed by the law of *Shari'ah*, which does not recognize community property. As the argument goes, the woman is entitled to what she owns and Islamic law does not allow more than a year of spousal support. Of course, after twenty years, the wife owns nothing but a few pieces of jewelry, and perhaps this plagued jurist who provides a shoulder upon which she could weep.

The husband brings in an army of imams, guardians of the Divine, most of them volunteers. They testify that it is written in all the sublime books that the woman is entitled to nothing but her health, some good wishes, and the service of the Divine Will. Such is the law of God or at a minimum such is the consensus of the overwhelming majority.

So the woman plows through her tears, and says that every imam she approached has turned her away because it is shameful to second-guess the order of the Divine regardless of what the suffering might be.

And, here I sit in this witness stand being asked what does your God command? My God is your God—the God of beauty and equity.

Your honor, if I speak truthfully do I provide an accounting of each tradition and precedent, and present a list of juridical decrees? Do I pretend that whatever offends me cannot possibly be the Divine Will, spew the rhetoric about the liberation of women, and ignore the text's integrity? Do I say that although the Qur'an commands support for a woman during the waiting period, or, if pregnant, until she gives birth, these are guidelines, but the overriding concern is compassion and mercy? (65:1–6) Does it make all the difference that a few jurists held that a repudiated woman is owed support until she remarried or dead? Do I say that whatever laws God decreed, they are premised on a prerequisite of human decency?

What I find myself saying in the end is that rules without a moral course are nothing more than signposts, each signpost pointing to the other in an endless circular hell.

CHAPTER 67

Searching for the House of God

There is a raw intuition, a reductionism, a fundamental illumination, simple and basic like the proof of life, the engagements of love, and the devotions of belief that pervades this Conference. I often ask, why this singular pursuit of beauty—basic and amorphous as Divinity? Are there measurements, detachments as irrefutable as numbers that could define the search for beauty? Isn't this Conference and its core belief in beauty a reductionism as crude as intolerance, essentialism, and purity?

And, yet, I know that existence, and consciousness like time and numbers are adamant constructions, real but unreal. Even mathematics and equations hold true only if you believe. There is no one plus one, but legions that engage legions—there are convictions that restore convictions with stone faced commitment and belief. This cramp and pain I feel in my hands is a wonderful affirmation of faith, believed in my mind, projected to my hands, but my very mind is a conviction not a reality. Is there really skin that I can touch or cells bonded by a purpose, a sense of mission, commitment, and belief? All my intimate realities are descended from my mind, and the reality of my mind descends from the reality of God. I am as real as God wills me to be. It is this reductionism that empowers me to see that God is the noncontingent and immutable reality. My belief in God is simple and fundamental and yet this does not mean that God is reduced to essentials. The presence of God is beauty, but the product of this beauty is an overwhelming complexity. Like a trail left behind, and like the consciousness that demonstrates life, beauty is the presence of God—my consciousness is incapable of extracting ugliness from Divinity.

Are there detachments as irrefutable as numbers that could define the belief in God? Yes, if you are willing to believe in equations of consciousness and love, and if you are able to believe that beauty and morality are but computations. Otherwise, you must be content with the commitments of the mind that conceives, defines, and believes affinities and associations. Even reason makes sense only to those who believe in reason.

The essence of being is the mind, and the essence of the mind is God. What is filtered through the inventions of the mind could be measured by the mind, but what created the mind is beyond an objective realization. We objectify what we create, but we touch the Creator only with the humility of subjectivity. What I know as a matter of consciousness and love is the presence and absence of God, and in that sense, only good and evil are real; everything else is a figment of my imagination. The beauty that is God, and the ugliness that God is not, are realities perceived through the subjectivities of the mind, but all else are fictions susceptible to objectification. God and beauty, like the truth, cannot be objectified, but they also cannot be invented by the mind.

My friend, I see you sitting in the forgotten corner of the house of God, a bundle covered by clothing crowned with a mind. Has the serenity of the house of God escaped you, or is it at times hard to find beauty in an abode exploited by human beings? You wonder if a structure that aspires to be a mosque is pervaded by anxiety, is it still the home of Divinity? Or, are these Islamic centers dispersed in the land nothing more than fiefdoms ruled by self-declared nobility? Doctors, engineers, computer specialists, bubbling evangelists, and technicians of piety, bearded and unbearded, have set themselves up to dabble in the game of divinity. Each center a mosque, and each mosque a suzerainty where the potentate can try his hand at playing king. Here again, you crouch in the prayer area of an Islamic center with the difficult and ambitious goal of coming and leaving in dignity. I will confess to you that even I now enter every center in the grip of anxiety. All I want is to be able to enter and worship without instructions, directives, commands, or without relinquishing my autonomy to some custodian of divinity—to enter and leave in dignity. I recall, my sister, once I entered a center, and found literature on a table near the front. As I flipped through a pamphlet, a servant of the custodial majesty set upon me and promptly grabbed the pamphlet from my hand, and barked some irrefutable commands. If I approach a center, I anticipate to be told from which door to enter, how to sit, how to wash, how to pray, and how to breathe. May God forbid that you desire to distribute literature or hold an unauthorized class or attempt to teach! The truth is that over each Islamic center and its mosque sits a little despot nursing the plagues of his insecurities, and what better way to nurse these afflictions than to pretend that God owns the manor and that you are God's deputy? Every lord of these fiefdoms believes that the fate of God's message hinges on their delivery.

But this is me, my sister, and your problem is much bigger and more serious. Your problem is not only fiefdoms and despots, but also the banishment away from the realm of consciousness. Here, in this center, there is a wall separating existence from oblivion. The space called the women's section is accessed through the door of *fitnah* (seduction)—the gateway to irrelevance. Once you enter through the door you are indubitably branded as a seductive danger. Inside you can neither be addressed nor heard—if you listen carefully you will catch the echo of the yammer of men coming as an uncontestable contention. Here, in this house of men, the women's bathroom is locked because a good woman would do her ablutions before coming to the mosque, and a better woman would pray at home and keep her seductions away from the house of God. Is there a more profound statement of alienation than to claim that the best rows of women are those that are the farthest behind or that the best spot for prayer is the most secluded and dark? If you venture beyond this isolation, then every man becomes the guardian of confinement, chasing women into a prison constructed from the walls of modesty.

Such is the nature of autocracy; it feeds on nothing but power, and breathes nothing but anxiety. The nature of despotism is to objectify God and beauty into a quantifiable sum, but once quantified God and beauty could be realized and rendered an irrelevancy. It is this objectification that allows the despot to obfuscate the boundaries between himself and God and beauty. In the fiefdoms, intuitions, feelings, thoughts, claims, and complaints of people do not count. After all, how could they count if beauty is measured, quantified, and realized and so all challenges are an irrelevancy?

My sister, my subjectivity—my convictions tell me that the reality of the house of God is beauty. But if my subjectivities find that anxiety and degradation prevails in a house, I suspect that I am not in the house of God, but a human fiefdom, and I continue the search for what I know is the Divine reality.

CHAPTER 68

Incoherence

These long tedious stares, and I am incapable of returning the gaze. I am only capable of staring within, and what I find is a full universe. I stand at your podium frozen in my place—if I speak, I fear that my tongue will ignite an incinerating blaze. I stand shivering in this chill with absolutely nothing to say.

We paid your ticket—we brought you here, so speak and prove yourself. Entertain us, comfort us, invoke the symbols, bang the drums for the dance of egos and tell us everything we already know. Tell us the future is ours, the present is fleeting, the past was brilliant, and the world is going to hell—that we are saved by the truth that escapes us, but that is preserved in the immutable law. Speak of conspiracies, of plots, of enemies, of the promise of unity, of the power of the movement, of the wonders of brotherhood, and pay a passing tribute to sisterhood. Speak of our superiority, of our miraculous ability to reconcile action and thought, and remind us that we are destined to save the world. Tell us to be movers, shakers, bakers, and to be activists and scholars all in one single swoop. For God's sake man, we paid your ticket, we brought you here, be grateful, wave your fist, excite us, cheerlead us, shake the pompoms of pietistic phrases—speak of the dangers of the West, and the rest—sound the sirens against corruption, herald our liberation, and remind us that we are God's gift to the world. Tease our imagination with a speech about the seductions of women, and quench the dryness of our lives with rhetorical intoxications. Yes, it is true that Sunday television programs are an utter bore, but consider that we abandoned mid-day naps and succulent feasts to come and listen to you.

I stand here my mouth agape, my thoughts muting my words. My friends, you invited someone who is thoroughly useless, and I should have never accepted your invitation—I do not know any of the things that you know.

You expect me to speak and all I am able to say is that I am an echo and reflection dancing around in a nebulous mass, the truth of my being is the source of the light and the word. In the perennial, the intellect manifested in the word, but I am a hint—a mere glimpse of the glimmer. The "I," constrained by its form and indemnified by its transience, is the flash of beauty that resonates from the perennial intellect. So I don't chase words—they reside within me—expressions of Divinity—like this mind and soul. I stand mesmerized by a moment of grace. I don't think of beginnings or ends—in my existence there are no special occasions, no celebrations, no time or place. There is the solemn progression of days except for that moment of grace, and it is in this that I find the full meaning. I am repulsed by everything else.

Brother! You write so eloquently of the miracles of the Conference. Speak to us of the beauty of our religion—fill us with hope and fear. Tell us how we misunderstand our religion, that whatever the West thinks it has—well, we saw it first. We invented democracy, constitutionalism, and pluralism, and they copied it from us, but the rule of *shurah* is even better, for it is a system that knows the truth, protects unity, and guards against divisions. Islam defeated materialism, cured the ailments of capitalism, and don't forget to mention that the system of *zakah* is better than socialism, and even as to that, we saw it first.

My friends, I write because this is the only way I can maintain my silence as I speak. The beauty you seek is but a fondle of the ego—I cannot count points, and speak to fear. Beauty overcomes you, it cannot be declared. So does your love for God need the salvations of mythology and the intoxications of history, does it need stories of victories and defeats, does it need the assurance of conformity, and the crutches of the rhetorical flare? My friends, you've perfected the act of cheering, but have you won a game?

Brother, come to our level and be with us. Why does your mind speak in circles, and your incoherence is so profound. Speak to us of what we know. Tell us that Islam is a revolution against oppression, racism, and sexism, that it liberated women, and empowered the human being to submit to no other than God—that Islam elevated the dignity of people, and guaranteed freedom of religion and liberties of speech. Tell us that Islam is perfection, and that in this is our unwavering surety. If you speak in riddles then that is the *fitnah* of ambiguity; the best speech is that which affirms the familiar, but the rest is a *bidah*.

My friends, the most coherent communication is an advertisement, but what does it communicate? Can you express your love in a commercial, and can you address the beloved in a sales pitch? If I put the beloved before my eyes, I melt before we could embrace. I touch my beloved's soul every time I breath, and I cannot exist beyond his sphere. Don't you feel the exhilaration of his fragrance, and how can we stay coherent after inhaling his scent? I see his smile in the laughter of books, and I am enchanted by a sweet delirium. I am unraveled in the ecstasy and I no longer know where I am or what to do with myself. In this frenzy, I yell out, "Restore me long enough to drink from your beauty, and then dilute me again!"

My friends, I don't know the things you know. You see, if I speak, I speak only of my longings and aches. I come to you seeking pity for my affliction, and to describe my pains. You know things that I do not know. My whole being is too immersed in what I crave to know to either cheerlead for you or to keep scores.

CHAPTER 69

A Breath from God

And God blew into us from His spirit (32:9), and so we are—God's breath flows within and transcends. It is God "Who created from among you your soul mates" (16:72), and so we crave. The unity of existence is in the spirit that sustains the universe bonded in a single breath. This is your consolation my friend.

My friend, you are as if extinguished with every exhalation, and reborn with every inhalation. The breath of God that pervades your shell consumes you in an unrelenting but profound craving. My friend, how could you be laden with this magnificence and not crave the effacement of the shell and the embrace of the majesty of the universe?

The purity of creation is in the sublime and primordial breath—a breath like the purity of the first time a baby opens her eyes, the purity of a bird's first flight, the purity of the first realization of love, the purity of hope restored, the purity of a prophet's revelation from the One and Only God. The breath embodies the vigor, power, briskness, and divinity of life unsullied by the dust of the mundane—a life not trounced by betrayal and pain. It is the beauty of the dignity dwelling within. But after the ugliness of desertions, the cruelty of deceptions, the veils on perception, and the debasement of integrity, what remains is the contested self. Compromised, degraded, and hurt the human being is disfigured until the human being is obscured from herself. We travel through consciousness adorned by the Divine breath. But the squalors of indignity defile, despoil, and cast the veil. After the assault of rot, what remains of the flower's scent?

My friend, you say you search the Divine exhortations and primordial text, but you find no heaven on this earth. You search the signs God posted leading to the path, but there does not seem to be a promised land. But my friend, God did not post signs leading to a promised land nor is there a concealed garden ready and made. God's signs lead you to fertile grounds, but once you arrive, you plant the garden with your own sweat and hands. The Shari'ah is not a garden; it is a guidance that takes you to the fields of rich soil. It is your soul that plants and nourishes the beauty, and it is your soul that could leave God's gift barren and an uncultivated expanse. My friend, God implanted beauty in your heart by the touch of His breath, and guided you to the potential self. But whether you raise a garden or you are emaciated in a wasteland, that depends on the nourishment that your soul can bring and what your heart can plant. Don't you see that the rotted heart will pollute wherever it settles regardless of how rich or giving is the land?

My friend, you say that at times a person becomes polluted despite himself. There are injuries that fester and spread into infections that have no known cure. You ask me, when the person's soul is murdered and he continues to roam the earth, does God's breath continue to dwell within or does he become like the living dead, essentially a myth? If it is possible to kill a person and extinguish human life, isn't it possible to kill the Divine breath and yet keep the body alive? And if the living dead follow the signs and finds the fertile grounds, isn't the only choice left to them is to lie down and quietly decompose above the ground? You protest that I speak of the breath of God flowing in the soul, but if you feel that your soul is dead, how could the Divine breath stay alive?

My friend, I know what happened to you, and why your mouth bleeds words of pain. I know that one time you were assaulted with the explicit intent of making you gasp for a hint of bliss, and every time you gasped you found the poison of the devil instead. I know that you were beaten and then bound, and your body was used as a bridge to break a whole nation's soul. I know that in a moment borrowed from the devil, the unimaginable happened, and the excretions of hell injected into you the most venal venom. My friend, I know that at that moment the light in your heart dimmed and your mind was paralyzed with incomprehension. I know that at that debased moment you screamed: "Why! Why!" I also know that you remember your desperate plea: "What did I do? What did I do?" And, to this very day, the indignity of this scream haunts your mind. Your face contorts into what appears to be a smile, but the joy is a memory from a very distant past. And when the memories accumulate, you think that death would be a coveted gift. If your body had become objectified and has become the repository of unimaginable filth, what is the difference between the decay you feel as you walk above the earth or the inevitable decay that would take place under the ground.

But, my friend, I ask you, do you really think that the breath of God can be defiled as long as it is guarded by a vigilant guarding soul? My friend, please permit me to be more explicit, why would the violation of a hole in your body become the means of stabbing and puncturing the dignity and beauty of your soul? Isn't it possible that they only violated themselves? What I am saying is that even as to the ugliest of desecrations, the body of the victim is the one that suffers, but it is the offender's Divine breath that is surrendered to the devil. My friend, if a person defaces a book, that person only degrades himself, but the knowledge and thought survives nonetheless.

I know that you say that you feel abandoned, and lonely, and that you say that you cannot feel the breath of God inside of you. You say that on that accursed day all the beauty was sucked out, and you now simply wait for your body to expend itself. But, my friend, God's breath is always there, nestled inside, and it does not leave until God retrieves it back to Him. No human has the power to take what God has given, for God's gift can be retrieved or refused, but it cannot be stolen by a human or usurped.

You tell me that you want proof for what I just said then I ask you, when you met that woman with God's breath flowing within her with unbounded beauty, and majestic blessings, didn't you crave to be with her? Didn't you yearn to unite with her, and reside in her forever? Did you not crave to embrace her heart, and fill yourself with the supernal vivacity that you so clearly sensed? When you glimpsed God's beauty in her eyes, and felt the Divine aura in her presence, when you touched her hand and in an instant you felt thoroughly restored and cleansed, didn't you crave to transcend all the physical limits and drown yourself in purity and bliss?

My friend, I humbly submit, that this is the proof that you are far from dead—I submit that this is proof that the breath of God within you aches to be recognized and even aches to transcend your shell, and embrace the Divinity of the universe. My friend, if, as you claim, you are dead, you would not yearn to embrace her Divinity in your heart. Those who have truly died do not long, crave, yearn, or love. But the proof of the vigor of life is that the broken and hurt, once they feel the breath of God pulsating anywhere on this earth, they long to heal and love. Your craving to inhale the scent of the blessed spirit filling this woman's heart is clear and decisive proof that despite the agony and pain, my friend, that you have survived.

CHAPTER 70

Derangements

The books absorb the hours of the night, and the resonance of words expends the mind. This brain-mass has drowned in emotions more onerous than its comprehensions, and this heart has chased after longings that have always left it deserted. This is a mind at war with itself, with its time, and place. It aches to become unbounded in a paradise of love and poetry, but ends up banished to the wastelands of reality. It aches to hover in the heavens and intoxicate itself with rivers of beauty, but instead it is firmly implanted in the deserts of the earth. This is a mind that never had a childhood, adolescence, or adulthood, nor will it age—it has been simply decomposing since its birth. This mind has been born a Muslim, and with this came the truth of its fate—it is fated to watch the beauty of its tradition crumble, and the poetry of its civilization turn into profanity. This mind was born of a civilization that is thoroughly penetrated—punished, invaded, vanquished, and subjugated. A civilization whose passions have become neurotic fears—a civilization that contests its own existence.

As the hours progress, tired and drained, I feel that this body has endured to its capacity. My eyes can no longer make out the words as my eyelids insist on drawing the curtains on night. If only this body could understand that when I leave the Conference I dwell in derangements and mania, it would never surrender me. If only this body would realize what I see in my sleep, it would leave me in my mind's company. But every night I am confronted with the ultimatum of sleep, and when I resist, this body shuts down and leaves, and I am forced to confront the dreams. Nightmares are engagements at the extreme, and dreams are manipulations rooted in reality. But I can no longer differentiate between the two when I sleep. When awake I am salvaged and stabilized by the Conference, when asleep I teeter on the edge of unmitigated lunacy.

As I slipped in and out of consciousness at my desk, I finally surrendered and crawled to my bed. In a flash I saw Muslims rushing in long corridors, and meeting behind closed doors. They all gathered in an enormous lobby in the Biltmore Hotel, and everyone was yelling "brother, sister, brother, sister," everywhere I turned. Each one took the podium and extolled and thanked the other for being a leader and servant of the movement, and spoke at length about the importance of grassroots efforts, and Islam as a revolution against injustice and poverty wherever it may be. Every CEO of a company, medical doctor, politician, and non-Muslim in attendance was given an award for leading Muslims right into their grand destiny.

Suddenly, the Pokemans invaded the Biltmore Hotel, firing laser beams, maiming and burning everything in sight. In response, the Council of the Highest Learned and Enlightened Muslim Masters of the Universe thoroughly condemned the attack, and met to deliberate over the extent of the Zionist conspiracy. In another part of the land, the Israeli army was razing houses to the ground, and killing soccer players to save the free world from the terror of bombs. But the Council of the Highest Learned and Enlightened Muslim Masters of the Universe announced that, after engaging in a thorough review of the balance of dangers, it decided to confront the Pokeman evil. They issued volleys of *fatwas* that incinerated the Pokeman, and thoroughly defeated the Zionist conspiracy against Islam.

At that moment, the Buddha statues met in the heart of the night and conspired to sow the seeds for a great big civil strife. They decided to brainwash Muslims into spilling their brothers' blood, and to starve millions of refugees. But the undeniable power of jihad rose again, and a vicious battle defeated the infidel statues and scattered their remains across the lands.

It was then that we noticed that women were flocking to the graveyards, where their lure and seductions were raising the dead. But the council met again, and decided that since women are already dead in our consciousness, the dead should be banned from visiting the dead. However, before we could rest, the news arrived urgently. In a mosque in Toledo, the Zionists have conspired to tear down the curtains separating the women, and zombie-eyed females emerged from their coffins in a stampede firing seductions at unsuspecting men. For this, the Council decided to reconvene, but it could not agree on whether the Biltmore or the Bonaventure was a better place to meet.

The meeting on the fate of the Aqsa Mosque had to be postponed as well because we uncovered that the direction of the *qiblah* was most definitely wrong. But the *qiblah* meeting, itself, had to be postponed as well because Sharon had threatened to bring pigs to the Holy Mosque. After meeting in Washington D.C., the Council uncovered that Sharon's plot was far more sinister and profound than we had imagined previously. He had conspired to feed lard to every Muslim cow, and the Council, thank God, dealt with the problem by issuing a harshly worded condemnation of the anti-Islamic conspiracies. To thoroughly neutralize all the dangers, we decided to issue a new book on *halal* meat.

Before we could catch our breath, Indian troops invaded a village in Kashmir and raped every Muslim woman they could find. But we consoled ourselves because we responded by divorcing heretics from their wives. Tired and worn out, we decided to relax in a massive convention that will serve spicy Tikka and nice Biryani. We need to eat well and sleep for tomorrow, we have a long and arduous day confronting the world conspiracies of Pinkie and the Brain.

At that point I awake, and I pray in gratitude that this was nothing but my dreamt up derangements.

CHAPTER 71

A Leader Among Us

He was a clangorous and roistering man. He would storm through our meetings rip-roaring with Qur'anic verses and Prophetic traditions as if scooping from an indefatigable reserve. He would roar with frantic laughter expelling it from his throat without occasion. Startled, we would look at him and then look at each other puzzled by the impulsiveness of his jubilation. Yet, at times, he would fall silent—the silence of death—and appear restless as if unsettled by his existence.

Our friend was never late to a single class of fiqh (jurisprudence)—always pillared in the front row. The minute the Shaykh entered the room, he was the first to rise to greet him and kiss his hand. If the Shaykh's throat appeared to dry, in a frenzied move he would spring to pour the water or serve the tea. And, at the end of the halaqa (class) our friend would jump to take the Shaykh's hand, assist him to his feet, and shower an array of prayers and well wishes for the Shaykh's health and well-being. "Baraka Allah fik wa Shaykh, ma sha' Allah wa Shaykh, la fudda fuk ya Shaykh"— supplications and prayers without pause.

He would graze on the Shaykh's unbounded blessings, roaming around him waiting for a glance. No one sought to assert an intimacy with the Shaykh more than our friend, and the Shaykh, may God bless his pure soul, was often annoyed. At times, it felt like our friend was like the thick dampness of humidity clinging to the soul or like an irrepressible tune, the more you ignore it the more it persists in your thoughts. While pillared in silence during the halaqa, "Shaykh, I have a question," he would proclaim afterwards, and each question echoed from his contested identity, and not from the complexity of the material we were being taught. Once or twice he appeared

257

at the Shaykh's home prattling about his musings—"Shaykh, I have been thinking," and what followed was a self-deprecating litany of newly uncovered maladies that in a fit of honesty are now being addressed. But this was nothing more than mastication on an expunged history in order to nourish the cravings of a thriving egoism.

For him, the classes we took were remarkably painless. We strained to dismantle the barricades constructed by the sheltered habits, and the obsessions of routine—we struggled not only with what the text told us but also with what we could tell the text. We struggled not in pursuit of answers to questions—we struggled with the pursuit of questions to the answers. But our friend blissfully rested in the vision of coffins; in their confines and darkness everything is wonderfully clear because there is nothing to see. Each lecture and each book somehow confirmed what his intellect already held. He blistered with laughter before our bewildered faces, and proclaimed that our debates are like fevers that plague the ailments of faith. Only the infirm ponder the cause of their ailments and puzzle over the wonders of health.

Yes, my friend was so comfortable with his certitudes that to this day I wonder why he bothered with our class. We worshipped God through the ruminations of the mind. We honored the mind through the act of creating, and in doing so we honored the Creator of the mind. But our friend preferred to thank God for what, to him, was an entirely superfluous creation.

The most memorable part about him was his endless rants against the corruptions of society and government. People were living, he would announce, in dire darkness and must be purified, and nothing purifies the filth of the soul as much as blood. It is not that he called for mass extermination, but advocated focusing on the eradication of corruption. If it were up to me, he would say, I would burn every body part that a woman uses for seduction. The law would be simple and certain like the purity of his faith, he would proclaim—a chest revealed, is chest to be burned, and a hair revealed, is a hair to be put on fire. I must confess that he seemed to have a bizarre obsession with female breasts—every example of seduction, every example of corruption, and every one of his dreamt up laws all, somehow, came back to the female chest. Our friend was no less stolid about his proposed solutions to the oppression of the government. We should move with merciless resolve to kill the agents of the devil, and if only he had the chance, he would eliminate the President with his own two bare hands. Every night, he would jump in our conversations about legal preferences or the need for disciplined principles regulating the reliance on subjective notions of equity, and indulge in long stories about his valiant confrontations on behalf of God. He stared down an officer, he spat in the face of a policeman, he taunted a soldier, he defied an official, he would proclaim, and if this country was made people like him, our life would truly be blessed by the valor of men. One of those nights, he told us he beat his sister when he discovered that her low-cut dress showed her cleavage, and he destroyed the furniture in his home when his father refused to stop collecting interest on his bank deposits. That night, Samir, may God grant him the status of martyrs, lost his repose and yelled, "Perhaps, if you focused on your lessons, you would have a real thought in your head." It turned into an unpleasant evening, and he stormed out after counseling us to stop acting like women hiding behind their veils, and become real men for a change.

Then came that pivotal night. As we sat in class, listening to the Shaykh's lecture, suddenly, we heard dreadful and chilling sounds. In what seemed like a second caught in frozen time, soldiers dressed in black uniforms stormed and scattered around the mosque. There was a moment of silence as we stared at the Shaykh and then stared at the black suits and then we noticed some plain-clothed strangers dispersed all around. An officer with a mummified frown manifested at the narrow door, walked and then positioned himself next to the Shaykh. In an instant, long thick sticks were hurling down, and the place filled up with the terrible sounds emitted from electric prods. The shock from a prod felt like a startling burn and then every thing in your system tremors and you collapse to the ground. There is a strange instantaneous desire that overcomes you to ask for a chance to explain, to plead for a single moment to talk—as if the first impulse is to believe that this is a misunderstanding that could be easily resolved. But the impulse is swiftly treated by sticks that whistle through the air, and come crashing down at our faces and heads, and every presumption of dignity is thoroughly rebutted by cracking bones and spurting blood.

Bleeding and stunned into silence, we are herded into what are known as box trucks. And the trip to the unknown destination seems like an eternity marked only by the circular and anxious thoughts. In that truck our silent questions are no longer ponderings on received answers, but puzzlements over the certitudes of existence—on justice, dignity, mercy, and the worth of life. You think of your mother, your father, you think of the dinner set on the table, of the couch in your living room, of your bed, of the family pictures on the walls, of everything that could have possibly marked your existence as a person, and it all seems so distant and remote. Perhaps nothing ever existed, and only this and now is real. Does the fact that you were loved by a mother, a father—that you had friends, that you had a favorite meal, that you lost yourself in a beautiful song, or that you longed for the woman of your dreams make an iota of a difference or somehow plead your case as a human being?

None of it matters, and perhaps it never mattered. The truck stops, the doors open, and there is this maniacal yelling. We are rushed through an aging grim hallway plastered with chipped paint, and then you are herded into a large holding room. We are filed behind a short wooden railing and ordered to crouch down on the floor—no talking, no smoking, no begging or pleading—just sit and drown in your stomach acids, and battle the terror of the unknown. I looked around me and I did not see the Shaykh, but everyone else seemed to be there. Our infamous friend was crouching just a few feet away. His face was pale, and a large black bruise was growing on the right

side of his face. An officer appeared and stood staring at us as he sucked on his cigarette. He started cursing this miserable evening that brought us to him, cursing the
constant headaches of his life, and cursing us—the filth and scum of this earth, and
the sons of prostitutes and whores. He insisted that we shut up although no one was
speaking, and told us not to even dare to breath. I will show you a living hell, he yelled,
if he even hears a cough, a sneeze, or even the sound of our thoughts.

I confess that I kept thinking of my father and wondering if only there was a way
of letting him know what was going on. I fretted for our aging Shaykh, and wondered
if he could have endured a single strike during the beating in the mosque. We remained crouched until the pain in our legs and backs had become unbearable. After
an hour they collected our I.D. cards, but two of the students who did not have any
identification were led away. After another hour, they started calling some names, and
two soldiers escorted those named to another room. When our friend's name was
called he looked like the blood in his face had vaporized, and he started sobbing and
muttering incomprehensible words. When my name was called, I felt a moment of
relief because my feet and calves were seized by a merciless cramp, but this relief was
like escaping the heat by jumping into a fire. There is hardly a reason to recount the
painful memories, and speak of the hell that awaited us in these other rooms. We had
committed the infraction of an unlawful assembly, and for that there were insults,
slaps, kicks, cigarette burns, and other ungodly things.

It took me a short while to figure out that none of us were the target of the raid.
It was our Shaykh that the government wanted, and it is was him that they got. It took
us all a little longer to discover that our friend had struck some deal with the officers,
and unleashed his fantasies in bizarre inventions about our venerable Shaykh. Perhaps
we should be grateful—perhaps his cowardliness saved us the agony of further torture
—perhaps his fabricated confessions against the Shaykh was the reason that most of us
were released so soon. Three remained in detention, and the rest were warned not to
meet again, and we were reminded that the government knows when we laugh, when
we cry, and even the number of times we yawn or breath. Our Shaykh, may God bless
his soul, died within the span of two weeks.

These were days of remarkable agony—these were days that left a trail of crushed
dreams. I saw my hated friend years later. He had become the imam of an Islamic center in the United States. When our eyes met, we looked at each other in utter disdain,
and then mumbled a grudging salam. On a separate night I was invited to one of the
Muslim religious bazaars, and I heard that he was invited to speak. One of the rambling brothers extolled his piety and true understanding of Islam. He told me that he
is a hero, a true mujahid, not one of those people who go around trying to intellectu-
alize Islam. Later that night I remembered the blessed face of the Shaykh, and I cried.

CHAPTER 72

When God Asks the Child

In the endless sleepless nights of the Conference, the dark uncovers as much as it conceals. In the embrace of the Conference, the tracks of the mindless race dissipate. There are no trophies at the end and no glimmering rewards; there are only traces of journeys and the toils of legacies. There are mountains that are concealed by the night and that glide like clouds into the mind. In the embrace of the Conference, there is the history of those who walked the straight path and those who were mangled by the hard sharp rocks.

In the full embrace of the Conference, in a glimmer—in a glimpse that evades the inflictions of time, the curtains draw back and the skies are revealed. The stars dim and disappear, and the sun folds up and all we can see is the unadulterated face of God. Overcome by the dazzle of this beauty we float to the mountaintops, and stand within reach of the paradise that draws near. The night closes its gates and the dawn becomes nothing but a state of profound insight. We shed the deceptions of our projected weaknesses and fears, and we melt in a luminous unity that can finally see what the partitioned and fragmented intellect had labored so miserably to conceal. We open the ledgers of our lives—of our trials and feats, and see ourselves through the eyes of God—through the immutability of our innate Divinity.

At this instant of untainted and sublime probity, we are able to confront the inquest of virtue and ask: For what possible crime or sin have the children of this earth been put to death?

Yes, once upon a time in the dark ages of time, young girls were buried alive, and God has one question to ask the conscience of humankind: For what possible fault or crime has this innocent soul been killed? (Q. 81:8-9) Once upon a time, the distinction between the cant of ignorance and the call of Islam was the Divine remembrance that raised the conscience out of cemeteries that had buried humankind. The remembrance was simple but profound: No one will be hurt for the fault of another, and even in the prevalence of injustice, the mandates of justice may not be compromised.

Today, I surrender to the Conference with a broken and ravished heart. In the name of the remembrance, in the name of Islam and the beauty of the Divine, Muslims are now the ones who somehow justified the burying of children alive. The graves were not made of sand and dust, but concrete and steel, and instead of burying their shame in the earth, these Muslims hijacked the skies, and then buried themselves with their victims in a shameless shrine.

I ask the Conference, after fourteen hundred years, how did we manage to end where we started—how could we have buried the living and ended up confronting the same question that heralded the call of Islam? Have these self-declared martyrs ever bothered to read the Qur'an?

Yet, perhaps this has nothing to do with the Conference or our historical traces. Perhaps this is a simple aberration brought about by a viral infection that afflicts the brain, erases the remembrance, and eradicates any sense of moral responsibility.

But perhaps this is a state of insanity brought about by the sadistic rape of Muslim dignity and the systematic dismantling of Muslim memory. Perhaps the unrelenting cruelty inflicted on Muslims in the modern age—the memories of the horrific scenes of blood and the scores of innocents lost were bound to create this mindless savagery. Perhaps when you rob a people of their honor, they are bound to act dishonorably. Perhaps this is not our fault—perhaps this is the inevitable result of the depravity of our enemies.

But can all the injustice in the world explain to a child why he must suffer and die? Can the burying of a child under sand or rubble ever be justified? God proclaims His disdain for those who corrupt the earth and describes corruption as the act of violating the sanctity of life (Q. 2:205). And so God told the Israelites that whoever kills an innocent soul he has killed all of humankind—the earth is either corrupted or salvaged in the very act of extinguishing or preserving the breath of God (Q. 5:32). Thus, if in one time and place, the sanctity of the Divine breath is violated, is the solution to further snuff out the breath of life?

Yet the devils that pinch the mind in thoughts of destitution and desolation pull the soul toward the amoral logic of necessity. Protesting, the devils scream out aloud, if you throw a people to the ground and deny them the right to stand on their feet with dignity, why are you surprised when they lash out and kick back indiscriminately? No, I am not surprised, but the mere fact that a reaction can be anticipated does not make it right. When my acts as a human being implicates and impacts upon the rights of God, if I cannot assert dignity while standing on my feet, I will assert it in the act of self-sacrifice—I will assert it in my suffering and dying on the ground. We were raised by a man, who forbade the killing of innocents, a woman, a monk, or a child, a farmer, a laborer, or anyone that is engaged in nonbelligerent activities. We were raised by the man who forbade a victory at the expense of the indiscriminate destruction of life. And who more than the Prophet and his followers had the opportunity to invoke the logic of necessity? Didn't they have to clinch the breath of honor from the choke of an unrelenting siege? But these are a people who learned their morality and took their guidance from God, and not from their enemies.

So I come back to this endless sleepless night—truly the darkness uncovers as much as it conceals. At times, when the stars dim and die, and the sun folds up and disappears—the Divine ledgers open wide, and we can see the luminous face of God, but we can also see the true ugliness that has infested our beings.

We have dwelled in this profound alienation; haunted by nightmares we have become marred in delusions and dreams. Since the age of Colonialism, we have become the children of a lost civilization living on the thrills of imagined heroes, villains, battles, and victories. Our junk food has become the malnutrition of adolescent clichés and demagoguery. We feed on fast thoughts, apologetics, and an idealized history, and when challenged, we respond with indignant arrogance hiding our rampant insecurities. We rejoice at infantile acts of rejectionism—howling at offensive novelists, cheering at the blowing up of historical monuments, celebrating a Muslim's refusal to stand up out of respect for the national anthem, and vigilantly guarding the hair of women lest it may, God forbid, appear. Infantile acts of rejectionism, like the protests of a child as he stomps his feet.

Between the extremes of rejectionism and apologetics we have guarded our fragile egos; we have found it all too easy to rely on impulsive reactions, while evading the imperative of moral probity. We claim equality but deny it; we attack democracy but claim it; we brag about women's dignity but violate it; we praise freedom of speech but ignore it; we depend on the West but attack it; and we claim victories but live in defeat.

If schizophrenia is a disease, what explains this insanity? Easy oil-money, easy rhetoric, easy apologetics, easy claims, easy denials have thrown us at the shores of extremes. Rejectionism and apologetics has become the drug that numbs our pains, but it does not treat our underlying maladies. But both rejectionism and apologetics are necessary elements in the psychology of terror—terrorists must reject the worth of life itself, and utilize apologetics to nurture an inherent sense of superiority.

So when the ledgers are opened, and the innocent child is asked why she was buried alive, and her life was snuffed under the ruins of immorality, I fear that we will have to respond: considering how our generation has dealt with our religion, we all share the shame of this horrendous culpability.

The Sites of Purity

I wish this pen could flow unadulterated, like a thread through the fabric of being, until it can bring together the scraps of remembrance into a full vision of reality. I remember the first moment I opened my eyes to the bewilderments of consciousness, the comfort of love, and the longing to go back to sleep. And, it seems that I have spent a lifetime struggling to make sense of the befuddlements of the first moment of being. With every pulse and heartbeat, I know that I did not come from oblivion, but I came from a supernal nature, extracted and banished for the time being. But my birth and death are inextricably inseparable that I can no longer tell which of them has taken place and which will come to be. I struggle with the tracking of shadows, and the pursuits of roving dreams until the only real moment, when you embrace me.

When the dreams of union call to me, it is like the thrill of the first awareness of love—a promise, a craving, and a resolve to defy all reality. Suddenly the shadows of existence slip further into oblivion, and the senses are dulled to everything, but ignite with a single quintessential feeling—a longing to fuse the bonded and contingent self with an unconditional and absolute beauty.

Sites of purity symbolize the promise of union, like the lips of the mundane allowed to sip from the gourd of infinity. It is sites of purity that call upon the temporal to visit the covenants of divinity. Sites of purity found in the infatuations of my mind, in the silent overtures, in the unrelenting longing, and in the weary wonderings of my heart—sites of purity found in the human smile; sites of purity found in your eyes dissolve me. All I want of you is to capture these fluttering parts, chase them, grab them, expose them, and when you are done, leave nothing hidden or concealed. Take these cumbersome appendages that they call my body—take this incomprehensible mess of fluids and tubes, and leave nothing of them behind, dissolve these delusions, and dilute this arrogant façade of the ugly me. But I beg of you, salvage this intellect for it is but a testament of longing, and guide this pilgrim to a settlement in a site of beauty. You see, I wrestle the delusions of perception throughout the earth, and kick the dust into passing clouds of reality, and yet, my gaze is always drawn back to a flickering consciousness of my own perennial immutability.

My Lord, what is left in this earth for a Muslim to gaze upon—where can a Muslim turn his eyes and find a semblance of beauty? Our religion has become a peddled commodity packaged in cheap and shiny demagoguery with the manufacturers perched in the oil markets of the world. Wherever I turn these eyes I see oil and blood, the summation of our existence, while one is spilled, the other flows. I, at times, wonder, in the markets of today, how many barrels of Muslim blood are worth a single barrel of oil. In every site of divinity today—in Mecca, Medina, and Jerusalem while oil and blood can be bought and sold, one of them is artificially under priced, and the other is treated as if it has no worth. I ask You God, for a Muslim, where can a site of purity be found, and where can a dignified Muslim find a home? Forgive me my Lord, but is it conceivable that in the modern age Muslims have become those chosen to suffer at the hands of the chosen people of old? Is it possible that those once chosen to be the bearers of the Word are now the shufflers of sand and the porters of oil? Lord, I am lost in our fate; my heart has exiled my mind to wonder in words, and the intellect that once prospered in Islam is now banished and banned, after its olive trees have been destroyed by messianic settlers and excavators for gas and oil.

Daily, a Muslim is confronted by the spilling of blood. Does anyone, but You, know the number of Muslims that perished in Palestine, Chechnya, Kashmir, and Afghanistan? Does anyone grieve for the inconceivable miseries that abound in prisons built by Muslims, and for Muslims, all around this world? Every day, we keep meticulous count of the number of barrels of oil produced, the number of hamburgers consumed, and the number of Cadillacs bought and sold, but does anyone care about the number of Muslims destroyed?

In the sanctuaries of Islam—in Mecca, Medina, and Jerusalem—a Muslim cannot find self-appointed guardians that are more cruel, and at no place is a Muslim at a higher risk of being robbed his dignity. At the holy sites, when the arms of the skies extend to open the earthly gates to the Divine, how much human ugliness and beauty do they find? And, as we bear witness and take account of our lives, what contributions of beauty do we offer back to God? As we assess the beauty of our faith, how do we assess the ugliness of the grounds we have come to inhabit on this earth?

In remembrance, I mourn the holy sites—the sites of purity in the chosen lands and in the geography of our souls. I mourn, perhaps if we can remember then we can also hope.

Those who occupy Jerusalem have soaked it in misery, and those who are the servants of the two holy shrines have choked it in tyranny. Perhaps, I can comprehend the enmity of the "other," but what explains our own malignity with each other? A professor of Islamic law by the name of Abdul Hamid al-Mubarak organized a demonstration in Dhahran to protest the suffering of his Palestinian brothers, and, now, he is made to suffer. The Saudi government declared him mentally unstable, and he was arrested, tortured, and at the time of this Conference, continues to be in the category of the disappeared. The Saudi government explained that in the benign culture of submission—in the culture of the guardians of the holy sites—it is not acceptable for a Muslim to think or speak. In the city of Muhammad and Ibrahim—in the city of the Ka'bah, of faith nurtured by reason, and of reason tempered by compassion, at least fifteen girls are incinerated by the hellfire of impiety and sheer stupidity. A girls' school in Mecca caught fire, and before the eyes of their parents, the girls are allowed to burn to death by the *mutawwa'in*. Fearing that the girls might escape the building on fire while improperly covered, the religious police prevented them from leaving or from being saved. The servants of the holy shrines invoke the rule of necessity (*darurah*) in every affair related to their own power, and in protecting every male desire. They invoke it even in feeding their sexual appetites, and in allowing Uncle Sam to feed his appetite for the riches of their Muslim brothers. But quite simply, when it comes to the preservation of the lives and well-being of Muslim women, there can be no necessity. I breathe deeply in pain, and wonder, what swamp of insanity and ugliness raised the *mutawwa'in*? As we observe the agony of our holy sites, what sins have we planted, which we now so painfully reap?

Why is it that we fail to read the omens written on the pages of history, and we pretend that our suffering is without a memory? Why do we refuse to acknowledge the ugliness and fanaticism that has gripped our holy cites, at least for a century? Why is it that we are oblivious to the many stories of injustice that have come to devalue a Muslim's basic humanity?

We forget the horrific massacres of Muslims by Wahhabi forces in Karbala in 1802, and the terror inflicted upon the inhabitants of Mecca in 1804 and of Medina in 1806. Where are the gravesites of the untold number of Muslims who were executed after being accused of heresy?

Does anyone remember the *bid'ah* of taking roll call at prayers in the mosques of Medina and Mecca? In the early 1800s, and again in the 1920s, rosters of the inhabitants were drawn, and in order to check attendance at prayers, rolls were called, and those absent were flogged, sometimes to death. Since the 1920s, our holy cities have become free of music, free of beauty, free of everything except a piety fed by power, and anchored in brutality.

As I flip through the pages of the Conference, I recall that in 1926, a crisis between Egyptian and Saudi governments broke out because the religious police of

Mecca attacked and beat Egyptian pilgrims whose sin was that they played the bugles as they escorted their ceremonial palanquin. In the same year, 'Abdullah bin Hasan, the imam of the *masjid* of Mecca, beat an Egyptian chauffeur for smoking a cigarette. And the response of the government was to flog the chauffeur to death, and appoint 'Abdullah as the director of *da'wah* and the chief judge of the holy city. From the 1920s until 1960s, I read about a steady stream of protests by Muslim governments against the vulgar treatment of their citizens, and the forcing of all pilgrims to abide by the divinely inspired Wahhabi claim to orthodoxy. But in the 1970s, with the growing Saudi wealth, all protests came to a sudden end, as the Muslim world learned the lesson that Abdul Hamid Mubarak must now understand well, and that is: the black gold has long sold a Muslim's right to dignity.

For decades, the size and architecture of the holy sites have flourished, but what has become of the Muslim soul and mind? For all the stones and roads oil can buy, can it buy a single moment of honor and dignity? Can we Muslims earn God's mercy and justice when we have defaced God's blessed sites with injustice and cruelty? At times, I even wonder if we Muslims have been denied the trust of Jerusalem because we have proven ourselves otherwise untrustworthy.

But as I struggle to undo the folds of this night, I expunge such thoughts because I cannot bear them, and I do not want to become the miserable dweller in hopelessness and defeat. I force all the pain to the palms of my hands; I grip it, inspect it, study it, but in the presence of your beauty, I must then look beyond. I am not the pain, and it is not my faith. This pain is but a reminder to those who are tempted to forget—those who forget that the sites of purity and Divinity on this earth must first be honored in the heart and intellect. "Do not be like those who have forgotten their Lord and so the Lord has led them to forget themselves" (59:19). My Lord, may the memory of suffering call us back to ourselves, and may the sites of remembrance shine, not with misery, but beauty.

CHAPTER 74

Banning the Conference

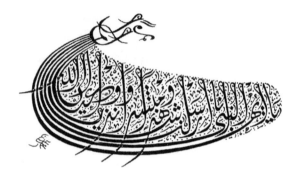

The night has surrendered its shelter to us. The music chants with supernal beauty, inviting God to reside in the midst of our dread and zeal. The Conference of the books never sleeps, but at times, as we stumble into the fissures of our contradictions, we fall upon the noise of our silence commanding that we seek You before we speak.

We are the breath of creation, enraptured by the beauty of the word that is You, and our words are but supplications, and so we do not have the right but the duty to speak.

God, here in this Conference are all the intellects that once prostrated before you, greeted you with the supplications of peace. "Greetings unto You, and the most blessed of prayers. Peace, blessings, and mercy for you our Prophet. Peace be on us and on the upright servants of our Lord."

These were the supplications of these intellects, for the intellects are but manifestations of the primordial word. With the intellect, we were taught, and the book is the pulse of our souls, and You are the infinite word. What is the Conference but a supernal chant supplicating creation, the intellect, and the word?

We have walked through creation, and found that it is nothing but the utterance of the Lord. Let the appendages, the ink, and paper vaporize until nothing remains of this mythology and lore. What remains, and what always was, is the soul of creation, the intellect and the word.

Kind You were to let us raise our heads, and then bear witness to the universe. In prostration we remembered our death, and when we rose we remembered our life, and in both we were blessed. If we prostrate to You, how can we prostrate to anyone else? In speaking to you, how can we refrain from speaking to everyone else? After we supplicated You, we honored ourselves. We partook in your beauty, for our prayers are like the communion of the heavens and earth. We prostrate on the ground only to reach for infinity. We kneel only to stand in dignity. We are expressions of God, so how can we be silenced by any human being? If the intellect is divine, and the word manifests the wonder of divinity, how can a human being be denied the right to speak?

Verily, my Lord, as you said: "My covenant is not given to the unjust" (2:124).

God, for twenty years, this Conference has tenaciously called for beauty, and reminded Muslims that the intellect is divine and the word its majesty. If we cannot listen, speak, and think, we cannot claim to believe. If we need the fortifications of darkness, and fear the penetration of speech, then what we shelter is doubt, not belief. How can we seek the light of God, but fear the divinity within humanity? How can we claim the light of divinity while forcing darkness upon human beings?

How can Islam and despotism coexist when despotism is the ultimate idolatry? What is despotism other than the displacement of God, and the denial of the supernal promise of humanity? While God has endowed us with the tools to think and speak, the despot confiscates the gifts of divinity. The unwavering mark of the despot is censorship, whether it slays the intellect or suppresses its speech. Whether the despot censors in the name of God, or seeks to prevent the triumph of Satan, censoring the word, by its nature, is an act of blasphemy. Censorship preempts the possibilities of creation, perjures the testimony, with which we have been charged, and voids the very logic of human accountability.

But censorship is the ailment of the despot, festering in a slough of cowardliness and fear. Seeking to escape the challenges of thought, the despot barricades himself in a stockade of arrogance that only shields his fears. But regardless of the fanfares of power and might, the despot is cowardly and weak. Any coward can fire a gun, or any tyrant can pluck out the tongues of those who dare to speak, but it takes the bravery of the sublime to confront ideas with ideas. It is impossible for a Muslim who has truly surrendered to the truth of God to refuse to confront thought with thought, and to indulge in the cowardly act of censoring speech. Light cannot exist if we ban the night, and if people cannot deny they cannot believe. Can there be heaven without its hell, and without hardship can there be ease?

Among the mythology preserved in our Muslim history is a story that claims: "Moses, peace be upon him, asked God to ban people from speaking lies about him (Moses). God answered that He would not censor people from speaking lies about Himself so how could he ban people from speaking about anyone else!" But no wonder! Wasn't the Devil ejected from the realm of God, and specifically put on this earth to speak? If the Lord allowed the Devil the freedom to speak, and say nothing but lies, how do we imagine that we can deny humans the right to speech?

Yet, this Conference is inspired neither by devils nor darkness for it is a primordial voice calling to the primordial inventor of beauty. The Conference is the echo of the voices that after traveling through the shades and shadows of all the deceptive delights, the only truth is the beauty of God. But after twenty years with the Conference convening in a magazine falsely called the *Minaret*, it now has been banned, and yet another voice of beauty has been terminated in the lands of Islam.

The Conference will persist—just because the night has fallen the sun does not disappear. Even in the somber gloom of darkness, the illuminations of the mind can ignite with such resplendence that even if the eyes cannot see, the heart will be the source of unhampered insight.

The Conference will live in the hearts and minds long after the dictators shuffling and hiding papers cease to be. But the point that I decry and what pains me is what we, Muslims, have done with the dominion of the Divine, and Sublime's sovereignty. A despot cannot exist without the hordes of people who acquiesce, and who submit themselves to the equivocations of apathy. When the restless absolutes of a despot confront an apprehensive people, unsure of their worth, and scared of their devils, more than they are confident in their divinity, invariably there will be the shameless birth of tyranny.

It is this that made many in Muslim history dream of the just despot, who will save people from confronting their failures, and deliver the bliss of God to their doorsteps as they simply confine their obligations to that of a joyous cheerlead. It is as if God has charged us with justice, only so that we can efface ourselves, and pass the charge on to an individual who is willing to pretend that he can shoulder the full responsibility. God has offered the trust to the heavens and earth, and refusing to carry it, they shrunk away in terror and fear. We human beings carried it, and we were elevated by its blessings, but also encumbered by its liabilities. How is it possible to relinquish the trust of justice to a just despot even if this person claims to be bound by God's decrees? Has God relinquished His Kingdom, appointed a successor on this earth, and transferred the possibilities of enlightenment to a person or group empowered by singular astuteness and perspicacity?

It was Hamid al-Ghazali who said that despotism and justice are two opposites that cannot be reconciled in the heart of one being. How can a human being who fancies that all of God's wonders and beauty can be deposited in a single person be just. And how is it just to ignore or void the bewildering richness of intellects, as we confine justice to the exclusive province of singular beings. It is as if God has given us an ocean of wisdom, but we confine ourselves to a single ship navigating the seas.

Yet, we must admit that even among this Conference's many participants, there are those who supported the myth of the just despot, and contributed to the profanity of censorship, and helped desecrate the word's sanctity. Among many, it was the Egyptian Shafi'i jurist, Ibn Jama'a, who said a thousand years of tyranny is better than a single day of anarchy. But this is akin to saying that a day of irreverence is better than a thousand years of blasphemy. It is true that without the anchor of discipline, and the

270

charts of divinity we might be overwhelmed and lost in an ocean whose majesty could be lethal, and whose expanse could be deadly. But worse than the possibility of being lost in God's infinite wisdom is to drown in place out of ignorance and fear. Despite the absolutions of historical contexts, and the right of the scholars of the past to respond to the call of conscience and the challenges of history, the burden remains on us to reach for greater perfection, and a higher moral fulfillment of God's indefatigable beauty. Prostrating to God, we stand free in dignity. But when we allow a despot, small or big, to deny a single man or woman from the natural right to speak, our very silence and our failure to rebel against the blasphemy of tyranny means that as a people and as a single nation we have surrendered our divine right to dignity.

"Because of what they've earned, We make the unjust rule the unjust?" (6:129)

CHAPTER 75

9/11

In the endless sleepless nights of the Conference, the dark uncovers as much as it conceals. In the embrace of the Conference, the tracks of the mindless race dissipate. There are no trophies at the end and no glimmering rewards; there are only traces of journeys and the toils of legacies. There are mountains that are concealed by the night and that glide like clouds into the mind. In the embrace of the Conference, there is the history of those who walked the straight path and those who were mangled by the hard sharp rocks.

In the full embrace of the Conference, in a glimmer—in a glimpse that evades the inflictions of time, the curtains draw back and the skies are revealed. The stars dim and disappear, and the sun folds up and all we can see is the unadulterated face of God. Overcome by the dazzle of this beauty we float to the mountaintops, and stand within reach of the paradise that draws near. The night closes its gates and the dawn becomes nothing but a state of profound insight. We shed the deceptions of our projected weaknesses and fears, and we melt in a luminous unity that can finally see what the partitioned and fragmented intellect had labored so miserably to conceal. We open the ledgers of our lives—of our trials and feats, and see ourselves through the eyes of God—through the immutability of our innate Divinity.

At this instant of untainted and sublime probity, we are able to confront the inquest of virtue and ask: For what possible crime or sin have the children of this earth been put to death?

Yes, once upon a time in the dark ages of time, young girls were buried alive, and God has one question to ask the conscience of humankind: For what possible fault or crime has this innocent soul been killed? (81:8–9) Once upon a time, the distinction between the cant of ignorance and the call of Islam was the Divine remembrance that raised the conscience out of cemeteries that had buried humankind. The remembrance was simple but profound: No one will be hurt for the fault of another, and even in the prevalence of injustice, the mandates of justice may not be compromised.

Today, I surrender to the Conference with a broken and ravished heart. In the name of the remembrance, in the name of Islam and the beauty of the Divine, Muslims are now the ones who somehow justified the burying of children alive. The graves were not made of sand and dust, but concrete and steel, and instead of burying their shame in the earth, these Muslims hijacked the skies, and then buried themselves with their victims in a shameless shrine.

I ask the Conference, after fourteen hundred years, how did we manage to end where we started—how could we have buried the living and ended up confronting the same question that heralded the call of Islam? Have these self-declared martyrs ever bothered to read the Qur'an?

Yet, perhaps this has nothing to do with the Conference or our historical traces. Perhaps this is a simple aberration brought about by a viral infection that afflicts the brain, erases the remembrance, and eradicates any sense of moral responsibility.

But perhaps this is a state of insanity brought about by the sadistic rape of Muslim dignity and the systematic dismantling of Muslim memory. Perhaps the unrelenting cruelty inflicted on Muslims in the modern age—the memories of the horrific scenes of blood and the scores of innocents lost were bound to create this mindless savagery. Perhaps when you rob a people of their honor, they are bound to act dishonorably. Perhaps this is not our fault—perhaps this is the inevitable result of the depravity of our enemies.

Yet, can all the suffering in world explain to the mind of a child, why she was buried alive? No, this is simply too easy—every aggressor in the world was once a victim, and the bedrock of every injustice is a litany of injustices, both imagined and real.

CHAPTER 76

Divine Threads

I clench my books, and recall the vows inscribed on the pages of this Conference. I struggle to stay the course, believing in beauty as the straight-line path of our faith. But sometimes, in such strange and odd days, the straight way narrows until it hides, and I lose my way. When the scales of life are filled with ignorance on one side and with pain on the other, what can come from our lives but hate?

I open my mouth, but flooded by pain, I am thrown around by surges of agony, and then the words drown. Although my heart bleeds, I think, if only I can scream then perhaps this can end, and I can awake. Don't screams break the grip of sleep, and don't they become the catalyst for transporting the dreamer from the reality of nightmares to a more profound reality?

If I could silence the memories of beauty, perhaps I could accept the ugliness of today. Perhaps, if history could be silenced, then I would no longer agonize over our fate. Perhaps, if I could convince myself that Muslims are real, I could wake up from this hellish nightmare.

I wish I could find the beauty that is the unwavering truth—the perennial beauty shrouded by the mist that embraces divinity. I know I can find it guarded and concealed by a million clouds that seem like vapor, but when touched, they turn into me. What could possibly be more truthful than timeless souls standing rejoicing in the intoxications of this beauty? The souls of beauty are nothing but light threaded from light. Hasn't God proclaimed the fulfillment of the divine beauty in His Being? And hasn't the beauty of our Lord been entrusted to human beings? Entrusted with the covenant of beauty, can we but weave this creation with the light of divinity? But, my

God, when we scuttle in darkness, and tear at shadows, what in our hearts remains of the threads of light or Your divinity?

My God, You are beautiful—the beauty of the unadulterated insight when it travels unhampered by the obscurities of shadows, and freed from its own conceit. At a time where the scales are weighed by ugliness, the only measure to which I steadfastly adhere is to clench the threads of divinity. As I confront myself with my own existence, I ask, am I a part of the weave of beauty, or am I among those who undo the threads uniting all existence in a single divinity? In life, there seems to be those who are content to be like the encrustations of dirt on the seams of beauty; there are those who add their thread, but marred in ignorance, they only deform the tapestry; and there are those who are like the obnoxious moth, they exist to feed on, and ultimately, decay the tapestry. There are also those who live in the self-denials of awe, and supplicate Your beauty. But then who are we?

I am a Muslim because there is nothing in this heart and mind but a single, unified, and unadulterated glory. I feel no "I," and there is no "me." There is no law, but there is the overwhelming innate compulsion of divinity. It—it is in the beat of the heart, the pulse of being, and the secret that enshrines the word in the mind of infinity. God, I am a Muslim not by faith, but by the simple fact of being. In every instant, I am reborn and transformed into a Muslim to the extent that I uncover Your beauty. I am a Muslim to the extent that I am beautiful, for if Islam and ugliness combine, life becomes a slothful slumber, and nightmares become the reality.

God, in my mind is majesty. It is this certitude that drives me into puzzlements, and so I sequester my senses in the sanctity of the Conference. But today's Conference is as if sitting in a wasteland seeded by immorality. If I can open my mouth at the bottom of dew, and quench this painful thirst, perhaps I can rise again and anchor this soul in this majesty. But our life is barren, and we—well, we are a blasphemy.

God, look at your people! Look at those who have wrapped themselves in your religion like a cloak of hypocrisy. Look—are they your people? On their splattered banners, bombastic slogans, and rolling banter, do you see or hear beauty? Does their labor carry the fragrance of Your breath—do their acts resonate with mercy and bliss? Is the bliss of Your touch found in the misery of their follies? Can the agonies that they spread, and the suffering they inflict possibly represent divinity? If the nature of a people is measured by their tragedies and glories, what if for them tragedy is glory? No, they are not Your people for with certitude and conviction, I know that Your people are known by the love they earn, not by the hearts and minds they mutilate and burn, as they convince themselves that they are the bearers of Your majesty.

I sit in the Conference in long and solemn nights, remembering the past and picturing the future. Here is a chorus of intellects sublimating the majesty of the word and Your unbounded beauty. Through the centuries, intellects, transforming to words, reigning in books, they sit on thrones of shelves built for Your glory. What a kingdom this is—a kingdom illuminated by words, adorned by books, paved by intellects, and spirited by humility. Here, every intellect is sovereign, and every brain is noble. Here, in the Conference, is the record of those who consumed themselves for the love of knowledge, longed for You, and understood that the intellect is a miracle that is both a trust and mercy.

So many times, the intellects of the past and present met to confer with a visitor to the Conference, and console him in misery, but tonight, I am my own visitor, I am my own seeker, and I am the porter of misery. This Conference has witnessed betrayals of scholars throughout the centuries, but I have been betrayed by ways that are shamelessly vile, and by people who are of unimaginable cruelty.

People that I once imagined as brothers have cloaked themselves in Your name, and caused me to suffer by targeting my work and name. The worse treachery comes from those I once called friends, from those I prayed and laughed with, and with whom I experienced genuine moments of love and beauty.

This portly-burly leader that walks as if bumbling from side to side has fed his rotted stomach from the corpses of murdered minds. With his oversized skull and vitreous eyes, he wears the face of the dead, as if his putrid and putrescent mind is encrusted in a feculent head. He is a medical doctor, because it was written in the Ancient Sacred Tablets of Adversarius Islamicus, "Only By Homo Fatuus Medicus Thou Shall be Led." This is a man who, in his despotism, has used a mosque as if a depository for his ego, and a consecrated space for a megalomaniac Godhead.

This vindictive man was enthroned in his ignorance by nothing more than the indolence and apathy of the Muslims, who surrendered to him their stretched and slothful necks. He grabs these slothful necks, as he declares God's will to be whatever he pleases. He then hoists it before the eyes of his constituency of idle sleepers, and if one dares to as much as lift an eyelid or even sigh in protest, he proclaims to all, that as far as they are concerned, they are to consider the troublemaker as good as dead.

This is a man who prides himself on speech that is an invective bite, and declares his monthly printed sneer "unique." This is a man who in his bygone days when arrested by the political police sold out his brethren, and once let an injured women die because he wanted to finish a meal. This is a man who pompously dismisses generations of thought because he finds in the prattling of his head a full replacement for the need to read. This is a man whose truth and *fiqh* is built on nothing more than whim, and his truth and speech is entirely contingent on who, at a particular moment, he wishes to impress or please. Your Prophet said, "As you are you will be led," and the truth that is agonizingly painful to admit is that in the United States, this is also a man who is genuinely and truly equipped to lead.

This Conference, searching for beauty, and celebrating the intellect, has ascended to so many hearts and minds. It grabbed the slumbering eyelids, and breathed life into so many languished intellects. Search your God, it said, that perennial beauty known and nestled in your hearts. Its voice burrowed deep to the core of the earth, and rose to the azure and firmament with the imperishable call honoring the beauty of the human mind. There is no God but God, this Conference said, but there is a wealth of diverse intellects, and all carry a piece of the secret of the divine. This life is as if a banquet, with God the host and we the guests, and no human can decide who may or may not be invited to dine. But it is moral that all guests leave God's house, at the end, as beautiful as it was originally found. We have not been invited to dine on food and drink—we have been invited to know the Word and be nourished by thought. Such is the generosity of our host because we have been invited to partake in nothing less than the very essence of the divine. Such was the message of the Conference, and it was heard by nations near and far.

Our corpulent leader also heard this, except that, in his mind, the banquet exists for him; he is the host and guest, and humans exist to feed on the scraps of his intellect. Declaring outrage and great offense, he banned my books, my writings, and even my presence from his kingdom, and announced to all: "This heretic from hereon is to be treated as if dead, and any who dare acknowledge him are banished from my kingdom and my mosque as well." God, I confess that his megalomania is a cause for laughter and weeping—laughter because the kingdom he rules exists only in his mind, and weeping because if it had not been the apathy of your people, he would not reign supreme in a mosque.

God, you know that the Conference is not scripted on the pages of a book or journal; it is scripted in the hearts and minds. Has a tyrant ever banned history from speaking, or beauty from being, or from life becoming a word?

But as many a tyrant before him, and many that will come, when censorship and bans fail, they employ the infliction of agony and pain to break the resolute will. It is not that the infliction of pain can overcome the power of the word, or, as some have said, that the sword is mightier than the pen, but it is like water and fire, they are different powers, yielded by different natures, although they exist in overlapping instants of time. Like evil and good, they are of two natures, but if combined in an overlapping moment, the results are so murky and contingent to such an extent that the moment experienced obfuscates the truth, and tears the heart. Each encounter between the different natures yields a situation, but it ought not result in an absolute conviction. In an overlapping moment, torture and pain might undercut the means to the word, and inflict confusion, but once the moment passes, and tranquility is restored to the mind, the word invariably returns calling the conscience to return to God.

My God, it is one of those moments of confusion that I now experience. All the slander and all the threats, and in disbelief I remember that those who today do the tyrants deeds were once brothers and friends. Truly, "these are people whose hearts have been hardened and the devil has made their deeds seem most pleasing" (6:43). But of all the evils of this world, none is as deceptive, hallucinatory, and self-forgiving as jealousy. Every slanderous effort they undertook against me has failed, and even their threats only propelled ahead in my journey toward the divine. I have walked through shadows, screamed at demons, and forced even the devil to run and hide. The books on my shelves have emitted threads of light that pierced the darkness, and flew with words to unparalleled heights.

God, I have been made to suffer, and my sin is that I stood up to tyranny. In my confusion, I remember your verse: "Is that who has been given the certitude of his Lord no better than those to whom the evil of their deeds seems most pleasing? Is that who has been given certitude like those who follow their whims?" (47:14) I sit in the Conference, clench the books, and remember your verse. Is that who has taken the vow of beauty, and lived weaving the divine threads, like those who undo the tapestry of existence by persecuting the intellect? God, my certitude in You is my salvation, but my shock at the ugliness of those who pretend to be your people is the source of my confusion. I pray to You my Lord, grant me patience, perseverance, and the wisdom to transcend the moment to see the end. I know, that this Conference, long after its persecutors are forgotten and dead, through the miracle of the intellect, will continue weaving the divine threads that are as if glimpses of You, and of our innate, and sometimes lost, beauty.

Embraced by the Beloved

Your beauty overwhelms me to the point of pain. In obeisance, I feel nothing but you. Those who speak of obedience do not know. They do not know. Submitting myself to you, all that remains is to partake in your beauty. My beloved—my beloved, there remains no hate, no rancor, ugliness, agony, or strife.

What remains is us anchored without flesh—embracing shrouded in light—surrounded by an existence that spreads behind a veil of mystery. Absorbed in you, I have no use for my eyes—I see through my beloved. And in your embrace we float through existence and through your eyes, I realize that this existence is what you will it to be. Engulfed in your will it is impossible but to be jubilant about the beauty that surrounds me.

My beloved, I am compelled to know myself so that I will know you. If I do not who and what I am, I will project myself onto you. Then, my beloved, you would become the excuse of the narcissist who loves himself and is unable to love any one else. I must know myself so that I can know you—I need to confront the self with the truth, so that I can know your truth. My beloved, I discovered myself before I discovered you. My beloved, I was forced to confront my own ugliness before absorbing your beauty. Before knowing myself I could not surrender—I could not possibly surrender what I did not own.

My beloved, in truth I must confess that I was struck by my own ugliness and I was forced to wonder: How in God's name could you ever come to love me? I am folly standing in a ridiculous shell. How ridiculous the folly and how ridiculous the shell!

But for your sake, I ripped myself to shreds, and stood unveiled without my shell. My folly evaporated in your love and my body was but a myth.

The unrelenting pain of self-recrimination and self-reprobation removes the folds of deception, and clears the way to penetrating perception. With piercing and perforating eyesight, we puncture through the shells and shields, after which we know not what we see but what we can feel.

It is then that I discover that I am bright and luminous—shining like a Muslim sun. I sense the Divine potential weaved into the fabric of all existence, like light concealed by grit and grime accumulated by ignorance and egoism. My beloved, with you I am divine, and luminous—partaking in your beauty, I am entirely at peace.

CHAPTER 78

The Shaykha's Endless Jihad

The Conference of the Books is soon to begin, and he sits eager to abandon himself to the debates of the long-past—to the tradition that once defined us as Muslims. Once, it defined us as Muslims—but now it has denounced us, as we have disowned it.

The Conference of the Books—the sum total of our convictions, thoughts, ideas, dreams, hopes, and aspirations; the sum total of our disagreements, disappointments, fears, and failures—it is a legacy that is profound and great, but it has become long abandoned to mythology—it stands abandoned like the rooms of a great mansion: grand but dead. It is a tradition of Muslim speech, speech by Muslims, speech about Islam, and speech inspired by Islam. It is the tradition of the search for the Divine in our land and souls—a tradition that now stands as a glorified tombstone or as a long abandoned gravestone. We, Muslims, have turned it into a sepulcher of roaming ghosts haunting our memories and delusions and foreboding terrors. It is as if a castle of irredeemable dreams and devirginated ordeals.

We the people of Islam have been raped by the twin beasts of despotism and Colonialism—animals of the same nature and identical in their objectives and cause. In shame, we turned against ourselves, exchanging blame, and indulging in the death of self-hate. Torn from our roots and soil we were thrown to a Western wind. Neither could we stand our ground and then firmly march ahead, nor could we avoid the turmoil and ravishes of the modern world. We did not bandage our injuries with the dignity of the self, and then stand on the anchor of our tradition in order to progress. Instead, our injuries festered inside ourselves until our dignity became listless and ill.

We are not defined by the Conference, our tradition, or religion—we are defined by our hurts, pains, and injuries. Our visions are blurred by the ceaseless flow of blood, and our ears are plugged by the thunderous clouds of agony encircling our world. Mercy and compassion, which we owe ourselves and others, have been buried under incrustations of salivations over power and obedience to the rules of obedience, but without the discipline of law.

Torn from our roots, orphaned in modernity, alienated from ourselves and each other—our ethical actions have become an indulgence in computational configurations or whimsical divinations. That imperceptible and ethereal thread that ties brothers and sisters together in empathy and love has been torn, ruptured, and unraveled from every side. What remains is the arrogance of supremacy claimed by the pretense of knowing the law of the Divine. Law by its very nature is power, and only arrogance can empower ignorance and its pretenses—so ignorance transforms into the key to the law. But it is this corruption of the law that rips apart the threads of love, and overrules empathy, compassion, and mercy in favor of egoism and in favor of the lust for dominance. In the clutches of egoism and ignorance, the corruptions of law are inseparable from the evils of power—they exist in unity and unwavering reciprocity—extinguishing love and mercy from the body of the religion and its plighted community.

Yes, the Conference of Books, the citadel of knowledge, stands in all its grandeur enormous and supreme—but it does often seem that there are no more Muslims for it to teach.

He sat in the Conference as the years raced by and it is but a very short while before he will stand before God. "Interrogate yourself before you are interrogated," the Prophet said, and God warned us to remember ourselves before we are forgotten.

Have we already been forgotten?

The pains only draw him closer to God—pain exposes that the truth of material reality to be indeed fragile. Pain divorces the soul from its body—the body enslaves the mind within the confines of its reality, but pain declares to the soul and mind their right to liberty.

He has spent his prime in a microcosm of the Muslim world—the communities of Muslim minorities in the West. In a past long gone after years of studying Islamic law and its many fields and disciplines, despotism made him covet the pure air of liberty. And so he traveled to the country founded on the principle of freedom, and to a people who forever have struggled with their fear and love for liberty. But in this country, the Muslim minority has for long struggled with its fear and love for authority—perhaps even power. It is a minority that is zealous in its search for identity but so often what it finds and then fights to guard and protect is reactive and false—like a promised land forever elusive; lost in the fogs of broken, enervated, effaced, and then invented memories.

His long jihad—with its torments of rejection and acceptance, envious denouncements and shared moments of love, appreciative criticism and callous ingratitude, but worst of all, treacherous betrayals—left his body ailing, mind exhausted, and spirit worn out. His memory traveled to the days of fantastic excitements, frenzied thoughts, and eruptions of enlightenments—the days of his *shaykhs*, his teachers—the days when he was but a novice and a humble disciple.

Most of his *shaykhs*, may God bless their souls, had passed on to the next life awaiting the final judgment. But he traveled to Egypt in search of the few who were rumored to be alive. His heart longingly embraced his hope as he visited the mosques of his past and the many sights of the conferences once held and the circles of knowledge (*halaqas*) that died with the death of their teachers. Most of his leads and searches took him to the graveyards in which the blessed bodies of his teachers rested.

He heard, however, that one of his teachers was now holding her *halaqa* in her apartment in Cairo. Umm Umar was a lighthouse of knowledge, but she was the only female teacher in the circles of knowledge that he frequented back then. The secular schools are full of women teachers, but sadly the religious circles of education are not similarly enriched.

Despite the fact that a single woman founded one third of Muslim jurisprudence; that the first centuries of Islam were replete with women jurists such as Umm al-Fadl bint Harith, Maymouna bint Sa'd, 'Amra bint 'Abd al-Rahman bin Zarara al-Ansariyya, Nadba mawlat Maymuna, Fatima al-Khutha'iyya, Hind bint al-Harith al-Farisiyya, Umm 'Abd Allah al-Dusiyya, 'Aisha bint Sa'd al-Zuhriyya, Umm 'Umar bint Hassan al-Thaqafi, al-Salam bint al-qadi Abu Bakr bin Shajara al-Baghdadiyya, and many others, and despite the fact that Islamic history boasts hundreds of women jurists throughout and until the Ninth Hijra/Fifteenth century AD, today the number of women jurists are abysmal. All the founders of the main Islamic schools of law, such as al-Imam Malik, Ahmad Ibn Hanbal, al-Shafi'i, and Abu Hanifa were tutored partly by women. In this very country and city, Egypt and Cairo, the granddaughter of the Prophet, al-Sayyida Nafisa filled these lands with the wisdom and knowledge teaching hundreds of people including Ahmad Ibn Hanbal and al-Shafi'i themselves and the disciples of Malik, Abu Hanifa, and al-Laythi.

Data rushed through his mind as he remembered the kind face of his teacher. She used to teach her *halaqa* at the Mosque of Khalifa al-Ma'mun in Misr al-Gadida. He wondered what made her teach from her apartment as he struggled to climb the aged and deteriorated stairs of her building,

The door to her small and crowded apartment was open, and so he bashfully entered. He held his breath in anticipation as he approached the *halaqa* in the living room at the center of which sat a figure curved over a book, speaking in a tired and slightly trembling voice. Sitting at the edge of the circle, he clearly recognized his old teacher, Shaykha Umm Umar Zaynab al-Laysi, and a wave of love overcame him, bringing back the memories of the happiest days of his life. He humbly waited until the Shaykha finished her class and then approached her.

"The days have taken you away from us! It has been so long that I thought the lands of Cowboys and Hollywood made you forget us!" the Shaykha softly spoke after her eyes lit up with the joy of recognition and familiarity.

"Shaykha, may Allah bless and honor you and allow you His peace and well-being, if I forgot you I would deserve to forget myself. May Allah honor you, I have held all my shaykhs deep in my heart and I owe them and you everything that I am. The Prophet, peace and blessings be upon him, taught that scholars are the inheritors of the Prophets, and he also taught that the ink of scholars is more valuable in the eyes of God than the blood of martyrs. Shaykha, haven't you taught us that in the Sunnah of the Prophet, peace and blessings upon him, that respect and gratitude towards one's teacher is among the most honored moral qualities? To forget or to deny the worth or value of one's teacher or to forget or deny the debt owed to one's teacher is among the greatest of sins. Even to deny that someone who taught you *is in fact* your teacher is a vile sin. I have not forgotten you—you and all my shaykhs have been with me every night I spent searching the beloved Will of God through reflection and reading."

"May Allah reward you my son—I thank God Who decreed that I see you before I die. You take me back to days that I feel were so close and yet so far. I recall I taught you Qur'an and then hadith—now time has taken its toll and I teach only once a week, and one year I dedicate to hadith and the other to the Qur'an. I praise God that the spark I saw in your eyes back then is still there. But now the spark is touched by exhaustion, perhaps touched by pain, perhaps sadness, perhaps disappointment—my son, your eyes are full of battle scars."

"My Shaykha, does it show that much?"

"Yes, but my son, it is like luminous glass that has fallen many times. It is cracked, perhaps—but the light within it still shines."

"My Shaykha, so many of my teachers passed away and as I visited their graves, I could not help but wonder if I was on their mind." A tear slipped away. "I find so much peace in your presence—I wish I could glue myself to you until the end of times."

The Shaykha smiled: "Glue yourself to me! You wish to escape your troubles—like a child that longs for the womb. Your faith ought to guard you, but instead you seem to be plagued with anxieties. Your speech about the duties of a student to his teacher only betrays your fears and anxieties."

"My Shaykha, as always—your perceptiveness humbles me, and I do apologize. I did not mean to lecture my teacher, and in your blessed presence, far be it for me to give a speech. I ask your permission to say that I respectfully disagree—I am not anxious and I have no fears. Rather, it is sadness and even agony that squeezes and suppresses my heart.

"Shaykha, you have planted seeds and I can attest that all your students learned the lessons well. You taught us that the heart and mind must be put at God's service, and that to know oneself and know His creation is to know God. God cannot be truthfully served unless God is first known. And knowledge of God brings about the realization that God is served by *al-ta'aruf wa ta'mir al-'ard* (serving human beings through genuine empathy and intercourse and preserving creation). At the same time, it is imperative to observe *'adam ifsad al-'ard* (not to corrupt earth or creation through violence or other means).

"Shaykha, we learned these lessons well and we spread on the face of this earth—peace in our hearts, seeking to spread peace. Ours was jihad for peace and in peace. But. . ."

"But what my young shaykh?"

He smiles because he feels older than the Conference itself. Nothing in him has remained young—not his mind, not his ailing body, and not his worn out heart.

"Shaykha, there are so many buts—so many buts!"

"Let us start with you my son. What makes you so anxious to the point that your words seem to come out seethed and parched with heat?"

"Shaykha, the seeds I've planted in the U.S. have not borne any fruit. In fact, the rule is that many of those that I taught have met my favor with ingratitude. I can't tell you how many of those that I taught and helped the most have responded to kindness with betrayal and arrogance, and acted as if they could respect the knowledge and dishonor the teacher."

"Subhana Allah!"* the Shaykha exclaimed, "Haven't they heard the Prophet's report: There is no piety in that who is ungrateful and betrays? But my son, you should remember the old proverb: The more a scholar cares less about the way people react and respond to him, the closer he approaches the truth."

"My teacher, perhaps it is me—perhaps the problem is the way I teach. But what I suspect and fear is that the problem far exceeds any personal idiosyncrasies. Shaykha, what I fear is that throughout our history, the love of knowledge has been the barometer measuring our relationship to God and the thermometer reflecting our moral well-being. I fear that as a people, instead of God's guidance we are guided by egotistical idolatry. Shaykha, what is the love of knowledge but a part of *husn al-khuluq* (upright morality and good manners)? It is good manners—basic human decency and the exploration and internalization of ethics—is the very fabric of our religion. Muslims in the West seem to think that they can pray, fast, give alms and so on but do not have to worry about reflecting upon, understanding, and abiding by good manners and common decency."

"Subhana Allah!" the Shaykha exclaimed, "Haven't your brethren and sisters in America heard Ali's, may God be pleased with him, saying: 'People are of two types, either your brothers in religion or your peers in morality immune from wrongdoing'?

---

*Subhana Allah is an exclamation praising the wonders of God. It is often pronounced in prayer or when one is surprised or dismayed by something.

Haven't they heard the Prophet's saying: 'The most beloved by God and the closest to God in the Hereafter are those who are adorned by the best manners'? Or, the Prophet's saying: 'The most pious of you are those who are best mannered'? Or, the Prophet's saying: 'Those of you who are the most like me are those who are the best mannered and the most forgiving'? Or, the Prophet's saying: 'The source of all good is sound manners'? The Prophet's report that best summarizes the truth and nature of Islam is the Prophet's response to a person who asked him what is Islam? The Prophet responded: ' Islam is the pursuit of good manners and virtue.'"

"Shaykha, may Allah bless you, your words comfort my heart and mind. You say what is rarely heard among Muslims in the U.S. In the U.S., Muslims have forgotten these basic foundations, and these types of traditions are rarely heard. For instance, Shaykha, the U.S. is full of the homeless, of those who are sexually and physically abused. The U.S. is full of poverty, prostitution, and drug addicts. Yet, Muslims live oblivious to all that surrounds them—they rarely help and they rarely engage their communities in such a way as to set a moral example."

"Shaykh," she said, "you had your fair share of learning—you are not a novice. If the Muslims in the U.S. do not know why did you not remind them?"

There is a stern look in her eyes; he pauses and lowers his head. What can he tell her of his struggles? To complain is not dignified and he has already complained enough as it is.

He says: "Shaykha, you are better than myself—I do remind and teach to the best of my ability. In fact, shortly before coming to Egypt I was delivering a lecture and I spoke about the tribal chief Aktham bin al-Sayfi who sent two messengers to the Prophet, peace and blessings be upon him, to ask about Islam. Among other things, the Prophet instructed the two men that God commands justice in all things and goodness in all things. Upon hearing what the two messengers had to report, Aktham addressed his tribe saying that Islam in summary enjoins the best of moral qualities and forbids what is immoral and reprehensible.

"Shaykha, the problem, however, is not reminding Muslims of this or that. The problem is the prevailing moral and intellectual climate. The problem is one of emphasis—what gets emphasized in Islamic centers, mosques, or classrooms. Often the difficulty is the difference between the principle and application—the difference between the general claim and frame of reference. For instance, many concede that good manners are imperative but they claim, for instance, that a Muslim should not assist a non-Muslim. Put differently, the problem is that people claim: How do we know what constitutes good manners and virtue? Many respond to this by saying: We know good manners and virtue are imperative but we define good manners and virtue only by reference to the religious text—to rely on intuition or reason is strictly prohibited."

Umm 'Umar took a deep breath and exhaled. She felt the burden so heavy and so she smiled. "My young Shaykh, first do not say I am better than you—do not plant the seed of arrogance in my heart. Only God knows who is better than who for only God knows the nature of the piety that fills one's heart.

"My young Shaykh, you know that what these people say is nonsense and God knows best. We know good manners by referring to the text, intuition, and the intellect—each of them complementing the other. For instance, numerous texts tell us that the Prophet, peace and blessings be upon him, while being in a state of war with Mecca, he sent five hundred dinars to be distributed among the non-Muslim poor living in Mecca. In addition, the text tells us that Ibn 'Abbas, may God be pleased with him, explained that God commanded in the Qur'an that the *sadaqa* (alms) be given to the needy—whether the needy is Muslim or not. Thus, I wonder on what basis those people claim that Muslims may not assist or help non-Muslims. Indeed, it is virtuous to help a needy human being regardless of their creed.

"As to recognizing good manners and virtue, reason, intuition, and the text all do their parts to guide a Muslim towards what he should know.

"We know by text and reason that two essential qualities of God, justice and graciousness, give rise to God's mercy, compassion, and love. Simply knowing this allows us to explore the nature of good manners and virtue.

"As the Hanafi jurist al-Dabbusi said, we know through the application of reason that ignorance, justice, and frivolity are ugly and undesirable conditions and qualities.

"It is through reason that we know that objectives rationally known to be necessary for rational people are in turn necessarily permissible and whatever obstructs rational people from attaining their rational objectives is forbidden (*yuharram bi'l 'aql ma tafut bihi aghrad al-'uqala*). Thus, we know that what is needed for self-preservation and the promotion of well-being is legally obligatory. This opens the door to knowing that actions that lead to justice, graciousness, mercy, compassion, and love is virtuous.

"It is intuition and reason that inspired Umar, may God be pleased with him, to declare: People were born free and so who can claim the right to enslave them. Yet, this intuitive position reached us through the text that transmitted this report to us. From it we learn that the original condition for human beings is freedom, and there must be a compelling reason to deny a person their freedom. We also know that all that unfairly takes away human freedom is contrary to virtue.

"We also read that through intuition, Abu Hanifa reasoned that human beings are deserving of dignity and are entitled to live a dignified life. Therefore, Abu Hanifa freed his slave girl Halima, and refused to own slaves.

"Sometimes reason and intuition can allow us to know ultimate and foundational values. Through intuition and reason, for instance, Zayd bin 'Ali, may God be pleased with him, proclaimed: By God, if I heard a voice call out from the skies that Allah has made lying permissible, I would never lie. From this we learn that certain virtues are inherent and fundamental and it is impossible for any text to deny or negate these virtues.

"Sometimes, reason is the instrument that we rely upon in order to scrutinize textual claims. As you will recall when I taught you hadith, we have what we call *'ilm al-Diraya* according to which we assess the authenticity of reported traditions by analyzing if such traditions are in accord with the Qur'an and also if they are consistent with reason. Therefore, as you will recall we rejected a report in which a conversation is said to have taken place between Abd al-Muttalib and the Prophet on the eve of the Prophet's migration to Medina."

He quickly commented: "Yes, I recall the report is not authentic because Abd al-Muttalib died three years before the Prophet's migration and so it is logically impossible to claim that the incident took place."

"Yes, yes, that is correct," Umm 'Umar responded, and then she quickly continued, "The dynamic interaction between text, intuition, and reason can yield specific knowledge of what is virtuous and well-mannered. Therefore, the text tells us, for instance, that there was a Muslim man named al-Husayn bin 'Awf and he had two daughters who were Christian. He asked the Prophet, peace and blessings be upon him, for permission to force his daughters to convert to Islam and the Prophet strictly forbade him from doing so. We learn from this text that it is not virtuous to use coercion and duress against people even in order to achieve a noble end. But the ugliness of coercion is intuitively and rationally known because it is contrary to freedom and dignity.

"By text, intuition, and reason, we know that good manners include smiling in the faces of people and speaking to them kindly. Al-Hasan, the Prophet's grandson, said: good manners include meeting people with a cheerful face and being gracious with all. He also summarized the nature of good manners very well when he said: good manners mean living with people without causing them harm. The Qur'an commands not to spy against one another or to defame each other. This is a textual command but it is also known rationally and intuitively because spying and defaming is contrary to freedom and dignity."

"May God bless you Shaykha," he commented, "what you've just said reminded me of something I read in *al-Durr al-Mukhtar* the commentary on al-Qaduri: In that book the author said: In all legal matters, when one is forced to choose one position or determination over another, one must consider the practices and customs of people and their condition. Then, one must choose the legal position that is less cumbersome and more kind and merciful towards people. And if one cannot determine which legal decision is more kind and merciful then one should return to the legal presumption of innocence, nonobligation, or the nonexistence of a legal duty. It is the duty of a jurist to seek the alleviation of hardship and to choose the legal solution that is most merciful and kind."

"Yes my son," the Shaykha said, "doesn't every Muslim know that the Prophet taught us: You (Muslims) have been sent to people to bring ease and kindness to people—you have not been sent to bring hardship and suffering upon people."

With a hint of sarcasm he smiled to himself. "Shaykha, at times I wonder what Muslims really know about their religion. There are things that you just said that if you repeated in an Islamic center in the U.S. would get you promptly ejected out of the door. But even leaving aside the Muslims of the U.S., how about the actions of some Muslims in the Muslim world? Consider the repulsive actions of some Muslims who grab hostages and then make films of themselves cutting the throats of their victims. I remember studying the well-known incident that took place during the Caliphate of al-Mansour. At that time, the Romans kidnapped Muslim hostages and then murdered them. The Caliph brought the great jurist Abu Hanifa and asked him if it would be lawful for the Muslims to retaliate by killing the Roman prisoners of war. Abu Hanifa resolutely refused, arguing that doing so would violate Qur'anic prescriptions and would be contrary to virtuous behavior. The Caliph was unhappy with the response and it got to the point that he imprisoned Abu Hanifa; but then later the Caliph forgave him. But Abu Hanifa never changed his position, and later the vast majority of jurists praised Abu Hanifa for his moral uprightness. How did we ever get from this to where we are now!"

Umm 'Umar lowered her head and then shook it. "Yes. How did we get to where we are now? That is the question."

"Shaykha," he continued as if answering himself, "What amazes me is how the tradition is broken down, reinvented, and corrupted. Why this particularly horrifying way of killing the hostages? Why the cutting of necks? The Qur'an does mention the striking of necks in the context of urging Muslims to be steadfast and vigilant in battle. It is a figure of expression anchored in its historical context. Therefore, the Qur'an speaks of fast horses, sharp swords, and striking the necks of the enemy. If the Qur'an would have been revealed today it would have said shoot your enemy in battle instead of cut their necks.

"In fact, the hostage takers do not fight with swords and knifes—they use guns. So what is the point of this gruesome demonstration of bloodletting except to spread fear and terror! The irony is that the only other place that the traditions speak of cutting the neck of anything is in the context of slaughtering animals. The Prophet, peace and blessing upon him, is reported to have urged Muslims to slaughter livestock by using a sharp knife to swiftly cut at a certain point of the throat so that the animal will not suffer and so that all the blood will flow out. But it seems to me that killing the hostages this way increases their suffering—it does not minimize it. Even when fighting our enemies, we are commanded to be merciful and we are barred from using torture or mutilation."

The Shaykha exhaled heavily again before cutting in: "I doubt that any of this is relevant for the folks who commit these acts. The Qur'an warns us not to let our grievances against a certain people lead us to become unjust. I fear that these folks allow their morality to become framed by their enemies instead of by their faith. They are obviously angry because their country has been invaded and because the invader has committed many indiscretions and they have every right to be angry. But they seem to believe that in order to fight and repel the invasion they have a right to use any method regardless of how inhumane or cruel, and that is clearly wrong."

He moved closer to his teacher and lowered his voice as if trying to hide his words: "But Shaykha Umm 'Umar, don't you think that the problem has become greater and our plight even worse—don't you think that instead of mercy, there is a culture of cruelty and inhumanity that seems to have become an affliction plaguing many in the Muslim world? Shaykha, I remember in the 1970s when we, in the Usuli circles, used to have heated arguments with the Wahhabi students. I recall that among our primary criticisms of them were that they were too extreme, harsh, and even cruel—especially with regards to women. In the 1970s it was not clear, but now it seems that their ideas, attitudes, and influence have become widespread."

Umm 'Umar shook her head from side to side and then exclaimed in pain: "Ah! Ah! Ah! This is a painful matter that leaves so many open wounds. If you recall, in the 1970s, there were many shaykhs right here present in the mosque I used to teach in that stood up to the Wahhabis and debated and refuted their claims. But then everything changed. There came the lucrative sabbaticals and invited lectures in Saudi Arabia, and the profitable book contracts with Saudi presses and the Saudi government and its many semi-official institutions. In a short while, the shaykhs who dreamt of owning a car, marrying off their kids, paying their medical expenses, or creating secure retirement funds—everyone knew what they had to do. No one had to use a whip or gun to coerce the scholars around here. There was so much self-censorship until it became official. Before we knew it, the Azhar seminary itself changed its curriculum on many issues including the Shi'is, philosophy, and *kalam*—after all, the seminary itself needed funds. Before long, the Azhar started to demand that the Egyptian government ban books that the Wahhabis found troublesome. Even at the level of students, there was always money for those who wanted to study in Medina or study with certain shaykhs friendly to the Saudis. It was all downhill from there—it is a long complicated story but a very unhappy one. Believe it or not, for the first time in modern Egyptian history, we had people imitating Saudi Arabia in banning books of tradition that are hundreds of years old. People actually had the gall and arrogance to ban books written by the great masters of the Islamic tradition. If you took the intellects of a thousand of those so-called scholars issuing the recommendations as to what ought to be added to the blacklist—a thousand of their despotic intellects would not equal the intellect or knowledge of one the great masters they banned. No, no, the circles of knowledge and even the quality of students are nothing like what they used to be in your days. Things have changed my son and for the worse."

---

*Speculative theology.

A solemn and sad silence flowed between them as they both gazed at the floor. He felt the peace of silence and the sense of tranquility defied the limits of time. However, he started to feel that the prolonged silence is too familiar and forward or even brazen toward his teacher. He mumbled: "Shaykha, things in the U.S. are not much better at least among the Islamic centers and institutions. The same ideology and attitudes have found their way to the institutions that claim to represent American Muslims."

"This is what I find puzzling," Umm 'Umar commented, "Money was the key that opened the door to the Wahhabis here and in other places. But in the U.S aren't Muslims affluent enough to be immune from this kind of influence?"

Despite himself, he found himself smiling: "Yes, but Muslims are too miserly to support their own institutions financially! But the problem is not just money but ignorance, egoism, and arrogance. Shaykha, I'll give you an example of the type of nonsense that goes on in many of the Islamic centers. I know of a shaykh who taught this married couple for many years. During these years, he helped out the couple financially, morally, and many other ways. The wife's father is a medical doctor, they are an affluent family, and this father on top of that is the chairman or president of a local mosque. The shaykh got gravely ill and his family sought to ask that student's wife for help. You know what her response was?"

"Considering the rights owed to a teacher, and the compelling entitlements of the ill in Islam and considering that her father is a doctor and a leader in the Muslim community—her response must have been favorable."

"Shaykha, no—her response was I am sorry I cannot ask my father for any favors. Even her father knew that his daughter's and son in law's teacher was gravely ill and he did nothing to help. The so-called students and the doctor father did not even bother to call the shaykh in the hospital."

The Shaykha's jaw dropped and her eyes jutted out: "May God protect us from His anger and the evil of Satan. How could this doctor be a leader in the community? How could this be the daughter of a leader in the community? How could these be students of Islam?"

"Shaykha, I will tell you an illustrative story that is even worse. A Muslim woman belonged to an Islamic center. This woman excelled as a student, she became a well-renowned journalist in one of the most prestigious newspapers in the United States and she published a book with one of the top publishers—a book that spoke about her faith and femininity, in general. For being a shining example of a Muslim women in the community, her reward was that the Islamic center she belonged to formed a tribunal, tried her, and then expelled her. Her charge was that she exceeded her proper bounds as a woman."

The Shaykha's face changed to anger and he knew her anger. "May God guard us from ignorance and arrogance, and from the worst of deeds! May God protect us from the trickery of Satan and from his likes! By what right do they judge her or expel her! By God, do these people know that the Prophet, peace and blessings upon him, suffered so much from the trickery of the hypocrites of Medina and yet simply because they declared themselves to be Muslim the Prophet never gave himself the right to harm or expel them. Hasn't the Qur'an affirmed the principle that it is not permissible to expel Muslims in 11:29; 26:114; and 6:52? How can those people give themselves the right to expel anyone from the house of God? Has God put them in charge of His house!

What does that mean 'she exceeded the bounds as a woman'! How many times has the God reminded us that men and women are equal in accountability, responsibility, and deserve before God? In 3:195; in 4:124; in 16:97; in 40:40; and then again in 49:13. Has not the Prophet, peace and blessing upon him, taught that men and women are the partners and counterparts of each other!

"Shaykh, I want to tell you something—did you know that in the first century al-Sayyida Aisha, the Prophet's wife, may God be pleased with her, taught Islamic law to 232 men and 67 women; al-Sayyida Umm Salama, may God be pleased with her, taught 78 men and 23 women; al-Sayyida Hafsa, may God be pleased with her, taught 17 men and 3 women; Asma' bint Abu Bakr, may God be pleased with her, taught 19 men and 2 women; Asma bint 'Umays taught 11 men and two women; and Ramla bint Abu Sufyan taught 18 men and two women. This is our history—so what bounds are they talking about! Yet, I am not surprised for those influenced by the Wahhabis imagine women to be no more than cattle or slaves to their husbands!"

"Oh my Shaykha, the stories that I could tell you!" he said as his head started to ache, "I am a man with a modest knowledge of Islamic jurisprudence and yet I often feel aggravated by the false assumptions and closed mindedness. Shaykha, you on the other hand, with your vast knowledge, I don't know how you would survive in this environment. Shaykha, the things I've seen have broken my heart. Because of this ignorance, Islamic law as a discipline—as a scholarly field, is not respected by non-Muslim legal scholars. Non-Muslims think that Islamic law is all about oppressive and inhumane rules that are not susceptible to any change.

"Shaykha, I was once arbitrating in a case in which a woman left her marital home because her husband mistreated her. He would yell at her, call her names, leave home for long hours, and rarely take her out. The woman left her marital home and returned to her parents. The husband was informed by the imam of their local mosque that the wife owed her husband the duty of obedience and patience. Therefore, she had no right to leave the marital home. As the arbitrator I ruled that the woman was within her right to leave the marital home and that unless the husband improves his treatment of his wife, she was under no obligation to return to her marital home. Upon reading the judgment the imam jumped up from his seat and pointing a finger at me, he declared that I one of those Americanized feminists who rules according to whim and not

Islamic law. I calmly noted that in the *Fatawa al-Hamidiyya* and in the *Tahdhib* both sources stated that mistreatment that does not rise to the level of abuse (*su' al-mu'ashara*) was sufficient grounds for a wife to refuse to co-habitat with her husband."

"Yes, many jurists have held this position, and of course, all the sources you cite, and all the jurists who wrote these sources lived long before America ever existed and at a time when Europe lived in the dark ages."

"Yes, Shaykha but that imam dared call me a liar and so I went got the relevant books and showed him. His response amazed me. Over the tip of his nose he looked at the texts for about half a second and then said, 'Yes, I know about this—but it is wrong. Much of what is found in these books is wrong.'"

Umm 'Umar struck a hand against another and exclaimed: "Subhana Allah! Truly the words of God are true: 'Say: Are those who are knowledgeable like those who are ignorant. It is only people of sound reason who will know' (39:9)."

"Shaykha," he continued with an unmistakable fervor, "There are so many things that would make the hair turn white! Shaykha, I was involved in a divorce case in which a man divorced his wife and with the help of another local imam, these guys wrote a divorce settlement dictating that the ex-wife is entitled to alimony. However, the ex-husband put in the settlement that he reserves the right to observe the behavior of the ex-wife. If he deems her behavior to be sufficiently appropriate and pious, he continues spousal payments. If, however, the ex-husband does not deem the conduct of his ex-wife to be sufficiently pious or Islamic, he has the right to complain to the imam, and if the imam agrees with the ex-husband, the imam will terminate the spousal support. When consulted about this I said that in my opinion this arrangement is in direct contradiction with the Qur'anic verse: 'For divorce women there a right to maintenance at a reasonable level—a duty upon the righteous'" (2:241). In fact, I said, if they check the books on the occasions of revelation, they will see that no discretion was granted to men on this matter at all. The continuance of spousal support cannot be made contingent on the approval of the ex-husband or an imam or anyone else. In fact, the very reason this verse was revealed was terminate any discretion men have over spousal support. Pre-Islamic Arabs used to make spousal support subject to the whim of men, and this verse terminated this unfair practice.

"Upon hearing my view the imam went ballistic—accusing me of being one of those Westernized liberal men who want to encourage women to become promiscuous. But Shaykha, as you said, all these texts were written at least a thousand years ago. How could I be Westernized when I rely on determinations that come from the heart of the Islamic juristic tradition?

"What made this whole encounter even worse is that the divorced couple had a fourteen year old boy. The imam of course said that custody belongs to the father. I, on the other hand, said that in my opinion the boy should be consulted as to where he would prefer to reside, and only if he has no preference custody should go to the father. I explained that this was the view of the jurist and traditionalist al-Tirmidhi and that a very large number of the early jurists held this view. Apparently, this imam had never heard of this view. This only increased his anger and it further confirmed that I am a Westernized corrupt jurist. He eventually stormed out saying that he refuses to be in my presence."

The Shaykha stared at him as if she was at a loss for words. Finally, she murmured: "Truly, as God says: 'The blind are not equal to those who could see, and darkness is not the same as light' (13:16; 35:19; 39:9). The light of knowledge creates facility, flexibility, and ease, and the darkness of ignorance makes people immobile and frozen with fear. The darkness conceals the growth of so much that is deformed, twisted, and unseemly."

"But Shaykha," he said with a puzzled look, "Many of these imams spend a considerable amount of time in prayer, and they often recite the Qur'an beautifully, and often on that basis they become the leaders in their Islamic centers."

Umm 'Umar cut him off: "My young shaykh this reminds of a story reported about Umar bin al-Khattab, may God be pleased with him. Umar once asked if anyone knew a particular man. A fellow came forward and said: Yes, I know him. Umar inquired: Have you dealt with him on some matter involving money or have you perhaps traveled with him? The man said no, I have not. Umar said: Perhaps you saw him in the mosque praying or moving his head back and forth while reading the Qur'an? The man said: Yes, this is what I observed. Umar then said: If so then you do not really know him.

"Piety my son is in the heart for God to judge. When piety turns into a public performance it tells us nothing. We judge people according to the way they treat others, and according to their knowledge, which ought to be used in the service of others.

"But my son, I have two questions: Who are those leaders? What is their background? And, how are these Islamic centers governed? Are they plagued by the narcissism of individual despotism or the cult of personality or by institutional structures guaranteeing that the best can rise to the top and a free flow of information and open criticism?"

He smiled for he knew that his teacher with her typical perceptiveness cut to the heart of the matter. "The leaders of the Islamic centers are for the most part medical doctors, engineers, and computer scientists. Alternatively, they are controlled by individuals who traveled abroad, typically to Saudi Arabia, for a couple of years and then returned to declare themselves experts on the whole corpus of Islamic law. And no Shaykha, there are no institutions guaranteeing anything. Certain cliques form around an individual and they cling to power with all their might and strength. Each Islamic center is like a fiefdom owned by a group of self-declared noblemen. Each center has its group of owners and rulers and they believe themselves entitled to control. They treat those who come to their centers as customers—not a congregation. Ironically, the same attitude prevails in their treatment of Islamic law—it is as if each group in control assumes the power to define Islamic law within its territory. The bases for the claimed or asserted Islamic legal rules are the general impressions and attitudes picked up haphazardly from the moral and ethical climate prevalent among Muslims in the U.S. Of course, this fiefdom-like territoriality and the prevalence of despotic governance in the various Muslim institutions in the U.S. permits the abysmal condition of Islamic law to continue for the most part unchallenged, and the quality of our thinking about our own intellectual heritage and tradition remains stagnant and unimproved."

He was quiet for a second but then recalling something, he raised his eyebrows and wrinkled his forehead as he exclaimed: "Shaykha, at times I do think that the condition of Islamic law in Muslim countries is not much better than it is in the U.S. A few days ago I read something that really made me wonder as to what kind of pit and abyss we've fallen. Two Saudi shaykhs issued a fatwa claiming that it is a sin for women to access the internet without a male *mahram*.* According to this fatwa women have 'bad intentions, are weak, and are susceptible to corruption.' Therefore, the fatwa goes on to say, the *mahram* must be someone who is aware of women's 'bad intentions and their conniving tricks.' Shaykha, this is not jurisprudence—this is an exercise in bizarre paternalism. I assume that these Wahhabi shaykhs are basing this on the idea that men should not travel without a *mahram*, but on what basis do they assume that women are full of bad intentions and are conniving? This reminds me of another Wahhabi fatwa that held that women should not wear brassieres if they intend to deceive men into thinking that they have ample chests. What insanity brought us to this level of thinking when our history is full of women jurists and scholars, and there are hundreds of Islamic law books written by women?"

The Shaykha smiled despite herself and then a small chuckle slipped out: "You know my son, it is not women who usually access the pornography sites!"

He looked surprised that the seventy-year old Shaykha knows about what goes on in the internet.

The Shaykha perceptibly noticed his surprise: "Oh my son do not be surprised—a true jurist must know his time and its ills!" She paused in reflection then continued, "As you know, my young Shaykh, the *mahram* rule was decreed for the physical safety of traveling women—it was not intended as a form of custodianship. This is why most jurists held that if physical safety could be insured—for instance, if travel routes are safe from highway robbers—women may indeed travel without a male companion or *mahram*. The issues raised by the internet are entirely different than travel—this fatwa is like saying men have the right to decide what women may or may not read or that men may control what women may or may not learn. In Islamic law, women have the right to be educated, and in our age, the internet has become a method of education. As to the internet access, who says that as a rule that a man will

---

*A man enjoying a blood relation to the woman like her husband, father, uncle, brother, or son.

be more sagacious, pious, or discerning than women? Men are the ones who indulge in the sins of the internet and they are also the ones who go to London and spend millions of pounds on prostitutes! Sometimes I think that in the age we live in it is women who should act as the chaperones of men and not the other way around!"

"As to what is behind these masochistic determinations?" the Shaykha wondered smilingly, "Forgive me for saying this, but in the modern age men have not done a very good job protecting the Muslim nation or keeping Muslims united or advanced and competitive in relation to the rest of the world. And so they blame women—they project their failures on us women! What is most striking about this internet fatwa is its despotism. We have moved from insuring the physical safety of women to controlling them. This fatwa is about controlling women. Until we learn to treat women with serious respect and dignity we will go nowhere."

His eyes sparkled as his lips parted in a wide smile: "You know Shaykha! The Wahhabis and fanatics are going to say, you are one of those wild feminists suffering from West-intoxication!"

"Yes, for sure," she retorted, "although your teacher has never been out of Egypt, only reads Arabic, and does not even own a television!"

In reaction both laughed wholeheartedly as automatically their hands rose to cover their mouths. The laughter tapered off and the silence between them seemed to grow deeper. The somber reality set in again and as if weighed down by their thoughts, they both looked down at the floor.

The Shaykha's face had grown sad—her advanced age showed, and the wrinkles covering her face seemed much more pronounced. But she remained silent. The pain in his heart was such that he wished to throw himself in her arms, weep for a long time, and then jointly pray. He wanted to weep for all the learning that now seems to have been lost, to weep for the suffering of Muslims everywhere, and to weep for all the aborted Conferences of the Books that could have taken place.

After what seemed like moments of silence that lasted forever, the Shaykha sadly smiled and still looking at the floor she said. "You know my American shaykh," she commented, "The All-Wise warned us not to erect from amongst ourselves Lords other than God (3:64). The Prophet, may the best blessings and peace be upon him, told us: 'As you are so you will be led.' Didn't the Almighty say: 'Because of what they've earned, We make the unjust rule the unjust?' (6:129)."

He nodded his head solemnly.

The Shaykha raised her head and looking straight into his eyes she spoke in a steady and firm voice: "My son, my dear American Shaykh, this is our reality—this is our situation. But we are never to despair and we must struggle in an endless jihad against ignorance and despotism until one day in all the lands of Islam and among all Muslims the just will lead the just again."

They parted that day promising to see each other again, and indeed he saw her two times again, each time he attended her classes and she honored him by having him sit next to her facing the class—a sign of respect and honor. After each class he lost himself for hours browsing through her voluminous library, and conversed with her at length. But not two weeks had passed and the Shaykha passed away in her sleep with a serene smile on her beautiful face. Shortly before he returned to the U.S. he attended her funeral and spent hours praying at her grave. Although she is dead, her endless jihad continues to this very day.

Waves and Rocks

"I hope that being an Islamist will in of itself—without necessarily having ties to violence—be grounds for keeping aliens out of the United States, much as being a communist was grounds for exclusion in an earlier era."

The Conference of the Books stands every night reviewing and retelling what we did. The Conference of Books is our record—moments of victory and moments of loss, moments of darkness and others of light, moments of morality and moments of sin, moments of conscience and others of death—moments when we acted as Muslims should and others when we betrayed ourselves. The Conference speaks to us—who else is responsible for our legacy? Who else is charged with the duty and right to exhume the full record and subject it to scrutiny? Who else must unearth the devilish ugliness when it exists and transform it to divine beauty?

As the Conference of Books marched deep into the night, the books took their toll on my mind. With the progress of hours, the chair seems to harden and the muscles of the back feel as if they are about to collapse and crumble. As the head wrestles with the entangled and unyielding words the eyes feel strained and the neck grows weary of its weighty load.

The keeper of the Conference usually lasts until the sun puts the Conference to sleep, but that night exhaustion overtook the keeper and he passed out on his papers and desk. Often he dreams of scholars and angels, but that night he dreamt of a well-known Islam-hater. But in his dream the Islam-hater stood supreme recognized by all as a sage to be obeyed in all matters of religion and belief. He had become the authoritative voice defining what ought to be considered as acceptable and moderate and what is militant and extreme.

In this dream, a group of Islamophobes stood on an enormous stage—they were many and their names were even much more. On this huge stage, stood so many among them: Tom Boy the Sharkasi, Ibn the Towel Head, Spencer the Denser, Banji the Danji, Lucifer the Miller, Emerson the Terrorson, Kelvin the Fascist Schmidt, Farroosh the Terrortoosh, and many more. The names phased in and out in my dreamy mind, but it did not matter because they were all exactly the same. They perjured themselves before their lord and call their lies insightful "witness." The master of this group and the most infamous of them was Poops the Tubes who stood in the center of the stage and before all. In this dream, Mr. Tubes, as he always wanted, had become the grand master for all Muslims, and appointed himself the Grand Shaykh. He was the honored guest of all the Gulf States, and all the kings' and princes' men and queens stood sunny and beaming. The Al Jazeera television channel had hundreds of televisions broadcasting so that the audience could comfortably see Tubes' angelic face on huge screens.

Before him stood heaps of Muslims all eager to hear from Tubes the truth about their faith, and he stood eager to oblige and please. To the right of the stage stood a group of Jews and to the left stood a group of Christians present to attest and learn from the Master's speech.

With his arms spread out on the podium, Tubes started out his speech: "Oh Muslims, hear me out for I am a knowledgeable author about your religion. I speak the truth with complete fairness and justice, and I do not conceal any ill will or hate against you or your religion. I learned your history and faith because I am a friend, and all my hope is that you will thrive and excel. I, and some of my standing friends, have been on Al Jazeera channel many, many times and this is further proof of my bona fides. So, hear me now and hear me well. To be Muslim is fine but to be an Islamist is bad—it is to be a fascist, militant, and extremist who deserve to be deported from the face of the earth."

The Muslim audience yelled in unison, "We see, we see."

Two people from the Christian and Jewish camps came forward to the stage raising their hands: "Master, sir," they said, "We have a question if you will permit. We heard of the bad Islamist but is there such a thing as a Judaimist or a Christianist?"

Tubes roared in response: "What a silly question this is! Of course, there is no such a thing as a Judaimist or Christianist! There is only an Islamist, and only Islamists must perish!"

From the thick crowds emerged a Muslim with his face to the ground and said: "Master Tubes if you please, we all know Islam but what exactly is an Islamist—we have not found this term in the Qur'an, traditions of our Prophet, or any of the books we read."

Tubes folded his arms and smiled: "You! Listen carefully to me—you do not know Islam! What qualifications do you hold to make such an audacious claim?—I hold a doctorate, I wrote books, very important people set up a whole institute for me, and other very important people bought me a whole journal to edit and lead! The idiotic universities did not hire and tenure me, but this is because they are controlled by Islamists who night and day plot and scheme against ME! I know Islam—and you don't! I know the secrets of that faith and all that Muslims conspire to hide and conceal. Your question betrays your audacity! You sir are an Islamist! The evidence against you is compelling and clear!"

In a second, the INS and FBI swooped in and took the miserable dunce to suffer the consequences of his misdeeds.

Having calmed down Tubes spoke softly: "O' people, Islamists are extremists and fanatics—they are militants and zealots. But moderate Islam is fine and good, and that is the Islam that Muslims should learn and believe in, and this is the kind of Islam that ought to exist in the world. The most authoritative voices on moderate Islam my friends are those of people like Ibn Warraq—a good man who knows what type of Islam is good. Also you should focus on extremely knowledgeable books like: *Islam Revealed*; *Islam Unveiled*; *The Trouble With Islam*; or even better the author of *What Went Wrong* with Islam—these my friends are the real voices of moderate Islam so focus and learn the truth about your beloved faith. Ah yes, moderate Islam is wonderfully set out in *The Great Divide: The Failure of Islam and the Triumph of the West*. This book proves you guys are losers—ah, I mean that moderate Muslims know that they have much to learn from the West. But because I know you Muslims well, I know that you do not read, so get the book on tapes and listen to them attentively."

A Muslim man came forward from the crowds with his eyes glued to the floor. "Master, sir, I have a question if you may. Ibn Warraq is the author of books with titles like *Why I Am Not a Muslim* and *Leaving Islam*—how could someone who clearly detests Islam be the authoritative voice of moderation about the faith? Bertrand Russell wrote a book titled *Why I Am Not a Christian*—can anyone claim that Russell was the voice of authentic Christian moderation? Can someone who writes about the evils of the Jewish faith and becomes a Jewish apostate become the voice of Jewish moderation?

"Sir, forgive me, I also cannot help but wonder. If you are objective and fair, why do you celebrate those who leave the Islamic faith, create links to their writings on your website, and promote and praise their works at every occasion and everywhere? Why do you celebrate the circle of hate—all these writers cannot read any of the original sources, and they are but a circle—they feed from each other, repeat the same stories, which they learn from each other, and they cite and endorse each other. It is like a circle of hate!"

Tubes' eyes flared with heat and fire, and his face became inflamed: "You! Stop right there! This is the type of babble Islamists say! I am a man who loves the truth and nothing else, and Ibn Warraq and all the others, may God bless them, reveal the full truth about the Islamic faith. I respect them because they testify with the truth about all the ugly and vile actions and beliefs of your religion. Ibn Warraq, for instance, had the courage to abandon this religion and he showed that many other Muslims have dared to do the same. Now, some of the faithful may not have the same strength or courage, and I respect their right to believe and practice their faith, but on one condition—they must know the truth about their religion regardless of how this knowledge may hurt or induce pain. Islam was spread by the sword! Islam is a violent religion! Muslims collected the poll tax, humiliated, and degraded non-Muslims and called them infidels. Islam divided the world into the abode of Islam and the abode of war, and this shows that aggression flows in the blood of the Muslim faith. From the beginning, this religion and its followers have been bad, ugly, and inhumane, and until Muslims realize this about their faith, they are extremists and militants by definition! In the same way these books reveal and unveil the secrets of this religion, I have unveiled your secret sir! Sir, you are an Islamist! The evidence against you is compelling and irrefutably clear!"

In a second, the INS and FBI swooped in and took the miserable dunce to suffer the consequences of his misdeeds.

At this point, two men, followers of the Christian and Jewish faith, politely approached the illustrious sage. In unison they spoke: "Mr. Tubes, if you will excuse us sir, we have questions that will help us learn and compare. In our religions, there have been many mistakes—in Christianity we cannot forget the violence of the inquisition, and the way Christianity treated native populations and the untold numbers of forced conversions whether in medieval or colonial age. Sir, for instance, Christianity remained the faith of a very small and weak minority until Constantine and his assistant Licinius forced his whole empire to adopt Christianity. Sir, the spread of Christianity under the rule of Constantine involved bloodshed, torture, and pain for all who resisted or abstained. If you read history, Constantine convened the Council of Nicaea in 325 and violently suppressed paganism and idolatry, and spread Christianity by violent punitive measures. This initiated a development that in the Middle Ages led to the forcible conversion of, among many others, pagan Germans, Slavs, and Jews. Also, we cannot forget the bloody crusades and the thousands of Muslims, Jews, and even eastern Christians who were massacred during a level of violence that bordered on insanity. In addition, historically the poll tax has been a part of the world system that prevailed back then. There are many instances when Christian states had Muslims pay the poll tax including, for instance, the tax imposed on Muslims by the Crusader states, and the Spanish authorities in Toledo and Marbella. Those who know anything about medieval world systems know that Christian states always imposed special taxes on religious minorities, whether Muslims or Jews. Furthermore, our learned sir, the dichotomous view of the world was part of Jewish law and Canon Law, for that was the prevailing logic back then. Christianity saw the world as either

Christians or heathens. For example sir, we are sure that you read the monumental work: *How the Idea of Religious Toleration Came to the West*. So you would know that medieval Canon lawyers practically had no conception of tolerance, accordingly they divided the world into true Christians on the one hand and heathens, idolaters, and heretics on the other. Similarly, Judaism saw the world as either Jew or *oved kokhavim u-mazzalot* or for short, *akkum* (idolater). Furthermore, Israel has many Palestinians under its dominion and it has imposed on them both special taxes and exceptional laws, and as an occupier, it has often mistreated and abused them."

Tubes was smiling smugly until that last sentence. Upon hearing it, fire blazed out of his eyes, steam exploded out of his ears and perspiration tried in vain to cool the heat burning his face. Tubes yelled: "All the stuff you've said are complicated matters that cannot be so easily judged. It is the Islamists who confuse things in your minds so that you will think that Islam, like the two great religions, Christianity and Judaism, have mixed records of good and bad. One cannot generalize about the two great religions, Judaism and Christianity, or discuss their legacy in this sweeping fashion. But in all cases they are nothing like Islam! This confusion induced by the Islamists can be forgiven, but that last statement cannot be uttered except by a self-hating Jew or an anti-Semite. Israel has never, never, and ever wronged the Palestinians or any Arab in any way or fashion. To say that Israel has mistreated or wronged the Palestinians is nothing but lies and deceptions and to accuse Israel of misdeeds is a sure sign of an Islamist."

The poor two men started trembling with fear, but Tubes interjected: "Fear not—I forgive you for Islamists are stealthy and conniving creatures, but never repeat such heresy about Israel again."

Nodding and bowing the two men backed up into the crowd, but at the same time, a Muslim came forward. Looking at Tubes, he said: "But sir, how about the Islamic civilization and its humanism. The Islamic civilization made great humanistic contributions and non-Muslims such as Montgomery Watt, Hamilton Gibb, Joel Kraemer, Norman Daniel, and many others wrote as much. Lenn Goodman just came out with a first-rate book titled *Islamic Humanism*. Islam inspired a great civilization that contributed a great deal to humanity. In fact, sir, in the opinion of many, the European Reformation and Renaissance would not have been possible had it not been for coming into contact with the Islamic civilization, and the works of the great Islamic thinkers such as Ibn Rushd. Haven't you read *Aristotle's Children* by Richard Rubenstein or *The Ornament of the World* by Maria Rosa Menocal? Sir, even Thomas Aquinas himself cites and debates Ibn Rushd among other Muslim thinkers in his works. In the opinion of many scholars, sir, the very idea of toleration and idea of tolerance came to the West from the Islamic civilization.

"Sir, this is a civilization that was full of *awqaf* (legal trusts) that financially supported professors, students, grand universities, and enormous libraries. There were trusts that financially supported the homeless, abused or divorced wives, widows, the

302

freeing of slaves, the feeding of prisoners of war, the construction of gardens, the support of artists and musicians, and even trusts that paid for broken musical instruments and things like bottles and dishes—these trusts paid for dishes or other wares broken by waiters and workers so that these people would not get fired from their jobs. Sir, at the time Europe treated the mentally ill by putting them in chains and abusing them, the most popular method in medieval Muslim hospitals was the inducement of laughter. Muslim physicians back then believed that if you cheer up the mentally ill and get them to laugh and listen to music, this will cure them.

"Sir, have you forgotten the *mozarabs* (the Arabized) of the West, the large number of Christians who in medieval times adopted the Arabic language without adopting Islam. We cannot overlook the complaint of the Bishop of Cordoba, Alvaro in 9th century C.E. Spain who wrote:

> Many of my coreligionists read verses and fairy tales of the Arabs, study the works of Muhammedan philosophers and theologians not in order to refute them but to learn to express themselves properly in the Arab language more correctly and more elegantly. Who among them studied the Gospels, and Prophets and Apostles? Alas! All talented Christian young men know only the language and literature of the Arabs, read and assiduously study the Arab books . . . . If somebody speaks of Christian books they contemptuously answer that they deserve no attention whatever (*quasi vilissima contemnentes*). Woe! The Christians have forgotten their own language, and there is hardly one among a thousand to be found who can write to a friend a decent greeting letter in Latin. But there is a numberless multitude who express themselves most elegantly in Arabic, and make poetry in this language with more beauty and more art than the Arabs themselves.

"Furthermore, Sir, if Muslims mistreated non-Muslim minorities to the extent that you claim, why did the Egyptians celebrate the defeat of the Byzantium forces that occupied Egypt and welcome Muslim rule? Isn't it a fact that when the inquisition in Spain heated up against Muslims and Jews, Jews escaped to Muslim lands? When the inquisition reached Venice didn't the Jews escape to the Ottoman Empire and didn't they establish solid financial institutions in Muslim lands? Sir, even Maimonides, the great Jewish thinker, and many others, were secure in Muslim lands when he wrote his theological and legal works, and in fact, he was directly influenced by theology and Islamic law. Isn't it a fact that in pre-modern times Muslims who lived in Europe were eventually forced to convert or leave while Christians lived securely in Muslim lands to this very day? Jews lived in Muslim lands until the 1967 war when most of them migrated to Israel? Aren't these facts that clearly attest to the humanism and tolerance of Islam?"

Tubes enjoyed a hearty laugh before responding: "These are all lies! Islam was never ever humanistic or tolerant. If you read the great works of Ibn Warraq you would realize that these are lies. This is a telling difference between Islamists and moderate Muslims—people who make such claims are Islamists, and militants. Muslims who know that Islam was never humanistic or tolerant are the real moderates! The problem is that you and the authors you cited are reading Muslim sources, which are full of lies. If you want the truth about Islam you must read the non-Muslim sources—the non-Muslim sources tell you the truth about what Muslims said or did. This is another huge difference—militants and Islamists believe the lies you just said and know history by reading Muslim sources. Muslim moderates, on the other hand, know history by reading non-Muslim sources."

"But, Sir, Master Tubes, Alvaro the Bishop of Cordoba is not a Muslim source, and non-Muslim sources had a much weaker sense of historicism than their Muslim counterparts in the medieval age. As proof, medieval historical sources faithfully documented the deeds and misdeeds of Muslims while Western sources at the time could not differentiate between mythology and history."

Tubes had grown impatient: "You sir, are argumentative," Tubes yelled, "and what you say is nonsense. All I have to say is that you are clearly a militant and a stealth Islamist!"

In a second, INS and FBI swooped in and took the miserable man to suffer the consequences of his misdeeds.

Two men from Jewish and Christian groups came forward looking worried: "Master Tubes, we have a question if you please, you said that if we want to learn the truth about Muslim history we should read non-Muslim sources."

"Most certainly," Tubes confidently interjected.

"But sir, we are most concerned because if we followed this methodology we will have to rewrite the whole of Jewish and Christian as well as European history. Western historians would have to learn Arabic and read Arabic sources before exploring history. We would have to write non-Muslim history by reading Muslim sources because we would not be able to rely on Western sources in writing Western history."

"No, no gentlemen," Tubes exclaimed, "the logic is not the same—Muslims are a special case. The problem is that Muslim sources are inherently unreliable and full of prejudice, bias, and pietistic fictions. This is because Muslims do not know factual incidents or the truth—they fundamentally cannot understand it."

A Muslim sprang out of the crowds protesting in a confrontational tone: "Master sir—Master sir. This methodology is odd indeed! You are basically saying that we should write the history of Muslims by relying on and trusting the texts of their enemies! What makes you believe the sources of those enemies would be any less prejudiced or biased or sincere? Even the grandfathers of this methodology, Patricia Crone and Michael Cook, have not trusted it—look at their recent works. They rely nearly exclusively on Muslim sources. How would you like it sir if we wrote the history of Israel by relying exclusively on Palestinian sources—the sources of their enemies!"

On the mention of Israel, Tubes' face once again blazed with anger and heat: "I have already said: Muslims are a special case—their sources cannot be trusted. Muslims lie and this is a fact proven and affirmed by history! You should take your so-called Palestinian sources and throw them in the trash. As Golda Meir already said, those people do not exist! Now, your sins are too enormous to ignore—first, your hostility proves you're a militant and your arguments are decisive proof that you are an Islamist. The case against you is compelling and clear!"

Tubes regained his composure and after taking a deep breath, he resumed his speech: "People listen to me! Islamists are a stealthy and tricky bunch—they try to sound progressive, educated, logical, and smart, but you have to be very careful indeed. You need experts like myself to snuff them out—to uncover their lies and deceits. They may appear reasonable and scholarly but far from it—as I have shown today, their tricks are many and they seek to do no less than the full destruction of the West and all that is moral and good. They may claim that they believe in democracy but they lie. They may say they believe in human rights but they lie. They may say they believe in tolerance and co-existence but they lie—this is who they are! The problem, people, is in their Divine law—the so-called Shari'a or Islamic law. Shari'a law is simply vile, full of the most ugly commands and inhumane laws. Islamic law commands the beating of wives and indeed Muslims beat their wives if they say a word or even smile. Islamic law commands the veiling of women as if women's hair was obscene. Shari'a has the evil doctrine of jihad that ought to scare everyone. This is why anyone who believes in Shari'a or defends it is clearly an Islamist and a militant."

At this point a Jewish woman came up from the crowds and cut in: "Mr. Tubes, excuse me please, but what you are saying is rather troubling and needs careful scrutiny. Following your logic are you saying that anyone who believes in or defends the Halakha or Jewish Law is also a fanatic militant? The Halakha contains rules that to say the least is not friendly towards women—I am sure you are aware of problems surrounding the *get*, and the rebellious wife or the *agunah*. There are also problems regarding the rules mandating obedience of wives to their husbands, and regarding the permissibility of husbands physically chastising their wives. Rachel Biale has already written about these problems. Carol Goodman Kaufman and many others wrote about the problems of spousal abuse in Jewish Orthodox communities. Furthermore, in fact, Halakha law, in the opinion of many, demands that women cover their hair."

At this point, another Jewish woman and a Christian woman came up to join their friend and they continued to question Tubes: "As to the doctrines of jihad, sir, have you read the rules of war in Deuteronomy, which demand that the defeated be entirely wiped out—whether men, women, or children? Have you read the Canon laws associated with Crusading? They pose no less a problem than that of jihad. The point is, sir, are you saying that anyone who believes in Halakhic law or Canon law is also an extremist and a militant?"

Tubes looked very irritated: "No, my friends, I am not saying that because it is very different. The issues you raise are very complicated and we cannot make sweeping generalizations about them. These are quite complicated matters that need much analysis and discussion. For one, all these problems you've raised have been discussed and debated by many scholars, and these scholars have found innovative and original solutions to these medieval issues. People, the difference is that Shari'a is nothing like Jewish or Canon laws. Shari'a law has remained frozen since the 4th or 10th century so it is archaic, medieval, and old. It has never been changed or developed—what can you expect from such a law? For a thousand years, Islamic law has been in a frozen state after the doors of *ijtihad* (independent thinking) were closed. It is idiocy to compare Muslim thought with Christian and Jewish thought—the former is archaic. Medieval, and clearly not fit for the modern world."

A Muslim walked up to the podium with a steady stride: "Master Tubes," he said, "I have a question if you would permit: Who said that the doors of ijtihad have been closed for at least a thousand years?"

Tubes immediately replied: "My son, this is an established fact—beyond dispute. It was said by many among them the immutable scholar and sage Shaykh Joseph bin Schacht, the non-Muslim, the Great!"

"But," the man continued, "greater scholars like Baber Johansen the non-Muslim the German, Wael Hallaq the Christian the Canadian, and David Powers the Jewish the American have proven that Schacht was clearly wrong. Shari'a law dynamically continued to develop until the Colonial age. Even after the Colonial age, there were the great liberal reformers such as Muhammad Abduh, Abd al-Rahman al-Kawakibi, Taha al-Rifa'i, Abd al-Razzaq al-San'ani, al-Shawkani, Rashid Rida and many others. The liberal project of these reformers was aborted by the oil-rich Wahhabis and this is the real Muslim plight. So just as in the case of Jewish law, the story is complicated and not susceptible to sweeping generalizations, which you are so fond of promoting. Schacht's scholarship was careless, ideologically motivated, and decisively flawed. For instance, Master Tubes, I personally own thousands of books on Islamic law—I wonder how many of these books you've read so that you give yourself the right to generalize sweepingly about the whole Islamic juristic tradition. If it is true that Islamic law stopped developing as you say why did Muslims write thousands upon thousands of books on law and philosophy? Do all these books redundantly repeat the same exact ideas and thoughts? If as you say Islamic law and thought stopped developing wouldn't we find just a few books written by Muslims and all Muslims studying the same exact texts again and again? Isn't it possible sir that Muslims are not aware of their rich intellectual heritage and tradition?"

Tubes' voice roared to the point that the Jazeera technicians rushed to adjust their instruments and sound monitors. "You little intellectual pipsqueak! How dare you question the great master Joseph Schacht, the towering founder of Islamic legal studies! I don't care about the other intellectual pipsqueaks that you've cited—it is not a matter open to debate that the doors of ijtihad have been closed and firmly shut since the 4th/10th century and that is the end of the matter. Muslims do not have the intellectual aptitude to engage in serious thought for very long, and as to the thousands of books you claim to own, you can dump them in the garbage can. I have read all the books written by Muslims and there is no thought or thinking there! There is just repetitive babble and prattle—most of it entirely incomprehensible. All these books demand the murdering of infidels—the killing of innocent peace-loving civilians. All these books demand the stoning of women and the chopping off of the hands of thieves on the most flimsy and tangential evidence. All these books demand that Christians and Jews be degraded and humiliated and forced to pay your jizya (poll-tax). Those who defend the Shari'a are stealth Islamists plotting to establish an Islamic state where women are forced to be veiled, where hands will be chopped off, where women will be stoned, and where non-Muslims will be forced to pay the jizya. You, sir, are one of those stealth Islamists and the evidence against you is compelling and beyond question."

In a second, INS and FBI swooped in and took the man to suffer for his beliefs.

Hardly had the soldiers left when a Muslim woman immediately sprung forward. "Sir, sir," she called out, "why do you seem to cling to anything that makes Islam look bad! For instance, sir, if you really read these texts you would know that the real meaning of jihad is to struggle and exert one's best efforts and hence the word 'ijtihad.' You would also know that the Prophet taught that the highest form of jihad is to struggle and to cleanse oneself. You would know that Muslims long debated whether pre-emptive strikes can constitute just wars, and they debated whether proper jihad can be offensive or defensive wars. You would know that the evidence required to apply the punishment for theft or adultery is very difficult to satisfy. In fact, stoning is not mentioned in the Qur'an but it is mentioned in the Old Testament or the Torah, and Muslim jurists have long debated whether stoning is part of Islamic law. If you read Muslim texts you would know that the legal logic behind the jizya is that it is money paid in return for Muslim protection and that according to the Shari'a, if Muslims are unable to protect a non-Muslim population, they cannot collect the jizya. The fact that there were misapplications or abuses committed in Islamic history does not change the nature of the textual and intellectual legacy. No doubt some Muslims have stubbornly defended archaic aspects of the legal tradition but here is where the reforms of progressive Muslims become particularly important. Progressive or liberal Muslims engage the tradition from a critical perspective and keep the Shari'a living and dynamic. Nevertheless, in a review you wrote about a recent Rand report, you claimed that the progressive and liberal movement is a failed and useless project. So following your logic, the classical Shari'a tradition is no good, and modern thinkers who try to work with the Shari'a tradition to update it are also no good. So we and our tradition are just no good!"

Tubes was growing visibly impatient: "You militant Islamists are good in twisting facts and corrupting my arguments. I told you, those who believe in Shari'a believe in something that is inhumane, and I don't care what your texts say. Towering figures like Schacht already told us what the Shari'a has to say about the different topics, and all this mumbo-jumbo about what Islamic texts say is apologetic nonsense. Look at what Muslims did! But, as I said, in order to know what Muslims did don't look at Muslim sources, look at what their enemies had to say about them. Now, the so-called progressives and liberals are actually quite reactionary because they respect and defend Shari'a instead of solidly and unequivocally condemning it. To know the real liberals and progressives of Islam, read books like *Leaving Islam* and *Why I Am Not a Muslim* —I already said all of this—what is wrong with you people! Don't you have the ability to listen and understand! The real moderates are those who condemn Shari'a law in all its forms because it is too evil to be fixed or reformed. As I already said, those who defend Shari'a in any form, or speak of reform, what they really want is to establish an Islamic state and a theocracy! There is no such thing as an Islamic democracy. Organizations like the Muslim Brotherhood and men like Ghanoushi or even worse CAIR and others in this great country who all pretend to believe in democracy have no place among us whatsoever—they are all Islamists who want to establish a theocracy. As to you missy, whoever you are, I have seen through your guise and conspiracy—you are but another stealth Islamist conspiring against this great democracy—the evidence against you is overwhelming and compelling, and your status does not warrant a bit of scrutiny!"

In a second, INS and FBI swooped in and took the daring women to suffer the consequences of her speech.

At this point, a group of Christians and Jews approached rather bashfully, and spoke hesitantly: "Mr. Tubes, we are a bit concerned about your analysis and speech. As you know, sir, in Israel there are several religious parties all competing for power within a democracy—and all these parties strongly believe in the Torah, Talmud, and Halakha. Through their participation in the process, they seek to give effect to God's law and will. Also in several European democracies, there are Christian parties that are actively engaged in the political process. Should all of these be barred from participating in the political process—are all of these a source of danger for our Western democracies?

Tubes smiled before replying: "No,` my friends it is not so—the issues are very, very complex in Israel and Europe. You cannot compare apples and oranges—things are different in the Muslim Middle East. Indeed, things are different for the Islamist organizations in the United States—these are front organizations for terrorist conspiracies. Don't you notice that these organizations sponsor the entry of so-called Shari'a scholars into the United States? These Shaykhs and specialists in Shari'a are an incredible danger to civilization! They are the source that feeds and nourishes the Islamists! The real moderates denounce and condemn the so-called Shari'a scholars of new and old. Read *Why I Am Not a Muslim, Leaving Islam,* or *The Trouble with Islam* to see how the real moderates unequivocally condemn the people Muslims call the *fuqaha*—those fanatic militants that have always promoted the Shari'a among Muslims. Can you imagine that these *fuqaha* get involved in politics, and then they dare speak of democracy! These reactionary fanatics get involved in politics and then they dare speak of democracy—this is nothing short of a joke!"

Men from the Christian and Jewish groups immediately replied: "But Mr. Tubes, priests and Rabbis are often involved in politics in Israel and Europe." A Rabbi spoke alone: "Pipes, listen carefully to me. In the Shulkhan Arukh the rules say that it is a great sin to humiliate or hate Rabbinic scholars. Indeed, one who holds the Rabbis in contempt has no portion in the World to come. Denigration of the sages leads to the mocking of Rabbinic authority and eventually the Halakha itself. I fear that what you say about moderate Muslims will be taken to encourage so-called moderate Jews to attack and denounce the sages and their Rabbis. Be careful, Tubes, with what you say! Because you will have few friends if you are attacking all religious authority."

Looking stressed Tubes said: "I have never attacked religious authority and nothing I said should apply to Judaism or Christianity. Things with Judaism and Christianity are very complex and we cannot generalize sweepingly—I am talking only about Islam and nothing but Islam! Islam is a special case—an exception—an idiosyncrasy."

Another Muslim woman marched forward—confident looking and she spoke defiantly: "So Tubes, you've made perfectly clear that you think that Islam is an exception—apparently, an exception to all of humanity. We have listened to you carefully, and we have listened with deference and even fear. Thus far, all we have learned from you is that an Islamist is a Muslim who is proud of his heritage and who thinks Islam is a living religion that can contribute to humanity. All we understand from you is that an Islamist is someone who claims to herself the rights other people enjoy. The type of Muslims you call moderates and who you like are self-hating Muslims who detest everything in their law and history. I wonder if you would demand the same from Christians or Jews."

In response, Tubes screamed: "This is nonsense! You Islamist militant! You are indeed part of the Islamic conspiracy! For your information, there are self-hating Jews—they are Jews who, for example, criticize Israel! So what are you whining about?"

"This is such a non-answer!" the women yelled back, "And you savagely attack these so-called self-hating Jews. The difference, however, is that if a Muslim dares criticize Israeli policies towards the Palestinians you accuse them of being Islamist militants and then claim that they deserve to be purged from history! Isn't it a fact that the only reason you commend books like *The Trouble with Islam*, and take such books to be an example of moderation is because they vindicate Israel of wrongdoing and are entirely oblivious to Palestinian suffering? Isn't it a fact that what you consider moderate Muslims are people who are willing to find everything wrong with themselves, but at the same time place Israel above scrutiny?"

Tubes shouted back: "Yes, of course—those who criticize Israel are criminal Islamists conspiring to destroy the Jewish state!"

She quickly retorted: "Although many of them are human rights organizations or Christian Palestinians like Edward Said and Hanan Sha'rawi! In other words, they are Arabs, but not Muslims—so what will you call them? Arabists!"

In a rage, Tubes pounded the podium with all his strength.

In a second, INS and FBI swooped in and took the defiant woman to suffer the consequences of her opinions.

Without pause an elderly Muslim man jumped in the place of the woman who disappeared behind the democratic sun. He challenged the speaker standing on the stage: "Sadly, sir, I have to concur with the sister who said you simply dislike Muslims. You enthusiastically celebrated the well-known statement: 'Fears of a Muslim influx have more substance than the worry about jihad. Western European societies are unprepared for the massive immigration of brown-skinned peoples cooking strange foods and *maintaining different standards of hygiene*. Muslim immigrants bring with them a chauvinism that augurs badly for their integration into the mainstream of European societies. Put differently, Iranian zealots threaten more within the gates of Vienna than outside them.' (emphasis added) This is clear bigotry. It reminds me of Nazi writings in the 1930s that claimed that Jews can never be integrated with German society or be loyal to Germany because their loyalty belongs to the halakha! Yet you attempt to legitimate your bigotry by exploiting the Islamist label. In your writings, you supported the decision of our government to deny Yusuf Qaradawi and Tariq Ramadan a visa to our beautiful country."

"That is right," Tubes responded, "Qaradawi is a Muslim cleric who is a known supporter of terrorists, and Ramadan is one of those so-called moderates who in reality is a stealth militant Islamist."

"But you also supported the decision to deny a visa to Yusuf Islam (Cat Stevens)—a Muslim singer."

"Well, unlike you American Islamists," Tubes retorted, "I trust my government—if they denied him a visa, they must have had their very good reasons."

The Muslim man replied, "But at the same time when our government has granted visas to other Muslim moderates, you still protested and accused our government of ignorance, naiveté, and even incompetence. So it seems that you support our government when it fits your whims and you oppose our government also whenever it fits your whims."

Tubes spoke condescendingly: "Because you're an Islamist, you don't understand the nature of our democratic governance. The whole point of a democracy is the freedom —even the duty—to oppose the government when a citizen believes the government is following the wrong policy. This is a matter of freedom of speech—a sacrosanct right in our constitutional history. But of course because you are an Islamist you can't understand concepts such as the right to speak freely."

Folding his arms, the Muslim said: "Precisely! So why is it that when Muslim citizens oppose the U.S. government's policy in the Middle East—such as the invasion of Iraq or the policy of unequivocal support for Israel, you typically accuse these Muslims of being Islamists, militants, or even traitors! You claim to respect freedom of speech yet in one of your endless flood of e-mails you celebrated Tariq Ramadan's decision not to pursue his academic post in Notre Dame, but you claimed it is not a perfect victory. You went on to support a guy who wrote: '*I hope that being an Islamist will in of itself—without necessarily having ties to violence—be grounds for keeping aliens out of the United States, much as being a communist was grounds for exclusion in an earlier era.*' Excluding people we rather not hear is hardly consistent with the principle of freedom of speech. You're 'hope' sir would make the United States in violation of a dozen international conventions guaranteeing the right to religious freedom and forbidding discrimination on the basis of religious convictions and beliefs. If your concern, sir, is to protect the U.S. from religious militants—I wonder if you would support a similar exclusion against European militant nativist groups that detest Muslims or the exclusion of members of extremist and militant religious groups from Israel! No, sir, you care not for the integrity of the U.S. constitution or even for the principle of freedom of speech. You want to use the immigration laws of the U.S. to serve your own ideological agenda and your own religious prejudice.

"Tubes, I have another question as to the exclusion proposal that you endorsed. If a Muslim criticizes Israel, they become Islamists and are excluded from the United States. But I read books like *Speaking the Truth: Zionism, Israel, and Occupation; Towards an Open Tomb: The Crisis of Israeli Society,* and *The Other Israel: Voices of Refusal and Dissent.* All of these strongly criticize Israeli policies and Israel's human rights record. The authors of these books are not Muslim and so they will not be excluded. Meanwhile, if these same books were written by Muslims they would be excluded as Islamists! "

Tubes looked very irritated and impatient—he was silent for a couple of seconds then in frustration he pounded the podium with all his strength. The Muslim man anxiously looked around him—the room was entirely quiet as all expected the forces to come swooping in but no one came. Hesitantly, the man slowly walked back and joined the crowds and waited.

Encouraged by the lack of response another Muslim man walked up to the stage. Tubes rolled his eyes and puffed then he started shouting: "When is this mockery going to stop! I am growing tired of you people and your endless rant—obviously you are pea brained, nit wits—you are blockhead dunderheads who cannot understand the obvious difference between a good moderate Muslim and an Islamist!"

The man standing before the stage protested: "But I have a very important comment to make." Speaking fast so that he would not be interrupted, he continued: "You wrote a book about Muslim conspiratorial thinking. You claimed that Muslims believe that the whole world is conspiring against them, that Muslims are irrationally suspicious and that they constantly think there are schemes and plots being weaved to rob them of independence and liberty. You even claimed that Muslims are always suspicious of Jews and so they are anti-Semitic—whether consciously so or subconsciously. But Tubes, I look at your own writings and I notice a constant and persistent theme—that theme is the Islamist conspiracy. You repeatedly speak of stealth and undercover Islamists. You consistently accuse progressive or liberal Muslims who do not meet your fancy of being deceivers, liars, and dissimulators. You even supported Joseph Bodansky who during the Bosnian Genocide wrote about the 'International Islamist'—a massive worldwide Islamist conspiracy being woven to dominate the world. Obviously, the label used here has grotesque references to the Nazi era and its terminology, and in fact, it is an eerie reminder of Nazi anti-Semitism. In fact, during what Human Rights Watch called an act of 'human extermination,' you publicly advocated that the USA should abandon the Bosnians to Milosevic and Karadzic rather than rescue them.

"You proposed that all Islamists—whatever an Islamist means—be summarily excluded from the United States regardless of whether these Islamists believe or do not believe in violence. You also endorsed the idea of every single Muslim as constituting a terrorist sleeper cell—a source of constant danger that might be triggered and explode at anytime. Sir, in short you accuse Muslims of conspiratorial thinking but you sir are the master of conspiracy thinkers. Assuming you actually believe what you teach, you are obsessed with the idea of Muslim conspiracy. I do think this is decisive evidence that you are an Islam-hater or better put 'an Islamophobe.'"

Tubes could not contain his anger: "Me, an Islamophobe! The concept doesn't exist! Your speech exhibits all the symptoms of an Islamist who excels in sophistry. I don't doubt for a second that you are a sleeping cell endangering national security!"

The man turned around and started heading toward the crowd, but before he could reach his position suddenly INS and FBI agents swooped in and took the surprised man to suffer the consequences of his protests.

A group of Muslims marched forward and confronted Tubes—a woman spoke on their behalf: "Tubes you personify our sense of alienation, suffering, and persecution. You are not an academic, researcher, nor a seeker of truth, but a propagandist and legitimator. What you promote and legitimate is fear—the type of fear that fuels social and economic discrimination. You contribute to a process of dehumanizing Muslims by categorizing, labeling, and demonizing—you stroke the ego of the persecutor so that those who wish to do harm to Muslims may do so without guilt—you provide such persecutors with a laundry list of feel good-excuses and justifications."

Tubes yelled in frustration: "Ah! People, do you see! Muslim conspiratorial thinking emerges again! They constantly whine and complain about feeling oppressed, discrimination and alienation, while there is not a shred of evidence that anyone has done them harm except that they harm themselves. Especially here in the West, they live a life of luxury that they could not have dreamt of if they stayed in the countries where they belonged. They come to the land of freedom and complain about unfair arrests and unjust prosecutions—here Muslims have shown themselves for what they are and I need not say more!"

The Muslim woman yelled back at the man at the podium: "I am a native-born American and a convert to Islam, and I know no other country. You conveniently ignore that whether you like it or not, more and more Muslim are citizens and this *is* their only country. Whatever your loyalties might be, most Muslim citizens are only loyal to this country.

"But the real problem is that you and people like you are our persecutors and our persecution! The problem, sir, is that you define instead of letting us define ourselves—you slice and dice us into black and white blocks—this block is good and this other is bad. You want a Muslim who dances to your tune—who says only what you want to hear and does only what you want to see. You want a Muslim who hides in his home, performs his rituals, and dutifully leaves the world for you and your friends to run as you please. You want a Muslim who does not define his history, his law, his politics, or even his holy book but leaves everything to you and your friends to decide what is acceptable and what is objectionable—what is false or true—what is mythical or historical. You and your friends with their meager credentials appoint yourselves as the owners of the truth—you decide who is good and who is bad, you even know what is in the hearts and conscience of Muslims. You accuse journalists, politicians, academics, and citizens of being bamboozled and fooled by this and that Muslim. In truth, you are the quintessential trickster—putting on the robe of the sagacious and objective judge of everything Muslim but you have an extremist militant agenda that despises Muslims and vindicates all the interests that you fancy that Israel needs.

"You speak of democracy! But what democracy do the occupied Palestinians enjoy! You speak of democracy but you had high words of praise for the dictatorships in Algeria and Tunisia because they slaughtered and tortured what you call Islamists. You even praise the dictatorship of Saddam Hussein because it went to war with Iran and because it exterminated what you call Islamists! You speak of terrorism, but you had the highest words of praise for Mujahideen Khalq because they blow up civilians in Iran!

"You write with vigor and sensitivity about rising anti-Semitism in Europe, the U.S., or the Middle East. But this vigor and sensitivity is entirely shut off when it comes to Muslims. Regardless of the evidence, you deny with all your will and might the rise of an anti-Muslim feeling in Europe, the U.S., or Israel! But how could you admit the existence of a problem that you work very hard to create!

"We are no longer afraid of you or believe that you are a master. It suffices that you call all those who affirmatively condemn and demonize Islam and then leave the faith the moderates—the 'real moderates'—and you encourage all Muslims to follow their lead. And before you gleefully exclaim that according to Shari'a law, apostates should be executed and this is proof of how vile Islam is, let me remind you that the Qur'an mentions no punishment for apostates. Progressive Muslims who come along and say that 'we respect Shari'a law but death for apostates is not Qur'anically supported and should be abolished because it contradicts the Qur'anic command that there be no duress in religion,' you accuse them of being liars and insincere and call them stealth militants.

"Let me remind you that unlike the Qur'an, Deuteronomy 13:7, 9–10 says: 'If your brother . . . or your closest friend . . . entices you secretly, saying, Come let us worship other gods . . . do not assent or give heed to him . . . but take his life.' Did you know that the word Marronos given to Spanish Sephardi Jews forced to convert to Christianity in reality means 'swine'? Do you know that in Halakhic law an apostate is considered dead, and relatives are commanded to go through the rituals of mourning for the dead, but when an apostate actually dies, however, no actual mourning period is observed? How shameful for you to demand that Muslims celebrate, be proud of, and give heed to their apostates! Perhaps. sir, you should go focus on learning your tradition, and leave it to us to deal, and at times, struggle with our own tradition! As you yourself repeatedly pointed out to our Jewish and Christian brothers and sisters, matters related to religion are complex and need to be worked through with empathy and care and with the exactitude of surgical precision not with the mentality of a butcher or meat processor!"

Suddenly, in this dream, all the keeper of the Conference could see is Tubes' stern face speaking calmly and very carefully: "As to your invitation that I focus on my own tradition and leave you alone, thank you very much but that will not happen. As to all your complaints about who has the right or power of definition, this is a free country. If you do not like what I have to say, you are free to speak. I carry no weapons and I have not pointed a gun at any of you. Whatever influence or power I have it is through my hard work, and if you wish, you can work as hard to gain or achieve what you please. These are my final words—all of you go and do what you will, but I will always be right there in your faces, and I will—I promise that I will—say whatever I want or please."

At this point, the dreamer felt an overwhelming sense of panic. Will the FBI and INS officials come swooping in to pick up the Muslim woman and the group standing with her?

• • •

Hearing the decisive roaring vow and feeling the intense sense of panic, the keeper of the Conference was jolted from his uncomfortable sleep. His neck hurt and he felt sorry for the books that pillowed his head through the night. The sun was threatening to rise and he realized that he had but minutes left to catch *fajr* prayers in time. He rose promptly to do his ablution, but as he washed up for prayer he could not help but think of this strange dream. What did it mean?

Despite the truth that sustained this Conference for fourteen-hundred years, in this age, the Islam-haters and Islamophobes have multiplied. They arrogantly claim to have discovered the truth that over a billion people have missed: Islam is an evil religion that managed to deceive its followers for centuries. The absurdity of this proposition was challenged by the contemporary reality. Printers of books keep spewing out trash about this majestic religion, and the logic of supply and demand and the temptation of profits make this like a tidal wave that can only be broken and stopped by a will that is as hard as rocks. But the solution is as simple as buying books—it is the simple act of purchasing books that determines the strength and height of the wave. Where is the Muslim will? Where are those rocks? Will they ever come to exist?

The Lord of the Essence: A Fatwa on Dogs

The Lord of the essence, the silence, and the void; the Lord of the truth, the light, beauty, and the word, I am a Muslim who searches for beauty—I search for beauty as I search for my religion—as I search for myself.

You have taught me by the Word, the truth of being, which is nestled in our souls: justice, equity, love, mercy, compassion, trust, dignity, well-being, and safety is the fabric of beauty, and You are its essence—the very essence to which we are drawn. Yet, the sad reality documented by this Conference is that although we long for the light, it is in darkness that we drift to an abominable void. In arrogance, we stumble over our inflated selves until our hearts are made stale by lust and whims. In the walk of life, we crumble over delusions built as if high walls of pretense invented to stockade, fortify, and protect our forgetfulness and confusions. We confuse submission with dominance—we imagine that suffering and misery could be divine, and that those who long and compete over riches and lands could ever catch a glimpse of the Divine.

We forget our own divinity, and that only through the remembrance of God can we submit to the truth of beauty. "Know yourself and you will know God," the Prophet is reported to have said. But as the pretense of longing becomes desire, and pretense of beauty becomes power, our egos weave an impenetrable blindfold, and we pretend that life could mean anything without beauty.

The Conference of the Books would soon begin, and I was eager to abandon myself to the debates of the long-past—to the tradition that once defined us as Muslims and that has denounced us, as we have disowned it. The Conference of the Books—

the sum total of our convictions, thoughts, ideas, dreams, hopes, and aspirations; the sum total of our disagreements, disappointments, fears, and failures—abandoned after being raped by Colonialism. Ashamed, we indulged in the death of self-hate and sought to forget. But we only managed to forget ourselves.

As I readied myself, I tried to clear my mind and gather my strength for the debates of our predecessors were nothing like our own—they were marked by vigor, intensity, complexity, and above all honesty, and to be the honest keeper of the Conference, I needed my full wits about me.

May God forgive whoever it was who interrupted me and put before my eyes something full of the ugliness—an ugliness that has become the earmark of our contemporary Muslim discourse. It was a printout from the web, and how much I detest this technology. Every ignorant moron has now acquired the means to become an author, publisher, and distributor, all in one step and without the benefit of peer review, editorial review, or any other serious scrutiny. In fact, how much it pains me that students in respectable universities when writing papers now cite the rubbish on the web more than they cite well-researched, documented, and published texts.

Someone whose qualifications do not exceed translating a book on Islamic law—a book that is fully embedded in its ideological, and socio-historical context, and sadly even a book that has done much damage to the reputation of Islam in the West—but the benighted dunce is not aware of any of this and thinks that this book is beginning and end of the world of Islamic law. This man was told that the keeper of the Conference owns dogs and is convinced of their purity. In response, he pompously declared this matter is well-settled in the annals of Islamic law—this man, the keeper of dogs, but lives according to his whims, and he uses whatever he knows of the law to legitimate and justify nothing but absurdities. Dogs are impure, the pretender declared, and owning a dog without a compelling necessity is a sin. No Muslim jurist has ever said otherwise, this is the unanimous consensus of the scholars, and that is absolutely clear!

My heart fills with sadness over what has become of our intellectual pluralism and its methodologies. My heart fills with sadness over the inescapable reality that practically anyone can appoint himself as the spokesman for God and put on the garb of the sage and pretend to be the true Will of God as it should be.

I try to return to the Conference and ignore the calamity of knowledge among modern Muslims—what has become the plight of knowledge itself—the despotism that has invaded its epistemology. How could the venues that lead to God become despotically narrowed down to a single venue or means? Who has the right to rob Islam of its long tradition of diversity of opinions and intellectual pluralism? Who has the right to rob Muslims of their hard won achievement of realizing that the sheer fact of God's unbounded Majesty, infinite potentialities, and perennial and immutable beauty necessarily means that the richness of the means leading to God's Will are in direct proportion to the overwhelming richness of God's Being?

Returning to the Conference proves to be difficult—the more I look at that web printout the more I am struck by that man's arrogant tone, air of self-importance, and the adeptness in adorning the attire of piety. These displays with their intricate system of symbolisms have become so prevalent in Western Muslim communities, and sadly such displays are effective and they do work very well. Symbolisms of piety by their nature are deceiving because piety is in the heart, and that which is in the heart is compelling only with God. We human beings are expected to measure the authoritativeness of other human beings and our deference to them should be in accordance to what we can observe of their knowledge, sagacity, wisdom, and the beauty of their behavior in dealing with God's creation and creatures—which includes, but is not exclusive to how they deal with human beings. Umar Ibn al-Khattab, the Prophet's Companion and the second Caliph, once taught that if one sees a man praying and supplicating in a mosque that does not mean that one knows the true character of this human being. And the Prophet, peace and blessings upon him, taught that the measure of piety on this earth are the manners to which a person adheres to in dealing with other human beings.

How do you honor and serve the Creator? By honoring and serving God's full Creation. That obvious and perhaps self-evident proposition has drifted from our memories. All of creation supplicates their Lord—we in turn serve creation by extending our hands to the world bearing compassion, mercy, and beauty. Every act of destruction or cruelty against what the Lord has made is an abomination against the One and Only. This is our faith—this Islam—submission to the Lord does not mean arrogance and hostility toward what God has molded and shaped—submission to the Lord means recognizing and fully affirming, by actions not words, the inherent dignity found in every living thing from human beings to a tree and doing so with complete humility. This is the truth of the Islamic message, which was sent as a mercy to human beings. This is the truth that allowed Muslims to a build a civilization that enjoyed endowments (*awqaf*) for the care of street dogs and for the feeding of house pets whose owners could no longer afford to feed.

Confronted by the grim reality of all those who have wronged this tradition—from the terrorists, to those who imagine that piety is an exercise in anger and hate, to the hadith hurlers, to the confessional critics who know nothing about the object of their critique, to the apologists who refuse to confront and correct our mistakes, to the self-appointed muftis and imams who believe that knowledge and hard work are an inconvenience, to the cruel and inhuman experts on God's law who do not understand that God is beautiful and that God loves beauty, to the self-haters who project upon Islam their chaotic insecurities, to the arrogant authoritarians who do not realize that despotism is a form of idolatry and care not that God portrayed the arrogant as iniquitous whose egos reach the height of mountains, and to those who think that rules define the limits of mercy, and those who forget that a smile, a kind word, a caring hand, and a loving kiss are at the heart of Islam—confronted by this reality, I could not help but to escape to memories of happier and more innocent times.

Rummaging through my memories I could not avoid remembering the circles that formed me—the circles of learning. Once the circles of learning—the *halaqa*—were my life. The humility of sitting on the ground reminded us that the dust beneath us embraced the inescapable question of life: Who sat beneath us and eventually who would sit on top of us? These bodies are projects of dust, and also dust that reached a charted Divine potentiality.

But the Shaykh—this Shaykh, Shaykh Wadi—sat like a luminous source encircling this orb with an infinite truth: After the dust remains the eternal Word.

This *halaqa* was an exercise in disputation and jurisprudential analysis—an exercise in *tarjih* (probabilities). The students came from different backgrounds but had passed a test to join the circle of learning by Shaykh Wadi. We were about fifteen men and three women—the women sat to the right of the Shaykh. Back then there were also a Wahhabi *halaqa* and a Tablighi *halaqa*—we were known as the Usulis: those who used rational methods to analyze jurisprudence. In the 1970s, the Usuli circles of learning were in the hundreds and the Wahhabi circles were in the tens. Every once in a while, we would clash with the Wahhabis, who tried to cleanse the mosque of those who they considered to be followers of *bida'* (heretical innovations) and the servants of Satan, but back then, their numbers were fairly small and they never succeeded.

The Shaykh started out by posing the problem: "We start in the name of God the most merciful and compassionate and praise the Lord for the gift of reason, speech and the word. As you know, I have here a *fatwa* issued by a Saudi shaykh and we will discuss it today." We had already picked up copies of this *fatwa* two days earlier and prepared it for the discussion but perhaps for emphasis the Shaykh started out by reading the text of the *fatwa* to us. The gist of this *fatwa* was that a man told the Saudi shaykh that he once had a dog for a number of years. The man then heard that owning dogs is unlawful for Muslims and so he put his dog out in the streets. The dog, however, would not leave, and kept hanging around the front door of the man's house. Feeling sorry for the dog, the man and his children would put water and food outside the house for the dog to drink and eat. The problem the man said was that since the dog refuses to go away and the dog lives and is fed outside the house, is this situation lawful? May he continue to give the dog food and water outside the house although that necessarily means the dog will not go away? The Saudi shaykh responded that this situation is not acceptable because technically he still owns a dog, which is forbidden. The shaykh advised the man to stop supplying the dog with water and food, and if he stops feeding the dog, the Saudi shaykh claimed, it will only be a matter of time before the dog goes away.

After reading the *fatwa*, the Shaykh paused and looked around at his disciples sitting on the ground. "Let us breakdown this *fatwa* and analyze it," the Shaykh said.

"Who believes the *fatwa* is correct?"

We all looked at each other knowing fully well that the first to speak is always the fool. With every passing second the silence grew more uncomfortable but Shaykh Wadi seemed intent on not moving on until someone willingly sacrificed himself.

A student who usually did not speak often in class mumbled, "It seems awfully cruel!"

"Yes, yes," the Shaykh said thoughtfully, "if I was this poor dog, I would not like this *fatwa* very much!"

The sanctity of the mosque prevented us from laughing out loud, but many of us chuckled.

The Shaykh straightened up and said, "Since the *fatwa* does not explain its logic let's break down its reasoning. What was in the mind of the shaykh who issued this *fatwa*?"

Again, we looked at each other—humility always obviated our participation even when the possibilities were clear.

One of the outspoken students finally blurted: "I think the author of the *fatwa* believes dogs to be impure."

The Shaykh appeared to ponder the matter: "The impurity of dogs," he repeated, "now but do we know the color of this dog and why is this question important?"

Amira, a woman who we nicknamed Smart Mouth, said with much skepticism in her voice: "We don't know the color of the dog, but it is important because it was reported in *Musnad Ahmad* that black dogs are devils in animal form."

"And I am sure you have investigated the authenticity of this report," the Shaykh said putting the women on the spot.

"Shaykh," she responded, "I did and the consensus of the scholars is that it is apocryphal."

The students smiled at each other—we all knew the dialectical hell the woman would have suffered if she had not done her homework.

"That's right," the Shaykh said, "black dogs in Arab culture and many cultures including medieval Europe as well have been the victims of much prejudice and myth. Black dogs were considered a sign of foreboding omens, and their appearance at night invoked images of monsters and demons. Among the horrific practices of old was that in some instances in history, the rulers used to hang the bodies of dead rebels and hang the bodies of black dogs with them—as a form of humiliation. In Europe, they would burn black dogs with victims of the inquisition. There was a time in history my sons and daughters when it was truly miserable to be a black dog. So if you see a black dog in the street, be kind—the poor creatures suffered from our superstition and fears for centuries. But even apart from black dogs, in medieval times there is evidence of a wide prejudice against dogs in general. Similar to the medieval European practice, pre-Islam and after Islam, as an expression of contempt or deprecation, dogs of any color were hung or buried with the corpses of dissidents or rebels. This was done to demoralize and break the spirits of would be rebels." The Shaykh paused for effect then he continued, "Now, assume that the dogs are indeed impure, why would the author of the *fatwa* suggest not only that the man put out the dog, but that he even stop feeding it so that it will go away?"

One of the students well known for his wittiness responded: "I don't know—the author of the *fatwa* seemed to have a dog-complex!"

Again, we dared not laugh but there were a few muted chuckles.

"Thank you for this brilliant analysis brother Ibrahim," the Shaykh sarcastically said, looking somewhat annoyed, "Can anyone here give us something a bit more useful?"

The one woman who at that time was the harmony of my heart and the princess of my dreams remarked in that voice that used to send tremors down my spine: "Shaykh, clearly the author of the *fatwa* could have suggested to the man that dogs are impure but left it up to him to avoid this impurity. So for instance, the dog could have been kept in a backyard or allowed to exist in front of the house even if it is a sorry condition for the dog. The author of the *fatwa* is not just concerned about the dog's impurity but that the very act of taking care of a dog represents a violation of the law. The only evidence the author could have relied upon are what we might call anti-dog hadith or hadith hostile to dogs, in general. Some of such hadith state that angels will not enter the abode of a dog keeper. Other hadith state the company of dogs voids a portion of a Muslim's good deeds. There are other hadith, Shaykh, that claim the Prophet commanded Muslims not to trade or deal in dogs, and even to slaughter all dogs, except for those used in herding, farming, or hunting. If the author relied on these traditions this might explain his *fatwa*."

"Thuraya," the Shaykh continued, "as you said there are anti-dog hadith, but are you aware of any other part of the tradition that points to a further cultural prejudice against dogs—I mean the type of prejudice that we saw associated with rebels?"

I thought of one possible area, but as I watched Thuraya think, I held my breath. After a few seconds and what seemed like an eternity to me, Thuraya replied: "Oh yes, Shaykh, these are reports that express an association between women and dogs. In some such traditions, it is claimed that the Prophet said that dogs, donkeys, women, and in some versions, non-Muslims, if they pass in front of men in prayer, they will void or nullify that prayer. These reports are mostly found in *Musnad Ahmad* but they also occur in some form in *Muslim* and *al-Tirmidhi* as well. Most are reported by Abu Hurayra but A'isha the Prophet's wife, may God be pleased with her, strongly protested these reports—Aisha even confronted Abu Hurayra saying, "Who gave you the authority to make women equal to dogs and donkeys!" Consequently, it is mentioned by *al-Nawawi* and others that most Muslim jurists ruled that these traditions are not authentic and are unreliable. Hence, most jurists held that the crossing of women or dogs in front of men does not negate their prayers."

The Shaykh seemed pleased because he smiled. My mistake was that I allowed him to catch me beaming with pleasure—as if I wanted to jump up and congratulate my Thuraya for her thorough response, and so of course the Shaykh picked on me.

As the Shaykh's smile slowly disappeared he pointed at me: 'So brother Khaled, aside from the traditions on women and dogs voiding prayers, what do you know about what our sister aptly described as the anti-dog traditions, and what can you tell us about them?"

Feeling embarrassed that the Shaykh has noticed, I tried to quickly collect my thoughts: "Shaykh, may Allah bless you," I answered, "some of these traditions were reported in *Tirmidhi*, the *Muwatta' of Malik*, *al-Nisa'i*, and *Muslim* and some variants in *Bukhari*. But I researched their authenticity and there is no consensus on the matter. All the traditions are of singular transmissions, most were declared weak or apocryphal—for instance, the tradition about the slaughtering of dogs, a number of scholars found that it was invented at a time of a rabies plague in Medina. In fact, the traditions mandating the slaughter of dogs were the most troubling for jurists. We find in the discussions by *Ibn al-'Arabi* in his *'Aridat al-Ahwadhi*, in *Nayl al-Awtar*, and in *Nawawi's Commentary on Muslim* that the vast majority of jurists rejected the traditions mandating the killing of dogs as pure fabrications because, they reasoned, such behavior would be wasteful of life. These jurists argued that there is a presumption prohibiting the destruction of nature, and mandating the honoring of all creation. Any part of creation or nature cannot be needlessly destroyed, and no life can be taken without compelling cause. For the vast majority of jurists, since the consumption of dogs was strictly prohibited in Islam, there was no reason to slaughter dogs. Such behavior, they argued, would be against the moral assumptions of Islam. Also, Shaykh, for another example, we find that the tradition about the angels not entering the home of a dog keeper has been seriously questioned and doubted in several sources such as *Tuhfat al-Ahwadhi*. Many of the commentaries on hadith have pointed out that these traditions conflict with stronger traditions; other sources argued that these traditions are inconsistent with the principles of Islam. . . ."

I suddenly stopped myself because I noticed I was becoming redundant and I feared that I might have succumbed to vanity by showing off. But my heart danced when the Shaykh smiled and a quick glance at Thuraya found her smiling as well.

The Shaykh remarked: "Have you checked the commentaries on the Qur'an as well?" I shook my head in the negative, and as if expecting my response, the Shaykh commented: "You should have! You would have found a wealth of information about these traditions in these sources."

I dutifully nodded my head. However, still keeping me in the hot seat—or more accurately, since we all sat on the floor, the hot ground—the Shaykh held his beard and raised his eyes to the ceiling before inquiring: "Despite your oversight, you read the material written on all these traditions, and I am sure you analyzed all the technical points being made in this context, but why do you suppose, aside from the killing dogs tradition, that the jurists had such a hard time with these traditions in general? I am not here speaking about conflicting reports—I am speaking about God's creation, instinct, and the will of God in nature."

I had been a student of Shaykh Wadi long enough to know what he was getting at and so I replied:"Shaykh, the instinct of these animals seem to be inclined towards becoming domesticated. They understand love, kindness, and compassion, and they respond to them. They recognize and know their owners and exhibit loyalty. If God created them this way, this fact of nature must be considered. On the other hand, if they were not created this way but we, humans, domesticated them and changed their natures so that they have become dependent on human beings, we owe them a duty of care. The rational question presented is how could God create these creatures and endow them with such qualities only to command us to hate them—why would God make them drawn to us by nature and yet command us to detest them. The well-known tradition says: 'The angels are pained by what pains human beings.' The issues that we must confront are: We must celebrate all of God's creation. Furthermore, the Qur'anic principle states: That kindness only deserves reciprocal kindness. Why would God create these creatures only to punish them by constant deprivation and suffering? Why would angels in turn be hurt or pained by those creatures while those creatures do not hurt or cause pain to human beings?"

"And Khaled," the Shaykh quizzed, "are the questions that you pose decisive and conclusive in our analysis?"

"No Shaykh," I responded, "these rational factors or points of reflection regarding creation and its purposes are but an element in our overall analysis." Hoping that the Shaykh would relieve me from questioning for the time being, I stared at the floor right ahead of me.

The Shaykh adjusted the way he was sitting and straightened his back as if he had reached a particular point in the road map in his head. "Now my sons and daughters the picture is far from complete yet. Let us focus on the issue of dog's purity—what is the specific problem here?"

Mahmoud, an unusually attractive man who was known among us for memorizing two thousand hadiths with all their variants, in his typically calm and serene fashion raised his hand: Shaykh, may God bless you and prolong your life," he said, "the issue is known as *wulugh al-kalb*—the focus here are on Prophetic reports instructing that if a dog, regardless of the color, licks a container, the container must be washed seven times, with the sprinkling of dust in one of the washings. Different versions of the same report specify that the container be washed once, three, or five times, or omit the reference to the sprinkling of dust altogether. The essential point conveyed in these reports is that dogs are impure animals, or, at least, that their saliva is a contaminant that voids a Muslim's ritual purity. As to the references, Shaykh, most of them can be found in the commentary on *Bukhari* by *Ibn Hajjar al-Asqalani*, and the *Commentary on Muslim by al-Nawawi* as well as most of the books of jurisprudence. But Shaykh, I respectfully say that the authors of the *fatwa* could have warned the questioner that the saliva of dogs negates ritual purity, and leave it to the man to perform ritual cleansing when he comes into contact with the saliva. The issue of ritual impurity would definitely not call for the extreme measures recommended by the authors of the *fatwa*."

The Shaykh commented: "Yes, but also note that the Prophet, peace and blessings upon him, is advising us about an elementary point that is easily missed today: do not eat and feed dogs from the same plates without first thoroughly cleaning them. Today, this may seem to us a rather obvious point, but not back then. Back then it was not uncommon for families to own very few plates or houseware, which they used for all kinds of purposes including feeding themselves, guests, and even cattle. Clearly, the problem is partly solved by designating certain plates for feeding dogs. Also, take note that although many people today think that washing containers or plates with dust is a central point in fact versions of these traditions do not mention washing with dust at all. But why do we have these different versions that say wash the plate seven times, five, or three times or even once?"

Volunteering, one of the students named Isma'il who we nicknamed "the officer" because he seemed to have a military style about him cried out: "Shaykh, it is an indication that the point is that if you share containers with your dogs, clean the containers thoroughly—but the memories of the transmitters of hadith conflicted as to whether a certain number of washings are necessary. The question this raises Shaykh is, assuming the saliva of dogs is a contaminant, is the washing an act of ritual, the operative cause (*'illa*) of which is worshipping; or an act of cleaning, the operative cause (*'illa*) of which is attaining good health. Shaykh, the conflicting reports on this is a strong indication that the operative cause is the attainment of good health."

"That is good Isma'il." This response indicated that the Shaykh was not entirely pleased and wanted more. And indeed, the Shaykh commented, "Before we can analyze operative causes, we still need to consider the totality of the evidence. Your inclination to consider whether we are dealing with ritual-based or reason-based legislation is basically correct. But we need to refine this point so we could be precise in our analysis. My son, you are right that generally the evidence supporting a ritual-based law needs to be strong and precise. But what is the full evidentiary picture here?"

The officer was silent. However, Mahmoud came to his aid speaking in his serene and calm voice as if the knowledge was at his fingertips: "Despite the attribution to the Prophet of a large number of traditions hostile to dogs, we know from a large number of sources such as *Ibn Hajar al-'Asqlani in his commentary on Bukhari*, from *al-Mubarakafuri in his commentary on Tirmidhi*, and *al-Nawawi in his commentary on Muslim*, there are several reports indicating that the Prophet's young cousins, and some of the companions owned puppies. Other reports indicate that the Prophet, peace and blessings upon him, prayed while a dog played in his vicinity. In addition, there is considerable historical evidence that dogs roamed freely in Medina and even entered the Prophet's mosque. In another report, the Prophet, peace and blessing be upon him, warned his companions against evicting a dog weaning her puppies from her chosen spot. In other words, the Prophet taught that if a dog is found weaning her puppies, people should not disturb her. In one report, it is transmitted that the Prophet, peace and blessings be upon him, changed the course of his marching troops in order to avoid disturbing a pair of dogs and their puppies. However, one of the most important and well-documented report states that the Prophet taught that a prostitute, and in some versions, a sinning man, secured their places in Heaven by saving the life of a dog dying of thirst in the desert. These various reports are in clear tension with reports prohibiting the ownership of dogs or reports that de-value the moral worth of dogs."

The Shaykh smiled but Mahmoud's face remained serene like a sculpture; it showed no reaction. The Shaykh again shifted his seat and straightened his back indicating he had reached another road mark in the discussion. "As you learned, when we have conflicting evidence we weigh and balance. So which way does the evidence point here?"

All those who were permitted to attend this *halaqa* had learned the fairly complex methodology for balancing out competing evidence.

Side stepping the Shaykh's question, Smart Mouth seemed to have become impatient and she surprisingly exploded: "Shaykh, may God bless you, if a person saved the life of a dog and with that their sins were absolved and forgiven, I think the authors of the *fatwa* are in serious trouble. This *fatwa* was issued in Saudi Arabia where it is very hot, and animals may easily die if they do not find water. Effectively, the author of this *fatwa* might have sentenced this poor dog to death by advising the owner to stop feeding the dog. That constitutes a wasteful destruction of life and this is what really upsets me about this *fatwa*: its cruelty! Shaykh, a dog urinated in the Prophet's mosque and he, may peace and blessings be upon him, would not let anyone hurt the animal. Shaykh, the Prophet, peace and blessings upon him, also taught that a woman, and in some narrations a man, imprisoned a cat until she died, and for that God decreed that the woman deserves the inferno of Hellfire. Yet, we have this shaykh who treats the well-being of animals so casually!"

Shaykh Wadi looked at her sympathetically and nodded his head, but then he turned to look at all of us: "The time will come for that! But as I told all of you many times before: first, we learn to analyze and then we sympathize—first we search for the law and then we find equity."

Confronted by silence, the Shaykh repeated his question: "Now, when we have conflicting evidence this means certain things—what are they?" Then the Shaykh followed his question with the type of comment that always terrified us. "Anyone, he declared, "who does not know the answer to this does not deserve to be sitting in this *halaqa*."

With so much at stake no one volunteered, but the Shaykh picked on the witty guy Ibrahim. The poor guy looked as if he suddenly found himself dumped before the headlights of a speeding vehicle. He was visibly anxious and he spoke in a nervous voice: "Shaykh, may God prolong your life, we have conflicting evidence, and so two things follow: we realize that we must balance the evidence and reach a decision based on probability, and this also tells us that different scholars will reach different conclusions—in other words, there will be a diversity of views and perspectives among the jurists."

The Shaykh smiled and we all breathed a sigh of relief including the witty guy. The Shaykh then remarked: "The two conclusions pointed out by our brother are correct. But they are the most basic conclusions that we can derive. There is more— among the most important is that the space available for the application of reason considerably expands. Put differently, the precedents are not airtight and this frees considerable space to apply rational principles of analysis. Furthermore, the available precedents permit us to narrow down and focus the issue considerably. Sister Thuraya," the Shaykh suddenly called out, "could you narrow down the issues for us?"

Thuraya, in her enthusiastic but typically calm demeanor, replied: "Shaykh, may God bless you, balancing out the relative strength of the evidence, we can safely exclude things like slaughtering of dogs, dogs as demons, dogs as voiding prayer, and most likely even the issue of the angels' repulsion against dogs as nonissues. None of these questions are supported by sufficiently reliable evidence, and in fact, they go against the ethical premises of the faith. Narrowing down the issues, the only serious questions are twofold: Is the saliva of dogs impure requiring the performance of ritual cleansing? And the second question: Are the bodies of dogs impure, similar for instance to the bodies of pigs, so that contact with the bodies of dogs requires the performance of ritual purity? I should add, Shaykh, that the issue of the repulsion of angels against dogs could be contingent on the issue of purity. Although, if you would permit me Shaykh, I want to say that this particular report is entirely inconsistent with the companions of the Prophet, peace and blessing be upon him, owning dogs. It is also inconsistent with the report of the Prophet, peace and blessings be upon him, praying in the vicinity of dogs, leave alone the entry of dogs into the Medina mosque. Moreover, Shaykh, this report is unfair towards herders, hunters, or anyone who has to rely on dogs such as people who have lost their eyesight and need a seeing-eye dog. And in my humble opinion Shaykh, theologically speaking, it is incongruous to believe that angels could be revolted by any creature that God created and endowed such creatures with the Divine breath of life—how could angels detest what God created, and God knows best."

The Shaykh beamed and fearing that I would start floating in the air, I stole but a glance at her beautiful face and gripped my notebook tightly. Again, the Shaykh woke me up when the firm uncompromising "Khaled!" being called out. I looked up at the Shaykh as if pleading with him to find a palliative for the affliction and pain that I had come to cherish and love and I never wanted to be cured of. As if reading me like an open book, the Shaykh smiled at me with such a tender and sweet smile— a smile that to this day soothes and consoles my heart. "Brother Khaled," the Shaykh repeated, "sister Thuraya has focused and narrowed down the issues for us. Do you agree with her? And what do you know about the specific issue that she untangled and distilled for us?"

I felt a sense of relief—the jurisprudence of the schools of thought had been my field of specialty and my point of strength. "Shaykh, may God prolong your life for us, I believe sister Thuraya is correct and God knows best. This seems to be the exact conclusion that *Ibn Rushd*, the grandson, *in his Bidayat al-Mujtahid* and *Ibn Taymiyya in his Fatawa* had reached. The jurists focused on the issue of purity or ritual impurity, and they particularly focused on whether there is a rational basis for the avowed impurity of dogs. As the Officer—ah, I mean brother Isma'il—alluded to earlier, are dogs impure as a matter of scientific and empirical fact, or are they impure because of a reason known only to God—like pigs for instance? As we find in the *Mudawwana* and *al-Bada'i' by al-Kasani*, a considerable number of jurists asserted that there is no rational basis for the impurity of dogs—like pigs, dogs must be considered impure simply as a matter of deference to the religious text. Consequently, these jurists allowed the ownership of dogs only for the purpose of serving human needs, such as herding, farming, hunting, protection, or because of blindness. But they prohibited the ownership of dogs for frivolous reasons, such as companionship, enjoying their appearance, out of a desire to show off. Although these jurists held that there was no rational basis for the prohibition, some of these jurists still rationalized this determination by arguing that dogs endanger the safety of neighbors and travelers. Some of the jurists that adopted the no rational basis approach did not focus on the issue of ownership, rather they focused on the cleanliness of the owner of the dogs. In short, they asserted that a Muslim may own a dog for whatever purpose as long as they perform ritual cleanliness after coming into physical contact with dogs, and as long as they make sure they do not share their foodware with dogs and also as long as they keep dogs away from the area in which they pray and worship."

The Shaykh remarked: "Okay, this is as to the no rational basis school of thought—how about the rational basis school of thought?"

I replied: "As reported by a large number of sources including *Ibn Rushd*, the grandson, *al-Dardir*, and *al-Sawi*, a considerable number of jurists particularly, but not exclusively, from the Maliki school of thought, reasoned as follows: Everything found in nature is presumed to be pure unless proven otherwise, either through experience or text. Establishing that the all the hadith we already discussed are not of sufficient reliability or authenticity so as to overcome the presumption of purity, they argued that dogs are pure animals. Accordingly, as reported in sources such as *al-Munif* the author of *al-Fatawa al-Khayriyya*, *al-Qarafi in al-Dhakhira*, *Ibn Nujaym in al-Bahr al-Ra'iq*, *Ibn Qudama in al-Mughni*, *Ibn Hazm in al-Muhalla*, several jurists maintained that dogs do not void a Muslim's prayer or ritual purity. In other words, that dogs and their saliva are pure. We are informed by *Ibn Rushd*, the grandfather, *in Muqaddimat al-Mumahhidat* that other jurists argued that the command mandating that a vessel be washed a number of times was intended as a precautionary health measure. These jurists argued that the Prophet's tradition on this issue was intended to apply only to dogs at risk of being infected by the rabies virus. Hence, if a dog is not a possible carrier of rabies, it is presumed to be pure, and therefore, there is no problem with owning or coming into contact with such a dog. As mentioned by *Ibn al-'Arabi in his 'Arida*, a number of jurists, building upon this logic, reasoned that rural dogs are pure, while urban dogs are impure because urban dogs often consume garbage or trash. Another group of jurists argued that the purity of dogs turns on their domesticity—domestic dogs are considered pure because human beings feed and clean them, while dogs that live in the wild or on the streets of a city could be carriers of disease, and therefore, they are considered impure. The point is, Shaykh, that for those who adopted the rational basis approach, as long as the cleanliness of the dog could be insured, they saw no problem regarding the dog's purity, and they also saw no problem as to the ownership of dogs."

The Shaykh nodded his head a couple of times, and then asked: "And brother Khaled which of the schools do you think is right?"

"Shaykh," I replied, "I agree with the rational basis school. Unlike the case of pigs, the Qur'an does not contain a ruling about dogs. The Prophetic traditions are conflicting on this issue, and so returning to the legal presumption of the purity of everything in creation is correct. The exception, Shaykh, is if we have reason to believe a dog is filthy or consumes filth. I do agree that especially in the case of domesticated dogs, their consumption could be controlled and their cleanliness could be insured, and thus, their ownership is allowed."

Once again, the Shaykh adjusted himself and straightened his back and after looking at us intently for a few seconds he said: "So now, how about this *fatwa* we studied— what do we do with it? Whichever school the author might have belonged to, how do we integrate the issue of equity into the analysis? We know that after doing our homework, and expending our energy in analyzing a problem, we have to reach a result but we have an affirmative duty to reach a result that is just and merciful. God told us in his Wise Book that Muhammad was sent but as a mercy to the worlds—note that the Qur'an does not say "sent as a mercy to humankind or even to the world;" it says as a mercy to the "worlds," which most certainly includes all living creatures. In the case of animals they do not participate in formulating our law, and so we have an added duty of diligence in not making them suffer the results of our heedlessness or our cruelty. The Prophet, peace and blessings be upon him, taught that Muslims are under a duty to bring facility and ease to the world and not hardship or suffering. In case of this *fatwa,* what was the right approach?"

Smart Mouth was clearly waiting impatiently until we reached this point in the discussion and so without pause she jumped in: "Shaykh, what I would note is that the author of the *fatwa* did not attempt to find a merciful solution and he did not at all consider the well-being of the dog, which is among the interests that must be taken into account when issuing this *fatwa.* It seems to me that the author could have informed the questioner about the various positions brother Khaled outlined and then let the questioner choose which precedent he wants to follow. Alternatively, the author could have informed the questioner that he, the author, believes dogs to be impure, but he should have also instructed the questioner to insure the safety of the dog so that questioner does not become a contributor to the death of a soul. Negligently contributing to the death or to harming an innocent animal that we are in a position to help or in a position to prevent the harm, in my view is a significant violation and sin, and God knows best."

The Shaykh again nodded his head and said in a matter of fact way, "I always remind you that when presented with a legal question, first you expend your best efforts investigating the evidence and the precedents. After you have done your homework, there always remains the question: What is the most merciful? What causes the least hardship? What is in the public interest? Your response to any of these questions should tip the balance in determining your choice of law. In all cases, you are under a duty to achieve the objectives of the law, which are compassion, mercy, and justice, and thus, you might have to fashion a solution in response to each particular case—each case with its own specific elements. But what you cannot do is to mechanically apply a set of rules without asking yourself: am I fulfilling the objectives of Shari'a in serving the public interest and achieving justice? Always remember, you are not applying the rules to corpses—you are applying the rules to living beings and this means the law must be as alive as those who are bound by it.

"Other than preservation of the life of the dog, there is a question of whether it is in the public interest to encourage the phenomenon of stray dogs. In days now bygone, there used to be Islamic *awqaf* (endowments) that took care of stray dogs—maybe something like the dog kennels we hear about in the West. In our discussion, we did not have a chance to talk about the rich literature of the Arabs on dogs. When you get a chance my friends read: *Ibn Al-Marzuban's* fascinating treatise, *The Book of the Superiority of Dogs Over Many of Those Who Wear Clothes*, which contrasts the loyalty and faithfulness of dogs to the treachery and fickleness of human beings." The Shaykh smiled, "It will add some humor and richness to your knowledge."

"Alright," the Shaykh prepared to conclude the *halaqa*, "We thank God for His bounties and the privilege of knowledge for God is always the most knowledgeable. We ask God to guide us from error, sin, and injustice. Those who betray God; betray themselves, and those who find God, they but find themselves. Next my sons and daughters we will discuss a *fatwa* that I issued—the *fatwa* has to do with a problem relating to a contract of adhesion. Pick a copy of the *fatwa* from my assistant, and come prepared to discuss it in two days."

Of course, the Shaykh was wrong—the kennels in the West that execute dogs are nothing like the *awqaf* that used to exist when the Islamic civilization was in its height. I did pick up a copy of the Shaykh's *fatwa* from his assistant—who was his most senior and promising student and the one we went to when we needed help in preparing our homework—and in two days the conference with Shaykh Wadi in the same mosque was held.

I eventually became the Shaykh's assistant and analyzed with him so many *fatwas,* half of them the Shaykh's own. In all the *halaqas,* and in the years I spent with the Shaykh, the single most important lesson I learned is that the essence of God's law is justice, compassion, and mercy. If it is not, this necessarily means human beings abused it, and deformed it into becoming what is at odds with the beauty that is God's nature.

The position I was chosen for, the Shaykh's assistant, did not last long because for reasons beyond him and me, I had to leave the company of my beloved Shaykh. I was forced to choose God's most beautiful creation—the beauty of freedom and liberty. And that beauty was no longer available in the lands of the Pyramids, especially after Sadat's assassination.

As to Thuraya . . .

She had to become a beautiful memory, although to this day when I go book hunting I still wait for the day that I find a book adorned by her name.

As to me, I thank God for the beauty of liberty and its challenges. In prayer, I read God's words: "And, we made some of you a trial and tribulation for others; will you be patient and forbearing?" (25:20) I supplicate to God to give me the strength so that I am always as the All-Knowing wants me to be.

CHAPTER 81

Thieves of the Dark

An abrasive darkness surrounds me in this cold and spiteful night—an unrelenting opacity shrouds me and I cannot see our divinity and not even confront my doubts. I struggle with myself and my fervor hope is to deceive myself—to believe that the tests of life have left me only stronger, but I fear that I am only fooling myself. "A believer sees through the light of God," the Prophet said, but in the prism of darkness, I see shadows borne out by the layers of clouds obstructing the soul and mind.

My beloved, my master, mentor, and tutor . . . some of my dearest disciples have forsaken me and forsook the Conference with me, but perhaps I forsook myself when I cared. This is what I tell myself—I say: "Stand by principle, tread your path, and let deserters find their own way," and the temptation is great to find fault and pronounce guilt. But again, Prophet instructed: "If you are tempted to dwell upon the faults of others, remember your own," and the Prophet, may he be blessed had said: "He who sees his own faults is truly blessed." Basked in Your supernal light, I confront the shadows of being and the mind, and I confront my faults and they pursue me without reprieve and so I throw myself upon your unbounded mercy. Yes, my Lord, a true Muslim does not dwell on the faults of others, and turns the critical gaze onto himself but what of a person who sees the faults of a nation and its failures are inseparable from his own?

The teacher of humanity, may he be blessed, taught: "He who is ungrateful towards people cannot be grateful towards God." But robbed of so much, we've lost even our sense of gratitude and our sense of loyalty. My Lord, we are a people consumed and excreted by jealousies and self-idolatry—we are a people that no longer honor the word, and we do not honor the sage bearing the word, although they are the inheritors of the prophets and the guardians of what has been revealed.

My Lord, You said: "God bears witness that there is no god but Him, as do the angels, and those who are learned standing on justice. There is no god but God, the Almighty, the All-wise" (3:18).

Time and again, You told us that you sent your messengers to teach us the Book and Wisdom—as if the two are wedded without the possibility of divorce.

And then You warned us: "God bestows wisdom upon whomever God wishes, and who is granted wisdom is given a great good but only those with probing intellects can take heed" (2:269).

Then, You taught us that what stands behind wisdom and the realization of justice is the scale, for You said: "We have sent our messengers with guidance and sent with them the Book and the Scale so that human beings will establish justice" (57:25).

What is the scale but the intellect that studies and realizes our divinely proportioned world? We are but a venerated word spoken in an ethereal moment but we have meaning only in a divinely proportioned world. It is by this divine proportion that Your beauty is manifested in our physical reality and it is by this divine proportion that justice is understood. It is by the divine proportion that Your command was received and by the divine proportion Your primordial covenant was entered before we were born.

It is by the divine proportion that we see Your light even when we ignorantly maim our own eyes behind self-imposed blindfolds.

The true sage is not just the guardian of the revelation, but also the bearer of the intellect which is systematically applied to realize justice in this divinely proportioned world. Such is the sage who inherited the role of the messengers, and whose knowledge furthers and guards the divinely revealed word.

But God, I am not delusional, and I know that it is to our shame that the role of the intellect in the existence of revelation remains sadly controversial. We honor the sage who memorizes and regurgitates the revelation, but not the sage who has the wisdom to realize that revelation must be placed fully within the scale of intellect—and without the scale of intellect neither revelation nor justice can be realized.

Today, scale and wisdom elude us and so we produce little knowledge or thought, and our creativity and inventiveness is for naught. Shamefully, we add little to the divine proportion sustaining the universe and contribute little of great value to our world.

My beloved, the Truth behind all beauty, and the Bearer of the Balance that sustains this divinely proportioned world, I do place Your revelation on the scale, and I am tormented by the darkness that engulfs our actions and thought.

"O' my people, give full weight and measure with justice, and do not withhold from others what is due to them; and do not go as spoilers corrupting the earth" (11:85).

Such is our Lord's charge, but what are our deeds?

"Invite to the way of your Lord with wisdom and kind advice and debate with others in the kindest of manners for your Lord knows best who has strayed from God's way and God knows best those are rightly guided" (16:125).

Such is our Lord's command, so what has been our speech?

"Believers be the establishers of justice as witnesses for God even be it against yourselves or your parents or relatives whether one be rich or poor God is more worthy than either [of your loyalty and fear]. Do not follow your whims lest you stray from justice and if you pervert justice or neglect it God is aware of what you do" (4:135).

Such is our oath, but what has been our testimony?

"Good and evil are not equals. Repel what is evil with what is good, and you will find that your enemy will become as if a close friend. But this will not be learned except by those who have been most patient and those who have been given a great deal (of wisdom)" (41:35).

Such is the speech of our Lord, do we have the wisdom to take heed?

"Tell My people to say the most beautiful things for Satan sows dissension among people; indeed Satan is a conniving enemy to human beings" (17:53).

Our Lord is a god of beauty, have we been faithful to manifesting the beauty of the Lord?

". . . God loves *al-muhsinin* (the benevolent, beautiful, and good)" (3:148).

If this is what God loves, are we worthy?

God, I know that your compassion, mercy, and love envelopes us even if we are not worthy. But how I fear that so much has been lost to the point that we have lost ourselves. I struggle to rid myself of dreadful fears, but the severity of our condition assaults me without reprieve.

God, I confess to you that we Muslims have been robbed of our brotherhood, empathy, compassion, and mercy; we've been robbed of freedom, thought, creativity, inventiveness, and even speech; we've been robbed of intelligence, reasonableness, and probity; we've been robbed of our security, land, wealth, and peace; we've been robbed of our serenity, hopefulness, and dreams; we've been robbed of our honor, bravery, and dignity; we've been robbed of justice, equity, and our sense of beauty . . . but the question is my Lord: who is the thief?

My Beloved, recalling the bliss of submission, as a Muslim, I submitted to the beauty of the light, and to the remembrance of the divine proportion that manifests Your beauty. But I admit to You, Sustainer of the worlds, we Muslims have been robbed of so much but nothing as valuable as our own memory and our history. So who is the thief?

Nothing remains of our civilization but the bodies . . . the intellects, the word, the beauty is gone. So what happened to us and what happened to what once inspired us to give the world a civilization that was full of beauty and such sparkling majesty?

I search our history for answers, and this history is like a blade, slicing then healing then slicing me. Who was the thief? Boredom and stagnation? Luxury and vanity? The Crusades and their mad religious zeal? Colonialism, imperialism, and Israel? The West with its unrelenting interventionism and endless conspiracies? Or, our passive acceptance of despotism and refusal to rebel and demand liberty? Is it projecting blame and refusal to accept self-responsibility? Is it that we relied on revelation to solve our problems without taking the role of the intellect seriously? Or have we surrendered our religion to those who abused it, and we passively sat refusing to wrestle it out of their hands and thus honor God's covenant and our agency?

My Love, the possibilities are numerous and each might have contributed to our plight in the age of modernity. In such a dark, cold, and lonely night, I remind myself that patience is a virtue and the true weapon of piety. So I leave all my books open and sit, reading, and researching with unabated zeal. The darkness tonight is too thick and the gash in my heart too deep. But even in darkness; even in this darkness, I see Your light. Although tonight this abrasive darkness hid my heart from my mind, Your empyreal light is firmly embedded in my soul. Soon Your luminous torch will come, and the heart will be reconciled with the mind, just like revelation placed in the scale of the intellect, and together they will search and find, and they will confront the thief who robbed us of so much, especially our memory.

CHAPTER 82

Quietus

"We do know that you are distressed by what they say. So supplicate in praise of your Lord and in adoration be of those who prostrate. And serve your Lord until certitude comes to you (15:97–99).

Now and then, it rears its head, the record in its hand, it summons the end. The hour is approaching midnight, and I hear the voice of the past crawling back in a procession of phantoms intoned in a lament. Every injustice committed has broken its veil, and I sense the footsteps of ghosts around me; each a specter of a fallen moment—each a wraith of an abomination and a sin. Surrounding me are disembodied indignities—the suffering of those exploited by others, and those who lost themselves. From every corner of my study rises a chant of mourning and from every side of my heart erupts a grieving hymn. This is the end, I tell myself—no, it is near the end. But when the time does come and the record is read, there will be no defense for the dead.

I ponder the birds chirping well into the night, do they celebrate the breath of life or do they grieve my impending demise? Now you lurk in the Conference, and I do notice your smirking grimace. But after all, every single participant in this Conference, if they have not already made your fatal acquaintance, soon they will come to know the dubious pleasure.

You burrow yourself, ensconced in the expanse between our delusions and fears—between our perceived realities and imagined dreams. You shroud yourself behind an impregnable veil, concealed from our senses and cloaked behind our apprehensions and fears.

My friend, why do you conceal yourself? Our lives are but variations on a singular theme—an interminable requiem full of deceptively resilient melodies. We are like sculpted ice melting by the moment and falling to the ground; the more we try to preserve ourselves, the more we die.

Quietus, why do you hide yourself and then strike by stealth? Why do you not stand proud and dictate your indisputable will?

Perhaps we are the ones who conceal you—we obscure and dissemble you by our arrogance, our deceptively constructed memories, and narcissistically reinvented selves.

You are the herald of the return to dust and light, the dissolution of these magnificent constructs, and the reversion to the truth of being. You are the absolute truth awaiting our souls, the reaper of pretenses, deceptions, and lies. You are the certain return; you are the reversion to the Straight Path leading to the only absolute, immutable, and perfect Beauty of all the worlds.

The folded hands of the beloved are so luminous and tender and their fragrance is so sweet. But our hands have sewn a world of perverse contradictions and contrarieties and infected it with so much suffering and savagery.

Death, the truth is we fear you, and marred in our apprehensions we abjure certitude and dread verity—we strive to celebrate doubt but drown in wearisome and nihilistic ambiguities.

"And serve your Lord until certitude comes to you." Quietus, the certitude mentioned by our Lord is you.

Enfolded in your firm grip, I feel the sorrow of regret. Tucked away in the folds of this ailing heart are the memories of ways that I sullied it. In your hands is a record where every single deed and misdeed is dutifully preserved, and at the moment of surrender inescapably we are forced to remember what we spent a whole lifetime trying to forget.

Her sobs remind me of the thousand ways I have died and this Conference resuscitated me again. But when this sculpted edifice unravels, it will be the end.

"I breathe, but I feel I am dead."

I look into the darkness outside—I can still hear the odd birds chirping. Maybe they hold their own Conference—it is due time the Conference of the Birds met the Conference of the Books—both supplicate the same Master and sing the praises of the Beloved who with merciful unfolded hands waits. Tonight, the thought of death has opened the floodgates to memories, and I am drowning in torrents of things that once in the distant past I imagined were pleasures and pains.

What brought this grieving woman to my door in the depth of the night to intrude upon my phantoms and ghosts?

"I came here because I didn't know what to do! I didn't know where to go and to whom I should turn! I was in your . . . class but I don't think you noticed me. I always sat in the back," upon uttering the last words her tears poured down as if that was her tragedy. Eager to console her, I was tempted to offer her clemency for sitting in the back, but blissfully, I realized that anything I'd say in that regard would be pure idiocy.

"What do I do now? How do I live with my shame—with this pain? How do I show my parents my face? I swear I should kill myself."

I did notice her sitting in the back of my class for she was a strikingly beautiful woman—may God forgive our omissions and sins. She was a quiet, bashful woman with an angelic face and a soft demeanor. The freshness of her skin and her unvarnished and demure eyes made me feel very old—may God forgive our frailties and weaknesses.

I offered her something to drink, but the only thing I had was diet coke. She demurred but restlessly I took a can from my mini-cooler, opened it, and placed it before her. I asked if her parents would worry about her, and with her eyes fixed on her lap, she whispered that they reside in another state and her mother would probably call her cell phone any minute now.

Hardly two slow minutes had passed before her cell phone rang. Hoping that her mother would dry her tears so that I could once again indulge my morbid thoughts, I left my desk and busied myself with studying one of my over-packed shelves. The conversation, however, was short, and I returned to find her drowning in more tears than before, stretching her neck to the ceiling and muttering as if speaking to God.

Tensely I sat down behind the desk, and tried to find the courage to once again intrude upon her sorrow to ask what happened, but mindlessly my eyes rolled over the rows of books surrounding us. Suddenly, in a jerk she stood up and dryly said: "I am sorry I bothered you—I am going to be fine; seriously I'll be fine. I've taken up your valuable time."

In a panic, I stood up and begged her to stay. "May God forgive me if I appeared less than eager to be with you or if I appeared self-absorbed or distracted. Please grant me the honor of serving you, for the Prophet taught that God is in the service of those who serve others. If you came here at this time then you felt you needed me; don't let me live with the torment of realizing my own feebleness."

She looked at me with those eyes that looked like sparkling crystals drowned in water, and without comment headed back to her chair. But for the first time, I noticed that the left blade of her blouse had a small tear, and as I suspiciously examined the rest of her clothing, I noticed that the top of her blouse was missing buttons as well.

Unless she decided to speak there was nothing that I could say. She did not leave me waiting too long. "A disaster took place tonight. He took from me everything, and now I am lost. But it is my fault—I feel it is my fault! I am a good Muslim, I pray although my father does not. My mother prays, and taught me to fear God. I fast Ramadan and read the Qur'an—. . . I love God—I do! I don't know . . . I really don't know. My life ended tonight—he took my soul, and then abandoned me. . . . I am alone—completely and entirely alone."

I feared that I knew what was coming, and as if overcome by a dazed anility my heart drowned in the ethereal longings of Nusrat Ali Khan's divine laments. Nusrat expressed the indefatigable truth that we are alone only if we choose to be alone. With human beings we are with a mere possibility, an unfulfilled potential—we are ever in the presence of a risk and at times a fearful threat. With God, we are in the hands of the Compassionate, the Lover and Beloved, and Beauty epitomized—the Savior who saves us from ourselves but only if we invite Him in and open up our souls.

"I am angry, I feel betrayed . . . no, I feel like a hypocrite. I really connected with this guy . . . at one time, I even felt like we were soul mates. We would talk for hours . . . can you believe—we even talked about Islam, and what goes on at campus. We talked about that disgusting professor . . . who seems to have a chip on his shoulder against Islam." Her sobbing increased as she continued, "He told me that he's never met someone like me that he thinks about me all the time, and that he can't imagine his life without me. He said that when he looks at me, he sees the best example of how a Muslim woman should be . . . he said so, so much—he talked and I started feeling like I was floating on clouds."

As my fears continued to accumulate, my head remained lowered as I avoided her tearful eyes. It takes considerable cruelty to look suffering straight in the eyes.

Love, love, love—an intoxication of unequalled ecstasy. It is truly ironic that love is sought by all but it practically exists for none, and hate is coveted but by a few, yet it is ever present in our world.

As soon as consciousness sets in, we feel a tortuous restlessness, a state of unsettlement, an odd boredom of the soul. As if refugees who lost all memory of their homeland or travelers on a lifeless deserted road, the faint appearance of love is as if the promise of a safe and secure abode. But more often than not it is a portentous hallucination or a perilous delusion like a house of phantoms and ghosts. Safety and security can only be found in the same place from which we originally came and in the very abode in which we were born.

"You must know the rest . . . but I do not know what I have ever done in my life to deserve this? I don't know how could he have turned out to be such a foul and disgusting person? I don't know . . . maybe God is testing me, but this is too much; I cannot endure this! How could I have known it would turn out like this? The filthy, disgusting, pig! I swear to God, my life has ended—what do I tell my parents? I feel as good as dead!"

My eyes cast down, I pondered the strange web my interlocked fingers formed. I recall what the Lord had said: "When a calamity befalls you that is not half as bad as that that you have inflicted upon others, you say: 'Where did this come from?' Say: 'It is from yourselves.' And God has power over all things" (3:165). I steal a glimpse at her and feel her inconsolable sorrow. With her face turned up toward the ceiling, despite the stream of tears glistening on her cheeks, she looked as if wearing a death mask. I mumble the words of the Lord under my breath: "Humans do not weary of asking for good things but if ill touches them, they give up all hope and are lost in despair" (41:49).

I started to suspect that she forgot that I was in the room or that this was a most irregular night visit. Staring at the ceiling, she said in a voice that had turned dead cold: "You must know I despise myself—I am a hypocrite—I've not only sinned but I am forever lost. . . ."

Hypocrite? Who has given us the power to condemn ourselves? Who has empowered us to sentence ourselves without the possibility of clemency or appeal? I feared intruding upon her intimacy, but I thought of the words of the Lord: ". . . and who despairs of the mercy of his Lord but will surely go astray" (15:56). But then I looked directly at her and said in an audible voice: "My servants who have transgressed against their souls, despair not of God's mercy for God forgives all sins, for God is most forgiving most merciful" (39:53).

She looked at me with withering eyes: "He talked me into going on a car ride. We parked somewhere where we could see the moon, the stars, and the river. He spoke about his many dreams and his strong sense of loyalty and dedication to me. We weakened . . . I weakened and started to kiss. As his hands dropped down to my breasts, I pretended not to notice. When he uncovered them and helped himself, I got scared and pushed him away. Before I knew it, he was on top of me. I tried to fight and resist, but he kept repeating, 'just let it happen; it will be over soon.' I don't remember if he hit me or not—all I know is that I was overpowered and he entered me."

A stunned silence overcame me. There are levels of ugliness that cannot be met with words. To put oneself at risk is stupidity, and to disobey God is a sin. But compulsion is the very undoing of all religion and beauty. When God said, "There is no compulsion in religion," this means that in a world of compulsion, of forcible domination, and of public and private despotism is the very undoing of religion, and of any possibility of purity.

The longing and passion for love that relentlessly beckons us is a call for a higher existence—a union to be achieved with the essence of purity. From the moment of birth, this restlessness of being is a longing for the dissolution of being into a perfect unity—from purity we come and to purity we return so that we are fully absorbed by Divinity. But how the fear of death—the fear of loneliness, of abandonment, and of vulnerability distracts, deludes, and misleads us. Sullied by anxieties and fears, we confuse domination for love, control for security, and the absolutism of lust for intimacy. On the Final Day, only those who return to God with a pure heart will return home to their original Divinity. Those whose hearts are not pure will taste the torment of banishment and alienation from God's unadulterated beauty. Coercion is the ultimate sin; it corrupts the essence of will, negates the possibility of purity, and undermines the very logic of responsibility.

"My sister," I finally said, "are you still wearing the clothing in which this incident took place?" She nodded. I stood up and said, "If you want my opinion or fatwa, if you will, if you wish to seek the certitude before the final certitude, then I will call upon my wife, and we will accompany you to the hospital for a necessary examination and from there we will call the police. As to everything else you said, we will talk about all of that later. I suspect much later."

CHAPTER 83

Notes of the Night

The night steadily progresses, embracing the Conference in its heart. The clock persistently circles and waves its arms, warning against the delusions of the fog. The body aches, I flip another page, and I know that I am approaching the point where this body ends, and my migration will start. In my travel I will leave behind all the silly and petty things that once distracted my mind. I will carry my words and my books, and I will present them to my God. I have been ugly and committed many, many sins, but I always believed in the beauty of God. I have transgressed, and been unjust to myself, but at the darkest moments I always longed for the light. If I lusted after this world, I always lusted in shame, and I never indulged my whims without the disruptions of a reproaching heart.

I will discard this crumbling body without regret or even a courteous farewell. There will be no eulogies for me for I am transcending my form, and beginning again. Stand at my grave, and mock the deceptions of this world, for this world only thrives on fear. It has taken a troublesome body, it has taken the shell it wants, but I took everything that I hold dear. I live in beauty and the word, and in Conferences that never end, untouched by the vermin this world needs to feed. This body is like an ill-fitted garment, full of dirt and holes, it neither protects from the cold or guards against the heat—perhaps the grub of the earth will find it more fitting to their needs.

The night progresses and I turn a page. The words caress my eyes, and I rub my head as my back aches. While my body complains, my heart is titillated by the promises of insight as my mind leaps at the brink of ecstasy. If my body could understand that God is not some bounded physicality, God is the perfection of knowledge, the unadulterated beauty, and a fully realized potentiality. If I long to share the heart of the One I love, how could my body blame me? I reach for knowledge, I reach for beauty, and I long to fulfill my dormant potentialities—what is of the essence of God is also of essence to share God's company. Don't we search with whom we love the bonds of our commonality? But since my Beloved is infinitely rich, and I am wretched in my poverty, I implore my Beloved to bestow upon me some of His splendid bounty. When I rest my body, I do not do so out of love, but because my Beloved loves equity. As soon as this body is able to rise, I race the clock begging for knowledge, wisdom, and beauty.

Of all God's bounties, there is one that I do not want, and that is power, for this frail and brittle mind cannot bear the responsibility. I pray to share what God loves to share, not to share God's dominion and immutability. Of all the felonious transgressions, nothing could be as perverse as coveting the throne of divinity. The felodese understands beauty and knowledge only as thrones of power, and basks in the spoils of authority. In time, it is outright suicide for, except with God, the nature of power eschews knowledge and beauty. The felodese is putrefied in a morbid and feculent self-fog infected with the depravity of arrogance and the defilements of vanity. To turn to God and plead for beauty and knowledge is to acknowledge the promise of the potential implanted in the human heart and mind. To turn to God is to recognize that the mystifications of beauty are superior to the power of certainty. But to believe that you have attained either or both is to claim the power to model all meaning after a shameful idiosyncrasy. Power and arrogance are lecherous bedfellows, indulgences of lust, in a bed of depravity.

The night progresses and I turn a page as the muscles of my back ache like mischievous children competing for attention. But I long ago surrendered any hope of teaching them discipline or any measure of docility. The bad parent that I am, I ignore my back, and continue to read the book at hand. I hear the voice of 'Imad al-Din al-Isfahani (d. 598/1201) say:

> I have yet to complete a book and to re-open it the next day without finding I might have included this, or deleted that, or considered a different thought, or I might have polished my words, or modified some others or transposed yet others. In short, a human being's work, his thinking, his revisions and changes are never perfect or complete. Such is the unwavering fact about the nature of humankind.

Bless the souls of those who have joined the Conference, and doubted the equity of those who have the answers. Yes, such are the affairs of human beings—their thinking is never complete. Praise be to God Who decreed that we perfect the questions, and entrust the answers to the One Who is complete. But we are plagued in this age by those who only want to learn what they think they already know. Islam to them is no more than a band that is tailored to fit on their sleeves. They fashion Islam tightly and snugly, in order to cuddle them and nurse their pathetic insecurities. It doesn't matter what the evidence or indicators are, what matters is that the entire world is deaf and God whispers in their ears. They impersonate the Prophet, and speak for God, and if you tell them let's look into the evidence, they say, "I know what I know. Don't bother me with complexities." In truth, what they demand is that God submits Himself to their comforts, and not disturb their pedantic simplicity. I quoted the jurist Qadi Khan al-Farghani (d. 592/1196) before, and I will quote him again:

> Know that a man becomes restless and bored, and is overcome by insecurities, ignorance, and a defective brain. This man's affliction only increases when he becomes surrounded by idiots who sing his praise. Then this man fills his mouth with the words of scholars, and spews out phrase after phrase. Neither does he understand nor do his followers understand the implications of what he says. It is better for the rational man to guard his mouth, for the ignorant only fall flat on their faces.

The truth of our situation in the States is that among the activists and leaders of today, this quote applies to the overwhelming majority. If you remind them of the apathy and laziness of their brains, they look at you, squint, and say, "Brother! In Islam, God has prohibited reason and rationality." What a horrifying thought, that if these restless and bored men had their way, Islam would become the creed of the stupids of this earth. What greater ugliness is there than to claim that God created human beings, prohibited reason, and then decreed upon all an unrelenting idiocy?

The night progressed to the point of inevitable retreat, the dawn announces its presence with unequivocal might, and the body moans without a shred of dignity. I rise to perform ablutions and pray *Fajr*, and afford this body a measure of equity. As I finally surrender to my bed, and feel the flirtations of sleep, I whisper to the vanishing night, "I know that the end and beginning is near. If God wills, and I visit you again, I beg of you, share with me your serenity. Please temper this mind with the knowledge of your temporality. May the words I read console the silence of the night, and sprinkle glimmers of majestic light. And, when the time comes, and I join the Conference, may I help another aching body and vigorous mind reach for knowledge and beauty."

CHAPTER 84

Notes of the Transformation

I look at this crowded room, the numerous books on the shelves, and the piles on the floor. I look at the old scratched desk that accompanied my journey since 1982. I look at the two computers and the two printers sitting on tables, the two telephones, the four desk lamps, the three humming fans, the many scattered tapes, the old torn leather chair, the numerous papers everywhere, and I know it's time to transform. It is time for the record of this Conference to be preserved, and have a life of its own. It is time for one record of the Conference to close and for many other records to grow. When I look at this room, I see the remnants of a long and demanding search that had but a single goal. It was the unrelenting search for beauty that defined this room, and every single piece of furniture and every single book or paper played a crucial role.

From a small crowded apartment in Princeton, New Jersey, to Yardley, Pennsylvania, to San Marcos, Texas, to Austin, to Los Angeles, in rooms blessed by their immeasurable powers and burdened by their keeper, the Islamic Civilization convened. The glories, the infamies, the victories, the ecstasies, the soft supplications, the tearful entreats, the dreams, the endless lessons of human follies, and the exacting record of the Divine covenant were all here. The resilient volumes stood side-by-side in a solemn procession testifying to our deeds. I listened carefully to the whispers and sublimations in the night, and heard the Conference of the Books calling upon me. I was to be the keeper of records documenting every breath the spirits of words exhaled in their search for beauty. How many nights I sat inebriated by the Conference's presence, feeling thoroughly irrelevant to its majesty. I sat listening, learning, thinking, humbly awaiting my transformation—my transformation into a book.

Now, the marks of exhaustion are everywhere in this room—the records of the search are heavy and full. The keeper is burdened by the weight of words, and aching to speak of what he knows and, even more, of what he does not know. I see the legacy everywhere in this room, and I know it's time to transform.

Mystified by the honor given to me, I prostrate in gratitude to my Lord. What greater honor could possibly be given to this small and marginal Egyptian boy than to humbly join the search for beauty? I never sparkled in my own mind, and I was never the center of any world. I always nestled in the arms of marginality, and nursed the aches of my soul. I escaped every moment of ugliness and cruelty by intoxicating myself with the beauty of the book and the glory of the word. I always deserted every center, and resigned myself to some corner staring with bewilderment at my world. But I know that now it is time to leave the corners of oblivion, and bravely transform.

I know that the migration to the Conference was a gift from my Lord, I know that I heard the call and marched to the source of the voice. I was never one to question a gift or doubt the call of a supernal voice. But I've always wondered, what opened this heart to the search for beauty despite its fogs of hurt and the scars of perfidy? I know that the beauty of creation is overwhelming, but when beauty is absent, ugliness often becomes all we can see. Ugliness, like pain and disease, often overcomes the soul with senseless despair, and the delusions become a fog that blinds the eyes to the truth of beauty. I often crouched in a corner enfolding my heart, guarding it from the terror of the feculent fog. I think of the long and arduous journey in the past, and how much more I need to do so that I may be able to see. But at this moment of transformation I think, with infinite gratitude, of all the remarkable visions that empowered this heart to transcend its fears. I remember all the beautiful people and thoughts that might have pushed this heart to open its doors to the search for beauty.

Perhaps it was the beauty of my mother's touch and the compassion of her heart, or it was her eyes that always looked as if bewildered, and yet remarkably serene. Perhaps what opened my heart is that my mother would always say, "Time is better spent thinking of the suffering of others than on one's own pain," and then after working for thirty years, having given everything away, she is rich only with prayer and without a dollar to her name. Perhaps it is because my mother was the first woman to drive in Kuwait, and she always engaged men without a hint of deferment, and with beautiful dignity. She always refused the curtains of exclusion, and marginality.

My mother would often proclaim that the scholars have said, "The one who initiates the *salam* is closer to God's and the Prophet's beauty." She would chide me for my frown and say, "Don't you know that the Prophet said, 'When you meet each other then initiate the *salam*, and shake hands, and when you depart, ask for God's forgiveness.'" How beautiful was she when she fumed over every act of discourtesy. Some men refused to shake a woman's extended hand, and claimed that the touch of a woman voids their *wudu'*. How beautiful and majestic was she when a man refused to shake her hand, and so she raised her head high, and said, "If that is what you believe, then shake my hand, and do your *wudu'* again." And, when I suffered a bout of chauvinism and tried to dominate my sister, she would delegate to my sister the authority to discipline me. She would stand, adorned in dignity, and announce, "Our Master is God—those who want to dominate others are but slaves to their own insecurities."

My beautiful mother bought me my first book, and she is in Egypt searching the crowded streets for books today, even as I speak. The deal was simple and sweet, she would say, "I will buy the books if you continue to read." Perhaps my heart opened to the Conference because I grew up in a home blessed by the Qur'an every single day. Every morning my mother would wake us up with the call of the Qur'an, reminding our hearts and directing our way. But perhaps it was nothing more than the search for the beauty of my mother that brought the Conference here.

Perhaps it was the stories of my father's torture that made me detest every act of ugliness, degradation, and perfidy. Or, perhaps it was the number of friends that I knew who were slaughtered, if not in some hellish prison, then in the hell of poverty. My father would proclaim, "The soul of life is murdered by every moment of indignity." I grew up repulsed by the arrogance of oppression and the ugliness of torture, regardless of the victim's creed or identity. I can't recall how many times my father would say, "Son, don't be like the living-dead, unable to think or speak. It is our thoughts and words that guard our humanity." My father would always sit on the same exact chair in our living room with a book in hand, and talk at length about our nation's suffering and misery. He would often declare, "We are a nation of sheep, existing for the pleasure of our shepherds. Our leaders lop off our heads as these heads are bent toward the ground searching for something to eat. We are a nation of sheep, and then we wonder why we cannot achieve a single honorable victory." "Son," he would say, "Don't believe in the myth of a just despot who will come to save the day. Even if just, despotism is still ugly, and God does not work in ugly ways." It was the legacy of my father that opened this heart to the beauty of dignity, and taught me that it is our sense of honor that teaches us to stand up straight.

Perhaps what opened this heart were the many blessed teachers and *Shaykhs* who taught me the beauty of knowledge, and who taught me that to ignorantly claim knowledge is the equivalent of blasphemy. They often repeated, "Search for God with confidence and determination, but never allow yourself the arrogance of believing you can ever capture God's full majesty. Yield to God with humility, and never claim to know the will of God with absolute certainty. Exert yourself in the *jihad* for knowledge, but always repeat what Abu Hanifa (d. 150/767) said, 'I believe that my opinion is right, but possibly wrong, and your opinion is wrong, but possibly right.' Know that it is beautiful to seek the truth, but every time you claim to have found it, you are flirting with a lie, and risking the ugliness of conceit." Blessed be those *Shaykhs* who implanted in my heart the enormity of God and God's unbounded beauty.

Perhaps what opened this heart is that it was weaned on the Qur'an, the most beautiful and majestic text, or that the love of the Prophet blows through this heart like a purified and celestial light. Perhaps this heart needed no more than the knowledge that God is beautiful, and that God loves beauty. I ache to inhale the Beloved's heavenly scent, and bask in whatever God chooses to give. Perhaps what opened my heart is any of these or all of these or perhaps it is simply an undeserved, merciful gift.

Yes, I wonder and think, and in the late hours of the night, I simply confess that God knows best. I stare at the scars marking this room like badges of honor commanding me to transform. I rise to pray, and thank my Lord, my Guide and my wondrous Love, for the gift of the intellect and the word, and for the Lord's glorious beauty. I thank my Lord for teaching me that, by submitting only to the Divine, I can stand in dignity and raise my head high. I thank my Lord for teaching me that the omnipotence and immutability of the Divine means my utter humility. I thank my Lord for teaching me that the love of God will open the heart to its dormant sense of beauty. I thank the Lord, and remember my mother, father, teachers, books, and scholars who taught me that the heart and soul of Islam is the search for beauty.

CHAPTER 85

The First Admission

The Trust was offered to the Heavens and the earth and they declined to bear it. Because they are foolhardy, proud and arrogant, humans bore it. So how have we done thus far? The Trust is to have the gift of rational faculties bear the truth of Divinity without arrogantly pretending that our comprehensions and will are divine. The Trust is to humbly submit to God while dominating no one; to praise God by honoring volition and will, and to abstain from coercion for it is the very negation of all that is divine. So how have we done thus far? The Trust is to supplicate God by spreading civilization, to refrain from corrupting the earth by infesting it with animosities, hostilities, hate, violence, and destruction. So how have we done thus far? The Trust is to venerate God by preserving the dignity and well-being of His creation and to understand that the measure of goodness is the divinity of beauty. "God is beautiful and loves beauty," this is what the Merciful revealed about the truth of divinity. What is Divine Magnificence but perfected beauty—the Trust is not an entitlement, it is the challenge of beauty. Have we furnished this earth with beauty or with fear, suffering, and inequalities? The Trust is God's Law, but entrusted to our hands have we used it to affirm and manifest, or negate and defame divinity?

The Conference of the Books was a nightly celebration of the Islamic civilization, of rationality, of beauty, of humanity, of Divinity, and of God's Trust. Every Muslim who honored the word, who wrestled with the challenges of thought, and whose pursuit of knowledge was a jihad for the sake of God, was transformed into a book, and all congregated in this sanctuary to deliberate how to manifest the divinity of beauty in human life.

Twelve years ago, a man heard the call of his Lord: "O you wrapped up in a mantle; arise and deliver God's warning; and praise and magnify your Lord. Purify and clean your garments and shun all abominations and ugliness. Do not expect any benefit for yourself but for the sake of your Lord be patient and constant" (74:1–7).

Over fourteen hundred years ago, this was the same call that awoke the Prophet Muhammad, and it continues to enlist the conscience of Muslims to this very day. Our friend had studied Islamic law all his life, but on that particular night he was called to go beyond the law, and embrace the soul and heart of his faith.

"Read in the name of your Lord and Cherisher who created all things; Who created humans out of a mere clot of congealed blood. Read and your Lord is most learned and most bountiful. He is the One Who taught by the use of the pen (intellect), taught humans that which they did not know, nay but humans do transgress all bounds, in that they look upon themselves as well sufficient. Verily to your Lord is the return of all" (96:1–7).

With this, the Conference of Books—the search for beauty—was forever engraved in his mind, and he learned that the love of knowledge is inseparable from the love of beauty and God. Beauty undisciplined by the mind is chaos, but reason, if not tempered by the sense of beauty is like a life constructed on mathematical formulas but without the breath of the Divine.

"God commands justice, the doing of good, and kindness to kith and kin, and God forbids all shameful deeds, and ugliness and injustice. God counsels you perhaps you will take heed" (16:90).

"Recall the benefits and bounties of your Lord and do not go forth spreading mischief and corrupting the earth" (7:74).

"Give just measure and weight; do not withhold from people their due (rights) and do not corrupt the earth after it has been organized and set in order (by God) that will be best for you if you have faith" (7:85).

"Say: peace be on you; your Lord hath inscribed mercy for Himself" (6:54).

The man recalled these Qur'anic verses as he realized that the heart of submission to the Lord is to avoid evil and ugliness and to seek justice and goodness in all its forms. The heart of injustice is to deny human beings their due, and if God created humans in dignity (17:70) then dignity is their due. The challenge posed by God to all humanity is to refrain from corrupting the earth for corruption is the antithesis of beauty. What can corrupt the earth but the absence of peace and mercy? Isn't peace itself a divine mercy given to humanity? If God charges us with peace, and inscribes mercy onto God's self isn't the pulse of the search for beauty to raise the salvation of the earth on foundations of mercy?

"Let there be no compulsion in religion," the Lord declared, "truth stands out clear from error" (2:256–7).

"If it had been the Lord's Will, all who are in earth would all have believed! So would you then compel humankind against their will to believe!" (10:99)

"You have no power over the matter; whether God forgives or punishes the unjust" (3:128).

The Conference of Books debates in history over the words of God. And hearing the voice of history our friend realized that coercion is the corruption of religion and life, it breeds hypocrisy, negates volition and rationality, and is an offense against God. If God endowed humans with choice, freedom is their due, and who is empowered to take away a right given by God? Coercion transgresses upon the Divine domain; especially if it is perpetuated in God's name it is a usurpation of the seat of God. Coercion is fraught with possible transgressions but despotism is coercion epitomized. What history taught our friend is that despotism is fundamentally inconsistent with Islam because it cannot be reconciled with the mandate that Muslims submit only to God. Despotism is inherent ugliness. It is a corruption of the integrity of our testimony.

"You were the best of nations brought out to humanity enjoining the good and forbidding the wrong and believing in God. . ." (3:110)

"Thus have We made you a moderate nation (justly balanced) so that you might be witnesses over all nations and the Messenger a witness over you. . ." (2:143)

The duty to enjoin the good and forbid the wrong is the first principle of morality; it is the essence to investigate and search for divinity—for the universal distinction between ugliness and beauty—the foundation of the Conference of Books and its testimony. We are a nation charged with the obligation to learn the good and evil, to bear witness and testify, and to stand in moderation for such is the nature of the balance, of justice, and beauty. But our friend understood that the best nation brought out to humanity—a nation of moderation for our beloved Prophet shunned all polarizations, all excesses and all extremes—was not given an entitlement or a status beyond accountability. Muslims are not God's chosen people and they enjoy no privilege founded on an inherent superiority. God warns Muslims that if they fail to discharge their duties and obligations, God will replace them while preserving the viability of Islam by sending those who can do it honor and preserve its integrity (47:38).

Islam is a faith geared to liberate humans from oppression—the oppression of those who claim to have an exclusive venue to the Divine and the oppression of tradition, and patriarchy—the book of God forbade blind obedience and anchored the principle of individual accountability. In submitting to God, Islam denies the legitimacy of submission to human beings. Arising from this thought and in fulfillment of these ideals, the Conference of Books was built on the principle of rich diversity. Thousands of scholars with a million competing ideas congregated every night, each arguing for his or her ideas. In this our friend thrived and felt intoxicated with the world of thought. Motivated by the dream that the Islamic civilization would once again rise to the benefit of all human beings, but concerned about what Muslims were doing in the name of their religion, and the infamy brought upon the faith by the failure to understand the Divine nature of beauty, our friend became the servant of the Conference of Books—each night, he preserved the books, listened to their arguments, and reported on their deliberations to the best of his ability. In short, he became known as the humble keeper of the Conference—the faithful guardian of the Islamic Civilization with all its beauty and diversity, and this lasted for twelve blessed years.

But in a night not too far long ago, the Conference of Books was found in a quiet and pensive state. The books were there and the endless murmurings of the debates could be heard, but ghosts and phantoms roamed throughout the place. The Conference of the Books stood in full dignity persisting in its search for beauty, but its keeper had disappeared.

Several disciples of the lost sage diligently searched the den and all the rooms, the rows of books, and even the attic upstairs but the keeper of the Conference could not be found anywhere. The disciples wondered where the Conference keeper had gone and whether he left a clue as to his whereabouts, but there was not a trace. The disciples inspected the desks, the diaries, and papers, and searched under the bed and behind the chairs, but all their efforts were in vain.

Inspecting the keeper's mail, the disciples found messages filled with bigotry, and a considerable amount of hate mail. But they also found a few letters expressing admiration and praise. They bumped into heaps of jealousies fallen harmlessly to the ground, and located trash cans filled with pedantic sophistry and dribble that once camouflaged itself and tried to infiltrate the Conference posing as thought. They found broken hearts that once pumped with love in the keeper's chest, and in an ethereal reality stubborn in their loyalty those broken hearts persisted in pumping away. Hidden in the annals of the keeper the disciples found a sad history of betrayals by one-time students, friends, and brothers in the faith. The disciples walked in on a magnificent garden filled with millions of flowers—a flower that sprouted for every ray of light and every moment of love and longing felt for the Prophet Muhammad, the most beautiful human being that ever blessed this earth.

Diligently searching, the disciples were shocked when they walked in on the grim sight of thousands of headstones. Upon closer inspection they discovered that lying under the tombstones was a huge corpus of theories and hypothesis that the keeper once proposed, lovingly embraced, and even defended before the world. But after being martyred in rapines of merciless self-critiques, they were respectfully laid to rest in the gravesite of ideas. After a sigh of relief, the disciples continued and found a ridiculous collection of green ink pens, which they assigned to some bizarre infatuation or strange eccentricity. They also found a large collection of the Diva Umm Kalthum next to numerous classical music CDs, so they reasonably surmised that the keeper was among those who believed that the transcendental beauty of music offered a gaze upon the supernal beauty of Divinity.

After exhausting the search, the disciples reluctantly were forced to concede that the keeper of the Conference had disappeared into thin air. After twelve years this keeper will no longer report on the Conference's proceedings. The search for beauty is but an eternal jihad—it is but a discovery of divinity, but in whichever way this jihad might now proceed, its reporter has ceased to be.

The keepers of the Conference—never do they surrender, quit, resign, or desert their posts, and they cannot be abducted, murdered, maimed, or silenced regardless of what might be inflicted upon their bodies. In essence, they are the keepers of memory and the remembrance, and although it may be deconstructed, misconstructed, or hidden and covered, at the end, history tells the truth about humanity.

A disciple suggested that at times of collective amnesia and defeat, Conference keepers tend to fade—they fade so much so that they become increasingly faint. In such a condition and state they become sufficiently evanescent that although present, they cannot be seen. Only the most perceptive or those who have been properly trained can detect their presence by the translucence of their being. Another disciple argued that at times like this—times when countries founded on the great traditions of liberty and tolerance betray their principles. Times when countries that afforded the Conference sanctuary and safety start slipping in swamps of religious bigotry, and abuses against human dignity; when these sanctuaries of beauty start desecrating holy texts and torturing captives, engaging in arbitrary and secret detentions, and justify such unmitigated ugliness in the name of national security—at times like these, it is the Conference itself that starts to fade, and eventually it hides from sight until it is impossible to locate. So this disciple concluded that the keeper of the Conference is out somewhere feeling lost because it is the Conference that has faded from sight. So the keeper must be roaming the whole country trying to find his Conference, but to no avail.

The third disciple protested declaring both theories—that of the invisible keeper and invisible Conference—as patently absurd. Conference keepers eventually become an anomaly discordant with every reality, he explained. If you search long enough for beauty, you become the search—you become an open question—a never ending inquiry. The keepers, the disciple claimed, inevitably lose their physicality and exist in an ethereal world that remains an unfulfilled potentiality gazing upon the consummate paragon, the immaculate and impeccable perfection itself—potentiality wonderfully and flawlessly fulfilled—God, the One and Only unblemished and faultless beauty.

You see my friends, the disciple said, the keeper of the Conference must have fallen in a fissure or rift—keepers of Conferences in their endless search for beauty are inevitably set for disappointment. Sooner or later, they fall in a gaping cleft—a space between our forgetfulness and delusions, our pleasures and gluttony, our anger and avidity, our ingratitude and voracity, our greed and betrayals, our jealousies and insatiability, our self-deceptions and rapacity, our competitions and cupidity, our falsehoods and endless excuses—a cleft between the lives lived, and the lives lost, between what we are and what we could have been. When trapped in this rift, it becomes impossible to reconcile what is sought with what is, between the dream of beauty and reality. At such a moment, the keeper transforms into a member of the Conference—he is no longer a keeper he is a participant. In short, the keeper can no longer experience life, but if we wait long enough we will hear his voice in the murmurings of the nightly proceedings of the Conference. The truth is my friends the Conference needs a new keeper; as to the previous one he has become part of the beauty of our civilization searching for beauty in the proceedings of the night, may they forever be blessed by God.

Glossary of Terms

'Abbasid

The second ruling dynasty of the Muslim empire after the Umayyads. Flourished in Baghdad from 132/750 to 656/1258. Thereafter, it survived as a shadow Caliphate until 923/1517.

'Adl

Justice, uprightness.

'Alim (pl. 'ulama')

A learned person, scholar. The word often describes jurists or religious scholars.

'Amm

Lit., common, general, universal, or comprehensive. Islamic law: the "general" as opposed to the "particular" (*khass*). A word in the text that applies to many things, not limited in number, and includes everything to which it is applicable.

'Aql

Mind, intellect, rationality, reason.

'Arafa

To know, to come to know (see *ta'aruf* and *ta'arafu*).

Ash'ariyya or Ash'aris

A school of theology founded by Abu al-Hasan al-Ash'ari (d. 324/935–6). The school argued that the anthropomorphic expressions about God in the Qur'an are to be accepted without question. The school was attacked by the Hanbalis for using rational arguments, and by the Maturidiyya for being too conservative. The Ash'ari school became widely spread during the 'Abbasid caliphate.

'Asr prayers

The afternoon prayer. The third of the prescribed five daily prayers. Also the name of a chapter in the Qur'an.

'Awra

Areas of the human body that are considered private and to be covered in the presence of others. A modest man or woman would cover these parts of the body with loose-fitting cloth. Whether cultural norms may be considered in defining modesty is subject to debate. The parts that should be covered are different for men and women.

Abu

From *abb*. Father of such and such. Abu is always a part of a name; it is never the full name.

Adab

Good manners, humaneness, propriety, good character, decency, culture, social etiquette, proper human conduct. Also means literature, belles-lettres, or literary products.

Adab al-ikhtilaf

The proper bounds and manners for juristic disagreement. The acceptable process by which jurists may differ.

Adilla or dala'il (sing. dalil)

See *dalil*.

Ahad

Solitary hadith, a report transmitted by one person or a limited number of people.

Ahkam (sing. hukm)

See *hukm*.

Ahl al-Suffah

An appellation applied to certain persons who were the "guests" of Muslims in Medina, i.e., supported by the charity of the Muslims. These were poor refugees and houseless men who passed the nights in the "*suffah*" of the Prophet's mosque in Madinah, which was an appurtenance of the mosque roofed with palm sticks.

Akhi

My brother.

Al-

An article, means "the."

amn

Safety, peace, security, protection.

Amr mushkil

Difficult matter, challenging problem, the solution to which is not clear. See *mushkil*.

Ansar

The native inhabitants of Medina who believed in and supported the Prophet.

'Aqd (pl. 'uqud)

A legal contract.

Asl (pl. usul)

Source, origin, root, or basis.

Azhar

Lit., the brilliant or the radiant. A mosque and university in Cairo established by the Fatimids in 358/969. The Azhar has graduated many religious scholars in the Muslim world.

Azhari

A graduate of Azhar or someone who studied there.

Barak Allahu fik

May God bless you.

Bay'a

To commit to something or someone, to purchase, to declare one's loyalty. Usually refers to the oath of allegiance given to the Prophet, and given to the Caliphs after the Prophet's death.

Bayt Allah (pl. buyut Allah)

Lit., the house or abode of God. Usually, used to refer to a mosque.

Bid'a

Lit., innovation. Often refers to a heretical or illegal innovation in religion. *Bid'a hasana* means a good or desirable innovation. *Bid'a sayyi'a* is a bad or undesirable innovation.

Bin

Son of such and such. (Ibn when it starts the name.)

Bint

Girl, daughter, daughter of such and such.

Buyut Allah

See *bayt Allah*.

Caliph

Arabic: *Khalifa (pl. khulafa')* lit., successor or deputy. Refers to the head of the Islamic state after the death of the Prophet. Also see *Khilafa*.

Dabt

Capture, restraint, accuracy, correctness, control, investigate, set right.

Dabtt al-isnad

To examine and investigate the chain of transmission of a report; to authenticate a report by examining the transmitters. The report is usually from or about the Prophet.

Daf' al-darar

An Islamic legal principle that establishes the presumption that whenever harm exists, such harm must be removed. This presumption serves as an analytical or interpretive tool.

Daf' al-haraj

An Islamic legal principle that establishes the presumption that whenever hardship exists, such hardship must be removed. This presumption serves as an analytical or interpretive tool.

Dalil (pl. adilla or dala'il)
Legal proof, evidence, or indicators. The indicators pointing to the law of God.

Dalil al-'aql
Rational proof, an element in the legal analysis dictated by rational proof or evidence.

Dalil al-sam'
Textual evidence or proof, evidence from a textual source.

Daraba
To strike, hit, rove, roam, travel, forsake, abandon, mount, copulate.

Dhaka sarih al-iman
"That is the solid and strong faith," or "That is the correct and true faith."

Dhikra
Remembrance or memory. This term is used often in the Qur'an to refer to the divine message, divine word, or the Qur'an. It connotes the idea that God is sending a reminder to people to invoke in their hearts and minds what is already known to them but what has been long neglected or ignored. God is reminding people of what already lies dormant within their hearts and minds.

Dinar
A gold coin used by the Arabs.

Dreyfus Affair
An incident in 1894 in which a French Jewish Captain, Alfred Dreyfus (d. 1935), was convicted of treason and sentenced to life by a military court in France. Dreyfus was wrongly accused and convicted because of anti-Semitism.

Du'a'
A supplication or prayer.

Dunya
The lower life, earthly life, this world, temporal.

Fahisha
A vile deed, grave sin often involving sexual misconduct. A grave sin.

Fahisha mubina
Refers to an obvious and clear commission of *fahisha*.

Fajr prayer
First of the prescribed five prayers, offered at dawn.

Faqih (pl. fuqaha')
A jurist, one learned in jurisprudence (*fiqh*).

Far' (pl. furu')
Branches, subdivisions, the opposite of *asl*, new and original problems or cases.

Fard
Obligation, obligatory, often connotes a serious religious obligation. Some schools of thought distinguish a *fard* from a *wajib*. See *wajib*.

Fasid

Corrupt, deficient, voidable.

Fasiq

Iniquitous, sinner, corrupt, an impious person, a vile person.

Fatawa

See *fatwa*.

Fatwa (pl. fatawa)

A non-binding legal opinion issued in response to a legal problem.

Fiqh

Lit., the word implies "an understanding." Islamic law: the process of jurisprudence by which the rules of Islamic law are derived. The word is also used to refer generally to positive law.

Fitna (pl. fitan)

Calamity, corruption, civil discord. Also refers to enticement or seduction.

Fitra

The inner essence of an individual or the intuitive sense by which one recognizes the right and wrong, and the moral and immoral.

Fuqaha' (sing. faqih)

See *faqih*.

Furu' (sing. far')

See *far'*.

Hadd (pl. hudud)

Lit., the limit or boundary. Islamic law: prescribed punishment for a crime. There are only a few such crimes in Islamic law.

Hadith (pl. ahadith)

Lit., a report, account, or statement. Islamic law: a Prophetic tradition transmitted through a chain of narrators by which the Prophet or his *Sunna* is known. The word may also be used to refer to a statement by one of the Companions.

Hajj

The fifth pillar of Islam; pilgrimage to Mecca at least once in a person's lifetime, if physically and financially able to do so.

Halal

Islamic law: the permitted, allowed. Most schools hold that everything is permitted unless there is evidence requiring that it be prohibited. Most schools adhere to a presumption of permissibility, and so, the burden of proof is against the person who is arguing for a prohibition. *Halal* meat is meat slaughtered according to the specifications of Islamic law. See *Shari'a*.

Halaqa

Lit., circle. The term is often used to signify circles of knowledge in which a scholar teaches his or her students who are seated (usually on the floor) in front of him or her in a circle. A *halaqa* is normally conducted in a home or mosque.

Hamdulillah, al-
Often used expression that means "thank God," my gratitude be to God.

Hanafi (Hanafiyya)
An adherent of the Sunni juristic school of thought named after its eponym Abu Hanifa. (See *Abu Hanifa*.) The school developed in Kufa and Basra but spread in the Middle East and the Indian subcontinent. The Hanafi school is one of the four main Sunni jurisprudential schools.

Hanbali (Hanbaliyya)
An adherent of the Sunni juristic school of thought named after its eponym Ahmad Ibn Hanbal. This school is one of four main Sunni jurisprudential schools of thought. Today, its adherents are found primarily in Saudi Arabia.

Haqq al-'Ibad
The rights of people.

Haqq Allah
The rights of God.

Haram
Islamic law: what is forbidden, the sinful, the prohibited. One of the five categories or values of *Shari'a*, connoting that which is forbidden or sinful. See *Shari'a*.

Haramayn (sing. haram)
The two *harams*, the two holy sites of Mecca and Medina.

Hasan
Lit., good, desirable. Islamic law: refers to that which is considered beautiful and moral as opposed to the ugly and immoral (*qabih*).

Hasirat
Women who uncover their faces or hair.

Hijab
Lit., obstruction, shield, shelter, protection, cover, screen, seclusion, obscure, and hide. The veil with which a Muslim woman covers her head, except her face. The face veil is called *niqab*. (see *Hujub*)

Hijra
Lit., migrate, desert, or abandon. The historical migration of Prophet Muhammad and his Companions from Mecca to Medina in the year 622 C.E. The Hijra marks the beginning of the Islamic lunar calendar.

Hudud (sing. hadd)
See *hadd*.

Hujub
Veils, obstructions, something that hampers perception or sight, partitions, or curtains. Here, used as moral or spiritual fog and confusion.

Hukm (pl. ahkam)
Lit., judgment. Islamic law: a legally binding judgment, rules of law, ordinances.

Humm rijal wa nahnu rijal

Lit., they were men and we are men. When used in legal discourses it means that our predecessors were men who were capable of interpreting the law but we are capable of interpreting the law as well. This phrase, which became popular in some modernist discourses, is intended to encourage the use of *ijtihad* in the contemporary age. At times, it is taken to mean that there is no reason to defer to the juristic opinions of earlier generations.

Husn

Beauty. Also see *hasan*.

'Ibadat

Worship and prayers. In jurisprudence, it refers to laws of ritual and worship.

Iblis

Satan, the Devil, Lucifer. See *Shaytan*.

Ibn

Son, son of such and such; "*bin*" or "*b.*" when it is in the middle of the name.

'Id

Religious occasion for celebration, festival, holiday. There are two 'Ids in Islam. The first is the Feast of Breaking Fast at the end of the month of Ramadan, the month of fasting. The second is the Feast of Sacrifice.

'Idda

The period of time a woman has to wait after a divorce or the death of her husband before she may marry again. The period for a divorced woman is about three months and for a widow is four months and ten days. During that period a divorced wife may re-marry her husband without a new contract or dowry.

Ihram

State of sanctity that a pilgrim assumes during his or her pilgrimage to Mecca in fulfillment of the fifth pillar of Islam (*hajj*). During *ihram*, the pilgrim must avoid all categories of foulness, anger, argumentation, and conjugal relations from one of several entry points into Mecca (the *miqat*) until he or she has fulfilled the rites of pilgrimage.

Ihsan

Lit., kindness, goodness, compassion. That which is commonly known to be good and moral. In a tradition, the Prophet defined it as fulfillment of the Divine Will as though one sees God at all times.

Ijaza

Certificate of authorization earned by a student from his or her teacher after having read a certain text or attained a certain degree of legal knowledge, as a license to teach others.

Ijma'

Lit., consensus, agreement. Islamic law: consensus of legal opinion. Jurists differed, however, about the binding nature of *ijma'*, requirements of eligibility, conditions for its nullification, whether or not it is limited by time and place, etc.

Ijtihad

Lit., exertion. The process of exerting one's utmost in an effort to deduce laws from sources in unprecedented cases. Novel or original legal solutions, the effort of a jurist in searching for and deducing the correct law.

Ikhtilaf

Juristic disagreement.

Ikhwan

Lit., brothers, siblings. The *Ikhwan al-Muslimun* is the name of an organization founded by Hasan al-Banna in 1346/1928 in Egypt. The organization aimed to establish an Islamic state based on Islamic principles and emphasized gradual reform. Its leader was assassinated in 1949, the organization banned, and its members persecuted in 1954 and 1965. Since the 1970s, the Egyptian government, at times, has tolerated the organization. The *Ikhwan* established branches in several Muslim countries such as Jordan and Syria, and in some non-Muslim countries such as the United States.

Ila'

An oath of continence or abstention by which a spouse swears not to have conjugal relations with their partner. See Qur'an 2:226.

'Illa (pl. 'ilal)

Lit., the cause. Islamic law: the operative or effective cause of a ruling, the *ratio legis*. In the language of jurists, *"al-'illa taduru ma'a al-ma'lul wujudan wa 'adaman"* [The rule exists if the operative cause exists, and the rule does not exist if the operative cause does not exist].

'Ilm

Knowledge, learning, science, religious learning, or religious knowledge. Also see *'alim*.

Imam

Lit., one who stands out in front. Islamic law: leader of prayer or of a congregation. In common usage it often means a religious leader.

Iman

Belief, faith, right belief. Also, belief in God, the Messengers including Muhammad, angels, and the revealed books including the Qur'an.

Insha' Allah

"God willing," or "if God wills." Often uttered to indicate an intent to do something, provided God permits it to happen.

I'rad

To turn away from, to be repulsed, to reject, to abstain from.

'Isha prayer

Evening prayer. The last of the prescribed five daily prayers.

'Isma

The power of divorce. Presumptively given to the husband alone, unless the wife explicitly reserves the right to herself.

Isnad

The chain of transmission for a report or tradition. The list of people who transmitted a particular report from one to another.

Istighfar

To seek repentance, to seek forgiveness (usually from God), to relent and repent.

Istihsan

Juristic preference, equity, something that is good.

Istinbat

To deduce, to infer a meaning from an ambiguous text.

Istishab

A presumption of continuity. A presumption in favor of the *status quo* until sufficient evidence exists to mandate a change.

Istislah

Juristic consideration of public interest in a case.

Ja'fari (Ja'fariyya)

An adherent of the Shi'i jurisprudential school of thought named after its eponym Ja'far al-Sadiq, the Sixth Shi'ite Imam. This was one of the main Shi'ite jurisprudential schools originally founded in Medina.

Jahiliyya or jahili

A state of ignorance, a state of misguidance. These terms are used to refer to the pre-Islamic period in Arabia. Often used to connote paganism or a state of darkness.

Jalabiyya

The cultural dress of the Arabs, a one-piece garment that usually extends down to the ankles.

Jama'a

Congregation, grouping, the majority, the righteous group.

Jayb (pl. juyub)

A *jayb* is the bosom of a human being. It could also be where the neck and chest meet, or the beginning of the cleavage area on a woman's chest. Furthermore, a shirt, garment, or pocket may be called *jayb* as well.

Jihad

Lit., exertion, struggle. *Jihad* is a struggle for the sake of God. The struggle could be one of self-discipline and self-purification or it could be an armed or unarmed struggle against oppression and injustice.

Jilbab

A *jilbab*, singular form of *jalabib*, is a garment worn on the body, like a dress or Arab robe. A *jilbab* could refer to what is worn by men or women.

Jinn

A species of creation mentioned in the Qur'an. Reportedly, the jinn share certain attributes with human beings, such as free will, belief and disbelief, morality and immorality, procreation, and so forth. Satan was from this species of creation. Both humans and jinn differ from the angels insofar as the angels do not have free will to choose between right and wrong. Hence, Satan is not a "fallen angel" in Islamic theology.

Jum'a

Friday; the day of congregation in which Muslims gather at noon to hear a sermon (*khutba*) in the mosque and offer the noon prayer. Unlike the Jewish or Christian Sabbath, Muslims are not required to refrain from work or rest on Friday or any other day. Although Muslims believe in six periods of creation, they do not believe that God needed to rest on the seventh period.

Jum'a prayer

See *Jum'a*.

Ka'ba

Lit., cube. Refers to the house of worship built by Abraham and his older son, Ishmael, in the desert of Mecca. Muslims face the Ka'ba in their daily prayers as a symbol of their global unity.

Kafir (pl. kuffar)

A non-believer, someone who does not believe in God or in Islam. Someone who is ungrateful toward God. Also see *Kufr*.

Kalam

Lit., speech. Theology and dogmatics, scholastic theology. Considered reprehensible in contemporary Wahhabi thought.

Karbala

A city in Iraq where a battle took place between the Prophet's grandson, al-Husayn Ibn 'Ali, and the Umayyad forces in 61/680. Al-Husayn and his supporters were massacred in that battle. Al-Husayn is buried in Karbala and his tomb is a place of pilgrimage for the Shi'i branch of Islam.

Kayf halak

Arabic: "How are you?"

Khalifa (pl. khulafa')

Successors, deputies, or viceroys. According to the Qur'an, human beings are the *khulafa'* of God on earth. Also see *Caliph*.

Khatib

Lit., a speaker. Usually, the term refers to the one who delivers the public address (*khutba*) before the noon prayer on Friday (*jum'a*).

Khawf

From the verb *khafa*, to fear, dread, or be frightened.

Khidr

This name is traditionally applied to one of God's servants as mentioned in the Qur'an (18:60–82), who demonstrated to Moses the secrets of Divine Justice and Wisdom through examples that he presumed unjust and unwise.

Khilafa

Caliphate. The system of government that existed after the death of the Prophet. The first four Caliphs were Abu Bakr, 'Umar, 'Uthman, and 'Ali. The Caliph was expected to receive the oath of allegiance (*bay'a*) from the people, and enforce God's law. Many leaders throughout Islamic history adopted this title. The last Caliphate was that of the Ottoman Empire.

Khimar

A piece of cloth that is worn on the head. A man's turban may be called a *khimar* as well, and a man wearing a turban may be called a *mukhtamir.*

Khul'

A quitclaim, no-cause divorce in which a woman returns her dowry or pays a sum of money in return for a divorce.

Khutba

Lit., a speech or lecture. Usually, the term refers to the public address delivered on Friday (*jum'a*) before the noon prayer.

Kufa

A major city in Iraq, especially in the premodern age. The city was established in 17/638 and played a large role in Islamic history.

Kufan Jurists

Usually refers to the early Muslim jurists in Kufa of the second and third centuries.

Kufr

Lit., to cover over something. In this sense, the term is found in the Qur'an in its plural form as a reference to farmers (57:20). Islamic law: covering over the truth once one has recognized it as true, i.e., rejecting the message of Islam. Also means ingratitude or infidelity, not believing in God or ungrateful toward God.

La ta'ata li makhluqin fi ma'siyyat al-khaliq

See *ta'a.*

Madhhab (pl. madhahib)

School of thought, juristic school, or orientation. A juristic school of thought is distinguished by its jurisprudential methodology for deducing laws. Disagreements over methodology often distinguish one school from another.

Maghrib prayer

Prayer performed at sunset. The fourth of the prescribed five daily prayers.

Mahr

Dowry paid by the groom to the bride upon marriage. The amount is determined by mutual consent, and the dowry exclusively belongs to the bride.

Makruh

Islamic law: not recommended, reprehensible, not preferred. See *Shari'a.*

Maliki (Malikiyya)

An adherent of the Sunni juristic school of thought named after its eponym Malik Ibn Anas. One of the four main Sunni jurisprudential schools of thought. The school originated from the early jurisprudential schools of Medina. Today, it is widespread in North Africa and sub-Saharan Africa. This was also the school of thought that predominated in Muslim Spain.

Mamnu'

Prohibited, forbidden, banned.

Mandub

Islamic law: recommended, commendable, preferred. See *Shari'a*.

Mansukh

The abrogated law or Qur'anic verse. Also see *naskh, nasikh*.

Maqasid (sing. maqsad)

Lit., objectives or goals. Islamic law: the ultimate objectives of Islamic law.

Ma'ruf

That which is commonly known to be right. Muslims have the dual obligation of practicing it and enjoining others to do the same. Also means kindness and generosity.

Ma sha' Allah

Lit., whatever God wills; Muslims utter the phrase to express awe, gratitude, or praise.

Masjid (pl. masajid)

Mosque, Muslim place of worship. Also see *bayt Allah*.

Maslaha

Public interest, the consideration of public interest, and general welfare in formulating the law.

Mihna

Lit., test, trial, difficulty, tribulation. Islamic theology: a test given by God to His servants that could either turn into a blessing (*ni'ma*) or a curse (*naqma*) depending on how the servant responds to the test.

Minhaj

Methodology; the way or method.

Miswak

Tooth-stick; a piece of stick with which the teeth are polished and cleaned, the end being made like a brush by chewing it so as to separate its fibers.

Mu'allaqa

A term used in the Qur'an 4:129. Refers to a woman in a suspended state not able to enjoy her rights. As used here, it means a woman neither in a proper state of marriage nor properly divorced.

Mu'amalat

Social dealings. In jurisprudence, it refers to the opposite of acts of ritual (*'ibadat*). The laws that deal with commercial and social dealings.

Mubah

Islamic law: the permissible, allowed. Most schools hold that everything is permitted unless there is evidence requiring that it be prohibited. Most schools adhere to a presumption of permissibility, and so, the burden of proof is against the person who is arguing for a prohibition. See *Shari'a.*

Mufti

Muslim legal scholar who is qualified to issue legal *responsa.* See *fatwa.*

Muhajjaba

A woman who wears the *hijab.* See *hijab.*

Muhajirun

The migrants, Muslims from Mecca who believed in the Prophet and migrated with him to Medina.

Muharib (pl. muharibun)

Lit., warriors or those who fight. Islamic law: criminals engaged in gross acts of violence. The term is often used to describe bandits or brigands.

Muharram

The first month of the Islamic lunar calendar.

Muhtasib

Market inspector, an official delegated to make sure that the law is being respected in the market place. Sometimes used to refer to an official that enforces moral and legal injunctions.

Mujtahid

A jurist who performs *ijtihad* or is qualified to perform *ijtihad.*

Mukallaf

A competent person in possession of his or her faculties and who has a legal charge or obligation. Any person who could be held responsible for a legal charge or obligation.

Munkar

That which is commonly known to be reprehensible, illegal, and sinful. Muslims have the dual obligation of avoiding it and enjoining others to do the same.

Muqatta'at

The abbreviated letters used in the Qur'an at the opening of certain chapters (for example, chapters 2, 3, 7, 10, 11, etc.) whose true meanings are known only to God. It is thought that such letters were a challenge to the Arabs who prided themselves on their eloquence, poetry, and mastery of the Arabic language, as a lesson that the true secrets of language are hidden with the Creator.

Muqayyad

Lit., bound, fettered, confined. Islamic law: limited, restricted, qualified.

Murji'a (Murji'ites)

A theological branch in early Islam that played a significant political role. Their ideas were often described as politically quietist or passive. The basic tenet of their belief was that those who committed grave sins do not cease to be Muslims. They also believed in the postponement (*irja'*) of judgment on political conflicts until God resolves all matters in the Hereafter.

Mushari'

The legislator, the one with authority to legislate, often refers to God.

Mushkil

Difficult, challenging, unclear. See *amr mushkil.*

Muslim Brotherhood

See *ikhwan.*

Musnad (pl. masanid)

A *hadith* with a continuous chain of transmitters. Also a book that contains reports and traditions about the Prophet and the Companions, organized by the name of the transmitter.

Mustahabb

Islamic law: recommended, commendable, preferred. See *Shari'a.*

Mutawatir

A *hadith,* tradition reported by a large number of people, a report having cumulative authenticity. A more authentic report because of the number of people who transmitted it. Also see *tawatur.*

Mu'tazila

A rationalist school in Islamic history that emphasized the role of reason. The term came to connote a variety of theological and juristic orientations. The basic tenets of the school were the belief that the Qur'an was created and that the physical attributes of God mentioned in the Qur'an are allegorical. The school also believed in the absolute necessity of God's justice and human free will.

Mu'tazili

An adherent of the Mu'tazila school of Islamic theology. See *Mu'tazila.*

Nafaqa

Alimony, spousal support.

Nashiz

One who commits *nushuz*—in this context, means a grave sexual sin. Otherwise, the term connotes defiance, arrogance, disobedience, and vile sin.

Nasikh

The abrogator. Usually, the Qur'anic verse that abrogated an earlier verse or *hadith.*

Naskh

The doctrine that God abrogated or repealed some verses or laws of the Qur'an after they were revealed.

Nass (pl. nusus)

The text from which the law is derived. Also, a clear injunction or textual ruling.

Niqab

A piece of cloth that covers the face.

Nun

See *muqatta'at.*

Nushuz

See *nashiz.*

Qabih

Lit., ugly, undesirable. Islamic law: refers to that which is considered ugly and immoral as opposed to the beautiful and moral (*hasan*).

Qadaya masiriyya

Problems or challenges that affect the fate of a country, people, or person. The decisive issues, the defining challenges confronting a people or person.

Qadi (pl. Quda')

Judge.

Qalam

Pen or intellect.

Qat' (qat'i)

Definitive, certain, not speculative.

Qawa'id

Foundations, principles. *Qawa'id fiqhiyya* means the maxims of law, the basic principles guiding legal analysis.

Qiwama (qa'im)

Support, supporter of, sustenance, providing for, subsistence, guardianship, guardian of, the foundation of.

Qiyas

Islamic law: The extension of the law by reliance on analogy.

Qubh

Ugliness. Also see *qabih.*

Quffaz

Hand covers or gloves.

Quraysh

The leading tribe of Mecca from which Prophet Muhammad was born. Quraysh spearheaded the early battles against the Prophet.

Rahba

Fright, fear, alarm, terror, awe.

Rahma

Mercy, compassion.

Rahman (Rahim)

Two of God's glorious names that connote mercy and compassion as extended to all of God's creation from God.

Ramadan

The fourth pillar of Islam; it is the month of fasting for Muslims in which the devotee abstains from food, drink, conjugal relations, and all sins and indecencies from dawn to sunset each day.

Rightly Guided Caliphs (al-khulafa' al-Rashidun)
In the Sunni branch of Islam these are the first four Caliphs, Abu Bakr, 'Umar, 'Uthman, and 'Ali. They are referred to as "the Rightly-Guided" because they were esteemed Companions of the Prophet. Sunnis also believe that they were exceptionally just. Some Sunni scholars consider the Umayyad Caliph 'Umar Ibn 'Abd al-'Aziz to be the fifth Rightly-Guided Caliph although he was not a Companion of the Prophet.

Riwaya
Narration, report, transmission.

Sahaba (sing. Sahabi)
Companions or Companion of the Prophet. Term is used for all those who converted to Islam and lived with the Prophet, but some Companions, such as Abu Bakr, 'Umar, and 'Ali, were particularly close to the Prophet or lived with him for a longer time.

Sahih (pl. sihah)
Valid, authentic. Often refers to a report or tradition considered to be authentic. The *Sihah* refers to the six canonical collections of *hadith* considered to be authoritative by Sunni Muslims: al-Bukhari, Muslim, al-Nisa'i, Ibn Majah, Abu Dawud, and al-Tirmidhi.

Sakan
State of spiritual and intellectual balance in which there is tranquility and repose.

Sakina
A derivative from *sakan* (see above); God-inspired serenity.

Salamu 'alaykum, al-
"Peace be unto you!" The Muslim greeting of peace believed to be the greeting used by all prophets of past generations as well as the greeting of the inhabitants of Paradise.

Sanad
The authority of a report or tradition, the proof, the basis.

Shafi'i (Shafi'iyya)
Adherent of the jurisprudential school of thought named after its eponym Muhammad Ibn Idris al-Shafi'i. This is one of the four main Sunni jurisprudential schools, and is widespread in the Muslim world today.

Shahadah
Lit., derives from the verb *shahadah* which means to witness, see, or testify. Islamic theology: a testament of faith, to bear witness that there is but one God and that Muhammad is His Messenger. This is the first of five pillars of Islam [namely, the five are *shahadah*, *salah* (prayer), *sawm* (fasting), *zakah* (almsgiving), and *hajj* (pilgrimage)].

Shari'a
Lit., the water source, the way, the path. In Islamic theology and law, the path or way given by God to human beings, the path by which human beings search God's Will. Commonly misinterpreted as "Islamic law," *Shari'a* carries a much broader meaning. It is the sum total of categorizations of all human actions. These categories are mandatory (*fard* or *wajib*), encouraged (*mustahabb*), permissible (*halal* or *mubah*), discouraged (*makruh*), and forbidden (*haram*). *Shari'a* is not restricted to positive law per se but includes moral and ethical values, and includes the jurisprudential process itself.

Shaykh (pl. Shuyukh)

Lit., old man, master, leader. The title is often used to describe a learned man or religious scholar.

Shaytan (pl. Shayatin)

Demon, demons, the devil, devils, Satan (see *Iblis*).

Shi'a or Shi'ism

Lit., party or faction; historically, a group among the Muslims that called for the rulership of 'Ali, the Prophet's cousin, after the Prophet's death. Today, the Shi'a are the second largest branch of Islam after the Sunnis.

Shi'i or Shi'ite

A follower or adherent of Shi'ism.

Shiqaq

Discord, strong disagreement, disunity, and dissension.

Shirk

Polytheism or the association of partners with God. Believing in gods other than the One God.

Shura

Consultative body, council, consultation, and advice. The Qur'an commands that the affairs of the community be run by *shura*. In very early Muslim discourses, accusing a leader of abandoning the *shura* was the equivalent of claiming that the leader lacked legitimacy.

Shurut (sing. Shart)

A condition. In Islamic law, a condition precedent for the validity of a legal act, or a condition inserted into a contract by mutual consent. Such conditions may qualify the obligations of the contracting parties. Conditions may be inserted into the marital contract that modify or define the legal rights and obligations of the contracting parties.

Sira

Lit., this word derives from the verbal "*sara*" meaning, "to walk." Islamic theology: the biography of the Prophet (i.e., how he "walked" through life).

Sufi (Sufism)

Lit., one who wears a coat of wool. This term has been applied to Muslims who seek to achieve higher degrees of spiritual excellence or those who pursue Islamic mysticism or those who belong to a mystical order.

Sunan

Books containing reports and traditions about the Prophet and Companions organized by topic. Also means supererogatory acts, additional prayers offered in addition to the mandatory prescribed prayers. The non-binding precedents and acts of the Prophet that are followed in order to gain favor with God. The cumulative and general binding precedents of the Prophet.

Sunna

Lit., the way or course or conduct of life. Islamic law: the example of the Prophet embodied in his statements, actions, and those matters that he silently approved or disapproved as reported in *hadith* literature. The *Sunna* of the Companions means the precedent or the conduct of the Companions of the Prophet. *Sunna* is also the name used to describe the main branch of Islam.

Sunni or Sunnite

A follower of the main branch of Islam, which accepts the legitimacy of the Caliphate of Abu Bakr, 'Umar, and 'Uthman as well as 'Ali's.

Sura or surat

One of 114 chapters of the Qur'an that are composed of verses (*ayaat* [pl. of *ayah*]).

Ta Ha

See *Muqatta'at*.

Ta'a

Obedience. Common Islamic statement: "The created will not be obeyed if it means disobeying the Creator (*la ta'ata li makhluqin fi ma'siyyat al-khaliq*)."

Ta'arafu

To get to know one another, to become sociable and familiar with one another. See *ta'aruf* and *'arafa*.

Ta'aruf

The process of getting to know another person, sociability, familiarity. See *ta'arafu* and *'arafa*.

Ta'dib

Derived from *adaba*. To chastise, discipline, reproach, punish, educate.

Tafsir

Exegesis, particularly as it relates to the Qur'an.

Tafwid

From *fawada*: to empower, delegate, or entrust. Often refers to a process by which a husband delegates to his wife the power to divorce herself from him if she so wishes.

Tahqiq masalih al-'ibad

To achieve the welfare or good of the people; purpose or object of *Shari'a*.

Takbir

The declaration of "Allahu Akbar," which means God is greater than all.

Takfir

Calling someone a *kafir* (see *kafir*).

Takhrij

Extraction and derivation of the law according to systematic principles.

Taklif

Legal charge or obligation to a *mukallaf*.

Takhyir

To grant someone a choice or option. To grant someone a *khiyar* (choice or option). Often refers to options recognized by law or contract. In the context of divorce, it means a process by which the husband gives his wife the choice of divorce.

Talab al-'ilm

Seeking knowledge. In Islamic theology, seeking knowledge is a religious obligation upon every Muslim man and woman.

Talaq

An Islamic divorce.

Tamlik

To grant someone possession of something or to grant a tenancy. Often refers to a process by which a husband transfers a co-equal power of divorce to his wife. This type of transference or delegation is irrevocable.

Tanqih

Checking, re-examination, editing, revision. In technical usage, it means to investigate and extract the relevant elements.

Tanqih al-Manat

To extract and distinguish the *'illa* of a *hukm* through a systematic process. To systematically investigate the operative cause of a law usually done by close examination of the textual sources.

Taqlid

Lit., imitation; Islamic law: The term signifies the imitation of more knowledgeable individuals, usually within a particular school of thought. *Taqlid* is often considered the opposite of *ijtihad*.

Taqwa

Piety; caution; being religiously cautious; the precaution of piety.

Tarjih

From *rajaha*: to incline, to prefer more, to give more weight to, to preponderate. In Islamic law, to prefer or give more weight to particular evidence or to an opinion according to systematic principles often when the evidence or opinions are conflicting.

Tasbih

Supplication, glorification of God by saying "*Subhan Allah*" ("Praise to God," or "God is far beyond anything").

Tashbih

Lit., comparison or likeness. Islamic theology: anthropomorphism.

Tashih

Verification, authentication. The process of verifying the authenticity of a report.

Tashri'

Legislation, production of the law.

Tawatur

Continuous testimony, cumulative testimony, continuous recurrence of certain testimony. Also see *Mutawatir*.

Tilka mahd al-iman

Arabic: "This is the origins or basis of faith;" or "This is genuine and correct faith;" or "This is the nature of the genuine faith."

Tulaqa'
Emancipated slaves, freed or liberated people.

'Ulama (sing. 'alim)
See *'alim.*

Umayyads
First Islamic dynasty after the death of the Rightly-Guided Caliphs. Established by Mu'awiya Ibn Sufyan after the death of 'Ali Ibn Abi Talib, and lasted from 41/661 to 132/750.

Umm
Mother, Umm such and such means mother of such and such.

Ummah
The community of Muslims.

Ustadh
Teacher, master, professor.

Usul (Usul al-fiqh)
Lit., the origins or foundations. Islamic law: the principles upon which Islamic jurisprudence is based or the jurisprudential methods of Islamic law.

Wa 'uhdirati al-anfusu al-shuh
Quoted from the Qur'an 4:128. "And human beings incline toward greed."

Wahhabi (Wahhabiyya)
Follower of the strict puritanical teachings of Ibn 'Abd al-Wahhab. Wahhabis are hostile to the intercession of saints, visiting of tombs of saints, Sufism, Shi'ism, and rational methods of deducing laws. The Wahhabi creed is very restrictive of women. This creed dominates in Saudi Arabia.

Wahy
Divine revelation, inspiration.

Wajib
Obligatory, mandatory. Indicates various levels of legal obligations with some obligations more serious than others. Often used as synonymous with *fard.* In some schools of thought, a *fard* connotes a more serious obligation than a *wajib.*

Waswasa
Doubt and suspicion.

Wudu'
Ablution with water in preparation for prayer.

Ya
Vocative and exclamatory particle: "O"; "oh." "Ya such and such," means "O, such and such."

Ya rabb
Lit., "O' God." A supplication, a person's call upon God, a call for God's aid.

Yaqin

Certainty, certitude, or solid conviction.

Yasturun

"What they write," or "what they think." From 68:1 (*Nun*, "by the pen and what they write.").

Zahiri or Zahirite

An adherent to the Zahirite school.

Zahiriyya

The jurisprudential School of thought founded by Dawud Ibn Khalaf. A literalist school of thought whose most famous proponent was the jurist Ibn Hazm. The school is now largely defunct although the works of Ibn Hazm are still in circulation.

Zann (zanni)

Speculative, speculation, supposition, uncertainty. The opposite of *qat'*.

Zaydi (Zaydiyya)

One of three major branches of Shi'ism. Named after Zayd Ibn 'Ali (d. 122/740) whom they followed as the Imam.

Zina

Fornication or adultery.

Zuhr prayer

Prayer offered at noon. It is the third of five prescribed daily prayers.

Selected Biographies

'Abduh, Muhammad (d. 1323/1905)

A famous Egyptian Islamic reformer of the thirteenth/nineteenth Century. He studied in Azhar. When exiled to Paris, he studied there as well and met Jamal al-Din al-Afghani (d. 1314/1897). 'Abduh emphasized that reform in society can only come gradually and must originate with changes in educational policies. 'Abduh emphasized the necessity of using reason in the development of Islamic law, and emphasized the need for *ijtihad*. After the 'Urabi rebellion in 1300/1882, he was banished from Egypt but was allowed to return in 1889. Shortly after his return, he was appointed the Chief Mufti of Egypt and died holding that position.

'Abdullah Ibn Ubayy Ibn Salul (d. 9/631)

He was among the leading men of Medina upon the Prophet's arrival in the city, and was nominated to become the king of the city. He outwardly converted to Islam but continued to bear a bitter grudge against the Prophet. Ibn Ubayy challenged and betrayed the Prophet on numerous occasions, and was thus considered to be the leader of the hypocrites (*munafiqun*) in Medina.

'Abdullah Ibn 'Umar Ibn al-Khattab (d. 73/692)

Son of the Companion 'Umar Ibn al-Khattab. He was ten years old when he migrated with his father to Medina. After the death of the Prophet, 'Abdullah refused to become Caliph on several occasions. He became an important juristic authority and a transmitter of a large number of reports about the Prophet. Ibn 'Umar was among the last of the Companions of the Prophet to die in Mecca.

Abu Bakr al-Siddiq (d. 22/634)

His full name was 'Abdullah Ibn 'Uthman Ibn 'Amir Ibn Abi Quhafa. He was the first noble and rich man to believe in the Prophet in Mecca and among the closest Companions to the Prophet. Abu Bakr spent all of his wealth supporting the persecuted Muslims in Mecca, and he was in the Prophet's company when the Prophet migrated to Medina. Upon the Prophet's death, Abu Bakr was appointed to lead the Muslim nation and became the first Caliph in Islam.

Abu Hanifa al-Nu'man Ibn Thabit (d. 150/767)
A famous and brilliant early jurist from Kufa who is the eponym for the Hanafi school of Islamic law. During his life, he was the principal jurist of Kufa. He also taught some of the most prominent early jurists of Islam. Abu Hanifa refused to ally himself with the ruling government and, as a result, was imprisoned, tortured, and died in prison.

Abu Hayyan al-Tawhidi (d. 414/1023)
A brilliant man of letters and philosophy. Abu Hayyan studied Shafi'i law and Sufism but devoted himself to the writing of *belles-lettres* and philosophical essays. His work is a goldmine of historical information, ethics, and philosophy. Abu Hayyan was accused of heresy in Baghdad and banished to Ray. Eventually, he was allowed to return to Baghdad where he died in poverty. Embittered by his marginalization and social persecution, he burned his library before his death, apparently because he did not believe the people deserved to receive his writings. Thankfully, many of his writings survived anyway.

Abu Hurayra (d. 58/678)
His full name was 'Abd al-Rahman Ibn Sakr al-Dawsi, and he was called Abu Hurayra because of his fondness for kittens. He was a late convert to Islam. Abu Hurayra joined the Muslims in Medina around the time of the Battle of Khaybar in 7/629. Although he was with the Prophet for less than four years, Abu Hurayra has transmitted more traditions from the Prophet than most other Companions. Knowing that he was criticized for this, he would often respond that he spent all his time with the Prophet and made a conscious effort to memorize as much as he could from him. Abu Hurayra died in Medina.

Abu Talha (d. 34/654)
Actual name is Zayd Ibn Sahl Ibn al-Aswad. He was a Companion of the Prophet and one of the leading members of the Ansar in Medina who participated in many of the early battles fought by the Muslims. He died in Medina.

Abu al-Thawr, Ibrahim Ibn Khalid Ibn Abi al-Yaman (d. 240/854)
A prominent traditionist and jurist who lived and died in Baghdad, and who studied with Muhammad al-Shaybani and al-Shafi'i. His views and methodology were original, and he is considered to have been the founder of an independent school of thought. Followers of his school were in existence until the fifth/eleventh century, but his school is now extinct. All of his writings have been lost. Along with al-Tabari, he was one of the few jurists who held that women may lead men in prayer.

Abu Ya'la, al-Qadi Muhammad Ibn al-Husayn Ibn al-Farra' (d. 458/1066)
Master of the Hanbali jurists in Baghdad. His father was a notable Hanafi jurist, but Abu Ya'la adopted the Hanbali school of thought. He was the object of a fierce attack by the Ash'aris in Baghdad who contended that Abu Ya'la believed in the anthropomorphism of God. Abu Ya'la died an occupant of a prestigious chair in law, and a judge.

Abu Yusuf, al-Qadi, Ya'qub Ibn Ibrahim al-Ansari al-K.ufi (d. 182/797)
A student of Abu Hanifa and one of the most influential jurists in establishing and developing the Hanafi school of thought. He also studied with Malik Ibn Anas and al-Layth

Ibn Sa'd. Abu Yusuf was appointed a judge in Baghdad and became the head of the judiciary in the same city under the 'Abbasid Caliph Harun al-Rashid. He died in Baghdad.

'Aisha bint Abi Bakr (d. 58/678)
Abu Bakr's daughter and the Prophet's wife. 'Aisha played an important role in Medina during the Prophet's life. After the Prophet died, she became involved in politics and led a rebellion against 'Ali, the fourth Caliph. After her defeat in the Battle of the Camel, she retired to Medina where she continued to teach. She became a substantial juristic authority in her own right. She is the source of a large number of reports about the Prophet, and the source of many early legal opinions.

Ahmad Ibn Hanbal (d. 241/855)
The noted traditionist and scholar, Ahmad Ibn Hanbal is the eponym for the Hanbali school of Islamic law. He is known for his refusal to adopt the Mu'tazili view on the creation of the Qur'an, which was enforced by the 'Abbasid caliph al-Ma'mun as official government policy. Al-Ma'mun demanded that scholars accept the position; Ahmad Ibn Hanbal refused to do so and was imprisoned for his opposition. He spent two years in prison, and thereafter, discontinued teaching until al-Mutawakkil became Caliph and discontinued 'Abbasid support of Mu'tazili ideology.

'Ali Ibn Abi Talib (d. 40/661)
Cousin, son-in-law, and a close Companion of the Prophet, 'Ali was one of the first converts to Islam in Mecca. 'Ali was, according to Sunnis, the fourth Rightly-Guided Caliph (*rashidun*). During 'Ali's Caliphate, Mu'awiya, the governor of Syria, rebelled against him, and this insurrection led to the Battle of Siffin in 657. After 'Ali was assassinated by a member of the Khawarij rebels, Mu'awiya declared himself Caliph. The supporters of 'Ali, *shi'at 'Ali* (the party of 'Ali), asserted the right of the 'Alid branch of the Prophet's family to the Caliphate, and led several rebellions against the Umayyads. This conflict eventually led to the sectarian division between Sunnis and Shi'is. 'Ali was married to the Prophet's daughter, Fatima, and fathered the Prophet's two grandsons, Hasan and Husayn.

Al-Amidi, Sayf al-Din 'Ali Ibn Muhammad (d. 631/1233)
At first a Hanbali scholar, he later studied Shafi'i law and became a noted jurist within the Shafi'i school. He integrated the methodologies of *kalam* with Islamic jurisprudence. He was often accused of heresy because of his intellectual acumen and penchant for teaching philosophy.

Anas Ibn Malik (d. 93/712)
A close Companion of the Prophet from the Ansar of Medina. He converted to Islam at a young age and remained in the Prophet's service until the Prophet's death. Thereafter, Anas relocated to Basra, where he died. Anas was among the last Companions of the Prophet to die. Anas was the source of a large number of reports about the Prophet.

'Ata' Ibn Abi Rabah (d. 114/732–3)
A famous jurist and a recognized legal authority, especially in all matters relating to Hajj. Raised in Mecca of humble origins. He studied with 'Abdullah Ibn 'Umar, 'Abdullah Ibn 'Abbas, and many other prominent authorities. He died in Mecca.

Al-Banna, Hassan (d. 1369/1949)
Founder of the Muslim Brotherhood in Egypt in 1927. At an early age, he was educated in Islamic sciences. He also had *Sufi* inclinations, and by the age of fourteen, was inducted into

the Hasafiyya order. Professionally, he was a teacher and held teaching posts throughout Egypt. The Muslim Brotherhood became a formidable political force in Egypt. As a result of his growing popularity and power, he was assassinated, presumably by a government agent.

Al-Baydawi, 'Abdullah Ibn 'Umar (d. 685/1286)

A Shafi'i jurist well-known for his commentary on the Qur'an and works on jurisprudence. He held the position of Chief Judge in the city of Shiraz, located in Iran. He was at times accused of being influenced by Shi'ism. There is a debate as to his date of death. In addition to the date given above, some have said that he died in 691/1292, 692/1293, or even 716/1316.

Bilal Ibn Rabah (d. 17–21/638–642)

One of the closest Companions of the Prophet. Originally a slave from Abyssinia living in Mecca. After his conversion in Mecca, he was tortured by his master, but Abu Bakr purchased and freed him. In Medina, Bilal became the Prophet's *mu'adhdhin* (the one who would make the call to prayer) in Medina. After the death of the Prophet, Bilal continued to live in Medina, but he accompanied Muslim troops to Syria, and reportedly died there. There is substantial disagreement on his date of death.

Bin Bazz, Abu 'Abdullah 'Abd 'Aziz Ibn 'Abdullah Ibn 'Abd al-Rahman (d. 1420/1999)

Grand Mufti of the Kingdom of Saudi Arabia and a major proponent of Wahhabi thought. Generally, his thought is puritanical and conservative. For an English translation of his *fatawa* on women, see Muhammad Ibn Abdul-Aziz al-Musnad, ed., *Islamic Fatawa Regarding Women*, trans. Jamal al-Din M. Zarabozo (Saudi Arabia: Darussalam, 1996).

Al-Bukhari, Abu 'Abdullah Muhammad Ibn Isma'il Ibn Ibrahim Ibn al-Mughira Ibn Bardizbah (d. 256/870)

He compiled the collection of *hadith* known as *Sahih al-Bukhari*. He began studying *hadith* at an early age. Bukhari spent sixteen years gathering reports about the Prophet, traveling widely between Egypt and Khurasan. Reportedly, he collected more than 600,000 traditions, of which only 7,397 found their way into his collection of *hadith*. Although he held that the Qur'an was uncreated, he adhered to the view that the recitation of it was created. As a result, he was accused of heterodoxy and was exiled from his home in Nishapur. He moved to Bukhara, but after encountering more political problems, he was again expelled. He lived the rest of his life with relatives in a village near Samarqand. Bukhari's collection of traditions is considered by Sunni Muslims to be one of the six canonical works on *hadith*. Some modern Muslims claim that all the traditions documented in Bukhari are absolutely authentic and are not susceptible to criticism.

Fatima al-Zahra' bint Muhammad Ibn 'Abdullah (d. 10/632)

Daughter of the Prophet and Khadijah born in Mecca. She was eighteen years old when she married the Prophet's cousin, 'Ali Ibn Abi Talib, and migrated to Medina. She had four children with 'Ali: Hasan, Husayn, Umm Kalthum, and Zaynab. Her date of death cannot be assessed with certainty, however, it is reported that she died within six months after her father's death. She was the only one of the Prophet's children to survive him. Fatima played a very important role in the life of the Muslim community in Medina, and was a woman of exceptional piety and purity.

Al-Ghazali, Abu Hamid Muhammad Ibn Muhammad (d. 505/1111)

A famous Shafi'i jurist, theologian, philosopher, and mystic. He was a distinguished student of the prominent jurist al-Juwayni, and was appointed to a teaching position at the Nizamiyya School in Baghdad while fairly young. His fame as a jurist and philosopher spread widely. Troubled by his fame, al-Ghazali resigned his prestigious post and traveled to Jerusalem and then Damascus, seeking spiritual purification. His spiritual journey lasted ten years, after which he wrote some of his most influential works. His works of law and jurisprudence, such as *al-Wajiz* and *al-Mustasfa,* are reference sources for Shafi'i *fiqh* and jurisprudence. His monumental work *Ihya' 'Ulum al-Din* was an attempt to revitalize religious sciences among the laity. Al-Ghazali also tried to integrate and reconcile between juristic and spiritual sciences. He wrote a famous work about his own spiritual journey, a pseudo-autobiography named *al-Munqidh min al-Dalal* (Deliverance from Error). He also wrote a refutation of philosophers named *Tahafut al-Falasifa,* which is translated into English as *The Incoherence of the Philosophers.* He died in Tabiran.

Al-Ghazali, Muhammad (d. 1419/1998)

An author of numerous works and one of the greatest Muslim jurists in the contemporary age. He challenged essentialist and apologetic Islamic reform efforts by reinvigorating inquiry and investigation into the classical sources. He wrote a scathing critique of essentialist *hadith* methodologies and of Wahhabi thought. This became his most controversial work, leading to a ban in some Muslim countries.

Hafsa bint 'Umar Ibn al-Khattab (d. 45/665)

She was the daughter of the Companion 'Umar Ibn al-Khattab, and the wife of the Prophet. She transmitted some reports from and about the Prophet. She also played a crucial role in the collection of the Qur'an. She was the keeper of one of the few written copies of the Qur'an. A committee appointed by the third Caliph 'Uthman Ibn 'Affan borrowed her copy to study it and then returned it to her for safekeeping.

Husayn Ibn 'Ali Ibn Abi Talib (d. 61/680)

Grandson of the Prophet Muhammad. He is the son of the Prophet's daughter Fatima and the Prophet's cousin 'Ali. He was born in Medina before the Prophet died. Husayn was extremely pious and particularly influential in the development of Islamic law. Upon the death of Mu'awiya (d. 60/680), the first Umayyad caliph, al-Husayn refused to give the *bay'a* (oath of allegiance) to Mu'awiya's son and successor, Yazid. Thereafter, al-Husayn sought help from his supporters in Kufa to start a revolt against the Umayyads. Upon his journey to Kufa from the Hijaz, he was met by Yazid's forces at Karbala in modern-day Iraq. Betrayed by many of his supporters, al-Husayn's small forces were defeated by the much larger Umayyad army, and al-Husayn was killed. The battle of Karbala is of central importance in Shi'i theology, and passion plays (*ta'ziya*) are performed regularly in Iran in remembrance of the events leading to al-Husayn's death.

Ibn 'Abbas, 'Abdullah (d. 68/686–88)

The Prophet's cousin and Companion. It is reported that he was born three years before the Prophet's migration to Medina. He was one of the founding jurists of the Islamic legal tradition, and was very influential in the development of the juristic traditions of Mecca and Medina. He died in Ta'if.

Ibn al-'Arabi, Abu Bakr Muhammad al-Ma'afiri (d. 543/1148)

A Maliki jurist from Seville in Islamic Spain. He traveled throughout the Muslim world with his father and studied with a large number of jurists. Eventually, he became a prominent jurist and was appointed as a judge in Seville. Many of his legal opinions are quite original. When the Almohads came to power, Ibn al-'Arabi was exiled to Marrakesh and imprisoned.

Ibn Hajar al-'Asqalani, Ahmad Ibn 'Ali Ibn Muhammad (d. 852/1449)

A prominent scholar of *hadith*. Of Palestinian origins, he lived and died in Cairo. He traveled widely in search of knowledge, taught *hadith* and law in Egypt, and served as a *mufti* and judge. He suffered governmental persecution at different points in his life. His commentary on Bukhari's collection of *hadith*, *Fath al-Bari*, is a very valuable and rich source.

Ibn Hazm, Abu Muhammad 'Ali Ibn Ahmad Ibn Sa'id (d. 456/1064)

An Andalusian scholar and jurist, Ibn Hazm is famous for spearheading the Zahiri legal school in Andalusia. As the name of the school suggests, its primary legal methodology was to investigate the literal terms of the text without recourse to analogical reasoning. Ibn Hazm was an author of remarkable breadth, writing on law, poetry, love, grammar, history, logic, and other subjects. Toward the end of his life, he was exiled to Labla where he died.

Ibn Kathir, 'Imad al-Din Isma'il Ibn 'Umar (d. 774/1373)

A Shafi'i jurist, traditionalist, and historian in Syria. He studied with Ibn Taymiyya and others. He wrote a famous chronicle of Islamic history and a commentary on the Qur'an. Although his commentary is very basic, it has become widely circulated in the modern age. He was arrested and tortured because of his legal opinions.

Ibn Majah, Abu 'Abdullah Muhammad Ibn Yazid al-Rub'i (d. 273/887)

He was the author of one of the six canonical works of *hadith*. He traveled widely in search of traditions, and ultimately compiled nearly 4,000 traditions from the Prophet. Although his collection is considered one of the six canonical collections by most Sunni jurists, some jurists, such as those in North Africa, refused to grant it that distinguished status, arguing that it contained many weak traditions.

Ibn Mas'ud, 'Abdullah Ibn Habib (d. 32/653)

A close Companion of the Prophet and one of the first converts to Islam. He migrated to Abyssinia and then to Medina, and participated in most of the battles during the Prophet's lifetime. After the Prophet's death, Ibn Mas'ud was appointed to oversee the treasury of Kufa. He was the source of many reports about the Prophet. Ibn Mas'ud also had a substantial impact upon the development of the juristic school in Kufa. During the Caliphate of 'Uthman Ibn 'Affan, Ibn Mas'ud is reported to have returned to Medina. There is a disagreement over whether he died in Medina or in Kufa.

Ibn al-Qasim, Abu 'Abdullah 'Abd al-Rahman al-'Utaki (d. 191/806)

Prominent disciple of Malik Ibn Anas. Ibn al-Qasim collected the opinions of his teacher and added his own commentary and opinions in a book entitled *al-Mudawwana*. *Al-Mudawwana* played an influential role in the spread of Malikism to North Africa and Andalusia.

Ibn Qayyim al-Jawziyya, Shams al-Din Abu Bakr Muhammad Ibn Abi Bakr al-Zar'i (d. 751/1350)

A highly respected Hanbali jurist and theologian in Damascus, where he was born and where he died. He was the most famous pupil of the renowned scholar and jurist, Ibn Taymiyya. Ibn al-Qayyim's works on law were inspired and influential. He was also influenced by Sufism. He wrote several works in which he criticized several intellectual orientations, including the Ash'ari school of thought. For political reasons, Ibn al-Qayyim was imprisoned with his teacher Ibn Taymiyya in Damascus. He was not released until Ibn Taymiyya's death in prison.

Ibn Rushd al-Jadd (d. 520/1126)

He was a great Maliki jurist from Islamic Spain. During his life, he held the position of Chief Judge and *imam* of the Great Mosque of Cordoba. His grandson, also known as Ibn Rushd, was the famous philosopher known in the West as Averroes (see below).

Ibn Taymiyya, Taqi al-Din Ahmad Ibn 'Abd al-Halim (d. 728/1328)

A famous Hanbali jurist and theologian. Despite his Hanbali training, Ibn Taymiyya's knowledge was so great as to render him an independent *mujtahid*. At an early age, he migrated with his father to Damascus to escape the onslaught of the Mongol invasion. While there, his father was the director of the Sukkariyya School, where Ibn Taymiyya would receive much of his education and where he was later appointed as a teacher. Because of his polemics against his opponents and his political opinions, he was expelled from Damascus. He traveled to Egypt where he was imprisoned in Cairo and Alexandria. Eventually, he was allowed to return to Damascus, but his continued attacks against what he considered to be religious innovations and against Sufism, as well as his refusal to cooperate with the government, landed him in prison again, where he eventually died. It is reported that the entire city of Damascus went to Ibn Taymiyya's funeral. In addition to his own prolific writings, much of his thought and ideas are preserved in the writings of his most famous student, Ibn Qayyim al-Jawziyya. Ibn Taymiyya's exposition on theology named *al-Wasitiyya* and *al-'Aqida al-Hamawiyya* was challenged as being heterodox. In the contemporary age, he has become a favored author among the Wahhabi movement, probably because of his criticisms against Sufism. His jurisprudence, however, is inconsistent with Wahhabi tenets.

Ibrahim Ibn Muhammad (d. 11/632)

He was the son of the Prophet from Mariyah. He is reported to have died as an infant a few months before the Prophet's own death.

'Izz al-Din Ibn 'Abd al-Salam (d. 661/1262)

A Shafi'i jurist who was posthumously named the Sultan of the Scholars. He was one of the most original and rigorous jurists of his time. Among the notable aspects about his work is his attempt to demonstrate the relevance of Sufi doctrines to jurisprudential doctrines. Originally from Damascus, he died in Egypt.

Al-Juwayni, Abu al-Ma'ali 'Abd al-Malik Imam al-Haramayn (d. 478/1085)

A famous Shafi'i jurist from Nishapur. He was a professor of law in Nishapur. Among his students was the famous Abu Hamid al-Ghazali. Al-Juwayni was a follower of the Ash'ari theological school, and when the Seljuq minister 'Amid al-Mulk al-Kunduri proclaimed the Ash'ari school to be heretical and persecuted its followers, al-Juwayni fled to Baghdad and then to Hijaz. He taught law in Mecca and Medina where he earned the title Imam al-Haramayn (the *imam* of the two sanctuaries). When Nizam al-Mulk became the Seljuq minister, he reversed the policies of al-Kunduri and even endowed the Nizamiyya School for al-Juwayni.

Khadijah bint Khuwaylid (d. 3 years before *hijra*/619)
She was the first wife of the Prophet and the first convert to Islam. A wealthy woman, she hired the Prophet before his calling and then proposed to him in marriage. She spent all her wealth supporting the persecuted Muslims in Mecca, and died before the migration to Medina. The Prophet loved her dearly and was married to her for more than twenty years before she died.

Khansa' bint Khudham (d. unknown)
A Companion of the Prophet from the Ansar. After her husband died in the Battle of Uhud, her father married her to someone against her will. She complained to the Prophet, who voided the marriage. She reported traditions from the Prophet.

Al-Khidr
Al-Khidr is a man of some mystery. He is referred to in the Qur'an in *Surat al-Kahf* (18:65–82). Although no name is given to him, later commentators identify the man as al-Khidr. In the Qur'an, Moses is said to have met this man, who is referred to only as a servant of God (*'abd*). It is not clear from the text whether al-Khidr is a prophet, but the Qur'an states that he received divine knowledge and wisdom.

Malik Ibn Anas (d. 179/796)
A prominent early jurist in Medina, often called the *imam* of Medina. He is the eponym of the Maliki school of thought. His treatise *al-Muwatta'* is one of the earliest written works on Islamic law, and is the basis upon which many later Maliki legal works were built. Essential to Malik's method of legal analysis was to ascertain the practice of the people of Medina (*'amal al-Madina*), which he considered authoritative on many matters. He argued that the *Sunna* of the Prophet is not only ascertained by reference to *hadith*, but also by reference to the prevailing practice of the Medinese, who collectively inherited the Prophet's *Sunna*. Reportedly, there was a Caliphal attempt to make his *Muwatta'* the uniform law of the land but Malik, himself, protested. Malik was flogged for supporting an 'Alid rebellion. Later, the government tried to appease him and consulted him on several legal matters. He died in Medina as a highly esteemed jurist.

Mariyah (d. 16/637)
Known as Umm Ibrahim. Anas reported that she was among the closest to the Prophet. She was a Coptic maiden given to the Prophet Muhammad as a gift from the Egyptian governor of Alexandria, al-Muqawqis, in 6–7/627–629. Ibn 'Abbas reported that the Prophet freed her and then married her. Mariyah bore the Prophet his son, Ibrahim, who died as an infant shortly before the Prophet's own death. Reportedly, the Companion Hatib Ibn Abi Balta'a played a major role in Mariyah's conversion to Islam. After the Prophet's death, Mariyah continued to live in Medina until she died during 'Umar's Caliphate.

Al-Mawardi, Abu al-Hasan 'Ali Ibn Muhammad Ibn Habib (d. 450/1058)
A prominent Shafi'i jurist who taught law in Basra and Baghdad. He was appointed chief judge in Ustuwa near Nishapur but he moved to Baghdad where he settled permanently.

He was close to the Caliph al-Qadir and represented him in negotiations with the Buway-hids. In the reign of the Caliph al-Muqtadi, he issued a *responsa* against the grant of the title Shahanshah (the king of kings) to the Buwayhid representative of the Caliph, and suffered persecution as a result. Al-Mawardi's enemies accused him of being a Mu'tazili. Aside from his many works on law, al-Mawardi wrote what would become a very influential treatise on government. It is reported that al-Mawardi did not publish his writings during his lifetime. After his death, one of his students collected, edited, and published his works.

Mu'awiya Ibn Abi Sufyan (d. 60/680)
The son of Hind and Abu Sufyan, both late converts to Islam. He was the governor of Syria when he rebelled against the fourth Caliph, 'Ali. After 'Ali's death, Mu'awiya became the first Caliph of the Umayyad dynasty and moved the capital to Damascus. He ruled from 41/661 to 60/680.

Al-Nawawi, Muhyi al-Din Abu Zakariyya Ibn Muri (d. 676/1277)
A prominent Shafi'i jurist. At first, al-Nawawi studied medicine in al-Rawahiyya School in Damascus, but he soon switched to the study of law. He was appointed to the Ashrafiyya School of *hadith* as a professor, but when he refused to sanction unjust taxes imposed by Sultan Baybars, he was fired and expelled from Damascus. He was appointed as chief judge in Egypt where he was, in time, fired again and imprisoned. Al-Nawawi died in his father's home in Nawa south of Damascus. Al-Nawawi's works on law and *hadith* became very influential in Islamic legal history and remain influential today.

Al-Nisa'i, Ahmad Ibn 'Ali Ibn Shu'ayb Ibn 'Ali (d. 303/915)
A *hadith* scholar whose collection, *Sunan al-Nisa'i*, is considered one of the six authoritative works on *hadith*, alongside *Sahih al-Bukhari* and *Sahih Muslim*. Originally from Khurasan, he moved to Egypt where he resided. However, because of petty jealousies he was forced to leave Egypt for Palestine. In Palestine, he was suspected of not believing in Mu'awiya Ibn Abi Sufyan's merits. Reportedly, he was asked about the merits of Mu'awiya, but when he refused to respond, he was badly beaten in the mosque. He sustained injuries and later died. Some reports indicate, however, that he died in Mecca while performing *hajj*.

Al-Qarafi, Shihab al-Din Abu al-'Abbas (d. 684/1285)
A Maliki jurist and professor of law in the Salihiyya school in Cairo. Al-Qarafi is one of the most rigorous and systematic theorists in Islamic jurisprudence. His works of jurisprudence are notable for their sensitivity to issues of jurisdiction and enforcement. He died in Cairo.

Al-Qurtubi, Abu 'Abdullah Muhammad Ibn Ahmad (d. 671/1272)
A Maliki jurist born in Muslim Spain, he traveled to the East and settled in Egypt where he died. He is most notable for his remarkably rich commentary on Qur'an.

Rida, Muhammad Rashid (d. 1354/1935)
Originally from Lebanon, he was perhaps one of the most influential Muslim reformers of the late nineteenth and early twentieth centuries. Early in his life, he was attracted to Sufism. He was heavily influenced by the teachings of the reformer Jalal al-Din al-Afghani. In 1314/1897, he moved from Syria to Egypt and, with his mentor Muhammad 'Abduh, he established the journal *al-Manar* in 1898. He was the editor of *al-Manar* from its founding until his death. In it, one can find Rida's commentary on the Qur'an as well

as the collection of his *fatawa*. Rida remains one of the most original and innovative jurists, although he has come under attack by Wahhabi writers.

Ruqayya bint Muhammad (d. 2/624)

A daughter of the Prophet from his wife Khadijah. She married 'Uthman Ibn 'Affan, the Companion of the Prophet, who was later appointed as the third Rightly-Guided Caliph after the death of 'Umar Ibn al-Khattab. She died during the Prophet's lifetime.

Sahnun, Abu Sa'id 'Abd al-Salam Ibn Rabi'a (d. 240/855)

A Maliki jurist from Qayrawan. Sahnun is credited with being instrumental in the spread of the Maliki school to North Africa and Muslim Spain. In his *al-Mudawwana al-Kubra*, he compiled the opinions of earlier Maliki jurists, including Malik Ibn Anas. His work continues to be a very valuable source on early Islamic legal practices and opinions.

Sa'id Ibn Jubayr al-Asadi (d. 95/714)

One of the early jurists of Kufa. He was described as the most distinguished jurist of his time. Although a student of Ibn 'Abbas, it is reported that Ibn 'Abbas referred legal questions to Sa'id in recognition of his superior knowledge. Sa'id joined the rebellion of Muhammad Ibn al-Ash'ath against the Umayyads. When the rebellion failed, he was arrested in Mecca and executed in Kufa.

Al-Sarakhsi, Muhammad Ibn Ahmad Abi Sahl Abu Bakr (d. 483/1090)

One of the most influential Hanafi jurists of all times. He was a prolific jurist who systematized and developed Hanafi legal doctrine. He wrote his most important work on law in prison.

Sawdah bint Zam'a bint Qayyis bint 'Abd Shams (d. 54/674)

One of the wives of the Prophet Muhammad. She was an early convert to Islam and was among those who migrated to Abyssinia prior to the general migration to Medina. At the time she migrated to Abyssinia, she was married, but her first husband died in Abyssinia or shortly after the return to Mecca. She was left without family or support, and the Prophet then married her. It is debated whether she was the first woman the Prophet married after the death of his first wife Khadijah, or whether he married Sawdah after his marriage to 'Aisha. She remained married to the Prophet until his death. She reported a number of traditions from and about the Prophet. She died in Medina.

Shaltut, Mahmud (d. 1383/1963)

He was the rector of al-Azhar university in Egypt from 1958 until his death. An influential author on Islam and Islamic law, he pursued a policy of Islamic reform along the lines of Muhammad 'Abduh. As rector of al-Azhar, he implemented various reforms of the curriculum. One well-known aspect of this reform, known as *da'wat al-taqrib*, was a reconciliation and cooperation between the Sunni and Shi'i branches. He hoped that a rapprochement between these two branches would pave the way for greater dialogue and unity. Reportedly, he was greatly dismayed by the extent of governmental interference with the policies and curriculum of al-Azhar.

Al-Shatibi, Abu Ishaq Ibrahim Ibn Musa (d. 790/1388)

A Maliki jurist from Muslim Spain. He is notable for his theories on the necessity of legal change in the face of changing circumstances. His work heavily relied on the idea of justice as the ultimate purpose of the law.

Sufyan al-Thawri, Ibn Sa'id Ibn Masruq Ibn Habib Abu 'Abdullah (d. 161/778)

An early jurist of Kufa. He established a school of thought known as the Thawriyya, but his school is now extinct. He had a reputation for relying on traditions more than on his own logical deductions. He experienced several political problems with the Caliphal authorities and was offered a judicial appointment, which he refused. He evaded persecution by escaping to Yemen. Most of his writings perished, although his *tafsir* of the Qur'an has survived, as well as other religious treatises.

Al-Suyuti, Jalal al-Din 'Abd al-Rahman Ibn Muhammad (d. 911/1505)

A Shafi'i jurist from Egypt known as Ibn al-Kutub (the son of books). He studied with prominent jurists, including a large number of women scholars. He held several professorial positions, including one in the Shaykhuniyya school in Cairo. Al-Suyuti was a very prolific and original scholar whose fame spread throughout the Islamic world. Eventually, he removed himself from public life and devoted himself to his writing.

Al-Tabari, Muhammad Ibn Jarir Ibn Yazid (d. 310/923)

A famous jurist and historian, al-Tabari was considered to be the founder of his own school of thought. He was first trained in Shafi'i law, however, his extensive learning enabled him to develop an independent school of thought. Unfortunately, much of his legal writings have not survived. What have survived are his Qur'anic commentary and his historical chronicle. Nearly the entire chronicle has been translated into English. He was offered many government appointments during his life but consistently refused all of them. Through much of his life, he was persecuted by members of the Hanbali school in Baghdad, who considered al-Tabari disrespectful to the founder of their school. In fact, their persecution was so great that people could not visit al-Tabari even if they wanted to, due to the efforts of the Hanbalis to keep him isolated. It is even reported that upon al-Tabari's death, the Hanbali students burned his books and buried his body in an unmarked grave in a Christian cemetery. His school of thought did not survive long, and apparently vanished a few centuries after his death. Notably, he was one of the few jurists who held that women may lead men in prayer.

Thabit Ibn Qays (d. 12/633)

A Companion and scribe of the Prophet. He participated in the Battle of Uhud, as well as others. He died in battle during Abu Bakr's Caliphate.

Thawban Abu 'Abdullah (d. 54/674)

A close Companion of the Prophet who transmitted several reports about the Prophet. Originally a slave, Thawban was purchased by the Prophet, who subsequently freed him. Thawban remained under the care and protection of the Prophet.

'Umar Ibn al-Khattab (d. 23/644)

An early convert to Islam who migrated from Mecca to Medina and who was a close Companion of the Prophet. 'Umar was a very important figure during the Prophet's life and after his death. His daughter Hafsa was married to the Prophet, and he often served as the Prophet's confidant. 'Umar became the Caliph after Abu Bakr and ruled for about ten years. 'Umar played a crucial role in the development of Islamic law, and his legal precedents remain very influential. He is also the source of many reports from and about the Prophet. He was assassinated by a mentally unstable slave.

Umm Kulthum bint Muhammad (d. 9/630)
A daughter of the Prophet from his wife Khadijah. Upon her sister Ruqayya's death, she married 'Uthman Ibn 'Affan, who would later become the third Caliph. She died during the Prophet's lifetime.

Umm Salamah, Hind bint Suhayl (d. 62/681)
One of the wives of the Prophet. Before her marriage to the Prophet, she was married to a man named Abu Salamah. She and Abu Salamah migrated to Abyssinia before joining the rest of the Muslims in Medina. When her husband died in Medina, she was a widow with four children. When the Prophet wanted to marry her, she told him that she was old, given to jealousy, and had young children. After marrying the Prophet, she played an important role in the Muslim community in Medina. She continued to live in Medina after the Prophet's death, where she taught and transmitted traditions from the Prophet.

Umm Salim (d. unknown)
She was an early Companion of the Prophet, who was reported to have fought alongside the Prophet in battle. Specifically, she is reported to have fought at the battles of Uhud and Hunayn. She was married to Abu Talha, the Companion of the Prophet.

Al-'Uthaymiyyin, Abu 'Abd Allah Muhammad Ibn Salih (1347–/1929–)
A *mufti* in Saudi Arabia and a member of the Senior Scholars Committee of the Kingdom. A proponent of Wahhabi thought and methodology. His *fatawa* are gathered in various collections, and some of them have been translated. For an English version of his *fatawa*, see Muhammad Ibn 'Abdul-Aziz al-Musnad, ed., *Islamic Fatawa Regarding Women*, trans. Jamal al-Din M. Zarabozo (Saudi Arabia: Darussalam, 1996).

Zayd Ibn Haritha (d. 8/629)
Among the very early converts to Islam and a close Companion of the Prophet. He was a slave given to the Prophet by his first wife Khadijah, but the Prophet manumitted him and adopted him as a son. Because of his relationship with the Prophet, he was often called Zayd Ibn Muhammad. In Medina, Zayd reluctantly married Zaynab but divorced her after a relatively short marriage. The Prophet then married her. There is controversy in the sources about the reasons for their divorce.

Zaynab bint Jahsh (d. 20/641)
She was the wife of Zayd Ibn Haritha and the cousin of the Prophet. By the time she married Zayd, she is reported to have been approximately thirty-five years of age. Upon her divorce from Zayd, she married the Prophet. See also Zayd Ibn Haritha.

Zaynab bint Muhammad (d. 7/628)
A daughter of the Prophet from his wife Khadijah. Her daughter Umama later married 'Ali Ibn Abi Talib after the death of his wife Fatima, who was also a daughter of the Prophet. She died during the Prophet's lifetime.

Index

About the Author

Dr. Khaled Abou El Fadl is Professor of Law at the UCLA School of Law where he teaches Islamic law, Immigration, Human Rights, International, and National Security Law. Dr. Abou El Fadl previously taught Islamic law at the University of Texas at Austin Law School, Yale Law School, and Princeton University. He holds degrees from Yale University (B.A.), University of Pennsylvania Law School (J.D.), and Princeton University (M.A./Ph.D.). A world renowned expert in Islamic law and an American lawyer, he is a strong proponent of women's rights and human rights and serves on the Board of Directors of Human Rights Watch. He was appointed by President George W. Bush as a commissioner on the U.S. Commission on International Religious Freedom, and also recently named a 2005 Carnegie Foundation Scholar. He regularly provides expert testimony in a wide variety of cases ranging from human rights and political asylum to terrorism, national security, and international and commercial law. As a critical and powerful voice against puritan and Wahhabi Islam, he regularly appears on national and international television and radio including CNN, NBC, PBS, NPR, and Voice of America (broadcast throughout the Middle East). Author of numerous books and articles on Islamic law and Islam, his most recent work focuses on issues of authority, tolerance, and democracy in Islam.